GW00685110

Brassey's Defence Yearbook 1993

Edited by
The Centre for Defence Studies,
King's College, London

103rd Year of Publication

BRASSEY'S (UK)
London • New York

Editorial Board

Michael Clarke, MSc (Econ)
Professor Lawrence Freedman, DPhil
Brian Holden Reid, PhD
Jennifer Shaw, MA BSc (Econ)
Major General (Retd) A J Trythall CB, MA

Copyright © 1993 Brassey's (UK) Ltd

All Rights Reserved. No part of this publication may be reproduced, stored in a
retrieval system or transmitted in any form or by any means: electronic, electrostatic,
magnetic tape, mechanical, photocopying, recording or otherwise, without permis-
sion in writing from the publishers.

First English edition 1993

UK editorial offices: Brassey's, 165 Great Dover Street, London SE1 4YA
orders: Marston Book Services, PO Box 87, Oxford OX2 0DT

USA orders: Macmillan Publishing Company, Front and Brown Streets Riverside, NJ
08075

Distributed in North America to booksellers and wholesalers by the Macmillan
Publishing Company, NY 10022

Library of Congress Cataloging in Publication Data
available

British Library Cataloguing in Publication Data
A catalogue record for this book is available from the British Library

ISBN 1-85753-092-6

Typeset by M Rules
Printed in Great Britain by
BPCC Wheatons Ltd, Exeter

Centre for Defence Studies

KING'S COLLEGE, STRAND, LONDON WC2R 2LS

Honorary Director

Professor Lawrence Freedman, formerly head of Policy Studies at the Royal Institute of International Affairs, has been Head of the Department of War Studies, King's College, since 1982, and has held research positions at Nuffield College, Oxford and at the International Institute for Strategic Studies.

Executive Director

Michael Clarke, formerly a lecturer in International Relations at the University of Manchester and the University of Newcastle-upon-Tyne, has been a Guest Fellow at the Brookings Institution in the USA and an Associate Fellow at the Royal Institute of International Affairs.

THE CENTRE FOR DEFENCE STUDIES was established in October 1990 at the University of London with a grant from the Ministry of Defence. It is one of the University of London's Institutes of Advanced Study and is supported in particular by the expertise of the Department of War Studies, King's College, and the Department of International Relations at the London School of Economics. The purpose of the Centre is to act as a focus for research on a wide range of defence and security issues, which it does by conducting its own research, by commissioning research from outside, and by organising working groups, conferences and seminars to draw together the work of academic and policy specialists on a wide range of subjects.

In November 1990 the CDS assumed responsibility for the work of the Council for Arms Control and in one of its programmes continues to monitor the progress of arms control (particularly in Europe) with special interest in developments from the CFE and CSCE regimes presently in place. In the past year the development and steady growth of the Regional Security Project, presently concentrating on Southern Asia but expected to expand to include security issues in East Asia and sub-Saharan Africa, has been a stimulating new area of activity.

In conjunction with Brassey's the CDS publishes the London Defence Studies in an annual package which includes 8 to 10 expertly researched papers and occasional briefings providing informed authoritative comment on current affairs and which reaches a wide and influential readership in the defence and security fields.

PUBLICATIONS

Discussion Paper: United Kingdom Defence Policy in the 1990s
An examination of the major dimensions of defence choices facing the government for the next few years, dealing with the challenges facing UK defence policy, the international institutional context, the budgetary constraints, equipment, manpower and nuclear dimensions.
Size A4, 38 pages, £9.50. Obtainable from CDS, King's College, Strand, London WC2R 2LS. (Cheques payable to King's College London, please)

The London Defence Studies: an annual package of 8 to 10 expertly researched papers plus occasional Briefing Papers; available on subscription at £65.00/US$123.50 from Turpin Distribution Services Ltd., Blackhorse Road, Letchworth, Herts, SG6 1HN UK. (Individual copies may be obtained at £10.00/$18.00 each). Titles to date are:

1 *The Gulf Crisis: Economic Implications.* Susan Willett
2 *The Gulf Crisis: Politico-Military Implications.* James Gow et al
3 *The Crisis in Soviet Military Reform.* Elaine Holoboff
4 *The Prospects for British and European Space Programmes.* Bhupendra Jasani

New Books from The Centre for Defence Studies
Published by Brassey's

IRAQ, THE GULF CONFLICT AND THE WORLD COMMUNITY

Edited by JAMES GOW

This study of the Gulf conflict places notions of a 'new world order' in a more realistic perspective. Limited possibilities for an emerging world order focus now on such issues as humanitarian aid, and the restrictions on the international community to intervene effectively in the domestic matters of individual states. Such collective efforts can so easily be constrained by the state's divergent interpretation of the right to domestic sovereignty.

As such, this volume will be not only a key point of departure for future study of the Gulf conflict, but also a significant foundation for those seeking to understand the nature of the world community, and the significance of internal affairs in relation to humanitarian intervention amidst the wider concept of a stable world order.

0 08 041780 9 £27.50 June 1993

NEW PERSPECTIVES ON SECURITY

Edited by MICHAEL CLARKE

The end of the twentieth century is almost upon us - a fitting time for an appraisal of the current basis of international relations. NEW PERSPECTIVES ON SECURITY examines the current state of international affairs from a series of different intellectual, historical, economic, legal and military perspectives, to suggest new ideas and priorities in our quest for stability and order in the twenty-first century.

The rise of nation states, the creation of new national boundaries, a dramatic rise in sectional and ethnic tensions - are all issues deferred by Cold War priorities. It is possible to see that those old ideas are fast approaching exhaustion. A vacuum has been created in international politics, and a reappraisal of values and behaviour appears to be essential. NEW PERSPECTIVES forms a creative synthesis of intellectual, political, historical, military, and strategic analysis.

0 08 041790 6 £22.50 Sept.1993

Of Related Interest

GOING BALLISTIC : The Build-up of Missiles in the Middle East
MARTIN NAVIAS
1 85753 020 9 £30.00 August 1993

Orders to: Marston Book Services
PO Box 87 Oxford OX2 ODT

Prices and Publication dates subject to change without notice

Preface

by MAJOR GENERAL A J TRYTHALL
and JENNY SHAW

This, the 103rd edition of Brassey's Yearbook, is the first to be edited by the Centre for Defence Studies, based at King's College, London.

Brassey's Naval Annual, the forebear of this Yearbook, was first published in 1886 by Thomas Brassey, a civil Lord of the Admiralty who had considerable interest in and influence over naval affairs for many years, both in the House of Commons and, later after his creation as the first Earl Brassey, in the House of Lords.

From 1974–1992, the Yearbook was edited by the Royal United Services Institute for Defence Studies.

Brassey's now welcomes the participation of the Centre for Defence Studies, (CDS) whose Honorary Director is Professor Lawrence Freedman. Michael Clarke, Executive Director for CDS has edited this edition, along with Bryan Watkins, Brassey's Editor. We believe the combination of Brassey's and CDS will provide a strong editorial team ensuring that this most prestigious Yearbook will continue the tradition of providing information on and analysis of national and international defence matters at a time of great change and uncertainty.

Contents

Perspectives on Security

INTRODUCTION

1

Recasting European Security

LAWRENCE FREEDMAN

Professor of War Studies, King's College, London

1992 seemed almost as far from the start of this decade as the first months of 1990 did from the start of 1989, let alone the pre-Gorbachev Cold War years. The mood then verged on the euphoric. The peaceful revolutions of 1989 were generally seen to be an almost unqualified bonus for international politics. The very manner in which power was transferred from communist to non-communist régimes, long-standing disputes resolved and the state system re-arranged offered an optimistic prospect for future crisis management. The end of superpower antagonism removed the risk of a catastrophic total war and made it possible to think of a 'peace dividend' in both economic and psychological terms. European security came to be discussed in terms of strengthened institutional structure, helping resolve disputes and enforcing norms of good behaviour by means of economic and political rather than military instruments. At the centre of this structure was to be found the European Community, building on the profound integrative achievements of the past and pushing forward to economic and monetary union, while at the same time exerting a benign influence in its regional neighbourhood and offering a hopeful prospect for would-be members as they restructured themselves following the liberation from communism.

This was once offered as the ideal 'post-Cold-War world'. So it might have been. What had become clear even before 1992 was that no new order with any degree of firmness was set to take over from the old bipolar order which had gone before. Even the old order was somewhat more fluid than it now seems in retrospect, with regional conflicts already taking on a life of their own, independently of the superpower confrontation. The stability in core political relations that had developed during the Cold War could clearly not withstand the steady deterioration of the economic fundamentals in one of the two blocs. However, the pace and complexity of change since the communist system broke in 1989 has been both breathtaking and profoundly disorienting. The idea of a stable world order with conflict well contained and prosperity and justice abounding has not lasted long. The cumulative uncertainties of the 1990s are now threatening the self-confidence of Western Europe and are demanding drastic reappraisals of basic assumptions.

Two sets of events in particular shaped this reappraisal during 1992. The first was the continuing turmoil in the former Yugoslavia. This illustrated all the limitations of the established institutional structure in terms of coping with crisis. The second was the unravelling of the Maastricht Treaty on the future development of the European community. Although the Treaty just about survived the year, with a new Danish referendum and British ratification still pending, the underlying thrust towards economic and monetary union had been compromised by the stresses and strains within the existing exchange rate mechanism, while the promise of a European defence entity had been undermined by the poor performance in the former Yugoslavia. Both sets of difficulties were linked directly to the upheavals of post-communist Europe. The link is obvious enough in the Yugoslav case, which has been presented as almost a prototype for what might happen if the sort of ethnic conflict prevalent throughout the old communist world is exploited by hard-liners, turning to narrow nationalism to sustain themselves in power now that the universalist appeal of communism has been discredited, and then allowed to get out of hand. The currency turmoil too was linked, for it reflected the consequences of German unification as well as the downward thrust of key economic indicators. This is discussed further below.

THE OLD ORDER

The violence of the conflict in former Yugoslavia produced the most disturbing images. The old order of the Cold War was not in itself violent, although it involved more than its fair share of fear and intimidation as well as active military preparations. The East-West conflict never came to a head, but was restrained by a combination of a recognition of the risk of total war and the clarity of the border separating one bloc from another. In those places – Berlin in Europe and Third World 'troublespots' – where the basic political relationships were ambiguous and shifting, the superpowers were liable to get involved militarily but took steps to avoid direct conflict with each other and at times were often able to restrain their clients when they clashed. There were understood 'conventions of crisis management', and over the years forms of communication developed (i.e. the 'hot line') to prevent conflicts where only 'non-vital interests' were at stake to get out of hand and to ensure sensitive treatment where 'vital' interests were at stake. Increasing care was also taken in the definition of truly vital interests. It was very evident that when international institutions were engaged it was either because they were the expressions of one of the two power blocs (NATO/WTO) or because, as with the UN, the two blocs had reached a stalemate and recognised the need for compromise.

Bitter and bloody warfare was most likely to take place in those regions where East/West interests were not directly engaged. It was a natural part of the game in Third World conflicts to find an 'anti-communist' or 'anti-colonial' rhetoric to help draw an external power in to help retrieve an otherwise hopeless situation. The vulnerable sought to manufacture a strategic imperative for the Great Powers which they dare not ignore, even when they suspected that it might be artificial. As the regional political configurations became more complex, and local powers were able to play the role once played by the external Great Powers, it became difficult to generate a strategic imperative simply out of a fear of Soviet – or Western – influence. Gradually, most regions other than Europe began to disengage from the Cold War system. When conflicts then occurred outside the main lines of East-West antagonism – in

South Asia, the Middle East and Africa – it was often difficult to contain violence. As these regions became more troublesome it became even less likely that external interests would become engaged.

At the same time the Cold War system did make possible the use of economic and political measures to solve the classic security dilemma of Western Europe – Franco-German antagonism. After the Second World War, American hegemony, in itself a function of the developing Cold War, was reflected in the Marshall Plan for economic reconstruction. The development of the European Community was made possible by a lack of contrary pulls from the East and the blocking off of a large chunk of not very digestible Europe as a result of the Iron Curtain. The durability and stability of the overall political framework was critical to a peaceful, integrated Western European development. In those areas where international relations became intimate, as a deliberate result of policy, enterprises transformed economic relations. Where relations remained closed they were unable to make much of a dent. Thus, activity within both the economic and military spheres was governed by fundamental political relations – but as these were remarkably constant it was possible to treat much economic and military activity as almost independent variables.

ECONOMISTS AND STRATEGISTS

The resultant apolitical tendency in both economics and strategic studies is now causing a lot of problems to both as they attempt to adjust to new circumstances. Economists are thus continually surprised by the fact that their old models are no longer working, while many strategists have been made redundant if they were the type obsessed with the minutiae of military balances. Strategic studies have been forced the hard way to rediscover the link between the military and political spheres that, since the days of Clausewitz, has been at the heart of the subject. Even so, they often appear woefully ignorant of economic tendencies. At the moment there is really no manageable conceptual framework for handling the relationship between economics and strategy. Discussions of 'economic security' tend to revolve around questions of protectionism and the vulnerability of raw material supplies. In current circumstances it is necessary to look much deeper into the economic foundations of political stability.

Such an exercise might help in the analysis of the use of economic instruments as substitutes for armed force. In the past, the East-West political stalemate made it tempting to use economic and political means to ease the strains of Europe's division. Economic measures employed during this period, in particular technology transfers and credits, failed to help modernise the socialist system and probably subverted it further. Communism collapsed because it lacked the legitimacy and self-confidence to cope with the consequences of chronic economic failure. The faults were structural and beyond intelligent reform within the confines of the system. This meant that local élites had little resistance to either internal or external demands for fundamental reform. In all of this, it was possible for Bonn effectively to buy compliance from Moscow in German unification by generous financial transfers (none of which, again, seem to have helped the development of the Soviet economy).

This confirmed one legacy of the pre-October 1990 Ostpolitik: the habit of 'pocket book' diplomacy. This causes problems not only in shaping other's expectations – as could be seen in German responses to the Gulf conflict – but also that when practised as diplomacy it results in so-called 'economic' measures; being bribes in return for political favours instead of transfers of resources to ease the pain of structural reform. This was evident in the pre-coup debate on a 'Marshall Plan' for the Soviet Union. So long as there was no credible process of economic reform in place the net result of assistance was to help the élite hold on to its precarious position. The desire was to 'help Gorby' but the net result was also to help the hardliners who were still well placed to block reform.

Recent developments in Europe are best viewed as the continuation, indeed the culmination, of the post-war processes of decolonisation. There is nothing in that history to provide encouragement to the view that economic measures will be of much value in dispute management. Aid does little good if it simply involves transfers of funds into the hands of an incompetent and bloated bureaucratic élite and fails to address structural problems. This is not to deny its value when reinforcing economies making the necessary structural changes, or on targeted projects and disaster relief. Nonetheless, regional political stability is most likely to depend on domestic political stability combined with market-oriented policies and access to Western markets. Of course, as the newly industrialised economies, the East Asian 'tigers', have discovered, success in this can also produce a defensive reaction in the West. Any East European 'tigers' may face the same reaction.

The post Cold War 'Ostpolitik' concentrated on Poland, the Czech and Slovak Federal Republic and Hungary – which could be seen as the most culturally sympathetic, geographically contiguous, politically stable and economically advanced. The current association agreement with these states facilitates exports to the EC except in those areas where these countries are best placed to export. The split of the Czechs from the Slovaks indicates that even these more promising states still have some way to go in consolidating their political progress.

The proclamation of a democratic constitution does not in itself guarantee democratic practice. Many of the post-communist states are still in the process of self-definition and so are vulnerable to civil upheaval and secessionist movements. They can tax the most established democratic system – never mind one that is still feeling its way and is having to cope with horrendous problems of economic adjustment.

It would be unwise to draw excessively close parallels between experiences in the 'Third World' and the current traumas of what was once the 'Second World'. In economic terms there are differences with both positive and negative implications. On the positive side, the obvious replacement to communism is seen to be Western liberal capitalism. Economic modernisers no longer have a credible state socialist model. There are authoritarian options for capitalism using Chilean or Korean models (although not necessarily viable in heterogeneous societies) and there are potential non-capitalist alternatives based on various forms of romantic nationalism, often with strong religious inspiration. However, most key political leaders accept – at least rhetorically – that they should be working to a West European model, and if possible eventual membership of the EC. This is the basis for optimism on the use of economic measures to manage the dynamics of change in post-communist Europe. It can be added that geographic proximity and an educated population tend to work in their favour.

The negative side of the comparison is in part structural and in part temporal. The structural aspects relate to the fact that before these states can become modern economies they must first de-industrialise on a substantial scale; and this creates high urban unemployment. As can be seen with the strains of German unification, it is difficult to explain why the full benefits of a welfare state should not be kept in place simply because there are no longer the funds to support it. This might be less worrisome were it not for the unfortunate timing of the events in terms of the international economy. They have come after the 1980s boom. Just when spare capital was needed it was no longer to be found. If the revolutions of 1989 had come a few years earlier the story might have been very different.

Nowhere is the link between economic and political developments clearer than in the case of Germany. Many of the post-Cold War prognoses of 1990 postulated the inexorable rise of Germany as the dominant regional power. East Germany simply appeared as an add-on to the successful industrial machine of the West. Its large population, geographic location and formidable currency meant that Bonn – and soon Berlin – must provide the pre-eminent voice in European politics. Yet the reality, at least in the short and possibly medium term, has been that unification has sapped rather than enhanced German power. Monetary union between East and West on over-generous terms, was followed by a collapse of the Russian market. The high subsidies to which the German government are now committed is exceeding the capacity of the economy to grow and is leading to indebtedness. This will be a drag on the German economy and the West European economy as a whole.

These problems come before any adverse knock-on effects from continuing economic weakness in post-communist Europe which may render nugatory some past investments, as well as create problems of refugees and environmental disaster. Obviously, if a virtuous cycle can be set in motion then this would allow for substantial benefits both to the local economies and to the German economy, which has been the major player. All that can be said is that before these pay-offs arrive, there is going to be a need for steady nerves. One requirement of a virtuous cycle in Eastern Europe is improved access to EC markets, especially for agricultural products and textiles. The defensiveness of France in this regard was another factor leading to tension in 1992, with Paris apparently ready to jeopardise a GATT agreement and risk a trade war rather than put even more pressure on its farming community.

There is a real risk of disillusionment in post-communist Europe. Concentrating on the more promising cases may be realistic but it does risk removing hope from other societies and even the future of these three is by no means assured. Moreover, if we think of economic measures as instruments of crisis management, then some preparation needs to be made for hard choices. Making economic support conditional on both political and economic reform as well as good behaviour in external relations becomes problematic when some, but not all, of these conditions are being met. It is always difficult to pull the plug on a whole society because of unacceptable policies by its government.

Sanctions are often adopted as the most natural 'non-violent' alternative to armed force. They can be effective over the long-term so long as it is possible to be patient, the target is effectively isolated and there is a link to an imaginative diplomacy (as perhaps happened in southern Africa). They can also provide the basis for the development of an international coalition that would be difficult to forge, in the first instance, on the basis of armed force (as in the Gulf). However, it is unwise to view sanctions as a non-violent alternative. Often to have an impact they must cause real distress (which has been a continual dilemma over the anti-Iraq sanctions) while to succeed they may well require armed force to prevent the target breaking the sanctions through superior strength (as with the defence of Saudi Arabia and the blockade in the Gulf). Furthermore, if a problem is serious enough to warrant all the effort entailed by effective sanctions – and these show little prospect of success – then it is hard to argue that it is insufficiently serious to warrant military measures.

THE ROLE OF FORCE

This is not to argue that military instruments will always be appropriate where economic instruments fail. Just as wealthy states will face domestic constraints on their ability to follow enlightened economic policies vis-a-vis developing states, so will they face even greater constraints when it comes to placing their young men and women at risk. Western states regularly insist that they have no desire to act as the 'world's policeman' even though, in practice, that may be the role they are expected to play. Decisive military intervention in armed struggles in the more disorderly parts of the world to enforce international norms will be no more than occasional, though humanitarian intervention may be more frequent.

Again it is instructive to look at past practice outside the main areas of East-West conflict. The alternative to direct intervention into the affairs of other regions is to promote some local balance of power. This can be done by one of two ways which can, for obvious reasons, soon come into contradiction with one another. Either support can be given – through military advice, training and equipment – to an otherwise weak power to allow it to defend itself, or to a relatively strong power to encourage it to take responsibility for regional order. The problem with the latter course is the risk of identification with the range of political objectives harboured by the potential regional hegemon and of the consequences of a sudden change in its élite.

The problem with the former course is that it requires an enduring commitment and may still not be enough – prompting requests for direct intervention to save a client in mortal danger. Much of the discussion on 'controlling the arms trade' presumes that measures can be found to remove armed force as an instrument of local power politics. This would be a dubious proposition even if starting with a clean sheet, but in circumstances where military instruments are already widely available it is hopeless. To end support for a weak client simply means aggravating its vulnerability. On the other hand, simply supplying equipment rather than manpower to a small state is rarely enough to stop it being overwhelmed by a neighbour which has ample supplies of both, as Kuwait discovered.

It would be unwise for the foreseeable future to assume that states wishing to use armed force will lack the wherewithal to do so. The eventual location of all the equipment and ordnance accumulated in the former Soviet Union is an obvious area of concern. In all of this, nuclear proliferation, while always serious, is probably less of an epidemic than much casual conversation suggests. The real problem is likely to lie with basic army equipment. However, to the extent that proliferation occurs, it has the obvious effect of strengthening the proliferator in its dealings with neighbours and of deterring external powers from getting involved in any disputes in which it is at the centre.

None of this need matter overmuch if we had a basis for confidence that states would find very little worth fighting about. Part of the previous optimism was a reflection of the fact that for Western industrialised states this may be increasingly the case. For countries such as Britain and France, almost for the first time in their history, there are no direct external threats to national security. The end of the empires has made it possible to redefine 'vital' interests in a much more restricted manner. Even with oil in the Gulf it was by no means clear that the Western interest in suppressing Iraqi ambitions was truly vital in this regard, although there certainly was an interest of some sort. For Western states the most perplexing question is whether 'stability' in other regions or more specifically a respect for the elementary principle of non-aggression, is worth fighting for.

Given the intractable nature of many of the problems and the forbidding character of local conditions, it is doubtful that there will be much enthusiasm when it comes to enforcing equitable solutions to bitter local disputes in the absence of a clear strategic imperative. If this is the case, however, then we must expect to see an upsurge in international violence. In many regions, and perhaps in particular in the post-communist world, there is still much to fight about. This gloomy prognosis in part stems from the sheer dynamism of the current situation which renders 'stability' – as defined as an objective in itself – as a forlorn hope.

The West has always found it difficult to devise adequate geopolitical concepts for Eastern Europe; this failure has triggered two world wars. State formation has always been patchy and weak, largely because of the classic mismatch between nationalities and state boundaries. Nations have more than one state; states have more than one nation. The extent to which individuals identify with a group rather than a state is, as we have seen, a recipe for disintegration. This has cultural roots which cannot be changed overnight and is, if anything, likely to be reinforced in circumstances in which political leaders can point to few practical economic achievements. Until well into 1991, the general Western view was that the existing state structure should be preserved, and that national aspirations should be accommodated by provisions for autonomy. Unfortunately, this was a secondary consideration. Even if it had not been; there was probably little that could be done to convince disaffected groups that they should persevere with discredited political structures. Moreover, the only way is which the centre in Moscow or Belgrade might have been prepared to contemplate the necessary concessions would have depended on a threat by the West to recognise breakaway republics.

The possibilities for constructive and non-violent Western intervention were greatest with Yugoslavia but they were ducked because of the implications for Gorbachev and the USSR. Once the USSR disintegrated after the failed August 1991 coup, there was no reason to sustain the Yugoslav Federation. There was then a sudden lurch towards support for self-determination. The result has been the worst of both worlds. Civil wars have been turned into inter-state wars but in circumstances in which national boundaries have not been protected.

The Yugoslav precedents are deeply unfortunate. Serbia-Montenegro has suffered grievous economic harm as a result of the international embargo but with a long-term perspective can see possible victory in extending its border to include the bulk of the Serbian population in the former Yugoslavia. The platitude that military force does not solve anything has been invalidated daily in the Balkans. The message is that a sufficiently bloody-minded local power can impose its will in the absence of significant outside counter-pressures on behalf of the likely victims. It is a signal unlikely to be lost elsewhere in the post-communist world. In this case, no external power has had an interest in direct intervention, although that possibly could change with Hungary and Albania. The need to protect vulnerable Russian ethnics is now being canvassed as the basis for a long-term role for the Soviet Army, especially where it still has garrisons in former Republics.

The international community has lost its bearings on the relationship between borders and self-determination, and the general problems of regional stability. The idea that the only satisfactory political arrangement for a self-conscious and anxious national group is its own state, no matter how lacking in viability, has now taken root and will be difficult to reverse. This means that we must expect even more secessionist pressures in the future and, to the extent these pressures succeed, a greater potential for inter-state violence.

The West will thus have to face some awkward choices in the coming months and years with regard to its tolerance of the use of armed force to promote the narrow interests of particular groups. These choices may be prompted by humanitarian concerns or to prevent a major initiative being seen to fail. It may be that the choice is to stay out. That will not be a victory for a more peaceful approach to international politics – indeed, it will be quite the opposite.

INSTITUTIONS

One of the difficulties of conducting a serious debate on the management of individual crises is that every discussion tends to be turned into a debate on the role of institutions. This is not surprising as the major participants in the debates have often been officials of these institutions – or have taken their promotion as an important policy end in itself. As a result, a disproportionate amount of time has been devoted to designing and redesigning institutions and working out the inter-connections between them. In part this is a question of competence and membership but it is also one of power.

The evidence of recent years is that the role of institutions depends largely on the readiness of major states to make use of them. There are a number of institutions which, allowing for significant variations, can serve as an expression of collective Western will and have real resources at their disposal: The North Atlantic Treaty Organisation (NATO), the European Community (EC), the Western European Union (WEU) and the Organisation for European Cooperation and Development (OECD), come into this category. There are other institutions which embrace all states but lack a serious decision-making capacity. One reason for this is that Western states see no reason in current circumstances to hand over effective power to institutions which they cannot control. As has again been seen with Yugoslavia, the problem with a broadly-based institution, such as the Conference for Security and Cooperation in Europe (CSCE), which works on unanimity, is that it is very difficult to reach agreement when one of the members is the guilty party. The United Nations has been well placed simply because the major Western states do have effective power through the Security Council (so long as they do nothing to touch directly on Chinese or Russian interests).

When coercion becomes necessary to enforce international norms, it is very difficult to see much being achieved without the agreement of the major states. Other institutions, such as the CSCE, are more likely to play a conciliatory role prior to crises coming to a head while there are still opportunities for quiet diplomacy. However, quiet diplomacy can lead to its own complacency and often requires for success credible warnings of the consequences of failure, especially in respect of political leaders who have convinced themselves that violation of international norms need carry no penalties. Lastly, there is an early warning function of a dispute which has hitherto been ignored starting to bubble. Again this is an area where in principle international organisations might be expected to play a role but which may still depend on the intelligence-gathering capacities of the major states – and even these are overloaded these days.

The problem is not that power politics are irrelevant in the new age but that we have yet to develop appropriate power politics. There is a welcome lack of destructive great power rivalry and certainly no obvious readiness to carve up the world. This is a major advance. The problem is the opposite: great power reluctance to get involved in the quarrels and squabbles of others. In these circumstances it is likely that each region will have its own power politics. The problem is particularly acute in Europe at the moment because so much is in flux. There are numerous potential points of contention but we do not know as yet how much these matter nor the weight and determination which individual states will bring to them. In this sense there is a lot to play for in what might be patronisingly described as 'political education' – bringing the new generation of political leaders who have taken over from the communists up to date in concepts and methods of security and crisis management.

In the absence of direct threats to our own political structures and societies, what are our responsibilities for international order and what sacrifices, in both the military and economic spheres, are we prepared to accept to achieve them? This question is almost impossible to answer in the abstract and so it tends to be answered on a case-by-case basis, with the result that the new security order is emerging less through a grand design than through particular responses to particular crises.

If none of these crises are actually resolved, let alone managed, then they become cumulative. If they break out of their current boundaries and start to spread, they could soon become linked – Slovakia's argument with Hungary over a dam on the Danube could extend into a challenge to the Hungarian minority in Slovakia, which could in turn link with the potentially vulnerable position of Hungarian minorities in Rumania and Serbia. The mechanisms by which the current set of Yugoslav wars could engulf Kosovo, extend into Macedonia or revive in Croatia are well known. They could well have come to pass by the time this chapter is published. Russia is watching the Serbian precedent lest it feels obliged to act to protect its own nationals – in the Baltics or Moldova, for example.

It is this combination of political instability and economic uncertainty which leads to the unnerving possibility that Europe is facing not so much a set of awkward but essentially localised problems consequential on the transition from the Cold War to the post-Cold War world, but is actually confronting a crisis of historic proportions. The starting point for a response will be a recognition by Western states that this is a crisis in which they have a direct stake.

BRITISH DEFENCE POLICY

2

A Decade of Change in European Security

THE RT. HON. MALCOLM RIFKIND QC MP
Secretary of State for Defence

Like everything else, the way we think about our defence is having to adapt to the rapidly changing political and security scene in Europe. I intend to discuss the changes we see, and how NATO is adapting and the kind of contribution we think Europe – particularly the Western European Union (WEU) – can make to Europe's own defence and to the common effort.

The world has changed dramatically in recent years. I do not intend to rehearse all those changes; it is sufficient simply to stress their unpredictability. As an example, some were forecasting Gorbachev's fall 'within six months' even in 1986 but few foresaw the eventual manner of his going, still less the transformation of the Soviet Union into the Commonwealth of Independent States (CIS), which may itself prove to be a transitory stage.

In 1986, the Soviet Union was still in Afghanistan, Poland, Hungary, Czechoslovakia, and the German Democratic Republic; the Berlin wall still stood; Germany was not united; Albania was a Communist backwater; Ceaucescu reigned in Romania; Yugoslavia was a single country. The Cold War was still intense, although defrosting somewhat, thanks to Gorbachev. The changes since 1986 have mostly been benign and welcome but the new Europe is a far less predictable place than that of the awful certainties of East-West, bloc to bloc confrontation. The events of the past few years suggest that certainties and predictabilities are unlikely to be found.

DEFENCE

Against this scene of hopeful yet volatile uncertainty, who would not be a little cautious in defence matters? I have referred to the unpredictability of the past because it is equally relevant to the present and the future.

It seems to me particularly appropriate to avoid the whims of fashion when tackling defence issues. The success of Western defence policy in the past 40 years, since the foundation of NATO is rooted in the continuity of policy which the Alliance collectively achieved. I am struck by the contrast between the success of that period and the defence and security failures of the inter-war years. In the post war era, unlike the 1920s and 1930s, we learnt the lessons of history, and accordingly we may not be destined to repeat them. I hope that we will manage to sustain that post war achievement in the more volatile times which we have now entered.

The dispositions set out in the White Paper 'Britain's Defence for the Nineties' are based on the blend of caution, continuity and adaptation on which I lay stress; keeping Britain prepared to play an active role in the new security issues of Europe and ready, at the same time, to meet all eventualities with our allies.[1]

We recognise the facts that: the Cold War is over; the Warsaw Pact no longer exists; the countries of Central and Eastern Europe and the Baltic States are free and democratic; democracy is beginning to take root in Russia itself; Russian troops have withdrawn from Hungary and Czechoslovakia and have a programme to withdraw from Eastern Germany and Poland; new arms control treaties have been negotiated which promise much if we can ratify them soon: new vigour has been breathed into such institutions as the United Nations (UN) and the Conference on Security and Cooperation in Europe (CSCE).

But, with change comes instability: Yugoslavia may not be the last place where the need for peacekeeping in Europe is defined; the Republics of the Commonwealth of Independent States have yet to settle finally their relationships one with another; there are massive uncertainties associated with nuclear weapons control and allocation of conventional forces; malign capabilities in the chemical and biological weapons field exist and may pose a threat; ballistic missile and nuclear proliferation are an increasing danger; Iraq continues to constitute a threat to security and stability in the Middle East.

Moreover, the new situation may bring forth new calls upon our resources. Peacekeeping is likely to be an important one. In the first 40 years of the UN's existence, it undertook 13 peace-keeping operations. Since 1988 alone, there have been 12 – an exponential rate of growth. The UK has undertaken new commitments in Yugoslavia and Cambodia in recent months, and NATO has agreed to provide resources and expertise in support of CSCE peacekeeping operations. At the same time, a different type of defence obligation, that of assisting former adversaries to place the control of their defence in a democratic and constitutional setting, will rightly call for a new investment of intellectual resources and experience by Western defence authorities. We are already engaged in developing and implementing programmes of dialogue and cooperation with almost all of the states of Central and Eastern Europe.

WESTERN EUROPEAN SECURITY

The intense, monolithic threat to our security of the Cold War epoch is being replaced by new, more complex risks. At a time of change and unpredictability, Europe will be wise to sustain those institutions – above all NATO – which firmly engage North America in collective western security. At the same time, however, it will be right also for European partners to play a proportionately greater part in securing our own defence.

THE ROLE OF NATO

Beginning with changes in NATO: what is most striking is the vigour and vitality shown by NATO in adapting itself to changed circumstances over the past two or three years. With the end of the Cold War, there were many who predicted an end to NATO; or who claimed that its integrated structure no longer had a *raison d'être*. Instead, thanks to a process of constructive debate involving all the Alliance members, NATO's policies and strategies have been thoroughly overhauled.

The November 1991 NATO summit in Rome saw the completion of the Alliance's new Strategic Concept. This published document sets out clearly the role which NATO will play in the future. Moreover, all NATO allies (including France – a point that strikes me as very welcome) participated fully in the formulation of the Concept and signed up to the final document.

NATO has also overhauled its military strategy and force structure to meet the changed strategic environment and the more diverse set of risks now facing us all. Central to this process has been the creation of the Allied Command Europe Rapid Reaction Corps, a multinational formation with a major and militarily highly effective European component: so far 10 European countries are participating, and there is a substantial US contribution. The corps will provide NATO with a flexible means of responding quickly and effectively to crises ranging from instability on its borders to all out aggression.

These developments illustrate a continued commitment by all NATO's 16 members to the future of the Alliance. They exemplify the resilience of NATO; its ability to adapt itself in the face of events and its vital importance to the future of defence both European and trans-Atlantic.

The creation of the North Atlantic Cooperation Council, which held its first meeting in Brussels on 20 December 1991, added an important new dimension. Now the 16 members of NATO are joined in this forum by the countries of the former Warsaw Pact in a new consultative institution. Nations once ranged against each other are now keen to understand and learn from one another. All the Republics of the Commonwealth of Independent States, the Baltic States and the five Eastern European countries which once belonged to the Warsaw Pact are now members. More recently, in April 1992 Defence Ministers and their Chiefs of Defence of these countries met to extend the dialogue further.

The nations of Central and Eastern Europe clearly see NATO as an important bulwark of stability in a changing continent and as a beacon of the determination of Western democratic countries to maintain the power of free democratic values in Europe.

Our European defence policy has, therefore, two important premises.

First, NATO will continue to be what Chancellor Kohl recently called 'the anchor of European Security'. It remains the primary instrument of Western collective defence for the Allies. It is the essential forum for consultation and policy-making on their security and defence commitments under the Washington Treaty. In addition, NATO will increasingly play a crucial role in broader European security. It will be active in security consultations, arms control and, where necessary, peacekeeping efforts on the Continent; NATO offers a means for a richer and more stable Western Europe to help spread democracy, military reform and security to its Eastern neighbours and the countries of the former Soviet Union. As such, it will be at the centre of the institutions that will in future contribute to the peace and stability of the continent as a whole.

Second, the United States is going to stay in Europe. The United States makes a vital contribution to European security through NATO, its new role in the CSCE, and through the leadership which it has given recently in the crucial area of nuclear arms reduction and non-proliferation.

THE ROLE OF THE WESTERN EUROPEAN UNION

Given the above, how can a stronger Europe and the United States work together in future to assure peace and security throughout the continent, and the defence of NATO members?

This requires us to look ahead, as NATO did at the November 1991 Rome Summit. NATO leaders reaffirmed then that development of a European security identity and defence role would reinforce the integrity and effectiveness of the Alliance. This approach was reflected in the Maastricht Treaty which presages the emergence of a European Union with implications for the way we think about and organise defence. NATO will remain the corner-stone of European defence and the ultimate guarantor of the defence of the European Union. Within that framework, we should expect a number of gradual but major changes ahead.

First, it was agreed that the European Union's Common Foreign and Security Policy should include the eventual framing of a common defence policy, which must be compatible with NATO.

Second, it was also made clear that the building up of a specifically European capability in defence will be achieved gradually and through the Western European Union. The WEU is an autonomous body of European countries founded under its own Treaty in 1948 and with long-standing links to NATO. It will remain independent of both the European Union and NATO, but with close links to both.

One crucial purpose of developing the WEU is as a means to strengthen the European Pillar of the Alliance. Work on developing an operational role for the WEU is now underway. The Petersberg Declaration, which was agreed by me and my colleagues at the WEU Council of Ministers meeting in Bonn in June 1992, set out ways in which WEU nations could take a practical step forward in European defence in accordance with what was agreed at Rome and Maastricht.[2]

Specifically, it identified roles and missions which would seem to be appropriate for the WEU. In addition to the common defence of European territory, these are: tasks of combat forces in crisis management, including peacemaking; peacekeeping tasks; humanitarian and rescue tasks.

One of the most valuable potential prizes to be gained through a more substantial and coordinated European Defence effort would be the ability to bring a more coherent European military contribution to the support of wider Western security interests. This would be right in itself, in furtherance of European interests; and would be of value to our US allies, with whom we would in all probability be working closely in such circumstances. This was what happened in the Gulf in 1990–91. We were lucky then to have time to make ad hoc arrangements: for the future we need to be able to move quickly if needed.

Much of what is contained in the Petersberg Declaration accords with the UK's own approach to the new European defence identity; that is, that it should be developed within the WEU and organised so as to maintain the core functions of NATO, while giving impetus to collective European defence efforts. A number of key principles underlie this approach.

First, it is essential that all WEU partners should be involved on an equal footing; and that the authority for deployment and command of European forces in cases where NATO is not involved should come collectively from the Council of Ministers of the WEU. WEU member states should make relevant forces available to the WEU, drawing on those with NATO or national roles. Missions by European forces where NATO is not involved – including any operation flowing from the Common Foreign and Security Policy – should be planned and executed under the authority of the WEU as a whole. We should therefore get ahead with planning for a variety of contingencies, recognising that there will always be a political decision of governments at the time whether to sanction or participate in a specific operation.

Second, WEU forces should be drawn from existing assets – i.e. by identifying NATO or other national forces for use by the WEU on such agreed missions. This would mirror the way US forces in Europe are assigned both NATO and national roles. It is both undesirable and unnecessary to set up standing WEU forces or a standing command structure to rival that of NATO. Indeed it is difficult to see how standing forces or a standing command structure would be possible without conflicting with the primary obligation to NATO of those forces assigned to them.

Third, forces made available to the WEU should cover as full a range of capabilities as possible, including land, sea and air forces. I shall return later to the subject of what type of forces the UK could consider putting at WEU's disposal.

The contingency planning for WEU military operations will be carried out by a central WEU Planning Cell located in Brussels with close links to the WEU Secretariat which moved to Brussels on 1st January 1993. This cell started work on 1 October 1992. Once fully operational it will, under the guidance of the WEU Chiefs of Staff, recommend to the WEU Council how the forces available to the WEU might be packaged and commanded to carry out anticipated tasks. In consultation with NATO, it will also make plans for exercising those capabilities when approved by the WEU Council.

We should make every effort to emphasise multinational military formations. This is increasingly happening in NATO, and is the right pattern for the WEU. The UK has long sustained with the Netherlands a joint amphibious force: France and Germany have been developing a joint land force unit. NATO is developing multinational reaction forces with Britain, the

Netherlands, Germany and Belgium as participants in a multi-national division.

Partners should be encouraged to contribute according to their capabilities. Some have particular expertise in deploying forces outside Europe; let them work together. Some have particular naval capabilities. Some have more plentiful infantry and lighter forces suited to humanitarian and peacekeeping tasks. There will probably be a need for rotation of some responsibilities (for example, four countries might take on part of a peacekeeping force contribution for six months every two years). Some allies have constraints, which we understand, on their participation in operations outside the NATO area. A flexible approach, making maximum use of existing assets, will be the most practical way of proceeding.

For real work to begin it is important for WEU countries to identify the range of assets they can each contribute on which the military planners in the WEU will then be able to draw in defining forces appropriate to particular contingencies.

The approach which the UK advocates is to sustain the clear assignment of allies' forces to NATO while at the same time providing an ability to employ them for WEU purposes when that seems necessary. A decision to do so would require prior consultation within NATO, of course, to ensure that they are not simultaneously required for their NATO assignments. We thereby greatly strengthen our ability to respond to security problems but without duplicating force structures which would be politically dangerous, unaffordable – and make no military sense.

In a conflict or crisis within Europe, decisions on the appropriate response will of course be taken in the North Atlantic Council. NATO would deal with threats to Alliance territory directly, using the command structures set up under SACEUR and the forces assigned to him by the nations. However, it is conceivable that some situations might arise on which a consensus view was reached within NATO that a purely European response was more appropriate – for example in the case of humanitarian aid in a natural disaster.

In a crisis arising elsewhere, where Europe's interests were engaged, it would be open to the WEU Council to determine upon a European response in its own right. There should be

prior consultation within NATO, both because this would make
prudent common sense and to establish that any forces to be
used were not simultaneously required for NATO assignments .

It is right to set out these mechanisms for decision-making
and consultation clearly. Even outside Europe, action by
European states in a given situation is likely more often than
not, though not necessarily, to be in concert with a response by
the United States – because the identity of interests between
Europe and the USA in defence and security matters is so
strong. The Gulf conflict bears this out. So one should beware of
emphasising separateness for its own sake. Rather, I stress again
the potential prize of a more effective Western European
response in any future crisis – alongside the United States and
other allies.

How then might a WEU force be assembled on the basis I
have described? I stress that what follows is illustrative, bearing
upon subjects about which we are consulting closely with our
allies.

First, any WEU sponsored operation, whether humanitarian,
peacekeeping or military intervention, would require a static
Joint Headquarters (JHQ) for command and control. We
believe that the WEU should take advantage of such headquarters offered by a variety of nations as being available to meet the
needs of a specific situation. For example, we in the UK have
two locations that have already proved themselves in war and
could be made available for any foreseeable WEU task. At
Northwood our joint maritime/land/air HQ master-minded
the Falklands Conflict, whilst the UK contribution to the Gulf
war was commanded from our other joint HQ at High
Wycombe. Both JHQs have extensive command, control, communications and intelligence facilities and stand ready to
support any WEU operation. Our mobile Joint Forces
Headquarters, which deploys forward for in-theatre command
and control, was well-proven in both the Falklands and the Gulf
conflicts and could also be made available to the WEU if
desired. Such an arrangement would be both efficient and economic, avoiding the unnecessary cost and duplication of
creating new, separate WEU HQ structures. Other countries
will have similar examples of what they could contribute. The
whole point is that the effort should be a common one, and led

on different occasions by those with the resources most appropriate to the particular task.

Turning to availability of forces, a WEU operation may require the provision of land forces. Here the UK could make a useful and substantial contribution on the basis which I have described. Since our modern army is designed as a professional, multi-role force, it is ideally equipped to adapt to any of the three main task areas facing the WEU – humanitarian, peacekeeping or military intervention.

We are also involved, with our Belgian, Dutch and German colleagues, in the NATO Multinational Division (Central), a highly mobile Division to which the UK contributes 24th Airmobile Brigade, forming up over the next two years. This is the kind of multinational formation which might be highly relevant to WEU purposes where not required by NATO (which would, of course, have to agree to its release for that purpose).

Maritime forces are an important tool in crisis management and are likely to feature high on any WEU shopping list. At the lower end of the spectrum they can enforce an embargo, carry out immigration control operations or conduct general surveillance and deter any counter threats to European interests; maritime forces can be used to evacuate European and other nationals from a trouble-spot. In addition to the contributions which could be made by a number of European navies, the well-practised UK/Netherlands Landing Force, could, for example, be a candidate for a range of WEU operations.

The Gulf War vividly demonstrated the role of air power in a major conflict. There is a range of tasks in which European air forces might play a part. In our own case, in addition to the rapid deployment of peacekeeping or intervention forces, our air transport aircraft have frequently been to the fore in humanitarian tasks, for example when providing much-needed food supplies to Ethiopia and Northern Iraq.

The essential message here is that the WEU should have available to it a variety of forces and capabilities: the Franco-German Corps may be one of these. There will also be many others. As long as they operate under the WEU and are compatible with our NATO obligations, the Alliance will be strengthened.

I have set out here some views on how we can give real impetus and substance to European defence over the next five years or so. What I have suggested represents for us an exciting challenge and could enable the Western European Union to make a decisive contribution to the peace and security within the trans-Atlantic partnership which we enjoy in NATO. It will give Europe more flexibility and capability of action without breaking the bonds of consultation and military organisation which keep NATO together.

I hope that WEU partners will share our approach and, in the spirit of the Petersberg Declaration, join the UK in responding to WEU requirements. This would enable us to complement NATO's strengths, and could contribute to a solid defence in future: a strong European Pillar, in a strong Alliance.

Notes

[1] *Statement on the Defence Estimates. Britain's Defence for the 90s,* Vol 1, Cm 1559 – I, (London, HMSO, 1991).

[2] The WEU Ministerial Meeting took place at the Petersberg, outside Bonn, on 19 June 1992.

3

Options for Change:
A Political Critique

BRUCE GEORGE MP and NICK RYAN

*Bruce George is Labour Member of Parliament for Walsall South
and Nick Ryan is his Research Assistant*

On 6 February 1990, in answer to an oral question in the House
of Commons on British defence policy after the European revolutions of 1989, then-Secretary of State for Defence Tom King
announced that the Government would be examining 'options
for change'. This first indication of a defence review – or, more
correctly, of defence cuts – was greeted with some scepticism:
MPs were concerned that any defence review should be undertaken on the basis of an understanding of the future security
environment and not solely under Treasury pressure. A further
concern was that Options for Change should be conducted in
full consultation with all parties concerned – that is, Parliament,
the Armed Forces, Alliance partners and the public.

Mr King repeatedly assured Parliament that *Options for Change*
– named after his initial reference – would meet these concerns.
His assurances have, however, failed to be fully realised. There
has been little consultation and three years after the initial
announcement there has still not been any strategic justification
for the cuts. The exercise has, in most commentators' opinion,
been more a Treasury-led cost-cutting programme than a thorough-going review of British defence needs into the new
century. Many individuals, political parties and the House of
Commons Defence Committee (HCDC) maintain that what is
necessary is a full defence review; but while the Government
continues to adhere to the initial decisions made in 1990, it may
well be left to a future government to undertake such a review.
By then, however, with resources substantially reduced, com-

mensurate reductions in commitments will probably have to be found, so that the eventual result of *Options for Change* will be a continuation of the post-war British defence policy pattern of contraction by fits and starts.

BRITISH DEFENCE POLICY:
THE STRATEGIC BACKGROUND

It hardly needs to be stated that the *Options for Change* process was initiated against a background of immense change in the global security environment. It would be superfluous to discuss here the reasons for the final collapse of the Soviet Union and the Warsaw Treaty Organisation or to look back at the Cold War which consequentially ended. It will suffice instead to note a few of the epochal events of 1990–92 which form the background to defence planning in the 1990s, for NATO and for Britain.

The final collapse of communism in Eastern and Central Europe and the emergence of democratic, pluralistic and democratising societies: the failed Soviet coup and the subsequent implosion of the Soviet Union leading to the Commonwealth of Independent States; the declarations of independence of the Baltic republics from what was still a Goliathan Soviet Union; the disbandment of the Warsaw Pact and the Council for Mutual Economic Assistance which raised the Iron Curtain; the reunification of Germany and its corollary – an eastward extension of NATO's borders; the historic Conventional Forces in Europe (CFE) and Strategic Arms Reduction (START) Treaties; and the European crises in the wake of the Maastricht Treaty, all had enormous consequences for the Alliance.

The quest for a restructured, rebalanced Alliance gathered momentum after 1989 as all NATO nations reduced their force levels and as the European community attempted to establish its own foreign and security policy and defence identity. The impending demise of NATO had been predicted since its inception in 1949. It has endured many crises, internal and external, real and imaginary, many of which were believed to be terminal. Critics now argue it is superfluous, yet it has shown a remarkable resilience and capacity to adapt to rapidly changing circumstances.

The NATO London Declaration of 6 July 1990 declared that NATO must continue to provide for the common defence but also 'be even more an agent of change'; accordingly, three reviews were launched:

1 the North Atlantic Council set up a political 'brainstorming' process to adapt the Alliance to the new circumstances in Europe;
2 the Ad Hoc Strategy Review Group prepared a new Strategic Concept 'moving away from "forward defence", where appropriate, towards a reduced forward presence and modifying "flexible response" to reflect a reduced reliance on nuclear weapons';
3 the Military Strategy Group was charged with implementing the decisions taken in the Strategy Review Group.

The outcome of these reviews were, particularly, the development of a liaison programme with the ex-Warsaw Pact member states and changes in NATO strategy, command structures and force levels. These changes were formalised at the Rome Summit of November 1991 in the creation of the North Atlantic Cooperation Council (NACC) – as an institutionalisation of the liaison programme – and in the announcement of the New Strategic Concept, which included replacing the 'layer cake' force structures of national Corps allocated to sectors within the three main NATO Regions with a concept based on multinational, mobile forces, and with the emphasis on flexibility.

These changes have been prompted by new perceptions of the threat environment. Gone are fears of a massive offensive across Central Europe. Instead, emphasis has shifted to a 'new arc of crisis'[1] which extends from the Mediterranean, through Eastern Europe and into the former Soviet Union. Not only do a variety of existing and potential conflicts threaten to further destabilise democratic state-building in the post-communist states, but knock-on effects such as massive refugee movements threaten the stability of Western European states themselves, as any German will attest. Furthermore, the huge arsenal which the Soviet Union bequeathed to its successor states presents a real residual worry. It is unfashionable to speak of a residual Soviet threat, but democracy is far from consolidated in Russia, it retains the largest army in the world and is still a formidable nuclear power; and the division of the former Soviet nuclear arsenal represents a form of nuclear proliferation which cannot be disregarded.

The threat environment has been further punctuated by developments outside Europe. Of most obvious relevance was the invasion of Kuwait by Iraq in 1990 and the international coalition's military intervention, an action with ramifications for NATO, as an example of how Out of Area operations might be required in support of the United Nations.

It is, then, wrong to claim that NATO has failed to adapt. That NATO has changed, however, is not tantamount to concluding that its adaptation is complete. It continues its restructuring – as, for instance, in the restructuring of the Northern, Central and Channel Commands – and the first manifestation of the 'transformed Alliance' came when the North Atlantic Council, meeting at Oslo on 5 June 1992, agreed to offer *inter alia*, Alliance resources and expertise for CSCE peacekeeping on a case-by-case basis. This overdue narrowing of the 'out-of-area' debate could serve as a precedent for further measures acting, as the NATO leaders declared at the November 1991 Rome Summit, upon the 'conviction that our own security is inseparably linked to that of all other states in Europe'.

POST-WAR BRITISH DEFENCE POLICY

The British Government's response to the new environment – *Options for Change* – must be seen against the continuities and changes of post-war British defence policy. This is not the first time that the British Government has examined defence forces and expenditure, although the epochal period of 1989–1992 has possibly posed more dramatic dilemmas for this Government than for its post-war predecessors.

It should not be forgotten that Britain was, during its imperial heyday, a superpower. Both the First and Second World Wars were a drain on British power, but the changes in the geopolitical balance caused by the latter marked the beginning of a steady shift to second-rank power. To most outsiders (and many insiders) post-war British defence policy has been characterised by continual, disorderly and, at times, major contractions caused by severe economic problems. The image of a 'pillar to post' process resulting in a military of 'brass bands and admirals' is inaccurate; however, a process of reshaping has occurred, with distinct elements of continuity and change.

Throughout the post-war period, successive defence reviews have sought to reconcile the conflicting demands of British commitments, resources and defence priorities. The reviews of 1957, 1966–68, 1974–75 and 1981 all had to find areas in which to make cuts while maintaining – to the most viable degree – the areas of greatest priority. A major consequence of these successive reviews has been a steady contraction in the size of British armed forces and the proportion of GDP devoted to defence expenditure. Britain has experienced the second-largest reduction (31.8 per cent) in military personnel in NATO since 1971, after Portugal – between 1951 and 1990 the figure fell from over 825,000 to 320,000[2]; and by 1 April 1991 fell further to 306,500[3] – while defence expenditure, as a percentage of GDP, has fallen from its 1951–53 high of 10 per cent to 3.8 per cent in 1991–92; it is projected to fall further to 3.2 per cent in 1994–95.

This change has not been an orderly, rational process, but has occurred erratically, with gradual change punctuated by more dramatic contractions after the four major reviews. It should be pointed out that there exists a distinction between an 'official' defence review and a review by stealth. Conservative governments have been reluctant to admit to carrying out defence reviews – although both *The Way Forward* in 1981 and *Options for Change* contain elements of a defence review – and therefore tend to minimise the significance of changes. It is often the case that creeping reductions are left to Labour governments to resolve through a review.

If a contraction of resources has been a noticeable feature of change in post-war defence policy, there has not been a commensurate contraction of commitments. While the mid-1960s and mid-1970s reviews withdrew British forces from a variety of colonial commitments, other post-war commitments had been developed which were no less substantial. The priorities which have been established and the continuance of substantial British defence and security commitments are illustrated by the major continuities of post-war defence policy. First, the commitment to

NATO – initiated through the Attlee Government's founding role in that organisation – continues to take priority in British defence planning. Britain contributes the highest proportion of national armed forces to NATO of all member states, and has been heavily represented within the NATO commands. While a restructuring of the NATO Commands has altered Britain's status slightly – the incorporation of what was the Major NATO Command of Allied Command Channel into a new Major Subordinate Command (CINCNORTHWEST) removes a UK Major NATO Command but creates a UK Major Subordinate Command – British prominence is nevertheless maintained through its new command of the Allied Command Europe Rapid Reaction Corps (ARRC).

The second aspect of continuity – Britain's Atlanticist orientation – is vividly demonstrated by the priority placed on NATO, in contrast to some European countries' attempts to invigorate the West European Union (WEU) as the defence component of European Union. Although Britain is a member of the WEU, and as a signatory to the Maastricht Treaty acknowledges a European defence role for it, the British Government nevertheless tends to play down the significance of that organisation. Britain's clear preference for Atlanticist institutions, rather than European ones, is paralleled by the importance attached to the Anglo-American 'special relationship'. Events such as the American invasion of Grenada in 1983 and the use of British bases to launch bombing missions of Libya in 1986 have spurred criticism of the special relationship as supine British endorsement of US policy. However, while the United States has, for instance, gained the use of strategically important sites such as Diego Garcia and Ascension Island, Britain has also benefited from excellent terms in the purchase of Polaris and Trident nuclear missiles; and received intelligence and other assistance during the Falklands War. The relationship, its supporters say, is clearly more mutually beneficial than critics would hold. It remains to be seen how the special relationship will develop under the Clinton Administration.

The third element of continuity is Britain's relatively high level of defence expenditure. While, as already noted, there has been a steady decline in defence spending as a percentage of GDP, in comparison to most members of NATO, the level remains high. Since 1970, Britain has regularly maintained the third or fourth highest defence expenditure of NATO's 15 defence-spending members[4]. While it has been pointed out that the 'percentage of GDP' model is not an accurate comparative measure of defence spending because of the effects of exchange rates, the costs of individual states' defence structures, the difference in states' defence commitments and the simple observation that states' GDPs are not identical, British defence expenditure is nevertheless relatively high using three different measures[5].

Finally, an important element of continuity in British defence policy is the defence consensus that has existed for the most part throughout the post-war period. Whereas the Conservative Party has often been portrayed as the party of defence, the Labour Party has had an equally large role in formulating and implementing Britain's post-war defence. Ernest Bevin, the Attlee Government's Foreign Minister, was instrumental in the founding of NATO, and the same Labour government oversaw the initial development of the British independent nuclear deterrent.

The issue of defence has rarely divided fundamentally the major parties. The period of Labour nuclear unilateralism between 1981 and 1988 was more remarkable as a deviation from the general consensus than as a continuation of division. The capital that the Conservative Party was able to make from Labour's stance, illustrated Labour's distance from the majority of the electorate which had not accompanied Labour on its diversionary jaunt. Labour's 1988 Policy Review saw a quiet abandonment of the unilateralist policy, with a renewed emphasis on electability in the wake of the 1987 General Election defeat. This revision of Labour Party policy, combined with the hugely changed geopolitical situation since the late 1980s, contributed to the virtual absence of debate on defence in the 1992 General Election campaign.

OPTIONS FOR CHANGE

Against this background of a rapidly changing security environment, an evolving NATO strategy and the enduring continuities of British defence policy, *Options for Change* was announced. The 6 February 1990 hint was followed up on 25 July 1990 with announcements of the scale of cuts being initiated: forces stationed in Germany would be roughly halved; the Royal Navy's surface fleet would be reduced by one-fifth; the conventionally-armed submarine fleet would be nearly halved; and overall personnel numbers would be reduced by roughly eighteen per cent[6].

Almost immediately after Mr King's announcement to Parliament, however, the invasion of Kuwait by Iraq intervened, initially to defer, and later to question, the 'options' process and some of its proposals. Although the costs of Operation *Granby* – Britain's contribution to the coalition – have since been offset by foreign contributions, and therefore have not significantly affected the MoD's budgetary targets, the implications of the war, coming so soon after ideas had been expressed of a New World Order and of an opportunity for a period of international peace and security, led to a questioning of the strategic justification for such force reductions.

Although the Gulf action interrupted its plans, the Government continued to pursue its initial objectives. The plans for the RAF and Royal Navy announced in the 25 July 1990 statement – that is, the disbandment of the RAF's four remaining Phantom squadrons, the reduction from 11 to six in the number of Tornado Ground Attack squadrons, the closure of two of the four RAF Germany bases, the reduction of RAF personnel from 89,000 to 75,000, the reduction of the Royal Navy's frigate and destroyer fleet from 'around 50' to 'around 40' ships, and the near halving of the Navy's conventionally-armed submarine fleet – remained unchanged after the Gulf War and remain mostly unaltered to this day. Furthermore, between June and July 1991, the extent of Army reductions was made more explicit than had previously been the case. The Army would be reduced from roughly 160,000 personnel to 116,000 by the mid-1990s; the British Army of the Rhine (BAOR) would be cut from 55,000 to 23,000 personnel; armoured regiments would be reduced from 19 to 11, and infantry battalions would be reduced from 55 to 38 by 31 March 1998; the Royal Artillery would be reduced from 22 to 16 regiments and the Royal Engineers from 15 to 10 regiments. In addition, cuts and restructuring in the Territorial Army were announced in December 1991. Reductions in personnel levels would be achieved through a combination of turnover and redundancies – the latter predominantly affecting officers and NCOs, with the first redundancies to occur in February 1992.

These changes have prompted opposition from virtually every quarter. The arguments which have been levelled against *Options for Change* highlight the dilemmas which have faced successive governments seeking to make deep cuts to British forces. One such dilemma pitted the requirement to produce a competent force for high-intensity conflict with the Warsaw Pact against the reality of an army dominated by its commitments to Northern Ireland and low-intensity conflict. A second dilemma has been whether, with a constantly declining budget, to spend most of the resources available on major platforms and systems that contribute to deterrence (and that look impressive in the annual Defence White Paper and the IISS's *Military Balance*) or to have fewer expensive systems and invest more in sustainability and infrastructure. Successive governments have chosen the former, and were very nearly caught out in the 1991 Gulf War when, for instance, forced to cannibalise all but a handful of the BAOR's Challenger tanks to provide spares for those sent to the Gulf.

RESPONSES TO *OPTIONS FOR CHANGE*

The criticism which has been aroused by *Options for Change* comes from three main perspectives. The first, representing a broad body of Parliamentary and military opinion, is not unsympathetic to the Government; it recognises the dilemmas of defence savings, but accuses the Government of failing to reconcile them in any way that satisfies Britain's defence needs within new realities; it also criticises the Government for failing to enter into debate or discussion over its choices, and for continuing doggedly to pursue *Options* in the face of strong opposition. The opposition to *Options for Change* from this quarter can therefore be grouped into criticisms of process and criticisms of content.

Criticisms of process

A major failing of *Options for Change* is the manner in which decisions about changes to British defence structures have been made. Great concern has been expressed over the lack of consultation that such swingeing changes necessitate, not only because democratic government demands debate, but also because it is felt that the Government has been able to avoid the strategic implications of its decisions which are suspected of being driven by pressure to reduce defence expenditure. While a discussion of the centralised nature of decision-making over national security is beyond the scope of this chapter, such major changes of policy and structure of forces, roles and missions should entail wide public debate and should be open to the influence of expert opinion.

The HCDC, in its 1990 report *Defence Implications of Recent Events* ('DIRE') – which was released only hours before Tom King's 25 July announcement – considered the moment to be ideal 'for a debate on the scale of resources which the country wishes to devote to defence', including a discussion over the level of British defence expenditure in relation to its NATO partners, and argued forcefully that:

> Decisions must not be announced in advance of discussion of the conceptual framework within which they are taken. In many cases decisions would in any event be premature, until the outcome of current international negotiations is known. There is ample time for debate. *Options for Change* should be published in a Green Paper format to permit full public and parliamentary debate, rather than as a promulgation of decisions already made.[7]

Tom King was adamant in 1990 that full consultation would be undertaken over *Options for Change*. In the 25 July 1990 debate he avowed that he would 'honour my pledge of a genuine opportunity for consultation so that the changes can be orderly and sensible, with the maximum involvement of those concerned'. Yet by 1992 the HCDC continued to point out that, where it had recommended public scrutiny and debate: 'None of this has happened'[8].

It has been pointed out that the study behind *Options for Change* was conducted by several dozen people within the

Defence Staff and the Office of Management and Budget[9]. The excessive secrecy and centralisation of this process, leading to an undebated statement of policy, is nowhere more apparent than in the decision to reduce the number of infantry battalions from 55 to 38 and to amalgamate many historic regiments. In a memorandum submitted by the Save our Staffords Campaign to the HCDC on behalf of the Staffordshire Regiment, it was stated that: 'The Colonel of the Regiment was told of the amalgamation [with the Cheshire Regiment] just twenty minutes before the Secretary of State's Statement to the House'[10]. The decisions concerning infantry cuts were made by the Army Board and endorsed by Ministers without informing the HCDC, Parliament or the regiments of the rationale for amalgamations and without giving details of the criteria leading to the decisions[11].

There was great concern, after Mr King's initial reference, that any changes, in the words of a HCDC report released also on 25 July 1990, should 'bear the imprimatur of the NATO consultative process'[12]. Mr King assured the House of Commons that such consultations would take place. In reply to an oral question of 6 February 1990 he stated:

> I certainly agree that any changes must be made after consultation among allies and must follow clear advice from the military advisers, under the leadership of Supreme Allied Commander, Europe, General Galvin, to ensure that whatever changes and reductions are made, they maintain the military credibility and effectiveness of Alliance defence.

Notwithstanding the Secretary of State's assurances, the announcement, *inter alia*, of a reduction in the Royal Navy's frigate/destroyer fleet to around 40 ships was, as the HCDC points out, 'not preceded by any formal discussions with NATO. It is regrettable that NATO seems to have been bypassed in setting new levels for the Royal Navy's surface fleet'[13].

Britain's was far from alone in cutting its defence expenditure and forces whilst paying insufficient attention to the NATO force planning process, but there remains great concern that Britain's specific failure to follow this process will weaken its ability to meet its commitments precisely at the time when it has taken on leadership of a core NATO force – the ARRC. This failure also weakens the Government's assertion that: 'It remains a key security interest to sustain the present network of multinational Western cooperation and to avoid any reversion to nationally-driven defence'[14]. The lack of any form of consultation about *Options for Change* is seen, then, as a big mistake.

Criticisms of content

The greatest concern from this perspective over *Options for Change* is the Government's continued failure to give any strategic rationale for its actions. Two years after the initial proposals put forward by Mr King, the *Statement on the Defence Estimates 1992* (SDE 92), for the first time, made some effort to redefine the security environment within which *Options for Change* is being implemented. However, this redefinition extended only to a replacement of the four main defence roles of the British armed forces[15] with three new overlapping roles:

☐ To ensure the protection and security of the United Kingdom and our dependent territories, even where there is no major external threat.
☐ To insure against any major external threat to the United Kingdom and our allies.
☐ To contribute to promoting the United Kingdom's wider security interests through the maintenance of international peace and stability.[16]

Arguing that these redefined roles reflect the transformation of the security environment over the past four years, Secretary of State for Defence Malcolm Rifkind states: 'We are reshaping the forces to ensure that they can cope flexibly and robustly with such change. We shall therefore continue to assess the demands likely to be made on our armed forces and ensure that the Services are of a scale and quality able to respond to those challenges'[17].

While acknowledging that these redefined roles were intended only as 'a new way of presenting the evolving situation', the HCDC found it strange that 'new force levels and structures were fixed in July 1990 with some precision before the basic roles which they were to fulfil had been determined even within the Ministry of Defence'[18].

A series of new developments, largely unforeseen in 1990, such as the violent dismemberment of Yugoslavia, the potentially violent break-up of the Soviet Union and growing instability in the Near and Middle East, have led to unexpected new commitments, exemplified by the British UN contingent in Bosnia. The Secretary of State suggests that such developments do not fundamentally challenge the assumptions on which *Options for Change* was based. Commenting on the Secretary of State's assertion, the HCDC stated:

> This implies that the 'key choices' made in 1990 have, by hook or by crook, proved to have been the right ones, and have produced solutions robust and flexible enough to cope with unforeseen changes, leaving the current administration the task of carrying through decisions already made.[19]

Reasoning from past experience, the Committee concluded, as diplomatically as it felt able: 'We find this barely credible'. The certainty with which national forces can be restructured to meet such changes is clouded by developments within and beyond the Atlantic Alliance, particularly in the expanding role of the Western European Union as the embodiment of an emerging European defence and security identity, and because of the pressure exerted on defence budgets by wider economic problems.

The HCDC suspects that the latter economic pressure has maintained a disproportionate influence over British defence policy in the 1990s, and explains the decisions made in *Options for Change* more than does any strategic rationale. This view is reinforced by SDE 92, which states that ' . . . we must ensure that, *within the resources available*, the cover is right for the nature and the scale of the risks we may face,[20] (emphasis added). When the Government, in SDE 92 (presented to Parliament in July 1992), projected continuing reductions in defence spending to 3.4 per cent of GDP in 1994–95, the point was made that even the reduced aims of *Options for Change* would be unsustainable at that level of defence spending; however, in the

Chancellor of the Exchequer's Autumn Statement, delivered only four months after SDE 92, further reductions of £570 million and £480 million were announced for 1993–94 and 1994–95 respectively, so that defence expenditure will fall to 3.2 per cent of GDP in 1994–95. The Chancellor stated that these reductions reflect the effects of lower pay and inflation, but he also goes on to say: 'Some changes will also be needed in commitments and capabilities in the light of the evolving security climate'[21].

Far from assuaging Conservative MP Cyril Townsend's concern, voiced in the 25 July 1990 debate, that *Options for Change* should be 'led by strategic needs and not by the considerable pressures of the Treasury Bench', these observations can only reinforce the view that changes are being driven to a great extent by pressure on public spending. As the HCDC stated in 1991:

> Anyone buying SDE 91 in order to discover the strategic rationale for the changes proposed would be sadly disappointed. What SDE 91 regrettably fails to do, and does not even set out to do, is to argue in any detail the rationale behind the changes proposed, or to provide a coherent strategic overview, in contrast to some previous White Papers which have proposed radical shifts in defence policy.[22]

The HCDC has repeatedly emphasised the importance of matching commitments to resources and *vice versa*. The HCDC's 1991 Report on SDE 91 concludes that either 'sufficient resources must be found, or the Government must acknowledge its inability to meet all the commitments, and take the political decision to reduce or abandon some of them'[23]. There is no evidence that the Government is prepared fully to consider either of these proposals, however. Whereas the HCDC calls for a thorough-going defence review to 'take stock of the totality of the proposals for the British Armed Forces for the next decade, in the light of recent changes in the strategic environment, and of pressures on the defence budget'[24], the Government seems determined to proceed with *Options* under the same assumptions which underlay its introduction. The Government is clearly set on avoiding a thorough-going defence review, and will instead continue the staccato post-war process of adjusting commitments to resources.

To many critics, this Treasury-led approach, is exemplified in the reduction of infantry battalions from 55 to 38 at a time when flexible and mobile force structures point towards enhanced roles for infantry. While inter-service rivalries and differing views of the priorities of continental and maritime roles will necessarily divide opinion over where the brunt of cuts should fall – whether through *Options for Change* or through a wider defence review – it remains true that far greater opposition has been voiced to the programme of abolition and merging of army regiments than to, for instance, the halving of the conventionally-armed submarine fleet. This can partly be explained by the higher public profile of army regiments; emotional attachments based on historical regional and national loyalties account for some of the weight of the public campaigns opposing the Staffordshire/Cheshire and Scottish regimental mergers, for instance.

The campaigns also, however, share concerns within the Army about overstretching capabilities as a result of the reduction in the number of infantry battalions. The HCDC states that, on the basis of evidence submitted to it, there exists 'grave scepticism within the Army, in particular at the claim that the target for the interval between emergency tours can be met'[25]. Even before the majority of *Options for Change* cuts has been implemented, one army specialist suggests, the interval between tours for major units can be as short as eight months (the MoD's target is twenty-four months) and secondment of units between battalions has seriously undermined training, not only within infantry units but also within Combat Support and Logistic units. To achieve the MoD's targets, the Army requires 120 full-strength units – under *Options for Change* the available number will be reduced to sixty-six. Not only will these changes further affect the strength, training and availability of units for normal and emergency tours, but many fear that they will also threaten Britain's ability to meet commitments, especially those such as the ARRC, which is to be a central Alliance commitment, and NATO peace-keeping operations, which will clearly grow.

The ARRC presents great potential for a crisis in Britain's ability to sustain its current level of commitments. Having fought to take a leading role in the ARRC, Britain finds itself committed to commanding that force and to providing two divisions. The corollary of this commitment is that whenever the ARRC is deployed, British troops will be on first call. However, as any discussion of army overstretch makes clear, units allocated to the ARRC are likely to be committed to other roles. The first occasion on which the ARRC is called upon – which, given a deteriorating security environment, could be in the near future – could also precipitate a crisis for the Government.

These observations make any arguments for further cuts unsustainable. Such arguments, which represent the second critical perspective, are based, overridingly, on the absence of any direct threat to Western Europe in the wake of the Soviet collapse and in particular to the absence of any threat to Britain itself. A whole host of groups which were much more influential in the early- to mid-1980s, some of which were associated with the left wing of the Labour Party, have seen their influence diminish. Nevertheless there are many groups calling for very substantial reductions in defence expenditure in the new strategic environment. Two recent papers, published by the Institute for Public Policy Research, a think-tank associated with the Labour Party, present such arguments. Malcolm Chalmers, of the Bradford University Department of Peace Studies, for instance, states that: 'Most of Britain's existing conventional forces can now be justified – if at all – only as a contribution to collective military efforts many hundreds of miles away from the UK itself: in the Third World or, possibly, in Eastern Europe'[26]. The Saferworld Foundation's '50 per cent Initiative', also, bases its argument for a halving of NATO defence budgets by the year 2000 on the decline of the then-Soviet threat and on continued deep cuts through multilateral arms control negotiations.

As is made clear in most debate about *Options for Change*, however, Britain's commitments remain surprisingly diverse. As well as Britain's continuing important contribution to NATO, there remains the important Northern Ireland dimension. With no immediate prospect of a political solution to the stalemate there to justify a reappraisal of the British military presence, this will remain a core commitment which is at the heart of the debate over infantry cuts. Furthermore, considerable attention is being paid to the huge uncertainties of the emergent security environment which – far from reducing commitments as Chalmers implies – threatens to increase them. The majority opinion emphasises the need to maintain British capabilities beyond the limited assumptions of *Options for Change*.

A third critical perspective is opposed to any substantial cuts. This group is somewhat unfairly dismissed as unreconstructed Cold Warriors. It asserts that although the Cold War is over and the Soviet Union fragmented, the levels of Russian forces, the continued ex-communist domination of the Russian armed forces, the ever-present threat of a reactionary backlash against reform and the wider perils of proliferation around the globe suggest that British defence expenditure should be raised to maintain British preparedness for a 'return to Cold War'.

This argument, however, would be difficult to sell to the public, which under present economic conditions clearly seeks a peace dividend. Most politicians, and many in the Armed Forces also, would accept the need for reductions in defence expenditure post-1990 and are therefore sympathetic to the Government's dilemma; hovering around the Government's position, this consensus seeks adjustments in forces on the basis of a clearly-defined security policy.

A defence review cannot be conducted merely in terms of numbers of regiments or ships, but must base its findings on an understanding of the requirements demanded by the security environment (although military personnel would often seek to ameliorate the results of such a study on the basis of traditional inter-service rivalry over resources). The current turbulent and complicated period poses great uncertainty – the nature of the threat environment, the US commitment to Europe and the future of *NATO vis-à-vis* the WEU and the European Community (EC) for instance – for Government defence decision-making. Nevertheless, given that decisions do have to be made, they should be made on the basis of a comprehensive defence review. The British Government claims that its actions create forces which are flexible enough for all contingencies, but there is widespread scepticism of this claim.

POLITICAL PARTIES AND *OPTIONS FOR CHANGE*

The impact of an increasingly volatile security environment after
the hopes of 1989 became gradually dashed by proliferating
conflict globally and, most importantly, in Europe itself – is
vividly illustrated by the defence policy changes of both the
Labour and Liberal Democratic Parties in the last few years.
The defence policies of the Liberal Democratic Party and those
of its leader have undergone a profound transformation, particularly on nuclear weapons. In 1989 the Liberal Democrat
policy document *After the Cold War* argued for a 'comprehensive
Defence Review, with the aims of ensuring a reduction in British
spending on defence in a coherent and managed way'. In 1990,
in the document *Reshaping Europe*, these ideas were elaborated:
citing the Saferworld Foundation's '50 per cent Initiative', the
Liberal Democrats argued that greater European defence integration through EC multinational forces would reduce the
proportional costs of defence for individual member states; they
also argued that the proposals contained in *Options for Change*
did not go far enough; in addition, they confused their earlier
call for a defence review by saying:

> Against the background of our proposed reduction in defence
> spending, government should float options for the future shape
> of UK armed forces for informed Parliamentary, military and
> public debate, rather than produce one single all-embracing
> 'Defence Review'; as the last year has shown, events are likely to
> move so rapidly that the conclusions of any such Review would be
> rendered quickly out of date.[27]

By 1992, although they were again arguing for a comprehensive Defence Review[28], they criticised *Options for Change* as
cutting infantry battalions too heavily and because it relies too
heavily on fixed monetary targets – notwithstanding their earlier '50 per cent policy'. The *Shared Security* document suggested
ways in which overseas commitments could be reduced, and
argued that the profound shift in the priority of roles after the
decline of the Soviet threat made certain British roles – such as
Atlantic maritime duties and British air defence – open to
reassessment.

The Labour Party's return to the security consensus was partly occasioned by the changing world environment and electoral considerations. The chasm which divided it from the Government in the 1980s was narrowed very sharply by the Government's substantial reduction in resources devoted to defence and by a greater robustness on the part of the Labour Party. This could be seen in its recommitment to nuclear weapons, staunch support in Parliament and outside for the US-led Gulf coalition, facing down its critics at Party Conference after the 1988 Policy Review, its strong support for the European Fighter Aircraft and its criticisms of *Options for Change*.

Both the Labour Party and the Liberal Democrats have criticised the excessively secretive and centralised nature of defence decision-making which led to the specific proposals of *Options for Change*. Both have also argued for heightened cooperation between Britain and its Alliance partners, although here the specific priorities of the parties are revealed. The Liberal Democrats argue particularly for collective defence arrangements through the WEU; the Labour Party, as exemplified in Neil Kinnock's presentation to the Royal United Services Institute on 23 January 1991, emphasises the continued importance of NATO. This is not just a matter of historical continuity – the 1945 Labour Government was instrumental in founding NATO – but hinges on the distinctive roles which the EC and NATO have established for themselves. Because the economic role of the EC will continue to define that organisation's evolving relations with the European Free Trade Area (EFTA) countries and with Central and Eastern European countries, Mr Kinnock suggested that too strong a defence identity will complicate those relations; instead, he suggested, the defence component of European security, and the concomitant increase in European defence cooperation, should continue to be pursued through NATO.

The Labour view was expressed succinctly by then-Shadow Defence Secretary Martin O'Neill to the 1991 Labour Conference when he stated that 'we will plan our defence expenditure in consultation with our partners in NATO and through negotiations [towards arms control treaties] with our friends in Eastern and Central Europe'. This point underlines a major cross-party criticism of *Options for Change* as being excessively nationally-determined. The threat which *Options* poses to Britain's ability to meet its commitments is an indictment of the Government's intent to uphold the 'key security interest to sustain the present network of multinational Western cooperation and to avoid any reversion to nationally-driven defence'[29].

The British Government now finds itself challenged on a wide variety of political fronts over *Options for Change*. The Labour Party, as its Shadow Defence team has repeatedly emphasised, has demanded a halt to *Options for Change* and instead calls for a comprehensive defence review to be undertaken in consultation with its NATO partners. Labour Junior Defence Spokesman Dr John Reid stated clearly in the 1992 General Election campaign that a Labour government would initiate such a review. The Liberal Democrats, while having to backtrack somewhat from an earlier pledge to initiate deeper cuts than those contained in *Options for Change*, have also stated their support for a defence review. The all-party, but Conservative-dominated, HCDC has released numerous reports examining every facet of *Options for Change*, all of which have been critical of the process and which call repeatedly for a comprehensive defence review. As Dr Reid pointed out, subsequent to the release of an HCDC report on *Options for Change* in March 1992, 'it is a sad day when [the Government] can't even gain the support of their own backbenchers. If they aren't convinced, then who is?'[30].

Given this high level of opposition to *Options for Change*, it is remarkable that defence policy played such a small role in the 1992 General Election. Both Conservative and Labour manifestos were circumspect about the specifics of defence policy. Whereas the Conservative Party had been able to exploit Labour's unilateralist policy in the 1983 and 1987 elections, it failed to replicate its success in the 1992 election. It certainly tried to play the defence card. Prime Minister John Major declared, in the 1992 election campaign, that: 'No issue is more important than defence. It is a vital issue at this election'[31]; and an entire Party Political Broadcast was devoted by the Conservatives to the issue of defence. However, whereas the Conservatives attempted to portray the Labour Party as a 'defence wrecker' by pointing to the 1991 Labour Party Conference motion which called for a cut in British defence expenditure to the average Western European level, Labour's rejection of another motion which sought to commit it to the decommissioning of the Trident nuclear submarine system probably did more to narrow the gap in the public mind between the parties on defence.

Despite the Conservatives' efforts, opinion polls conducted during the 1992 election campaign found little concern over defence as an electoral issue. Representative of the polls that were conducted, a MORI/ *Sunday Times* poll found that by April 1992 only six per cent of respondents identified defence as one of the two or three most important issues of the campaign. Confirming the Labour Party's understanding of its own defence reputation, in response to the question of which party would best handle the issue of defence, the Conservatives polled around fifty per cent and Labour between twenty and twenty-five percent in a number of polls. Perhaps of greatest significance was the tendency for between 20 and 25 per cent of the samples to either express no preference or to not know which party's defence policy was preferable.

These figures suggest that the issues generated by *Options for Change* have not found their way into the public domain and that issues dominated by the state of the British economy overshadow the defence question. In the House of Commons there have been Early Day Motions, Parliamentary Questions, Adjournment debates, and a handful of specific debates on defence policy, yet it must be noted that the annual debate on the Defence White Paper has been held in the calendar year of its publication every year since 1970 except 1974 and 1992. In the Parliamentary session 1991–92 there were no Service Day debates and the Government-inspired debates on nuclear defence in that session seemed more motivated by embarrassing the Labour Party in the run-up to the election than by promoting a rational debate in Parliament. There has been no full scale defence debate since 7 June 1991; which includes opportunities for the Official Opposition and the Liberal Democrats to select defence as a subject for debate. The bulk of the Parliamentary activity has been within the Defence Committee. Without extensive public discussion of defence needs and capabilities, and given the background perception that Western Europe has been relieved of an overarching threat, it would make sense for most people to seek a peace dividend. If this assessment is correct,

Options for Change has largely received public support by default. This public and Parliamentary passivity and acquiescence on the future shape of British defence policy has played into the hands of the Government. However, anyone with a sense of history or an awareness of the growing volatility of Europe and the wider world will judge the Government to be skating on thin ice.

CONCLUSION

The significance of the foregoing observations about public perceptions of the defence issue is that the government is spared a major pressure to revise its actions. The Government is not wholly immune to pressure – a vigorous campaign saved the Staffords from amalgamation with the Cheshires and several well-supported regiments such as the Black Watch and the Argyll and Sutherland Highlanders seem to have owed their survival to their support. However, by and large the Government has shown little willingness to accede to criticism or to re-evaluate the proposals of 1990. Without widespread public opposition to its plans it will undoubtedly press on with *Options for Change*, leaving its consequences to a future government to deal with. If, by 1997, the major provisions of *Options for Change* have been implemented, the choices facing that future government will be stark.

By 1997 the defence budget will, unless a major crisis intervenes, be somewhere in the region of 3.0 per cent of GDP – it could even be lower. The apprehension has already been stated that it is doubtful whether British defence commitments can be met with a defence budget of 3.2 per cent of GDP. Somewhere down the line, something will have to give. Either commitments will need to be reined in, or the resources will have to be found to provide the personnel, equipment and infrastructure to enable British forces to meet their obligations. The current Government appears determined to carry through *Options for Change*, with the implication that in the near future, with greatly reduced resources but with unadjusted commitments, a comprehensive defence review will have to be undertaken. Unless, at that point, new resources can be found, the result will be a continuation of the post-war trend of semi-organised contraction.

Notes

[1] B. George, *NATO and the New Arc of Crisis —Dialectics of Russian Foreign Policy*, Report to the Political Committee of the North Atlantic Assembly. November 1992.

[2] B. George (ed.), *Jane's NATO Handbook* 1991–2, p. 321.

[3] M. Nawaz, *Defence Statistics*, House of Commons Library Research Note No. 92/53, 28/5/92, Table 3.

[4] 'Financial and Economic Data Relating to NATO Defence', NATO press release M-DPC-2(91)105, Table 3.

[5] In addition to the percentage of GDP measure already referred to, the IISS *Military Balance 1991–1992* compares defence expenditure in per capita and in real terms using 1985 US dollars (p.212).

[6] Secretary of State for Defence Tom King, House of Commons debate, 25/7/90.

[7] House of Commons Defence Committee, Tenth Report 1989–90, para. 5.

[8] House of Commons Defence Committee, Third Report 1991–92, para, 3.

[9] House of Commons Defence Committee, Tenth Report 1989–90, para. 4.

[10] House of Commons Defence Committee, Third Report 1991–92, p. 81.

[11] House of Commons Defence Committee, Third Report 1991–92, para. 83.

[12] House of Commons Defence Committee, Tenth Report 1989–90, paras. 5–7.

[13] House of Commons Defence Committee, Third Report 1990–91, para. 3.

[14] Statement on the Defence Estimates 1992, Cm 1981 (HMSO, 1992), p. 8.

[15] The four major post-war NATO defence roles were: the nuclear deterrent; defence of the UK; defence of the European mainland; and the maritime commitment, principally the Eastern Atlantic and Channel. (SDE 92, p. 8).

[16] ibid, p. 9.

[17] ibid, p. 6.

[18] House of Commons Defence Committee, First Report 1992–93, para. 2.1.

[19] House of Commons Defence Committee, First Report 1992–93, para. 2.2.

[20] *Statement on the Defence Estimates 1992*, p. 8.

[21] HM Treasury Autumn Statement 1992, November 1992, para. 2.54.

[22] House of Commons Defence Committee, Eleventh Report 1990–91, para. 2.1.

[23] House of Commons Defence Committee, Eleventh Report 1990–91 para. 3.5.

[24] House of Commons Defence Committee, First Report 1992–93, para. 2.4.

[25] House of Commons Defence Committee, Third Report 1991–92, para. 50.

[26] M. Chalmers, *Biting the Bullet* (Institute for Public Policy Research, 1992), p. 1.

[27] Liberal Democrat Federal White Paper No. 3, *Reshaping Europe*, August 1990, p. 23.

[28] Liberal Democrat Policy Paper, *Shared Security*, February 1992, para. 8.1.

[29] Statement on the Defence Estimates 1992, p. 8.

[30] Dr. J. Reid, Press Release, 9/3/92.

[31] *The Independent*, 2/4/92.

4

Options for Change:
An Academic Critique

CHRISTOPHER COKER

Reader in International Relations, London School of Economics

The *Options for Change* process of 1990–92 is one of the most, contentious defence reviews to have been completed by a Conservative government, or any other government, since the Duncan Sandys review of 1957. Sandys, no stranger to controversy, sought to bring the Services into the world of the Cold War, to dissuade them from preparing for the last war rather than the next. Later years showed the absurdity of some of his convictions, in particular that the *Lightning* would be the last manned aircraft to be flown by the RAF. In retrospect however, Britain's armed forces did adjust remarkably well to the changes. The review was imperfect but not disastrous. The Armed Services survived. Britain's role in the Cold War, to the very end, was a creditable one – the professionalism of its forces was more creditable still.

Options for Change (the controversy it has excited apart) is unlikely to be so favourably received by history. Its title is strange indeed for a document which eschews any change which cannot be quantified and assessed in actuarial terms. Like most of the defence reviews of the past it is driven by Treasury demands, justified in terms that are intellectually shallow and in no way convincing except in the eyes of the government itself.

The world it conjures up is a twilight one, a world caught between two eras, a world in which 'threats' to British security are not threats at all but risks, largely of readjustment to a post-Cold War environment, to the 'political fallout' resulting from the collapse of Soviet power. Little thought is given to the profoundly important questions of security which may beset the post-1989 world. Even less thought is given to a more fundamental question still, of what we mean by 'security', now that the strategic certainties of the past are behind us.

Options is not a security review. It is a defence review crammed with images that are intensely narrow and inescapably British. It has little to say about the changing security environment. In the words of Lawrence Freedman:

> the flaw is that it sets in motion a dramatic restructuring of Britain's armed forces without attempting to describe the circumstances in which they will be likely to operate.[1]

It is a damning indictment, made all the more trenchant by the comments of the House of Commons Defence Committee. What the review fails to do, it claimed last year, 'what it does not even set out to do, is to argue in any detail the rationale behind the changes proposed or provide a coherent strategic overview'.[2]

It seems only right, therefore, to outline at least three of the major changes in the security equation which, if it has not ignored, the government has chosen to play down to justify not a restructuring but an emasculation of the armed forces.

THE NEW SECURITY AGENDA

We used to argue that security, like defence, was indivisible, that the interests of one NATO member were the interests of another. Since 1989 this argument is no longer quite so convincing, either in terms of geography or political responsibility.

In the first place, there are now three Europes, not one. Britain, as so often in its history, finds itself favourably placed, largely insulated from the problems plaguing Central Europe, in particular Germany. It is doubly fortunate in being geographically remote from the dangers facing France.

Germany confronts problems that have no military solution because they are economic rather than military in nature – the problem of refugees spilling across state boundaries, 2.5 million of whom have found shelter in Germany. It faces a potentially more acute threat still in the displacement of people within state boundaries; one million alone were uprooted from their homes in the Soviet Union in 1988.

In the Mediterranean the former 'southern flank' members of NATO no longer find themselves on a flank, but on a front; what the Spanish Foreign Minister last year called a 'frontier', a cultural interface between two very different but economically interdependent Christian, and Islamic worlds. The old Europe, the single indivisible, mutually dependent continent of the Cold War has vanished with the disintegration of the Soviet Union, the one state that straddled the continent from Murmansk to the Black Sea. Europe, in other words, is no longer a community of risk, its members defining their common security in the face of a common threat.

Nor are the barbarians any longer outside the gate, struggling to break in. They are inside, struggling to break out. The new barbarism is nationalism. The long-term threat it poses is the *renationalisation* of security. There are many illustrations of this phenomenon. Like the United States, for example, Britain has dismissed the risk of the failure of the economic reform programme in Russia, even though the former Soviet Union is the only putative enemy that could destroy the material base of Britain in thirty minutes. The British, pragmatic as always, tend to treat the prospect of economic failure in Russia as a residual risk – one that can be managed or finessed – not a challenge to which the country should devise a coherent policy.

For Germany, the challenge of economic disorder is a reality that cannot be ignored; perhaps it is already the central reality of security policy. It represents a challenge that can be met only in part by NATO, in part by putting trust in other institutions including the Conference on Security and Cooperation in Europe (CSCE). Many Germans, however, are beginning to see the Atlantic Alliance not as a solution, but part of the problem itself; the product of a world in which history had atrophied, of a world defined not by change but stasis. 'Historical change is now happening in a way it is not meant to happen', complained an anonymous Pentagon official on the eve of Germany's unification. 'History is accelerating' claims Jacques Delors, at a pace that Europe has not seen for 45 years.

On both flanks, West and East, the Germans are struggling hard to keep up. Through Maastricht they are attempting to extend the scope of European cooperation on security matters. In the East, they are trying to bring the former German Democratic Republic (GDR) into line with their own national standard of living, in pursuit of which they will spend nearly $1200 bn over the next ten years – a commitment which represents the largest transfer of funds in history, dwarfing even Marshall Aid (a mere $50 bn at 1991 prices).

It is the British who are refusing to keep in step with history, event though of all people they should know better. 'History never stops short, only governments do' claimed the liberal historian John Morley. Wedded to the past, to institutions such as NATO in which they still play a central role, the British are much happier confronting their own history than escaping into the future, embracing the French tactic of *fuite en avant*. Objectively, perhaps, they had no immediate need. Historically and geographically they are remote from the countries and peoples of the east who at the last moment are struggling to enter the 20th century. The Germans are not. For them the debate over the status of NATO and the Western European Union (WEU) represents more than a political trade-off. It demands a vision of the future, not a policy of marking time.

A second seismic change in the security environment is, of course, the re-emergence of Germany as the dominant European power. As yet Germany is not large enough to absorb Europe, though it is too large to be absorbed by it. We cannot predict with confidence how successful the Germans will be in shaping a European security policy. For, as Leo Strauss contends, 'we cannot define our tasks by our powers, for our powers become known to us through performing our tasks'.

At present, Germany is being called upon to shore up democracy in the CIS states and in Eastern Europe, to shoulder the burden of maintaining currency stability in the Exchange Rate Mechanism (ERM) and to kick-start the East German economy, just as it is entering a recession. What more will its European partners ask of it?

Whenever the British discuss Germany's role they tend to do so in terms of their own past, in terms of German hegemony, of traditional German politics, of old policies that still seem threatening 45 years on. What concerns many continental Europeans much more is not the extent of German power but the risk that Bonn may be unable to match its resources with its political ambition. In that sense the French, in particular, find British fears of hegemony entirely misplaced.

The point has been put pithily by Gunther Grass in his most recent novel *The Call of the Toad*[3]. 'Unified the Germans are more disunited than ever'. Their very disunity offers the Republican Party an opportunity to pass the 5 per cent threshold in the 1994 elections and gain a respectable block of seats in the Bundestag. The Party's opportunity, however, is unlikely to be Germany's. The presence of the Republicans in parliament, writes Anatol Lieven, could make the traditional working of coalition politics impossible. It will almost certainly put back plans effectively to make the Deutschmark the European currency, a prospect, it needs to be noted, that only 22 per cent of Germans at present would welcome.

Germany's problems offer Britain an opportunity while also posing a threat. They present Britain with an opportunity to remain at the centre of Europe (which is the government's declared aim), a chance to forge a credible 'point' defence together with the Germans and French, if necessary, for symbolic significance only, by joining the Franco-German Corps. The threat is that Britain will be excluded if it is not prepared to come to terms with its European future. And it is hard to see what the British will gain from a deteriorating situation in the East that would expose as self-deceiving much of the optimistic analysis on which *Options for Change* is based. As a former French ambassador to Bonn has remarked, a strong Germany is urgently needed in Central Europe; a weak Germany, like the Weimar Republic, would create a power vacuum at a dangerous moment in Central Europe's history.

It is Germany's lack of political will which has antagonised its partners and created tensions in the Alliance. Its absence in the Gulf War, its clear reluctance to allow the WEU's Adriatic patrol to stop and search suspect shipping is a disturbing reminder of a reluctance, which has become peculiarly if not definingly German, to initiate military action for *any* political end. That failure in Yugoslavia has given rise to a much broader crisis of identity which lies at the heart of the Community's sense of itself, of its *idea* of Europe, of what it understands by the term 'European'.

It may also represent a more disturbing phenomenon still, one more demanding of its allies. In his 1946 postmortem on Germany's tragic history, Friedrich Meinecke urged the German people to construct a state that would turn its back on military pretensions and accept instead the military status of Sweden and Holland. It looks as though Germany has done just that, becoming what is called a 'post-military' society. Germany may be in the process of becoming a secondary military power, by choice not necessity. The direction in which it is heading is clear. It is a direction which makes it doubly important for the British and French to play the leading role in defining a common security policy for Europe.

A third aspect of the new security agenda which raises questions for *Options for Change* is its open-ended commitment to NATO. It is a commitment which presupposes a continuing and significant military role for the United States in Europe. This is a pretty bold assumption. Even American commentators on the right, traditionally identified with maintaining a strong military posture for their country, are beginning to redefine, rather than defend, America's role in NATO. The American analyst, Samuel Huntingdon, for one, has redefined America's strategic interests in terms that are not only inconsistent with it remaining a military superpower (spending \$250–270 bn a year on defence), but which would actually require it to surrender that role of its own volition. If the United States is to remain ahead of Japan in terms of technology, it must look to the state of its own industrial base – something which may make necessary a contraction of its defence industry. If it is to be in a position to defend its security interests in the Gulf and Central America, it may well have to accept a troop level of 150,000 men in Europe as a ceiling rather than as a floor. If it wishes to remain in Europe at all, the decision may be determined by the extent to which CENTCOM can provide a necessary infrastructure for intervention – not in Central Europe but the Gulf, as proved to be the case in the build-up to the Gulf War in 1991.

America's role in the world still remains largely a function of the Cold War, driven by the political exigency of a former era, and still largely derivative of the role it played for 45 years, responding to an agenda originally set by the Soviet Union. In showing any initiative at all, the Bush Administration spent much of its energy attempting to shore up the old security order, in part because of the not unjustified fear that its European allies might be tempted one day to translate their former subordination to the United States during the Cold War into insubordination – not in the fields of security but the realms of international commerce and trade.

Like the United Kingdom after the Second World War, the Americans are trying to lock themselves into a security system in which they will continue to have the principal role long after their power has diminished. Like Britain in the late 1940s, the United States faces a similar challenge: to adopt an over-stretched and economically faltering superpower to a new world which at times looks just as menacing as the old.

James Baker spent his last years in office as Secretary of State trying to patch together a 'European-Atlantic community' in the hope of preserving 'a European/American outlook', on issues such as GATT. His concept of 'cooperative security', which was to be at the heart of the new world order, was predicated on the possibility of finding a consensus not between East and West but between the Western powers themselves. It was a vision with which the British were all too ready to fall in, not least because it offered an escape route from Europe, a belated chance to maintain some kind of special relationship with its 'closest' ally.

In this respect, perhaps more than any other, *Options for Change* offers no change at all, merely a script which is crafted, full of equivocations, insistent on the small print of history. There is little recognition that the relationship with the United States, if it was ever real, and for much of the Cold War it undoubtedly was, is unlikely to constitute more than a historical footnote in the future. It is ironic that the United Kingdom should be trying to define a defence posture which makes sense only if the United States remains a European military power, even a leading one. Unfortunately, America's decline is likely to prove as relentless and precipitous as Britain's.

OPTIONS FOR CHOICE

Clearly a country which, eleven years of Thatcherism notwith-standing, is still in decline, has enormous difficulty in understanding the fact of its decline, let alone dealing with it. Through *Options for Change* the British may have abandoned a past defined largely in Cold War terms but that does not mean that they have discovered a future. The mark of a declining country, it has been argued time and again, is the refusal not to *change* but to *choose*. There are three choices which the British should make if they wish to remain in step with history. None of them should be fudged in the name of pragmatism.

First, the divisibility of security requires the British to take seriously roles that only they and the French can undertake between them. In particular, both should maintain capabilities for what were traditionally, but are now misleadingly, called the defence of 'out of area interests'. Unfortunately, both the French and Germans have every reason to question Britain's commitment. Britain's role in the Rapid Reaction Corps (ARRC), part of NATO's new security concept of point defence, offers an admirable allocation of responsibility. But an exami-nation of plans for *Britain's Army for the 1990s*[4] disclosed that the 3rd (UK) Division (the mechanised unit based in Britain) is to be responsible for only half the force, the other half being an armoured division in Germany. Unfortunately, the 3rd Division has also been given responsibility for a whole range of purely British interests including the defence of such outlying areas of the world as Belize, Brunei and Hong Kong. Such military over-stretch might just have been acceptable when Britain deployed three divisions in Germany. It is *not* acceptable for the new responsibilities Britain has been allocated in the 1990s.

It is doubtful, for example, whether under the present setup *Desert Storm* could have been fought at all. The Gulf operation was the largest campaign the British Army has fought since 1945 (including the Korean war in 1950). It is also the war in which it suffered lower casualties than any other campaign. It was an immense effort getting just one weak armoured division to the Gulf. And that required largely nullifying the British battleforce in Germany. Only 16 Challenger tanks were still operational in Germany by the end of the war.

The part played by the British in the Gulf was, of course, exemplary. But, in his account of the campaign, General Sir Peter de la Billière was right to savage the British government for pressing ahead with *Options for Change*, knowing that if its manpower cuts are implemented, Britain will never again be able to make such a contribution.[5]

The very success of the British participation in that war carried with it the seeds of disaster for it completely blurred the need for a complete reappraisal of strategy and roles based upon the sort of resources that would be available in the years ahead. *Options for Change* carries reference to the problems of readiness, largely because the God-given six months breathing space enjoyed by the Allies in the Gulf obscured the frantic scrambling to form the 1st Armoured Division, the considerable modification programme needed to make even such equipment as we had fit for desert operations and worst of all, the need to bolster units from BAOR, supposed to be fit for war on the Central Front, with injections of manpower from regiments staying behind. Finally, as the Falklands Campaign had shown in 1982, British reserves of ammunition and spares did not begin to meet the needs of even so limited an operation. Forty years of nuclear bluff had allowed all sense of reality to disappear from British preparedness. The tinsel of a superficially impressive mechanised corps in Germany in the Cold War years will lend no sort of credibility in an era in which the requirement will be for swift and comprehensive reaction, with no time available for a last minute frantic reshuffle of the pack. Only a complete re-think of every aspect of our defence policy will meet the bill.

Secondly, apart from attempting to stay at the centre of the European debate, the British have fudged the issue of European security quite disastrously by insisting that NATO should remain the central institution of Europe's defence.

It is time that the British distinguished between a European security policy and a defence posture. In the short term, of course, there is no possibility that the WEU will constitute the nucleus of a European defence force. The somewhat unconvincing WEU patrols in the Gulf (1987) and the Adriatic (1992) reveal demonstrably enough that the union has neither the political will nor the military resources to conduct a policy independent of NATO. It has no reconnaissance capability, no space satellites and no data collection facilities in space. At the Defence Planning Committee meeting in May 1991, the NATO allies agreed that it would not be sensible to duplicate what the United States already provides its allies. Even the NATO Allied Command Europe (ACE) units that were deployed in Turkey during the Gulf conflict had to hire *Antonov* planes from the Russians to make up a serious deficiency in heavy airlift aircraft.

At the moment, nevertheless, the debate is not about defence – it is about security. And security can be the responsibility of a variety of institutions other than NATO, including CSCE, the European Community (EC) and the United Nations. Some of these institutions, especially the EC, have overextended themselves, notably in Yugoslavia. Others, like the CSCE, have hardly been employed. It is clear that unless there is a security dimension specific to Europe, the Europeans will continue to improvise, to show excessive caution and be plagued by differences and divisions within their own ranks.

At Maastricht the Community fell between two stools – accepting that the EC should have a security policy while also insisting, however, that the implementation of that policy must remain the responsibility of NATO rather than the WEU. This is clearly nonsense. It is nonsense to vote for a Common Foreign and Security Policy which is purely declaratory, and even then is not binding. It is nonsense for the Europeans to have a policy *for* Europe but not *of* Europe.

The British should declare themselves in favour of a European defence community while insisting that the European defence force must be made up largely of NATO units. The Americans have long pursued such a vision, that of a two-pillar alliance, the dream the Americans hoped for 30 years ago; a promise which could become real. In the absence of such a commitment Britain will never restructure its armed forces rationally. It will merely ensure that such commitments as its contribution to the ARRC are commitments from which it is possible to opt out. This is not the most sensible way of running an alliance. It is more likely to be a prescription for disaster, a signal of a commitment to Europe that the British are reluctant to make. It would be tantamount, in effect, to arguing that the defence of the continent, like that of Hong Kong, has become one commitment too many, the 'east of Suez' option of the 1990s.

Thirdly, both Britain and France have an interest in ensuring that nuclear weapons remain at the centre of Europe's strategic defence. They also have reason to question whether the United States will continue to provide them with the assistance both need.

Jaques Delors has hinted that one day a European deterrent might be necessary. Should that be the case it would have to be based on Anglo-French nuclear cooperation. The reason why attempts at bilateral Anglo-French cooperation have been unsuccessful in the past was expressed clearly enough by the Statements on Defence Estimates in 1987. Until now the two countries have not been able to agree on the criteria that a joint force would have to meet, the targets that would be targeted, or the details of complementary refits or the patrol cycle of sub-marines. A more important – because unstated – problem was that neither country had any real, tangible interest in coopera-tion. The British were not prepared to put at risk their special relationship with the United States, the French to cooperate with a force committed in part to NATO.

History has forced them to think again. At the Reyjkavic sum-mit (1986), both countries recognised that the United States might not want independent third party nuclear states to remain outside the strategic treaties signed between themselves and the Soviet Union. The Soviet Union may have gone but in its absence both Britain and France need a new justification for remaining nuclear powers. One option would be to treat seri-ously the possibility of creating a European deterrent, of treating Europe as a whole as a third force.

Such collaboration would pose no threat to the Anglo-American strategic link, if the British, instead of maintaining their sub-strategic nuclear weapons by attempting to buy the American SRAM-T air-to-surface missile, were to opt instead for joint development of the air launched long-range missile (ASLP) designed by Aérospatiale. Even if the French chose to see ASLP as a second leg of their strategic dyad in the early 21st Century, the British could rightly claim that it is not a strategic system at all, only an intermediate range missile. If politically the

French would gain much from this, so would the British. A joint nuclear deterrent would give both countries a major influence in reshaping the European security order of the future. And if the French are likely, in the end, to derive more from such an initiative, the mutual advantage rule in politics is always untrue. Governments cooperate when they have to, when it becomes necessary or is perceived to be necessary. The necessity today is pretty obvious.

CONCLUSION

Britain urgently needs to undertake a strategic review, based on an open and public debate about its defence policy. It should not be drawn up by what Martin Jacques tellingly calls 'the club class of Europe', the intellectuals and pundits who have treated European defence as they have every other aspect of the European Project, as something to be discussed and conducted in closed circles.

Options for Change is a step on a disastrous road, the renationalisation of Britain's armed forces. Renationalisation will be made inevitable by political marginalisation in Europe. But it would be equally disastrous to dismiss the fears to which the measures outlined here might give rise in the British public. That is why there must be a public debate about security, an exercise from which the government has deliberately shied away. It is quite remarkable, in fact, that a country which can claim, more than most, to have invented modern democracy should conduct its defence debate with so little attention to the popular will. Great changes, even on a national level, work only if they enjoy a consensus, in particular a consensus between the political class and the nation. What we have is a defence review conducted in the old manner by the old methods. In that sense *Options for Change* is a prescription for disaster for which one day the government may be held to account.

Notes

[1] Lawrence Freedman, 'Whom are we defending, and against what?', *The Independent*, 10 July 1991.

[2] House of Commons Defence Committee, Eleventh Report 1990–91, *Statement on the Defence Estimates 1991*, HC 394, p. vii.

[3] Gunther Grass, *The Call of the Toad*, (London, Secker and Warburg, 1992).

[4] Ministry of Defence, *Britain's Army for the 1990s*, Cmnd. 1595, July 1991.

[5] Gen, Sir Peter de la Billière, *Storm Command: A Personal Account of the Gulf War*, (London, HarperCollins, 1992) p. 197.

5

Technology and the Emerging Defence Environment: The Land Forces Perspective

LIEUTENANT COLONEL NJH HINTON MBE

The Royal Military College of Science, Shrivenham

The Duke of Wellington once said 'All the business of war, and indeed all the business of life, is to endeavour to find out what you don't know from what you do'. With this in mind, it is tempting to interpret military crises such as those in the Gulf and former Yugoslavia as examples of what we do know, and use them to try and find out what we do not. However, it is predominantly the political demise of the Warsaw Pact and disintegration of the Soviet Union which has plunged defence communities world-wide into debate by posing a number of far-reaching questions. What is now the threat? What are the roles of NATO and the European Community in defence matters? What is the place of the surviving superpower, the United States? At the same time, worldwide recession and constraints on government budgets in developed countries have made it all the more imperative to ensure cost-effectiveness in defence expenditure. This means that technology, now more than ever, has a role to play in achieving greater capabilities at lower cost, and this chapter looks at how it can be harnessed to help ground forces meet the challenges posed by the complex and fast-changing environment they now face.

THE THREAT AND RESPONSES

Current threat analyses point to a continuing need to plan on countering a range of threats. At one extreme, nobody has yet disinvented nuclear weapons. In the middle ground, and in spite of agreement on Continental Forces in Europe (CFE), there are still a large number of conventional weapons both in Europe and what used to be called the Third World. At the low intensity end of the spectrum, insurgency and terrorism persist.

The increasing assertiveness in defence matters of organisations such as the European Community, the Western European Union and Conference on Security and Cooperation in Europe, not to mention the continuing influence of the United Nations highlights the fact that future security risks may well emerge from economic, migratory, environmental or other civilian problems that cannot always be dealt with appropriately by military action. NATO, which unlike those organisations is possessed of a military structure and strategy, also acknowledges that these threats extend security considerations beyond straightforward military aggression.

Defence planning and any collective security arrangements need to take account of all of these possibilities. Colonel Richard Connaughton, whilst Colonel Defence Studies at the Staff College, Camberley, identified three main factors that he believes characterise the current security environment. These are: first, continuing instability in many parts of the world, and the continuing proliferation of weapons, including those of mass destruction; secondly, a new collegiality, as he calls it, among the members of the UN Security Council; and thirdly, the increasing difficulty of unilateral military action in the post Cold War environment, for reasons of cost, scale, and political acceptability. He sees these as pointing to the almost inescapable need to mount multinational rather than unilateral responses to the wide range of potential threats.

This is reflected in the decision to make the ACE Rapid Reaction Corps (ARRC) a centrepiece of the restructuring of NATO and British land forces, which will inevitably become a main focus for developing new weapon systems. Britain will provide a Commander, the framework of the corps and corps troops. It will have two British divisions and two multinational divisions, including a multinational airmobile division to which a British airmobile brigade will be committed. These and other national divisions and brigades will be combined as necessary to tailor the order of battle (ORBAT) to requirements.

Any such organisation, be it under NATO, UN or other multi-national command, is going to pose a number of new operational challenges. NATO has already embraced multina-tionality successfully in many aspects of its air forces functioning, but there are several specific problems the land forces will have to deal with almost from first principles. The first, and arguably most important, task will be to establish a common doctrinal, organisational and procedural basis for operations and their support, and particularly the relationship of this structure to technology and weapon procurement. There will be a pressing requirement for comprehensive and compatible Command, Control, Communications and Intelligence (C^3I) systems in the various elements of any multinational force (MNF). There will be the perennial problems of limited money and demo-graphic constraints on manpower. A MNF will therefore be under pressure to reduce the proportion of its budget spent on personnel, and achieve greater cost-effectiveness in its weapon systems, which will also need greater strategic and battlefield mobility to enhance its flexibility and speed of deployment. Such formations will need effective and responsive logistic sup-port, not to mention a coordinated approach to equipment management to ensure that sustainability, availability and relia-bility are optimised. There will also be a need for effective joint training if a MNF is to be battleworthy. Technology can help in all of these areas.

THE PLACE OF TECHNOLOGY

Before looking at the specific benefits that technology has to offer in coping with the changing land forces environment, it is worth examining how it is managed and its relationship with concepts and doctrine. There appears to have been little or no specific consideration by NATO of how technology can assist in improving the effectiveness of MNFs, nor has Britain focussed upon the specific benefits of technology in the con-text of the smaller but better Army – but then it is early days yet. The USA, however, is entirely clear that within its concept of Airland operations, technology is a vital force multiplier. This has enabled US forces to invest in key technologies identified as having specific relevance to their war-fighting doctrine.

The British Military Doctrine divides fighting power into three components: physical, conceptual and moral. This encourages us to think of military technology as an element of the physical category, separated from concepts in some way rather than inextricably linked. At a simplistic level, for example, does technology drive concepts, or vice versa – or both? There is no straightforward answer, which is indicative of the fact that there needs to be a better understanding of the relationship and closer, more direct links, between concepts, technology and procurement. In the context of MNF operations, this needs to be extended internationally which, in turn, means that collaborative organisations should take on a greater importance in future in formulating joint concepts against which equipment can be collaboratively procured.

Refining this link will be of little value unless we also look at resource management, especially money. Operational analysis (OA) provides a scientific means of assessing the cost-effectiveness of new systems and the force structures and support they need to function. It will always be tempting politically to go for 'shop window defence', that is to say expenditure on capital equipments rather than sustainability. We should be looking to more extensive use of operational analysis both domestically and internationally to establish how best to employ the proposed force structures and their equipment and how to ensure that they have the logistic and equipment support to function effectively. This can only be achieved if managers and planners understand OA, and what questions it can and cannot answer.

The pressures of a fast-changing defence environment and multinationality may also provide a stimulus to reassess our managerial approach to technology. For example, it makes little sense to apply a 10 year procurement cycle to fast-changing technologies such as information technology; the equipment is obsolescent when it is introduced into service. An alternative is, whenever possible, to maximise the use of commercially-developed software and lease hardware, initiatives which are now being pursued and could be greatly extended. Similarly, procedures such as using Cardinal Points Specifications may allow the speed of procurement to come more in line with the speed of technological development, and in some circumstances may have collateral advantages such as reducing or shifting the focus of risk. If we can align the conceptual and doctrinal basis of the component nations of a MNF, then we should also consider how collaborative procurement procedures can be brought more in line as well, for example by further developing more effective European or multinational staff targets – a task of considerable complexity. We should also consider whether confidence and certainty in the capabilities technology offers can compensate for the uncertainty of the security environment in which it is required to operate.

As warfare becomes less and less manpower intensive, the consequences of failure by an individual under stress will become more serious, particularly if he is manning either weapon or highly complex C^3I systems. This means that both the quality of the manpower and their standard of individual training must be very high, which imposes an additional burden on the designers of equipment and those planning its support in service. It is vital that technology has an effective interface with these human factors if the true potential of both man and machine are to be exploited to the full.

COMMUNICATIONS

Turning to specific technologies, communications will be a critical issue in any MNF. In the ARRC, interoperability between encrypted allied communications systems will initially require technically awkward and perhaps operationally limited interfaces. In the short term, the tried and tested method of exchanging liaison officers with their own communications is highly likely to proliferate.

There are no technical problems with Combat Net Radio (CNR) as there are NATO agreed standards for HF, VHF, and UHF bands to which all nations adhere. No such standards have yet been agreed for electronic protective measures (EPM) such as frequency hopping. By the end of the decade it is possible that we might see agreed EPM Standards, but if non-standardised on-line encryption is then added to the equation we are back to our original solution of the liaison officer. One practical, if inelegant, solution to these problems could be for each nation to purchase just enough of a single radio type to meet their limited international interoperability requirements within formations such as the ARRC.

The backbone of the British Army's tactical trunk communications system is PTARMIGAN, and there is a simpler system, manned by the Territorial Army, called EUROMUX. Britain is committed to supplying British trunk communications for the Corps headquarters and up to four divisions, but down to divisional headquarters level only. Below that we run out of resources at present except for the British brigades, which will have their normal trunk facilities. Elsewhere interoperability depends on which other divisions are operating in the MNF. As an example, should the multinational airmobile division be included, then additional PTARMIGAN will be deployed to the divisional headquarters and down to the British airmobile brigade, but not to the other brigades within the division. Our NATO allies, whose trunk systems may conform to the current NATO trunk interface standards, will be able to link in to the PTARMIGAN system, but there will be substantial limitations on the facilities available, as the existing NATO interfaces are analogue and only offer secure voice and telegraph. A STANAG (standardisation agreement) defining a digital interface exists, and although no nations have adopted it as yet, the need to communicate effectively means that this will probably happen eventually. The commitment of a PTARMIGAN switch to RAF Oakhanger will ensure that trunk networks can be established virtually worldwide and linked together via satellite, as happened during the Gulf War. This will allow PTARMIGAN support for out of area operations and permit joint command post exercises (CPXs) in Germany, Britain and elsewhere if required.

It is appropriate to consider the role of Electronic Warfare (EW) in this new security environment. There are no technical advances here which warrant particular attention, but reductions in the size of armed forces will make it all the more important to protect and conserve the remaining assets. EW capabilities provide a vital and very cost-effective way of protecting the reduced quantities of valuable equipment and manpower on future battlefields. It is therefore an area which warrants closer attention in the future, in spite of the national security problems this might involve in a MNF.

INFORMATION ACQUISITION AND HANDLING

One of the key lessons to come out of the Gulf War was the need to deal with the huge quantity of good quality information provided by modern surveillance means such as remotely piloted vehicles, battlefield radars, and airborne stand off radars. It was appreciated some time ago that we are approaching a point where our intelligence-gathering capability is outstripping our ability to process the information. The PHOENIX drone, COBRA locating radar and ASTOR stand-off radar are just three equipments which will yield large volumes of additional data when all sources' cells are already working at near capacity levels. In a multinational environment the addition of sophisticated battle management systems such as the US JSTARS can only exacerbate the situation further.

Britain has a Technology Demonstrator Programme called the Battlefield Information Control System (BICS) which is examining the flow and handling of such data. Algorithms to simulate the very complex mental processes that humans go through when evaluating information are exceptionally difficult to replicate, and it seems likely that further progress in fields such as neural networks and knowledge-based systems will be necessary before substantial advances will be made in this field. In the light of MNF commitments, we should also now consider jointly with our allies how these and similar systems can be integrated and extended to ensure all our combined national intelligence and information is effectively pooled and processed. This again raises the problem of national security caveats.

Just as Electronic Warfare will be vital to protect limited resources, so too will countermeasures enhance the survivability and effectiveness of weapons systems and their platforms. The use of the F-117A fighter-bomber in the Gulf War was probably the most spectacular demonstration of the value of stealth technology. Radar absorbent materials and paint, the reduction of heat signatures, and the design of weapons systems to minimise radar reflectivity are all areas in which Britain maintains an interest, for the benefit of land and sea as well as air systems.

In the broader field of surveillance and target acquisition, the very effective use of Thermal Imaging in the Gulf War, such as the TOGS system in CHALLENGER, heightened awareness of this system's value on the 24-hour battlefield, and makes it all the more necessary to stay ahead of the game by developing effective countermeasures.

WEAPON EFFECTIVENESS

In seeking to improve weapon effectiveness, it is often better value to upgrade current systems rather than purchase new ones. But there comes a point when existing systems cease to have any 'stretch potential' left. An early example of this might prove to be tank guns. The conventional 120mm tank gun is approaching the scientific limits of its stretch potential. To further increase performance we shall at some point need to decide whether we should go to a larger conventional gun and accept the design constraints it imposes on tank design, or look to new technologies such as the electromagnetic gun or improved anti-tank guided weapons (ATGW) to give us the enhanced performance we require.

Television footage of the use of precision weaponry in the Gulf War educated the general public in the extraordinary capabilities of some modern systems. Without wishing to dampen enthusiasm for the very real advantages of precision munitions, such footage may have raised expectations unduly. No army is yet close to fielding truly 'smart' weapons, and the nearest to achieving this is the US Army, whose in-service ATACMS tactical missile system could eventually carry Precision Guided Munitions of the sort envisaged for the Multiple Launch Rocket System (MLRS) Phase III. It is also worth noting that the effectiveness of air-launched weapons in the Gulf War depended crucially on achieving air superiority. What technology is achieving at the moment is progressive improvement to precision guidance and control and better lethal mechanisms, but a lot of so-called 'smart' weaponry is far from having comprehensive, autonomous and infallible decision-making abilities capable of operating in the harsh environment of the modern battlefield. It is also costly, and we should also continue to look at generating adequate capabilities rather than nugatory overmatch in every area, using less expensive, less complex, less sophisticated weapons. In this respect, the use of Global Positioning Systems, could well revolutionise the guidance of precision weaponry still further in the future, just as it has transformed the field of basic navigation in many other areas.

Another fast developing area is that of non-lethal technologies. One definition of these is 'technologies with potential for development into weaponry that can destroy an enemy's capability without causing significant injury, excessive property destruction or widespread environmental damage'. Examples are chemical immobilisers, traction inhibitors, entanglement munitions, blinding lasers, neural inhibitors, infra sound and non-nuclear electro-magnetic pulses. Such technologies are not in themselves new, only the emphasis they are being given in an effort to attract scarce funds. Politically and militarily attractive as they are, it should be recognised that some will turn out to be dead ends, with or without funding. As an illustration, in the field of Directed Energy Weapons, which includes lasers, particle beams, acoustic energy and radio-frequency weapons, much of the technology is far from mature. Only laser weapons are an area where some progress towards the development of practical systems has been made and warrants closer examination at present.

Britain's priorities in this field are first defensive measures, followed by offensive. 5000 sets of General Purpose Laser Goggles (GPLG) were sent out for use in the Gulf War. A number of laser warning receivers will be evaluated in the near future. The aim is not only to alert the crew of an armoured vehicle but to tie this in to a vehicle-mounted defensive aids suite of some sort. The cost involved makes it unlikely such systems will be retrofitted to existing vehicles, but they will be available for inclusion in future if required.

Turning to active systems, the use of lasers as adjunct weapons which affect sensor systems seems the most promising way of employing this technology. For example, in an air defence scenario they could take on those targets that are out of coverage of the main weapons system either because they are too far away, fast crossing or too close. They could also help with multiple targets. Specific laser frequencies can be filtered and defences developed, but looking to the future, tunable lasers will present real problems to the defender. Cutting out all frequencies will disable him; leave a window and it can be attacked. On the other hand this could be used to our advantage, as selectable filters, changed on a daily basis, would permit weapons free use of our own lasers.

Information on defensive laser technology is exchanged within NATO, so this is a feasible weapons system to adopt within the context of multinational operations. However, in this, as in many areas of emerging technology, we at present lack the close interaction of technology and concepts which would allow us to find a niche where the benefits of laser technology could be practically applied.

The last area of weapon system design of particular note is robotics. Britain's Mobile Advanced Robotics Defence Initiative (MARDI) Technology Demonstrator Programme is an unmanned vehicle based on an Alvis STREAKER chassis, mounting a TV camera, thermal imager, laser rangefinder and acoustic sensors, as well as an array of light weapons and a smoke generator. It is remotely controlled by radio or fibre optic cable by a crew of two. The second phase of the project, starting this year, will include getting the vehicle to do some tasks autonomously. In the long term, MARDI should hopefully demonstrate that cost and manpower savings can be achieved by robotics in this and other similar areas.

MOBILITY

The smaller, more versatile coalition forces of the future will rely in part for their versatility on strategic mobility, in order to be able to deploy quickly to crisis areas. It is worth noting that 85 per cent of US warfighting material for the Gulf War was moved by ship rather than aircraft, which continue to have limited payloads and require comparatively large amounts of fuel. The progressive decline of merchant shipping can only point to the strategic movement of ground forces as an area that needs continuing attention.

Mobility is also a key factor in discussions about whether helicopters are becoming a substitute for main battle tanks. This is a complex and finely balanced argument, and at present it is probably wise to assume that both weapon systems have a part to play on battlefields in the near-term future. Nevertheless, it is certainly true to say that the technology of attack and reconnaissance helicopters is maturing rapidly, and a number of highly sophisticated aircraft are becoming available: the Franco-German TIGER, in anti-tank and combat support versions; APACHE LONGBOW, which could enter service in 1998; the Agusta MANGUSTA attack helicopter, now in service; and the Boeing/Sikorsky COMANCHE armed reconnaissance helicopter.

Looking at medium-lift helicopters, Britain has ordered 44 EH-101 Merlin, but only the anti-submarine version. No orders have yet been placed for the transport variant. An alternative, the NH-90 European collaborative project, will result in a prototype flying in 1995, and possibly being in service by 1998. No decision has yet been taken on what to procure.

The very complex decision to buy a particular helicopter depends partly on the weapons used on, or with, such platforms. For example, Britain's national decisions on attack helicopters may well depend partly on the continuing success of projects such as the long-range TRIGAT anti-tank missile. The Ultra Light Weight 155mm howitzer, which can be underslung from a medium lift helicopter to achieve greater mobility, and thus significantly enhance the firepower and mobility of airmobile forces, could also influence the decision on which aircraft we buy. These and the other considerations outlined above mean that it is likely to be some time before the ARRC or any other MNF has a fully integrated force of interoperable, adequately equipped helicopters.

Aids to mobility and counter-mobility are another aspect of enhancing MNF effectiveness. Britain is procuring the Bridging for the 90s combat bridging system, which will greatly improve its capabilities in this area, as will the recent decision to procure the M3 amphibious bridging equipment. Improvements to the GIANT VIPER minefield breaching equipment are being considered, and the possibility of using fuel/air explosives for minefield clearance is being examined. In the field of mines, the decision to procure the MLRS II system of scatterable mines delivered by MLRS rocket will enhance our abilities in this field, and act as a significant force multiplier, for example when used in conjunction with MLRS I, the bomblet round, and MLRS III, the precision guided munitions, all launched from the same system. With a view to the future we should also keep our eye on the continuing development of sophisticated, autonomous off-route mines.

LOGISTICS AND EQUIPMENT SUPPORT

Turning now to logistics: any multinational force will require sustainability if it is to remain credible, the NATO definition of which is 'the ability of a force to maintain the necessary level of combat power for the duration required to achieve its objectives'. The introduction of sophisticated equipment has resulted in greater complexity and a larger volume of spares, and this will be compounded by the far greater variety introduced by the different national units and formations in a MNF. If multinational forces are to be credible there is a paramount requirement not just for commonality in operational matters, but also in logistics and equipment support.

A good starting point might be the gradual resolution of such issues at national level – for example, by phasing out the mixed fleet of tanks fielded by Britain. Such advances can only be achieved internationally if equipment is standardised or at least interoperable, something which becomes increasingly important the smaller the size of the formation. Standardising procedures and definitions, agreement on stockpile guidelines, and meeting stockpile targets and common support philosophies would all enhance Alliance sustainability, but to achieve this there is a continuing need to consider all aspects of effectiveness, not just politically high profile capital equipments. It also reinforces again the need for increasing commonality of concepts, organisations and procedures.

Looking at specific technological benefits on offer in the logistics area, the Technology Demonstrator Vehicle Electronics Research and Development Initiative (VERDI) is proving how vehicle electronics can be integrated more effectively, and increase the efficiency of maintenance functions by autonomous diagnostics. The CHALLENGER 2 tank and AS90 self-propelled gun are proving to be model examples of how to contract for and achieve a reliability growth programme. At the humping and dumping end of the scale, the Demountable Rack Off-loading and Pick-up Service (DROPS) proved in the Gulf War that this sort of equipment is vital if we are to achieve the flexibility and volume of logistic support needed in modern warfare. One area of concern is the use of automatic data processing in logistics and equipment support. Its routine use to cope with material management problems is now almost a *sine qua non* in peacetime, but it is at present and for the most part based on stand-alone commercial personal computers rather than integrated networks using purpose-built software. Unfortunately the vital importance of a unified automatic data processing system to manage support functions only becomes apparent in wartime, and as a result it attracts little funding.

In logistics and equipment support, the existence of the ARRC and other multinational forces will, one hopes, oblige allies to come to workable solutions, but the danger is that unless the realities of sustaining a MNF effectively are properly assessed and taken into account, they will be glossed over and compromises made. These will only be revealed as such if and when the MNF concerned has to deploy on operations.

TRAINING

The problems faced by a large multinational force in training will be considerable, particularly given the increasing pressures to cut back on environmental damage by reducing deployments and decreasing the use of training areas. Simulation offers considerable benefits, both at the individual training level, such as the Direct Fire Weapons Effects Simulator (DFWES), and in more complex and sophisticated trainers such as the Combined Arms Tactical Trainer (CATT). Looking to the future, funding may eventually allow the integration of weapon effect simulators and tactical trainers to permit simultaneous CPX and formation training exercises (FTX) to play up to and including formation level; an aspiration of the ambitious US SIMNET system.

A more intriguing possibility is that virtual reality – the substitution of a computer-generated environment for the real thing – may become a workable alternative to deployment. This might allow not only the replication of realistic training and manoeuvre without ever leaving barracks, but also, for example, the opportunity to rehearse an attack realistically while sitting in the assembly area, using computer generated virtual reality fed through the vehicle systems, based on the latest and most accurate intelligence of the actual layout of the enemy position. This is however a very immature, and costly, technology at present, which is seldom seen outside laboratories and electronic games arcades.

Mention should also be made of the issue of language training. The Franco-German brigade has been unkindly referred to as the most expensive language school in the world, and serious language problems affecting communications between UN troops have been reported in Yugoslavia. Technology can also help in this area. Fully autonomous computerised translation is not yet a practical possibility, but several multinational organisations have relied on partial translation systems for a number of years, and the Commission of the European Community, among others, is currently investigating a system incorporating more advanced artificial intelligence techniques. Large-scale multinational integration of forces might justify a similar commitment by a collective defence organisation. Interactive language training using some of the many commercial systems now available is also practicable, and vital if the MNFs are to be operationally effective.

CONCLUSIONS

The hard facts of time, cost and performance associated with technology might well be able to provide a measure of stability or direction in defence planning to compensate for the uncertainties of the security environment.

It is necessary to strengthen the relationship between technology and concepts to ensure that we and our allies have a common organisational, conceptual and managerial basis from which we can achieve cost-effective collaborative exploitation of technology, and above all to justify effectively the considerable financial resources likely to be needed for sophisticated future weapon systems.

Managerially, we need to have mechanisms in place to ensure that against such justified requirements we can react in a timely way to get vital equipment into service quickly. Increasing reliance, whenever possible, on commercially-developed equipment, the use of simplified procedures and the amortising of costs by leasing arrangements are all measures which we would do well to consider applying more widely.

It is interesting that at the moment there seems to be little formal awareness of the positive benefits which could accrue from more effective use of technology. Of course there is a requirement to take account of its practical limits as well as the legacy of existing equipment and the continuing need to take account of national rather than international imperatives, all of which will act against any sudden change. But the existence of multinational formations such as the ARRC and the UN forces in Yugoslavia should act as a catalyst to ensure that policies and management techniques come more into line in order to make them more effective.

Given an improved environment of this sort for exploiting technology, and the resources, there are a number of specific benefits it has to offer in the emerging defence environment. As we have seen, these are in the field of communications and data handling; in achieving greater cost-effectiveness to compensate for reduced manpower and shrinking budgets; through the provision of greater strategic and battlefield mobility; by improvements to sustainability and equipment support; and finally in improving training.

However, these benefits are not there for the asking. Technology can achieve a great deal, but only if there is general awareness of its potential and its interaction with operational concepts, sufficient resources to support its introduction, and the managerial basis from which to exploit it in a cost-effective and timely way. If this can be achieved then its advantages can be harnessed to improve the effectiveness of land forces in the future and their ability to cope with the complex and fast-changing environment they face.

6

Naval Planning
After the Cold War

PROFESSOR GEOFFREY TILL

Professor of History at the Royal Naval College, Greenwich

The main claim of the proponents of seapower of the early twentieth century was that navies had a crucial impact on the international situation and therefore on national security and prosperity[1]. But they acknowledged that the reverse was true too. Navies had always to respond to changes as well as cause them. As the same century draws to a close, those with responsibility for considering the role that navies might play in the future and for designing their future size and shape are having to respond to an international situation that is still quite unfamiliar to them.

The end of the Cold War has meant two things. First, that the basic structure of the international system has fundamentally changed. Old enemies are new friends; bipolarity has been replaced by multipolarity; order, apparently by disorder; the familiar alliance systems of the past are shifting beneath our feet. In much of the developed world, the effect on defence spending of expectations of a peace dividend, now that the military requirements of the Cold War are no longer with us, have been reinforced by the debilitating effects of recession. The result is that defence planners, naval ones included, are having to seek how to make do with less in a world in which it is very difficult to define the requirement. In many cases, this is their most immediate and their most difficult task.

But in some ways, the second consequence of the end of the Cold War has led to a more substantial conceptual problem. This is to arrive at some conclusions about the extent to which the future nature and employment of military force will differ from what we have become used to. This is more than the familiar, though often very difficult, question of identifying who one might have to be prepared to fight, where and when. Instead, it is the much more fundamental issue of deciding what the actual function of the military of the twentieth first century will be.

The current interest in peace-keeping operations is a case in point. Humanitarian and peacekeeping operations are distinctive and may call for the military units engaged in them to be specifically trained. The tasks and their aims will be quite different. The allies involved will be various and varying. There is little reason to suppose that the military qualities that fitted armed forces for their military tasks in the Cold War era will automatically be appropriate for the one that has succeeded it. On the contrary, the military units involved may need to be given a new role and re-trained in order to cope with a quite different but in some ways equally difficult set of challenges. The extent to which this is true remains a matter for debate and will, in any case, vary according to circumstances.

Navies are, of course, as subject to these pressures as any other military forces, but sailors have always prided themselves on their versatility, their particular utility in situations short of absolute conflict, their global reach and their adaptability. Naval planners[2] in the 1990s will no doubt be arguing that these same qualities are particularly relevant to the new international circumstances and keen to do everything they can to maintain them.

The spectrum of military requirement for navies, the Royal Navy included, appears to be along the lines suggested in the accompanying table. We will discuss each level of requirement

Table 1

War fighting	Against a major adversary
	Against a minor adversary
Naval diplomacy	Coercive
	Alliance building
	Suasive
Good order at sea	

in turn, and then turn to the very difficult force structure questions that flow from them. We will conclude with a brief review of the even more difficult problem of ways and means.

THE SPECTRUM OF REQUIREMENT

War-fighting

At the top, and most demanding, end of this spectrum is the most serious but least likely war-fighting dimension. The most demanding level of this would be the prospect of conflict with a major power. Simply for planning purposes, the Western naval planner might want to take the new Russian navy as a measure of the characteristics and capabilities required, rather in the spirit that the US and British navies used to regard each other in the early 1920s. Given Russia's internal situation and its likely retention of a large body of ships operating out of Kronstadt, the Kola and Vladivostok, there is just enough resid   ' possibility in this to make the exercise interesting. But in truth, this ploy is not likely to cut much ice with a Treasury able to point to Russia's urgent need for Western help and diminishing (though still substantial) military capability.

That being so, naval planners are in unfamiliar territory in two ways. First, since it is difficult for them to take the characteristics of the assumed adversary as a measure of the capabilities required, the question arises, 'what should be put in their place?' Perhaps it should be the requirements of allies, or the demands of the defence industries, or sets of capabilities extrapolated from basic natural interests, or maybe established precedent skilfully camouflaged?

It would be wrong to reject this approach simply as 'old thinking' if the reluctance wholly to change in fact reflected real continuities in Britain's place and situation. The need to defend Britain's maritime requirements against serious attack, for example, will surely continue to be derived, at least to some degree, from its geography, its continued and still crucial dependence on sea trade and its Atlantic links with the United States. Such characteristics are more than ephemeral and should provide an element of continuity in an otherwise bewilderingly fluid world.

But naval planners have also to cope with a second fundamental consequence of the end of the Cold War which will have a major effect on their ideas about maritime strategy and naval policy. In the past, much of the Royal Navy's effort, both theoretical and practical, was devoted to the task of preparing for the struggle for the command of the sea. This concept was at the heart of its concept of operations and of its naval policy. But now there is no one to challenge Western maritime power and it is hard, at least at the moment, to imagine a situation in which there could be a sustained conflict at sea. This is not to decry the continuing importance of sea control, which still underpins all uses of the sea, including the diplomatic. These uses, moreover, may well be contested. The fact that the Coalition's sealines of communication were not significantly challenged during the recent Gulf War should obviously not lead to the conclusion that such invulnerability can safely be assumed.

Nevertheless, sailors will need to recast their theories and their concepts to focus more on power *from* the sea and less on power *at* sea. It suggests there will need also to be a shift away from the practices and the weaponry of deep blue-water naval operations, as perhaps exemplified by deepwater antisubmarine warfare (ASW), towards what the Americans are increasingly calling 'littoral warfare', in which the emphasis might be on amphibious warfare, shore bombardment, mine warfare and so on. The disappearance of the Soviet navy, in short, implies the need to switch attention and resources away from securing control of the sea and more towards its exploitation.

At the same time, those same sailors will probably need to be on their guard against the simplistic conclusion that since there is at the moment no credible adversary who might need to be dealt with in a major war at sea, that there is now no need for significant navies. The point is that command of the sea was only ever a means to an end, rather than an end in itself. It is now up to Western naval planners to show not what they need in order to be strong at sea, but what they can contribute to national and global security, now that they are in that happy state.

This could well find expression in the second level of task, namely preparing against the possibility of serious conflict against a minor/medium adversary perhaps outside Europe. In

a world of multiple and unpredictable risk, it is difficult, probably impossible, to identify with whom this conflict might be, or
where and when. Each case would probably be unique in most
of its particulars. Both the Falklands and the Gulf conflicts were
fought in highly distinctive sets of geographic, strategic and
political circumstances. This makes it dangerous simply to
extrapolate the lessons learned there in an attempt to apply
them generally. The problem is that in dealing with a world of
multiple and unpredictable risk, almost every possible adversary and every capability can be made to look a necessary, even
essential, element in future planning.

Naval diplomacy

The second major dimension of naval activity is the diplomatic. Naval diplomacy is based upon war-fighting capacity and
seems likely to be an expanding requirement in a disorderly
world because of the contribution it can make to the defence of
international stability. This has always been a particular strength
of naval forces. As Corbett pointedly remarked, the first function of the fleet is ' . . . to support or obstruct the diplomatic
effort.' Naval forces are particularly suited for the diplomatic
role because they are inherently flexible and mobile, they have
surprising reach and their liability is limited. Hence, if things go
wrong, they can be painlessly extracted so much more easily
than their land-based equivalents.

It is important to realise, however, that this is *not* a new task
for navies, for they have been extensively engaged in this type of
activity since 1945. The rate has accelerated since the end of the
Cold War and shows little sign of abating.

Naval diplomacy is a continuum, that indeed shades into war-
fighting at the upper, most coercive, end of the scale. Coercion
may mean the deterrence or control of forces threatening
regional or global stability. Much of this sea-based stabilisation
can be expected to take place in a cooperative context of some
sort in which each nation makes its contribution to a joint force
operating under the aegis of international organisations like
NATO, the WEU or the United Nations This concept of
'Multinational Naval Cooperation' (MINCO, as it is increasingly being called) will also have important political benefits and

requirements in terms of alliance building. The maritime sanctions campaign against Iraq was, on the one hand, an example of coercive naval diplomacy aimed against Saddam Hussein. On the other, and much more importantly, it was a brilliantly successful piece of coalition-building which, in its turn, made all subsequent military action politically acceptable to domestic electorates and to the international community generally. From a Clausewitzian point of view, it was arguably the most decisive use of military force in the whole Gulf conflict.

The building and servicing of naval alliances will continue to be an important naval activity through to the next century. It is an activity conducted by a multiplicity of means including joint naval exercises, joint procurement, staff exchanges and so forth.

The creation of new standing naval forces for NATO is an interesting recent example of the way in which naval forces can thus be used. For all such purposes, naval planners may well be concluding that they need to provide forces that are designed with allies, rather than adversaries, in mind. In the future, navies will, like the other Services, be much less independent actors than they have been in the past. More and more will they perforce seek solutions to common problems in the company of others.[3]

The last type of naval diplomacy is something of a rag-bag, but an increasingly important one. The current preoccupation is with peacekeeping operations. This may involve activities such as the monitoring of cease-fires or embargoes, the separation of forces, caring for refugees and so forth. More generally, such naval activity may also comprise bilateral cooperation of various sorts, routine ship visits, the provision of assistance (for example, the mine-clearance exercise still continuing in the Gulf), the rescue of threatened citizens and increasingly, the furnishing of humanitarian relief. There have been many examples of this kind of thing since the Gulf War.

Two examples, both conducted by international forces led by the Americans, are particularly worth noting. The ability of navies to provide a *sustained* but controlled and acceptable limited presence was well demonstrated by the remarkable but barely noticed maritime force that was able to wait off strife-torn Liberia *for seven months* before moving in to rescue 2400 people. The potential reach of maritime forces was shown by the US

Marine Corps' ability to fly helicopters 460 miles at night from their amphibious warfare ships to pull 260 diplomats and foreign nationals from the US Embassy in Somalia[4].

Good order at sea

Finally, there is the last dimension of the new spectrum of naval requirement that seems to be emerging in the post Cold War world, namely the hum-drum tasks concerned with the maintenance of good order at sea. A first glance, the concern of a blue lamp rather than a bluewater navy, these constabulary tasks are nevertheless important, and getting more so.

The growing importance of sea-based resources (oil, gas, fish) and the vulnerability of domestic societies to the threats posed by drug-smugglers, illegal immigration and so on, suggest that these tasks could become crucial. The recent arrival of 10,000 Albanian refugees at the Italian port of Bari suggests the potential scope of the problem, and population pressures in the Maghreb tend to make the Southern Europeans nervous too. Environmental concerns may become a particularly important growth area.

Lastly there is the reappearance of the scourge of modern day piracy and armed robbery from merchant ships so particularly prevalent in such areas as South East Asia, West Africa and South America. Currently estimated to be costing ship-owners about £200 million a year, and involving the use of violence in about 25 per cent of cases, this could well prove beyond the capacity of local states to control, thereby requiring international action of some sort[5]. The collapse of the Somali and Ethiopian navies and the consequent increase in lawlessness in parts of the Red Sea and the Gulf of Aden is a worrying example of a general problem.

ISSUES OF IMPLEMENTATION

If this, then, is the new spectrum of requirement for the Royal Navy in the post Cold War era, what are the main issues confronting those who seek to implement it? Here we can look at only a few of them. But the question of the maintenance of

quality is certainly one of the most important issues confronting
naval planners at the moment.

A continuing need for quality

It might have been thought that with the effective demise of the
Soviet Navy as a rival for the mastery of the oceans, it would be
possible to accept a lowering of quality standards. This is certainly a seductive idea in that it would allow the acquisition of
much cheaper *materiel* and the provision of more platforms,
weapons and sensors for less money. Sadly, this notion does not
pass muster. In the first place, most of the force structure of the
Navy of, say, the year 2010 is already in place.

Procurement plans are already underway, resources are committed and the planners' ability to change course, even if they
wanted to, surprisingly limited. Simple reductions, however, are
easier to arrange!

But there is, secondly, considerable doubt that this is what
they should try to do anyway. The requirements of conflict with
a major or a minor power, and even those of coercive diplomacy, all point to a continuing need to maintain quality standards.
This is certainly true at the nuclear level. In the Commonwealth
of Independent States (CIS), large scale nuclear forces still exist
and must be a matter of concern to defence planners.
Nonetheless, greatly improved relations have facilitated reductions. In particular, the *Statement on the Defence Estimates* for 1992
announced that ' . . . we no longer need to retain a United
Kingdom maritime tactical nuclear capability.'[6] Royal Navy ships
and aircraft and RAF Maritime Patrol Aircraft will therefore no
longer carry tactical nuclear weapons.

But it is hard to disagree with President Bush that ' . . . the
proliferation of weapons of mass destruction (is) truly the fastest
growing security challenge to international peace and order.'
Over 20 countries have or are developing nuclear, chemical or
biological weapons and the means to deliver them. This requires
the maintenance of an independent nuclear force, of high quality as ' . . . the bedrock of our security.'[7]

Proliferation is taking place in less apocalyptic ways as well
and this also points to a need to maintain quality. Sophisticated
submarines, aircraft and missiles are being made available at a

worrying rate to countries whose future political allegiance is uncertain. Iran, for example, has expressed an interest in the acquisition of modern *Kilo* submarines and Tu-22M *Backfire* bombers, complete with upgraded hypersonic anti-ship missiles from a Russia forced by its parlous economic situation to increase its arms sales. Western arms companies, squeezed by recession and facing diminishing markets at home, thanks to the end of the Cold War, are having to follow suit.

It would therefore be safer for planners to assume that were they to be engaged in conflict in the outside world, they could well find themselves facing the latest Western or Russian arms technology. Public sensitivity to the loss of life in messy, distant conflicts also supports the retention of high quality in offence and defence. Lastly, the inevitable fact that most navies are likely to comprise fewer platforms in the future than they have become used to means that planners will want each platform to have the capacity to perform as wide a range of tasks as possible.

For all these reasons, naval planners faced with a need, perhaps, to prepare for conflict against a medium regional power will need to retain versatile and highly capable forces of the sort, if not of the number, that they once needed for Cold War purposes. In the Gulf War, high quality in platforms, weapons, sensors and personnel was the main force multiplier, and will certainly remain essential for 'battlespace dominance' in the future, especially for governments acutely sensitive to the loss of life.

The expeditionary concept

The end of the Cold War has led to a drop in the relative importance assigned to the level of effort to deep/bluewater operations. The cessation of attack submarine building in the UK, for the first time since the construction of the first Holland Boat in 1901, and equivalent reductions in the submarine capacity in the United States, France, the Netherlands, Denmark and Germany are all an indication of this trend.

Instead, the accent in the United States is on the protection of interests in the wider world through the development of a capacity to intervene in a local situation where American or allied interests, property or lives are at risk. This is thought to require the development of an 'expeditionary' kind of force, a pattern being followed also by several of our European allies (most particularly, France, Spain and Italy).

Given the continuing stress on quality, and the growing interest in expeditionary/littoral operations, especially, but by no means exclusively, in the Third World, what are likely to be some of the naval planners' chief preoccupations in the next few years?

The anticipated characteristics of such a force are reasonably clear. First, but in no particular order of priority, there will be an obvious need at least to maintain, and possibly to expand, light amphibious forces which can be more easily and more quickly transported to where they are needed than the tank-heavy forces characteristic of the Gulf War.

The concern that such 'light' forces might not be able to hold their own against local threats would be legitimate were they to be confronted by heavy armoured forces, but this is more likely to be the exception than the rule. Most analysts expect *Operation Haven* to be more of a model for future interventions than *Desert Storm*. In most foreseeable circumstances, the portability and speed advantages of amphibious, and indeed airborne, forces outweigh the vulnerabilities deriving from their lightness. In any case, 'lightness' is a relative concept. The United States Marine Corps interprets the phrase more heavily than their European counterparts can hope to do. Nevertheless, that interpretation is one which could provide a model to which the Europeans might, in some respects, aspire.

Expeditionary activity also clearly requires sea-lift, its protection and sustainability. In a general way, these rather more hum-drum requirements sometimes do not have the visibility that they should. Their importance is however always signified by the latest war, and so it was in the Gulf. That conflict reminded everyone of the continuing need to maintain a modern ocean-going support fleet for the Navy and the capacity to transport military personnel and equipment to possible remote theatres of action. The absence of opposition at sea in the Gulf War and the near unanimity of international support for Coalition operations, meant there was no particular problem in relying on foreign-flagged ships for sea transportation, but it would plainly be dangerous to assume that these happy circumstances will always recur. For this reason, the continuing decline of the

British merchant fleet remains, in the measured words of the latest *Statement of Defence Estimates*, a matter ' . . . of concern'.[8]

Littoral vulnerabilities

The ability of naval forces to operate for long periods of time in remote but littoral waters has many implications for the structure of a fleet, especially one more designed to support expeditionary activity. There is, for example, the continuing requirement for mine counter-measure (MCM) forces with strategic mobility. The damage to the USS *Princeton* and *Tripoli* and the still on-going mine clearance effort in the Gulf were potent reminders of the sea denial power of even quite old sea mines. Any expeditionary force of the future would need to be able to emulate the Coalition's remarkable success in containing this threat before, during and after the fighting. Such an aim would appear to require the maintenance of quality and a new emphasis on the mine counter-measure forces being able to travel long distances and to operate for long periods of time in remote and perhaps unfamiliar environments. This has obvious implications for naval planners who must make sure that their MCM forces have all the necessary afloat support, command-and-control and navigational facilities they need for the self-contained conduct of an increasingly complex job.

The need for navies to defend themselves against deep-water threats, especially from ocean-going submarines and long-range aircraft with anti-ship missiles may have declined, but the need for self-defence in littoral waters has increased. In general, there does not yet appear to have been much of the narrowing of the gap between the great navies and the small ones so confidently predicted 10–20 years ago. In fact, the Gulf War demonstrated that very large platforms and formations can, if properly configured, operate in much narrower waters than had hitherto been supposed.

The Coalition's naval activity was much aided by the fact that the Iraqi navy had no submarines, but it would clearly be unwise to ignore the steady proliferation of modern coastal submarines around the world. This development brings with it the need to maintain, or even to upgrade, current ASW capacities especially those usable and useful in littoral waters.

Ship-borne helicopters operating in a relatively benign air environment were able to dispose of the Iraqi Fast Patrol Boat and surface-to-surface missile threat much more easily than most pre-war commentators had imagined. With the exception of the shooting down of a *Silkworm* missile by HMS *Gloucester*, defence was therefore assured by the safest means, namely the preemptive destruction of the launching platforms. For this reason, naval planners will certainly want to develop new surface-to-surface missiles and helicopters and fixed-wing aircraft armed with air-to-surface missiles for the twenty-first century. Although ship-defences in the rest of the world are currently quite unsophisticated, decoy and close in weapons systems (CIWS) capacities are beginning to appear and can be expected to spread rapidly (especially as they can reasonably be represented as 'defensive'). Once again, the likely cause of events points to the need to maintain quality in naval missiles.

Nonetheless, the challenge of the future will be to maintain the level of security achieved in the past, against air or surface launched with fewer 'observables', more range, punch and electronic counter-counter measures (ECCM) capacities, and possibly delivered in saturation numbers. It is hard, however, to conceive of the emergence of a new adversary with the equivalent sea denial capacity of the Soviet Union in the Cold War era. For this reason, there is no real reason to suppose that prolonged sea-keeping, even in narrow waters, is an unrealistic aspiration, provided that the force is assured of adequate air-support.

Air support

This matter is so important that it warrants separate treatment. Naval planners will now need to consider how best the air support so necessary to the fleet's capacity to keep the sea, and to influence the outcome of events on land, can best be provided. In some circumstances afloat air support may not be necessary at all. Two alternative cases can be imagined, and were, in fact, both deployed during the Gulf War.

In the first case, offensive airpower can be furnished from totally secure air bases outside the theatre, quite possibly thousands of miles away. During the Gulf War, this type of airpower was exemplified by the B-52 bombing campaign against Iraq, which accounted for some 70 per cent of the ordnance dropped during the conflict. In the second case, all the necessary air support can be provided from friendly air bases within the theatre. This was demonstrated by the large numbers of fighter and ground attack aircraft able to operate from Saudi and other airfields during the Gulf War, flying thousands of highly effective air defence, battlefield support and interdiction missions in the area.

Each alternative has its strengths and weaknesses. B52s are largely invulnerable to attack and when the targets are large tank concentrations or industrial centres, this kind of air offensive will almost certainly be effective. But these conditions rarely apply. They have only occurred three times in the last 50 years, and in one of them – the Vietnam War – the strategic bombing offensive largely failed. Moreover, diplomacy by B-52 is virtually a contradiction in terms, and in unclear, confusing local conflicts as in the former Yugoslavia, this model of airpower might seem to have little to offer.

Locally-based land airpower can be politically discriminatory and much more sensitive to local circumstances. In the Gulf War, shore-based Coalition airforces had important advantages over their sea-based equivalents in terms of providing strategic land attack on Iraq and, to a lesser extent, in flying close air support, battlefield air interdiction and defensive counter-air missions. Land-based aircraft managed shorter turn-around times, and so achieved a higher proportion of offensive sorties than sea-based aircraft. Moreover, it was easier for them to make use of their own land-based in-flight refuelling, and so they were able to fly further, faster.[9]

Nonetheless, their total reliance on the use of existing air bases in theatre makes this type of airpower critically dependent on the good will of the host country and potentially vulnerable to attack from terrorists, ground forces, or enemy counter-air. The Vietnam War reminds us that defending air bases requires a much more substantial political and military presence than might be wise. Land air bases also take more time to set up or, as in Saudi Arabia, to build, and then more logistics to sustain, than might be available.

In situations which call for a speedy response, where the total obliteration of an adversary's war-making capacity is not an operational requirement, where political dexterity is required, where land air bases are doubtful either militarily or politically or where there is a desire to limit liability, sea-based air will continue to have a good deal to offer. This will be especially true for the provision of tactical air defence and ground support in expeditionary activity.

This being so, British naval planners will doubtless need to consider how best to provide the naval air capacities required in the next century. This will require the replacement of both the Sea Harrier FRS.2 and their aircraft carrier platforms. This will pose a number of problems. One is budgetary; like all air projects, both are likely to be expensive and it may seem best to spread the costs of the two obviously-related programmes in a way which would make their simultaneous implementation difficult.

The second problem has to do with the search for a follow-on aircraft. One interesting option, also now being actively considered by the US Marine Corps, is the 'Hovering Hornet' STOVL Strike Fighter (SSF) now being advanced by the US Defense Advanced Research Projects Agency, General Dynamics and British Aerospace. Such complex matters are unlikely to be resolved in the immediate future, and nor are they the only naval aviation issues confronting the planners. Others include provision for the new Merlin EH 101 helicopter with increased capacities. Clearly, the future size and shape of the fleet will be much affected by the outcome of air questions such as these.

Cooperative enterprises

Since, in the future, the Royal Navy is more likely to operate as part of a multinational force than on its own, the accent in sizing and shaping the future fleet must be on developing its already considerable ability to operate with friends. The point has recently been well made by Vice-Admiral Weyher of the German Navy:

> The increasing possibility of risks arising on the periphery of the area covered by the North Atlantic Treaty necessitates . . .

participation in operations of crisis containment and crisis management in the framework of the Alliance. Naval forces are especially suitable for accomplishing this mission because they are a flexible, effective instrument in the hands of the political authorities, one that lends itself to effective command and control over long distances.[10]

Naval planners need to think about what set of capabilities and characteristics will be most helpful to the solution of the most likely crisis situations. Being able to provide these qualities will also help Britain mould and sustain the system it wants for the future. Many of these capabilities will flow naturally out of the expeditionary requirements considered earlier, but three more points are perhaps worth looking at briefly.

The first is the issue of exercises. When times are hard, there is a natural tendency on the part of planners to reduce the operational tempo and to cut down on the exercise programme. Taking this too far could damage fragile international alliances which have to be constantly serviced. The fact that its air and land forces have been cut proportionately more than its sea services, reminds us that NATO remains in essence a maritime alliance. Last year, two thirds of its major exercises were either maritime or had a major maritime dimension. The political health of any alliance, and its operational effectiveness is therefore contingent on the capacity to practise together – at sea. This is the rationale for the formation within the Alliance of new standing naval forces for the Atlantic and the Mediterranean. The Royal Navy contributes to both.

The second is the vexed matter of agreeing harmonised rules of engagement. This is a complex and sensitive matter since it has to do with delicate issues of political control and political objective. But given the complicated and difficult situations in which multinational naval forces might well find themselves, it is plainly important to make progress in this field.

Thirdly, a multinational force is only as coherent as its Command, Control Communication and Intelligence (C^3I) system permits. Being able to distribute accurate intelligence data around the force and to act on it in good time is normally an absolute condition for success. But data links are technically complex and usually expensive; their wide variety even amongst

NATO and WEU allies, makes full communication difficult. In this connection the US development of the Mobile Universal Link Translator System (MULTS) is an important and timely development. MULTS has helped the disparate air and naval forces assembled under NATO and WEU command off the coast of the former Yugoslavia to carry out effective and coordinated monitoring operations and may prove a significant pointer to the future.[11]

COLLABORATION: WAYS AND MEANS

In conclusion, this review might seem to suggest that navies need every imaginable capacity in order to be ready for every conceivable contingency. But such a view conflicts with the obvious fact that they are all confronted by a certain decline in resources. Naval planners seeking to square this circle will, of course, seek to restructure their fleets and to reduce the tail at least as much as the teeth; this process is constrained by its political and industrial implications but is certainly going on. The recent announcement of the formation of a single Surface Flotilla may be seen as a means to that end. A greater reliance on the reserves as a contribution towards the principle of reconstitution will also help.

But such responses are unlikely fully to solve the problem. For example, it has become clear that reconstitution is far from easy and only creates substantial savings if forces and platforms are in deep reserve from which it takes a long time to recover. Nevertheless, partial reductions in readiness help to sustain force levels and remain a sensible response against threats providing substantial notice.

Inevitably, with declining force levels, medium sized navies will, perforce, have to cooperate more with others in the solution of common problems. With such projects as the Anglo-French Anti-Air Warfare Frigate, navies may follow collaboration in operations with collaboration in procurement. The more that requirements can be aligned, the greater the prospect of savings. This might, though, be at the price of the essential national distinctiveness of particular navies; it might make the protection of total national defence industries more rather than less difficult, and it is bound to cause considerable programming difficulties. Plainly there are no easy solutions to the various problems involved in planning medium navies for an uncertain and unpredictable future.

Notes

[1] The opinions expressed in this article should not be taken necessarily to reflect official opinion in any way.

[2] The phrase 'naval planner' used throughout this article means simply someone who plans navies; it does not imply that that person necessarily wears a naval uniform.

[3] M Pugh, 'Multinational Maritime Forces: A Breakout from Traditional Peacekeeping?' (Mountbatten Centre for International Studies: SPIP, No 1, 1992) p. 15.

[4] General Carl E Mundy, 'Expeditionary Forces: A Defence Concept for the Future', *Seapower*, April 1992, p. 48.

[5] *Sunday Times*, 24 May 1992. Also work done by Mike Pugh at the Mountbatten Centre, Southampton University.

[6] Statement of the Defence Estimates 1992, CM 1981, July 1992, p. 28.

[7] Ibid.

[8] Ibid., p. 42 .

[9] B Sweetman, 'Naval Air Power for 2000: Time to Change Course' *International Defence Review*, 9/1992.

[10] In 'The German Navy on its Way Ahead', *NATO's Sixteen Nations*, No 1/92.

[11] 'Integration in Action', *International Defence Review*, 10/92.

EUROPEAN SECURITY

7

Cooperative Security in Europe

STUART CROFT

Senior Lecturer in Security Studies, University of Birmingham

In the Helsinki Declaration of the Conference on Security and Cooperation in Europe (CSCE) of 10 July 1992, the 52 participants committed themselves to pursue cooperative security and to seek the development of mutually reinforcing institutions. Cooperative security is to be based on a notion that security is a shared responsibility and that decision making has to be based on consensus. On the relationship between institutions the Helsinki Declaration stated that:

> Essential to the success of our efforts to foster democratic change within the CSCE framework will be increased coopera-
> tion with other European and transatlantic organisations and institutions. Therefore, we are convinced that a lasting and peaceful order for our community of States will be built on mutually reinforcing institutions, each with its own area of action and responsibility.[1]

This chapter will seek to examine the meaning of cooperative security and its role in European relations. First, it will look at the meaning of cooperative security, and will make some distinctions between cooperative security, collective security and collective defence. Secondly, it will consider the contribution of the CSCE itself to the creation of a cooperative security order. Thirdly, the contribution of other institutions – NATO, the European Community, the West European Union (WEU) and the Commonwealth of Independent States (CIS) will be assessed. Finally, the chapter will conclude with some thoughts on the level of cooperative security in Europe, and on its varying applicability across the continent.

COOPERATIVE SECURITY

Cooperative security belongs to that tradition of thinking which in the early and mid 1980s was termed 'common security'.[2] Common security was based on a notion that in the Cold War period there had to be cooperation to avoid nuclear catastrophe. It was felt that by keeping that idea to the political forefront, there would be more cooperation over issues such as arms control and crisis management, and less emphasis on national rivalry, the arms race and competition. In this way, some hoped, the security dilemma might eventually be overcome. With the end of the Cold War, common security rather lost its focus, since its prime aim had been to overcome the more dangerous elements of the East-West rivalry. Yet at the same time, cooperative security – based on very similar notions – has come to the fore as the most agreeable way to manage security relations in the new Europe.

The concept of cooperative security focuses upon security interdependence. It is suggested that there are major international implications following from changes in national security policies and in the national procurement of new weapons systems. The deployment of a new weapons system in one country, for example, could lead to pressures to increase the level of armaments – either offensive or defensive – in other countries, in what Robert McNamara called an 'action-reaction phenomenon'.[3] Further, at a time when security is defined in wide terms, to include economic and societal issues as well as military factors, negative consequences may follow for third parties from insecurities in particular groups of countries. In its New Strategic Concept, announced at the Rome Summit of November 1991, NATO redefined security to encompass 'political, economic, social and environmental elements as well as the indispensable defence dimension. Managing the diversity of challenges facing the Alliance requires a broad approach to security'.[4] Clearly, under such a definition the security of the members of NATO could be undermined by economic or societal instabilities in Central or Eastern Europe. Thus it would be in the interests of the NATO countries, in this case, to work to eliminate insecurities in countries outside the NATO membership, which was the idea underlying the creation of the North Atlantic Cooperation Council (NACC) in January 1992. Cooperative security is thus based on a notion of interdependence, recognition of which, in the words of *The Report of the Independent Commission on Disarmament and Security Issues* under the chairmanship of Olof Palme which in the early 1980s did much to popularise the notion of common security, 'means that nations must begin to organise their security politics in cooperation with one another.'[5]

The concept of cooperative security is thus somewhat different to that of collective security. The latter implies the organisation of all states to deter or militarily reverse the actions of an aggressor.[6] This requires formal guarantees of states' sovereignty and the provision of the military means to defend that sovereignty. Collective security seeks to stress the equal importance of all states, and to work against reliance on a balance of power. The United Nations-sanctioned military activity of the Coalition of forces in the Gulf to expel Iraq from Kuwait in 1991 could be seen to be a classic example of the implementation of collective security; even though the deterrent effect of the United Nations guarantee to nations of their territorial integrity was not sufficient to deter the initial Iraqi aggression nor compel Iraqi withdrawal before the initiation of the war. By seeking to alter the cost-benefit analysis of aggressor states in international relations, collective security could ensure that conflict would be much less likely to occur, and that the values of national independence and self-determination would be supported. Above all, with such a system, it would be much less likely that a preponderant power would emerge and threaten domination, such as Napoleonic France or Nazi Germany.

Of course, collective security has been the subject of much criticism and controversy. The failure of the League of Nations to control the rise of the fascist powers in the 1930s has for many analysts condemned the concept of collective security to the intellectual scrap-heap.[7] However, it is not really necessary here to outline the counter-arguments. For the purposes of this

analysis it is important to note that the concepts of collective
security and cooperative security differ in one fundamental
area. While collective security focuses upon military security,
the focus of cooperative security is on wider security issues.
Consequently, while the former is concerned with hard questions of sovereignty and independence, the latter is also
concerned with wider economic, social and environmental questions involving non-state security challenges (over terrorism,
environmental degradation and the migration of peoples, for
example).

The third major conception is that of collective defence.[8] As
with collective security, collective defence implies that all in the
alliance or agreement will support any member that might be
attacked. However, whereas the former is designed to be inclu-
sive, collective defence is designed to be exclusive. Collective
security would protect all its members against the military
aggression of any other member; collective defence would protect its members against those outside the alliance. Thus NATO
was designed to protect its members against the Soviet 'threat';
were NATO to have been a collective security arrangement,
then it would have had to include the Soviet Union as one of its
members.

Unlike collective defence, cooperative security does not
require detailed consideration of the collaboration of military
forces between various members of the system. Collective
defence posits a state or group of states as an enemy, while cooperative security looks at the security challenges that may arise
from processes (poverty and underdevelopment, for example)
that could lessen security in a variety of different ways.

Cooperative security, then, is conceptually different from
both collective security and collective defence. This means that
in the discussion of cooperative security held in the CSCE during 1992 and at other times, it is not implied that the CSCE
should or could either develop into a collective security organisation along the lines of the League of Nations, nor develop
into a collective defence organisation such as NATO. The supporters of cooperative security have attempted to appropriate
(perhaps some might say reappropriate) the term security from
defence ministries and discussions of military requirements and
place it in foreign ministries and into discussions of political

needs; in this sense, it may be that it is the perfect concept for a grouping such as the CSCE. However, if the CSCE is not to be turned into a new League of Nations, nor a reformed NATO, then clearly an important series of relationships with the other institutions of European security has to be worked out.

COOPERATIVE SECURITY IN THE CSCE

The emergence of a cooperative security regime within the CSCE can be dated from the Vienna Document of November 1990 on confidence and security building measures. A few days later, the Paris Charter of the CSCE set up the Conflict Prevention Center in Vienna. Following this, in February 1991, the Valetta Report established a mechanism for the peaceful settlement of disputes. Finally, in June 1991, at the Berlin CSCE Foreign Minister's meeting, it was agreed to allow states to ask for clarification of any emergency activity from other states to be provided within 48 hours. However, these moves were widely seen to be very limited. There was little scope for flexibility in reacting to the new challenges in Europe, from the collapse of the Soviet Union to the bitter war in the former Yugoslavia.[9]

Thus, at the meeting at Helsinki in the middle of 1992, moves were made to enable greater response to be made to such new challenges. Cooperative security was to be the aim sought by all. No country would attempt to strengthen its own security, it was agreed, if this was to the detriment of other states. Although this seemed to apply mainly to the area of military security, it was agreed that security itself should be thought about in a wide-ranging sense, linking peacekeeping with human rights and democracy, stability and security with economic, environmental, scientific and technical cooperation, political pluralism with the market economy, and stability with cooperation against terrorism, drug trafficking and organised crime.

Perhaps most significantly, the Helsinki Document set up the Forum for Security Cooperation. The Forum is to be the successor to the former bloc-to-bloc negotiation which was the arena in which the Conventional Forces in Europe (CFE) Treaty was negotiated, modified and subsequently signed for implementation. The success of signing the CFE Treaty – and successfully modifying it in the light of the end of the Cold War and the collapse of the Warsaw Pact and the Soviet Union – along with the CFE 1A Agreement reached in Helsinki, are positive precursors to the work of the Forum. Open to all the states of the CSCE, the Forum is supposed to provide an arena for the negotiation of further disarmament, provide a framework for consultation, and further detail methods of conflict prevention.

On disarmament, the Forum will provide an arena for harmonising existing obligations of states, and pursue further confidence and security building measures (particularly in relation to verification and exchange of information). Conceivably the first concrete move forward might be driven by association of other states with the CFE 1A Agreement which outlined the maximum levels of personnel strength of conventional forces in Europe.

Attitudes towards the Forum's prospects for success can perhaps be divided into two categories. The negative view would suggest that the Security Forum is most likely to replicate the sterility of the MBFR talks; that is, there will simply not be enough political will to overcome the difficulties inherent in negotiations involving up to 52 states leading to agreements, or at least agreements that would have any significant political and military impact. According to this view, the CSCE Security Forum is likely to make far less of a contribution to security and disarmament than the work of NATO's North Atlantic Cooperation Council. The more positive view might suggest that although the likelihood of great progress in arms control might be limited, the Forum could play an important role in more intangible areas of arms control, involving the exchange of views, ideas and information: at the very least, in some particular circumstances, providing a context for discussion rather than armed confrontation. Further, the direct association of those states that used to be referred to as 'neutral' might bring further skills and ideas to the process of disarmament.

In terms of conflict management, the Helsinki Document introduced three significant developments. The first strengthened the role of the Committee of Senior Officials (CSO), responsible to the Council of Foreign Ministers. The position of the Chair of the CSO was enhanced. The Chair can call upon limited groups of states to assist in particular situations, and can appoint special representatives (following the practice of the United Nations), and may draw upon the assistance of the previous and successor Chairs (following the 'troika' principle of the European Community). In order to further strengthen the position of the CSCE, a second development was the creation a High Commissioner for National Minorities in order to provide early warning of crises involving conflict between ethnic groups. The remit of the High Commissioner is to look at potential crises, not from the perspective of human rights (which remains within the CSCE's human dimension), but in terms of tensions that might lead to more general conflicts. The High Commissioner for National Minorities will not, therefore, look at the cases of individuals. The third and final innovation is in terms of allowing the CSCE to enter into peacekeeping. In part, the terms on which peacekeeping might take place are to be those of the United Nations: operations must be non-coercive, impartial, and have the support of the parties concerned. In addition, the Helsinki Document stated that for the CSCE to enter into peacekeeping, there must be an effective ceasefire, written agreements with the parties concerned, and specific guarantees about the safety of peacekeeping personnel.

But does all this innovation and movement at Helsinki move forward the development of cooperative security in Europe? Clearly, at one level, it does. Agreement has been reached on the principle of cooperative security as an aim across the continent, and on certain measures to facilitate the dissemination of information and the provision of good offices up to the deployment of peacekeeping forces. However, at another level, all these moves are severely limited. It is difficult to identify concrete areas where cooperative security might be implemented in practice. In a continent in which, during 1992 alone, wars of aggression and secession multiplied and intensified in ferocity, the practice of cooperative security was, at best, regionalised. Further, the provision of information is only of limited use if there is little will to act. In the most bloody crises of 1992, peacemaking and peacekeeping efforts were not driven by the CSCE, but rather as part of the work of the European Community and United Nations in the former Yugoslavia, and of the Commonwealth of Independent States in parts of the former Soviet Union such as Nagorno-Karabakh, Georgia and Tajikistan.

Thus, although it may be argued that the agreements reached in Helsinki might take the CSCE process forward into some of the more difficult areas of security and stability in Europe, the CSCE clearly is not and cannot be the sole institution within which the development of cooperative security might be sought in Europe. Rather, as in the early days of the CSCE in the 1970s, while providing some mechanisms for the alleviation of tensions, the contribution of the CSCE to security is still limited in the face of the powerful political and strategic animosities which have characterised European security. This means that the other major institutions of European security – NATO, the European Community, the West European Union and, to a lesser extent, the Commonwealth of Independent States – all still have important roles to play.

COOPERATIVE SECURITY AND OTHER EUROPEAN SECURITY INSTITUTIONS

It would perhaps be wrong to draw too strong a distinction between the work of the CSCE and that of other institutions in the area of creating cooperative security. After all, the Helsinki Document made it clear that cooperation between the CSCE and NATO, the European Community, the West European Union, the Council of Europe, the European Bank for Reconstruction and Development and the Organisation for Economic Cooperation and Development was to be pursued and was important in terms of creating institutional linkages. Further, although the idea that NATO should be the primary military arm of the CSCE was rejected, it was agreed in the Helsinki Document that the CSCE could call upon NATO, the European Community, the WEU or the Commonwealth of Independent States for the provision of peacekeeping forces.

However, this illustrates one of the key issues in the debate over the development and depth of cooperative security. In Western Europe, strong, developing institutions exist. In the organisational void between Western Europe and the former Soviet Union, there are some bilateral arrangements, but nothing to commend itself as a sound security organisation. And in the former Soviet Union itself, the Commonwealth of Independent States appears to be a weak grouping of independent-minded states, fearful of Russian domination. This asymmetric structure is complicated on the one hand by the clear desire of Western countries to close possibilities of widening membership to the transition countries at least in the near term, and on the other hand the continued limitations of the pan-European alternative, the CSCE. Perhaps harshly, the CSCE has been dismissed as a body that can 'do little. It is a cumbersome body of 52 nations, able to operate only by consensus. Its structures are inchoate, its functions undefined, its original role as a bridge between East and West superseded. It has no forces of its own, nor charter to give it powers of peacekeeping or peace enforcement.'[10]

The CSCE, then, clearly needs to be supplemented. In fact, this is widely recognised, and was set out in a series of statements by major groupings of states during the middle of 1992. For example, the NATO communiqué of 4 June 1992 stated that 'stability and security in the Euro-Atlantic area will increasingly be built on a framework of interlocking and mutually reinforcing institutions.' The North Atlantic Cooperation Council statement of the following day noted the Council's role in supporting 'a new security architecture based on cooperative relations among states and a network of mutually reinforcing institutions.' The West European Union declaration of 19 June 1992 stressed the importance of 'the relationships between the CSCE and other mutually reinforcing European and transatlantic organisations.' In the Helsinki Document, as already noted, it was emphasised 'that a lasting and peaceful order for our community of States will be built on mutually reinforcing institutions, each with its own area of action and responsibility.'[11]

Such an interaction of different institutions with different memberships requires cooperation and resource coordination. There have been some positive steps. As we have acted, the CSCE and European Community cooperated over missions to the former Yugoslavia and there has been cooperation between the CSCE and the CIS over attempts to create peace in Nagorno-Karabakh.

Yet what does this web of institutions really mean? Clearly there is a desire to move away from the ideas of a neat and tidy European security architecture, to a recognition that stability might be enhanced by a coherent interaction of those bodies that already exist. Three important political realities must be noted in this. First, there is a strong desire on the part of political leaderships to prevent significant power moving from governments to international organisations. This debate is most notable within the European Community, as the concept of subsidiarity is used, in part, to reduce the influence of any organisational ethos. There is, then, no desire to move to the creation of a powerful organisation with elements of enforcement to produce acceptable behaviour, as was initially envisaged after the two World Wars. This has important implications for expectations of what might be achieved by international organisations. If the power and influence of organisations is to be constrained by national policies, such organisations cannot really be said to have failed in preventing the outbreak of wars and offences against human rights in Bosnia-Hercegovina and elsewhere. The fault, if that be the correct term, lies with the degree of political will and level of cooperation between particular states, along with the limits set to any action by the sheer complexity of many of the violent crises in Europe. There are still, despite the web of institutions and the commitment to cooperative security, regions of Europe in which particular institutions either have no competence or are vested with little authority by member states, and cooperative security has no coherent and tangible form. The desire for sovereignty, one of the most notable features of European politics in the period since 1989 throughout Europe, continues to constrain the role of organisations to that of being essentially the tools of the major countries.

Second, the caution within Western countries at the prospects of expanding the membership of major Western groupings – NATO, the European Community and the West European Union – or even to set any coherent criteria for other nations to join from the former communist bloc, means that the scope and competence of those organisations, although significant, will be geographically limited. Although there is frequent debate within the European Community about the possibility of a two-speed (Western) Europe, in reality there is already such a two-tier Europe across the continent. In other words, where cooperative institutions are most required, in the East, where problems of economic transition, political stability and ethnic relations are the most intense, those institutions are at their weakest or are absent.

Thirdly, although there is some discussion about a web of institutions, there is also institutional competition. It was a major aim of France at the Helsinki CSCE summit to prevent NATO from becoming the defence arm of the CSCE. The Franco-American argument over the role of NATO continues into the post-Cold War world. Within Western Europe, there is argument over the speed and depth of political union, and the consequent nature of the relationships between NATO, the European Community and the West European Union, with major differences between France, Germany, Britain, Italy and other countries – notably Denmark – on various points. The compromise agreement on these points reached at Maastricht at the European Community summit in December 1991 became increasingly stretched throughout 1992.

What emerges from this is much less of a web of institutions pursuing cooperative security than a renewed competition between different conceptions of central ideas – such as the meaning of Europe, the importance of integration, and the role of military forces, which is played out in a series of different institutions and fora, not excluding the G7 economic forum. This has led to a degree of paralysis which has been most evident in the uncoordinated responses to the crises in the former Yugoslavia and the Transcaucasus. A further indicator of this trend might be said to be the reemergence of the CSCE during 1992. In the period following the signing of the Paris Charter, the CSCE declined in significance; the meeting in Helsinki and the attempt to create yet more new initiatives and institutions illustrated the failure to obtain any more significant routes forward.

CONCLUSION

Clearly, if there is an institutional web of cooperative security developing in Europe, it is very uneven. One might question the use of the term 'developing'. There have been some measures, but there are tight limits. NATO has adapted to a certain degree to the new circumstances, but the scope for change is constrained by the desire not to widen membership. The European Community, with a similar constraint, also faces a series of challenges in obtaining the ratification of the Maastricht agreement that, amongst other things, would make the West European Union the defence arm of the European Union. The whole process of West European construction seems wounded by the Danish, and to a lesser extent, the French referenda on Maastricht, by the apparent collapse of the Exchange Rate Mechanism and the growth of the influence in many countries of the so-called Euro-sceptics. It is difficult to make a case out of this for any 'development'. This is compounded by the crises to the east and south east of the European Community, and by the apparent fragility of the Commonwealth of Independent States.

There is an interesting contradiction at work. On the one hand, all are convinced that the ideas of cooperative security are important, and that they should be the principles underlying the creation of a new order in Europe. Collective security seems incredible, particularly given the policies of the Western countries (with the partial exception of France) in attempting to avoid making decisions and taking action over the former Yugoslavia, let alone the wars in the former Soviet Union. Collective defence seems to be a principle that cannot presently be extended beyond the European Community/NATO countries, in part for fear of exacerbating ethnic tensions and risking escalation of conflicts; in part for fear of the financial cost. Thus the *concept* of cooperative security, for all its strengths and weaknesses, has emerged from the others, although perhaps as a 'worst best hope' for many. But on the other hand, there seems to be no institutional base which can give full effect to the implementation of cooperative security in practice. The Western institutions are clearly to be limited in membership; the CIS faces internal division and potential collapse. This leaves the CSCE which, despite its strengthening at Helsinki, still has not been seen as the key institution for the management and resolution of any of the bloody post-Cold War European crises.

Perhaps, however, too much is being asked of institutions. As William Pfaff amongst others has argued 'Groups do not lead. Individual governments lead.'[12] Movement over the former Yugoslavia was led, at different times, by Germany, France and to a lesser extent, Italy. It was largely the United States that created the coalition of forces that expelled Iraq from Kuwait. Yet the evolution of political influence in the years after the fall of the Berlin Wall has created something of a vacuum in Europe. With the collapse of Soviet power, Russian influence has dramatically declined, with the Federation beset by ethnic, economic and political problems, and geographically set far to the east of Europe by the independence of the Baltic states, Belarus and the Ukraine. The United States, while still a major power, has committed itself to redefine its world role (which should be read only in part as a euphemism for retrenchment), unwilling to take the lead in purely European issues. Within Western Europe, France has focused on its relations with Germany, attempting to develop Western European institutions to maintain a balance with the new Germany, while increasingly being drawn into a certain dependency, as illustrated by the crisis over the franc in September 1992. Germany, in contrast, still faces constitutional limitations which constrain action, while the costs of unification mount. In Russia, the United States, France, and Germany, as well as in Britain and Italy, governments have laboured with great domestic problems, relating to various combinations of economic recession, constitutional gridlock, a rise in organised crime and political unpopularity.

In short, for a variety of geopolitical and domestic reasons, 'Europe' as a political construct defined by the 52 CSCE states, lacks leadership. In such circumstances, it is easy to expect far too much of international organisations. But the CSCE, as with NATO or the CIS, is fundamentally dependent upon the actions of member states. In this lack of leadership and direction some may see a return to the political paralysis of the 1930s, or perhaps as creating the circumstances for the resurgence of German power, or, as a further alternative perhaps, as heralding a return to German-Russian cooperation.[13] Regardless of the validity of any of these assessments, the gap between rhetoric and reality is clear in many areas, and it may be that one of the most obvious of these is in the concept and practice of cooperative security.

Cooperative security, itself a second best for the establishment of collective security or the extension of collective defence, is a concept that is having great difficulty in being implemented. Institutionally, much has been achieved at the micro-level, with the work of the North Atlantic Cooperation Council (NACC) and the further steps forward being taken at Helsinki in July 1992 under the umbrella of the CSCE. However, at the macro-level, institutional paralysis seems to be growing in the face of wider and more numerous security challenges and a lack of leadership on the continent. Whether this growing anarchy is positive or negative for groups of people will inevitably depend in part upon where those groups of people live in Europe. It maybe that a *Europe des Etâts* will prove to be a natural state of affairs in Europe, with some states existing with higher levels of security and stability than others. Such a situation, which might loosely resemble the situation in the nineteenth century after the Congress of Vienna is not, however, the concept to which the states of Europe from 'Vancouver to Vladivostok' are committed. Commitment to cooperative security implies that efforts need to be made to spread the institutional web and so raise the level of security for states and peoples throughout the continent. The countries of Eastern and Central Europe undoubtedly need economic aid aιιu technical support to assist the transition to a liberal democracy with a social market economy. Indeed, the concept of cooperative security would imply to many that economic investment in the former communist countries would be one of the most important contributions to increasing levels of security for all in Europe. It may also be that the achievement of adequate politico-military security arrangements would be a precursor to addressing other security issues. In the late 1940s, many of the major problems facing Western Europe were related to economic recovery and political stability. Both were achieved in the 1950s, but were built upon the confidence of secure politico-military arrangements. Thus, if it is accepted that West European economic recovery and governmental stability were in part built upon the foundations of the Dunkirk Treaty, West European Union and the North Atlantic Treaty, it is possible that economic regeneration and political democratisation in Eastern and Central Europe in the 1990s may be dependent upon the fashioning of an adequate security arrangement for the countries of the region, within which the rhetoric of cooperative security can be given more concrete form.

These are serious issues for all in Europe, for the logic of cooperative security, to which all governments are publicly committed, is that because of the inter-related nature of security, insecurity in one area of Europe necessarily lessens the security of all. In the absence of a strong pan-European institutional base to give cooperative security practical effect, it remains to be seen whether the concept of cooperative security will prove to be as flawed as has been its practice.

More seriously, it is not self-evident that those in government who have committed their countries to pursue cooperative security actually believe in that concept. How relevant are the instabilities and insecurities in the former communist countries to the security issues faced by the countries that (in security terms) are now on the periphery of Europe, such as Britain? How deeply does the British government believe that the wars in the former Yugoslavia, for example, really affect the security of the United Kingdom? Is it hard-headed realism to view that conflict as not central to the national interest, or is it a narrow view that is unable to take on board the truly inter-related nature of security in post-cold war Europe? For the central issue raised by the phrase and concept of cooperative security is clear: is 'Europe' still the correct level of analysis for the 52 countries of the CSCE, or is that level of analysis a hangover from the Cold War? The repeated discussion about the desirability of a Conference on Security and Cooperation in the Mediterranean implies that for some countries in that region, 'Europe' is not the relevant security category. But this may also be true for other groups of states currently talking about developing cooperative security under the CSCE. The future for cooperative security on a pan-European basis is therefore not straightforward by any means, and alternative 'regional' levels of security might, for many countries and groups, become increasingly relevant.

Notes

[1] Helsinki Summit Declaration. 10 July 1992., para. 24.
[2] The Report of the Independent Commission on Disarmament and Security Issues under the Chairmanship of Olof Palme *Common Security* (London: Pan Books 1982).

[3] See Robert McNamara, *Blundering into Disaster* (London: Bloomsbury 1987), especially pp. 52–9.

[4] *Rome Summit – NATO New Strategic Concept* para. 25, p. 6.

[5] *Common Security, op cit,* p. 6.

[6] See I Claude, *Power and International Relations* (New York: Random House, 1962), for a classic treatment of the subject.

[7] See E H Carr, *The Twenty Years Crisis* (London: Macmillan 1939) reprinted many times subsequently. For a more contemporary critique, see J Joffe, 'Collective security and the future of Europe' Survival Spring 1992.

[8] See the classic A Wolfers, *Discord and Collaboration* (London and Baltimore: Johns Hopkins Press, 1962).

[9] The 'consensus minus one' principle was invoked by the Council of Foreign Ministers in January 1992 against the new Yugoslavia which was condemned for clear and constant breaches of CSCE commitments. Subsequently, Yugoslavia was suspended. These actions, which could be seen as rather late, had no noticeable effect upon the course and conduct of the war in Bosnia Hercegovina and elsewhere in the Balkans.

[10] Editorial in *The Times* 13 July 1992.

[11] These statements are collected together by Kari Mottola in 'Prospect for Cooperative Security in Europe: The Role of the CSCEP', unpublished paper prepared for the Panel on Conceptions of European Security, Inaugural Pan-European Conference, Heidelberg September 1992.

[12] See William Pfaff, 'Nations Must Lead When Collective Security Stalls', *Herald Tribune* 12 July 1992.

[13] There has been a great deal of literature on this, but perhaps some of the most interesting has been found in *International Security*. See, for example, Richard Betts, 'Systems for Peace or Cause of War? Collective Security, Arms Control and the New Europe' Vol. 17 No. 1 Summer 1992; Charles Kupchan and Clifford Kupchan, 'Concerts, Collective Security and the Future of Europe' Vol. 16 No. 1 Summer 1991; John Mearsheimer, 'Back to the Future: Instability in Europe after the Cold War' Vol. 15 No. 1 Spring 1990; and Jack Snyder, 'Averting Anarchy in the New Europe' Vol. 15 No. 1 Spring 1990.

8

The Collapse of the Soviet Union and Problems of the CIS

ELAINE M HOLOBOFF

Lecturer in War Studies, Kings College London

The collapse of empire, like revolution, must always be an *ad hoc* and unpredictable process. In December 1991 Boris Yeltsin, President of the Russian Federation, took advantage of the weakness of Gorbachev after the abortive coup and made him irrelevant as President of the Soviet Union. Three months had proved that neither the leader nor his country were any longer viable. Regional declarations of sovereignty and independence had been voiced openly since 1990. By the autumn of 1991 the Baltic states had broken from the Soviet Union, and Ukraine's definitive calls for independence were sounding the death knell of central authority. Whether Yeltsin possessed some grand vision of his place in history, or was merely concerned with gaining an impressive tactical advantage over an old adversary, only history can judge.

The Minsk Summit of 8 December 1991 quietly put an end to over 70 years of communist rule. The leaders of Russia, Ukraine, and Belarus founded the Commonwealth of Independent States (CIS) and *de facto* thrust independence upon nine republics, regardless of their nationalist aspirations. Eight more republics joined the CIS on 21 December at the Alma Ata Summit. Only Georgia and the Baltic states declined to cooperate in the new arrangement. Now a leader without a country, Gorbachev resigned as President of the Soviet Union on 25 December 1991.

In a similar fashion, the end of the Cold War was thrust upon the West. The collapse of bilateral competition had been anticipated by the revolutions in Eastern Europe in 1989. But few could conceive that this would be followed by the disintegration of the West's greatest ideological adversary. Should not the disappearance of a great empire have been preceded by events of at least equal significance to the final collapse? Yet there were no cataclysmic confrontations, bloodshed was almost non-existent, and mass organised political movements did not arise. It was as if a great bear had been nudged with a small twig and simply rolled over and died. As unprepared as many of the Soviet republics were for independence, so too, the West was unprepared for life without an adversary. Many queued up to befriend the unpredictable but now powerful Boris Yeltsin, NATO suffered an identity crisis of even worse proportions than after the events in Eastern Europe, and pundits discussed the transition to a 'generic threat'.

Yet whatever else it did, the end of communism in the Soviet Union did not immediately usher in an era of peace and democracy. Five themes which will continue to guide the security dialogue on the former Soviet Union are discussed below. These include succession issues, ethnic conflicts, nationalism, and political uncertainty. The search for effective Western policies also faces many difficulties. Predication in this case is a fool's game, and the most that can be done is to develop a steady gaze toward the horizon and hope for the best.

SUCCESSION ISSUES

Succession issues involve the terms of divorce between parties to the former Soviet Union (FSU): what names and status are maintained after separation; what is needed to set up a new 'house'; and who gets what. Divorce is difficult enough between two parties, but when fifteen are involved the case becomes exceedingly burdensome.

The practical problems of succession have proved to be substantial, and are reflected symbolically in the difficulty in even arriving at a name for what was the Soviet Union. The 'former Soviet Union' seems unproblematic, until one considers that the Baltics at no time considered themselves to be part of the union and are insulted by the implication. The Commonwealth of Independent States (CIS) seems an agreeable enough term, until one becomes overburdened by the qualifiers: the CIS/Baltics/Georgia/Azerbaijan.[1] And as explained with irritation in Kiev, one cannot visit or do business with 'the CIS'; only with individual countries. Succession though, has brought with it more serious problems than bickering about names.

One of the first difficulties was who was the rightful successor to the former Soviet Union? The West was quick to declare that Russia would be regarded as the successor, at least insofar as nuclear weapons and the United Nations Security Council seat were concerned. This was not so much a judgment based on international law, as a judgment based on expediency. It was simply easier to continue to deal with Moscow, than with a collection of sundry unknown actors. Though perhaps inevitable, this formula did little to ease relations between Russia and the other new states. Russia immediately interpreted its recognition as *de facto* international acceptance of its role as successor in all spheres.

Ukraine reacted most unfavourably to these and related events. For the first six months of 1992, Russia and Ukraine appeared intent on starting their own version of a new Cold War. Why should Ukraine, now the world's third largest nuclear power, stand as a second class citizen next to Russia? Why should Russia have the privilege of being the sole representative at major summits? What right did Russia have to the Security Council seat? Why should Russia receive priority for Western aid? Similar questions existed in a less accentuated form among others in the CIS.

What of new institutional structures? If Russia had in place most of the mechanisms required for security and diplomacy, the other states did not. Ukraine and Belarus were fortunate enough to have developed some foreign policy infrastructure due to their long-standing seats in the UN General Assembly, but most other states had nothing of the kind. New institutions require qualified personnel who are not to be found in great numbers outside Moscow, and ministries in many places are still not staffed to optimum levels.

There has also been the problem of establishing new embassies. Russia's appropriation of Soviet embassies abroad left the other states at an important disadvantage. Failure to establish embassies or consulates has stunted normal diplomatic activities, slowed investment, and made travel a confusing process as far as visas are concerned. New states have also had to establish embassies in each of the former republics of the Soviet Union. One of the most difficult tasks has been to find diplomatic staff with even the barest minimum of language and professional skills. Moscow, with a surplus of trained staff, has had the opposite task of convincing well-educated and urbane diplomats to relocate to obscure destinations in the former empire.

Lack of proper state structures and institutions can have unpredictable results. For example, border controls have yet to be established in many regions; a delay that has created a major security problem, especially in the Baltics and southern regions. People, weapons, drugs, and controlled commercial materials enjoy trouble-free transit in many areas. Some states, like Russia, have found it less costly to assist in closing the external borders of neighbours, rather than setting up extensive border patrols on their own territory.

The potential for disputes around the division of military assets has been great. The break up of the Soviet Union left Russia, Ukraine, Belarus and Kazakhstan with strategic nuclear weapons (SNW), and a number of others with tactical nuclear weapons (TNW). All TNW were returned to Russia ahead of an agreed July 1992 deadline, though some questions still remain about accurate inventories and secure storage facilities. The issue of SNW has not been so easy to solve. 'The Agreement on Status of Nuclear Forces', reached at the Minsk Summit of 14 February 1992, contained a provision allowing for the return all SNW to Russia. On 23 May all four nuclear states signed a START I protocol in Lisbon committing them to ratification of the treaty.[2] Ukraine, Kazakhstan and Belarus also agreed to sign the Non-proliferation Treaty (NPT) as non-nuclear states, however none have done so as yet.

Both Ukraine and Kazakhstan have equivocated on their stated intentions to become non-nuclear states. Belarus has said that it intends to be non-nuclear by mid-1995. Motives for foot-dragging include domestic opposition; utilisation of SNW for bargaining purposes (economic and security-related); and the pursuit of international recognition and status. Ukraine further hardened its position after the signing of the START II agreement in Moscow in January 1993, demanding security guarantees and financial compensation for the dismantling process. While much of this is posturing, there are no guarantees that Russia will be the only nuclear power in the region in another decade. Kazakhstan, lodged between Russia and China, and Ukraine, bereft of powerful allies, will find it easy to develop a nuclear rationale should they so desire. The logic of proliferation in other areas of the world suggests that finding such a rationale is by far the easiest step on the road to the development of a nuclear potential. There have been reports, denied by the government, that Ukraine is developing the capacity to generate its own launch codes for SNW. If true, they may not be alone in their nuclear ambitions. In November 1992 Azerbaijan's Interior Minister claimed that the country had six nuclear weapons and would use them against Armenia if necessary.[3]

Ukraine's claims over 'strategic forces', especially the Black Sea Fleet, served as a focal point for the Russian-Ukrainian confrontation. The dispute over the Black Sea Fleet looked as if it might spill over into a hot war when the Russian parliament threatened to examine, and later annulled, the legality of the transfer of the Crimea from Russia to Ukraine in 1954.   In August 1992, a temporary cooling off period was reached when Presidents Yeltsin and Kravchuk signed an agreement on joint control of the Black Sea Fleet until 1995. However, the matter has merely been delayed and the question of the Crimea simmers on.

By comparison, the division of conventional forces has proceeded in a relatively orderly fashion. There was some irritation on Russia's part that its western neighbours, Ukraine in particular, had been able to claim much of the most effective military equipment. However, agreement on limits for conventional forces was relatively easy to achieve. The Conventional Forces in Europe (CFE) Treaty was signed on the 19 November 1990, but the dissolution of the Soviet Union meant that eight new states had to ratify the treaty. (By mutual agreement the Baltic states were excluded from the Treaty in October 1991.) Members of the CIS were able to work out the basic entitlements for treaty-limited equipment at a summit in Tashkent on

15 May 1992. On 10 July, a provisional document was agreed at the CSCE Summit in Helsinki and the treaty formally entered into force on 9 November 1992. A CFE 1A agreement, setting upper limits for personnel, was also agreed in Helsinki. Russia initially had some concerns about setting upper limits for equipment entitlements. Other CIS signatories could build up to their equipment entitlements if they did not already possess maximum levels, however it had to be made clear that Russia was under no obligation to leave behind military equipment to enable them to do so.

There has also been the question of the future of the armed forces themselves. Initially, Russia had hoped that the CIS could form its own general purpose armed forces. Marshal Shaposhnikov, head of the CIS central command, would oversee not only strategic forces but also a 'unified' CIS army. Too many states though, decided on the development of their own national armies, in some cases well before the collapse of the Soviet Union. On 7 May 1992, Russia finally accepted the inevitable and declared that it too would form its own armed forces, leaving Shaposhnikov and the CIS defence establishment with an obscure role.

A collective security concept for the CIS has not fared much better with only six members showing any interest in cooperation: Russia, Armenia, Kazakhstan, Kyrgyzistan, Tajikistan and Uzbekistan. Some, like Belarus suggested that a collective security agreement would violate their aspirations of neutrality, and be ineffectual. Nor is a NATO model of separate armies likely to evolve in the CIS in the near future. In 1992, most national armies were too underdeveloped and ill-organised to defend even their own countries, let alone each other. Over the next several years these armies and their new Defence Ministries will be concerned with reducing troops to reasonable levels, while balancing economic and security considerations; gaining the allegiance of the former Soviet officer corps; training and equipping new personnel; and defining new concepts of national security, military doctrines and strategies.

REGIONAL CONFLICTS AND ETHNIC RETRIBUTION

When the Soviet Union collapsed, the newly independent states found themselves with the double burden of the territorial expansions of both Russian imperialism and communism. In a previous era, Stalin had added to the misery of ethnic populations by mass internal deportations and the systematic redrawing of regional borders to prevent ethnic or religious upheaval. Ethnic retribution, the perceived righting of historical wrongs perpetuated by one ethnic group upon another, has been the result. Usually less systematic and less organised than 'ethnic cleansing' in the former Yugoslavia, it is no less deadly for the populations involved. Regions of the FSU have already seen their share of ethnic retribution, in what may be only the beginning of decade-long conflicts.

At the time the Soviet Union collapsed, several conflicts were already raging within its borders, especially in the Transcaucasus. The Armenian-Azerbaijan conflict over the disputed enclave of Nagorno-Karabakh has been going on since 1989. Problems in North and South Ossetia also began in 1989, and not far away a conflict also erupted in Chechen-Ingushetia.

The Armenian-Azerbaijani conflict over Nagorno-Karabakh increased in intensity during 1992 with both parties fuelled materially and psychologically for war by independence. Armenia made strong gains in the war, especially in its opening of an overland route (the Lachin corridor) into Nagorno-Karabakh. Various attempts by the international community to find a peaceful solution to the conflict have failed, as have over six ceasefires. However the increasingly dire economic situation in Armenia, and the fluidity of the political situation in Azerbaijan may ultimately force a conclusion to the dispute.

At least three different conflicts, each of which are a result of Stalin's massive deportations, have been brought together in the north Caucasus. South Ossetia in northern Georgia has for some time, albeit unsuccessfully, fought for a merger with North Ossetia across the border in Russia. In June 1992 Russian-Georgian peacekeeping forces were deployed in South Ossetia with moderate success. The Christian Northern Ossetians, however, have become embroiled in their own conflict with the nearby Muslim Ingush in a struggle for control over Ossetian territory which the Ingush claim as theirs. The Chechens (also Sunni Muslim), led by the flamboyant General Dudayev, declared independence in 1991 leaving the Ingush in the autonomous region of Chechen-Ingushetia without a homeland. The Ingush voted to remain with Russia, and in a domino effect turned west to reclaim land from North Ossetia. Much to Russia's alarm, this is the first serious conflict on its own soil. Difficulties are likely to simmer for some time to come, and the potential for further conflagrations is great, with at least 16 ethnic groups in the north Caucasus region.

The Transcaucasus' fourth major conflict in as many countries is in Georgia's western region of Abkhazia. It began when Georgian President Zviad Gamsakhurdia was ousted from power in a bloody war in the capital Tblisi in January 1992. The ongoing conflict is a result of an attempt by Gamsakhurdia supporters to regain power, and the simultaneous demands for independence in the autonomous republic of Abkhazia. Instead of routing pro-Gamsakhurdia supporters, troops loyal to the Tblisi government immediately became embroiled in a conflict with the local Abkhaz population and its hardline government. The Assembly of Mountain People's of the Caucasus, formed in August 1989, gathered together over 5,000 volunteers to assist the Abkhazians in their fight against Georgia. Several ceasefire agreements have been reached but the conflict remains far from settled.

Two more serious conflicts, in Tajikistan and Moldova, were added to the list of existing disputes in 1992. The civil war in Tajikistan has claimed an estimated 10,000–20,000 lives and displaced up to 200,000 people, especially in the southern regions. Geographically disadvantaged by its remote position in the Far East, the conflict has generated little international interest, despite the fact that its implications for regional stability are rather serious. The coalition of Islamic opposition groups and 'democratic' Tajik nationalists, which overthrew the communist government of President Nabiev in September 1992, is still active. A new government appointed late in 1992 did little to incorporate members of the opposition, and the conflict still continues.

Difficulties in Moldova erupted simultaneously with independence. The Russian population on the left bank of the

Dniester river in the eastern part of the country declared the 'Dniester Republic' and their desire to reconstitute the Soviet Union, or a Russian equivalent. Russia's 14th Army played a major role in the conflict when its members trained and supplied a local force with officers and equipment. A ceasefire was brokered by Russia and Russian peacekeeping forces arrived in August to control the 14th Army. Figures are unreliable but it would seem that several hundred were killed in the conflict, and over 1,000 injured, mostly on the Moldovian side.

As the FSU is reduced to smaller and smaller constituencies, the danger is not only one of tremendous human suffering. The financial costs of these conflicts are great, especially for countries with already failing economies. In Tajikistan for example, few crops were planted, even though agriculture is the mainstay of the economy. The transition to democracy and market economies are often put on hold while governments or parliaments either dissolve completely as with Tajikistan, Georgia, and Azerbaijan, or they become entirely consumed with debates on the local conflict, as happened on Moldova. Regional conflicts also contribute to the growing illicit weapons trade. Finally there is the danger of instability resulting from large population movements. The conflict in Tajikistan for example, has already produced thousands of refugees in Afghanistan, Uzbekistan and Kazakhstan; and in the Ossetian conflict over 100,000 refugees fled from south to north.

In response to these regional conflicts Russian 'peacekeeping forces' have been deployed in three regions: Tajikistan, Moldova, and the Transcaucasus. But are these in fact 'peacekeeping forces', 'peacemaking forces', 'peace enforcement forces', or something more sinister altogether? In places like Moldova, Russia has clearly used these forces to the advantage of the indigenous Russian population. In the long term, Russia risks being accused of neo-imperialist intentions, not to mention regional geo-political opportunism.

On the positive side, the Russian armed forces, bereft of a mission for the past several years, are now occupied in increasing numbers as long as Russia is willing to continue to pay the costs. It is also apparent that Russian peacekeeping forces carry out the work which few others are willing to do. Neither the international community nor former republics have shown much inclination to contribute to the resolution of regional conflicts in the CIS, especially insofar as the contribution of troops is concerned.[4] Both Moldova and Georgia would have found Conference on Security and Cooperation in Europe (CSCE) or UN peacekeeping forces preferable to Russian troops; Uzbekistan requested UN assistance in Tajikistan; Armenia requested international peacekeepers in its conflict with Azerbaijan; and Lithuania asked for international observers to monitor the withdrawal of Russian troops, all unsuccessfully. The failure of an international response has left these regions with few options in the resolution of local conflicts.

THE TIDES OF NATIONALISM

Nationalism continually threatens to be the dark side of independence. Indeed, it has been suggested that only nationalism can replace communism as an ideology in the FSU.[5] In moderation, nationalism can be a positive force in nation-building, but unfortunately it has often manifested exactly the opposite tendency in post-Cold War Europe. There have been a number of instances where nationalist fervour has contributed to vitriolic exchanges of rhetoric and thinly veiled threats of aggression; for example, between Russia and Ukraine, and Russia and the Baltic states. There have also been moves to ban extreme nationalist political parties or groups, even by moderate states such as Kazakhstan.

The Yeltsin government has come under increasing criticism for its pro-Western inclinations, with the corresponding accusation that it has failed to support 25 million Russians residing beyond Russia's borders. The greatest concentrations of Russians in the FSU reside in Kazakhstan (36.5 per cent), Latvia (34 per cent), Estonia (30.2 per cent), Ukraine (21.8 per cent), and Kyrgyzstan (21.5 per cent).[6] The nationalist question is complicated by the fact that former Soviet military bases and personnel are still located in many far flung regions. Troops have become the target of hostility from local populations, something which Russia has indicated it will not tolerate. Russia is also especially concerned about Estonian and Latvian citizenship laws which disenfranchises large groups of Russians.[7] The

Russian Defence Minister Marshal Grachev and others have these considerations in mind when they suggest that Russia's sphere of interest extends the length and breadth of the FSU.

In response to perceived discrimination and regional instability, many Russians are moving home; for example half of those in troubled Tajikistan have chosen this option. Given that Russia is unable even to provide housing for thousands of returning troops, it will not relish the prospect of thousands more displaced persons on its doorstep, Russian or not. For those who remain in what are now alien regions, their future choice in elections may be to support conservative or former-communist leaders in the hopes of protecting some rights for persons such as themselves who are now seen as bankrupt colonialists.

There are other dangers of nationalism. In Russia there are fears that a strong nationalist-communist coalition could emerge, and even worse, that the military could become involved. The conservative All-Union Officers Assembly was formed early in 1992 and favours a reconstitution of the FSU or a Russian equivalent. There is also concern about ultra-nationalist reactionary forces such as Vladimir Zhirinovsky (who came third in Russia's presidential election in 1991), the now banned National Salvation Front, and Pamyat whose policies which are not easily distinguishable from fascism. Though numbers are small, the expanded influence of such groups cannot be excluded in the future.

THE CERTAINTY OF UNCERTAINTY

The situation in the FSU has been and will remain extremely fluid and unpredictable for the foreseeable future. The greatest uncertainties include the viability of the CIS framework, potential conflicts between and within former republics, and the fate of political leaders.

Between December 1991 and 1992 eight CIS summits were held, often with only modest results.[8] During the last part of 1992, CIS leaders showed less and less inclination to meet. There is still no enforcement mechanism for agreements, a dissolving common currency, no coordination of foreign policy, and an incoherent military structure. Open borders and the free movement of people exist more by default than intention. There are strong indications that new regional formations and bilateral agreements will make the CIS increasingly irrelevant. For example, the five Central Asian states have moved closer on regional cooperation. Most states have already signed extensive bilateral agreements on economic, political and even security issues.

An evaluation of the CIS should not however, be entirely negative. During a difficult transition period it was the only formal mechanism for dialogue between former republics. It is doubtful whether the division of economic and military assets would have proceeded as peacefully as it did without the CIS. Its future may rest in a long descent into irrelevance, followed in several decades by a nostalgic and ceremonial revival not unlike the British Commonwealth.

What potential is there for future conflagrations in the FSU? The withdrawal of Russian troops from the Baltic states will be a continued problem and potential flashpoints include Estonia, Latvia, and the Russian region of Kaliningrad. The latter, cut off from the rest of Russia by Lithuania, has been the dumping ground for many of the troops leaving the Baltic states. Should Estonia and Latvia continue with their discriminatory citizenship laws, they risk raising the ire of Russia and its local troops. Lithuania, with its new socialist government, may be able to avoid problems if Russia does not insist on lumping it together with the other Baltic states. On the other hand Russia and Ukraine probably have many battles to fight yet over the Black Sea Fleet, the Crimea, Moldova, and nuclear weapons.

Larger states such as Russia and Ukraine may also not be able to remain immune from future internal conflicts. In Russia various regions arguing for increased autonomy include Dagestan, Tatarstan, Bashkortostan (formerly Bashkiria), Yakutia, and Karelia. Ukraine has its own problems with the large Tatar population in Crimea and secessionist movements in Transcarpathia.

The stability of Central Asia is also open to question. There are potential problems on Kazakhstan's northern border with Russia. The large Russian population in Ust-Kamenogorsk objects to proposed Kazak language laws and is demanding greater autonomy. Even liberal Kyrgyzstan has been accused by democrats of not including enough of the Kyrgyz majority in government. Pro-communist governments in Uzbekistan and Turkmenistan have been able to avoid the eruption of ethnic tensions by an authoritarian approach which restricts, among other things, political parties and press freedoms. It is a fragile peace though, as populations seek to rid themselves of their communist heritage, economic situations deteriorate, and conflicts in neighbouring regions threaten to spread. Some regional resentments against Uzbekistan also exist because of its attempts to adopted an aggressive leadership role in Central Asia.

The staying power of political leaders is another uncertainty. Political intrigue and chaos will remain a way of life, at least until political parties and coalitions mature and institutional structures are strong enough to bear the burden of state. Former communist leaders have been overthrown in Azerbaijan and Tajikistan. Conversely, anti-communist reformers were thrown out in favour of a socialist government in Lithuania; and Georgia's anti-communist dissident leader turned autocrat, Gamsakhurdia, was also ousted from power.

A pivotal issue for former republics and the West will be the future of the Russian leader. Politicians in any country are continually forced to compromise, though in the FSU the stakes are inevitably greater because the progress of a nation can be at stake. This was demonstrated at the Russian Congress of People's Deputies in December 1992 when conservatives sought to alter Yeltsin's economic policies by ousting key personnel. It is with an eerie sense of *deja vu* that one discovers conditions similar to those under Gorbachev. Sacrificial lambs are offered up to the altar of the conservatives; many pre-coup faces are to be found in the military; the Minister of Security (formerly the KGB) still makes speeches denouncing Western influence; and the West asserts that there is simply no one to replace Yeltsin. Will Yeltsin, and indeed the West, be able to avoid the mistakes of the Gorbachev era or will historical forces beyond anyone's control repeat themselves?

THE CIS AND DILEMMAS FOR WESTERN POLICY

There are several important questions which will plague Western policy towards the FSU. First, how much effort should be made to integrate the region into the rest of the democratic world? With a few exceptions, the countries of the FSU have quietly been told to take care of their own business. There has been no Marshall Plan to support the great democratic experiment, and what used to be called the 'Common European Home' has shrunk to western Europe. To the dismay of many countries in Eastern Europe and the western FSU they have been offered the ceremony of membership into the democratic brotherhood, but not the substance. Membership or observer status in bodies such as the CSCE, the North Atlantic Cooperation Council, and the Council of Europe has certainly been welcomed, but more is desired. Realistically or not, some new states such as the Baltics and Ukraine will continue to seek security guarantees. For its part the West will have to be conscious that the dialogue on 'European security' is not simply reduced to a dialogue about Western European security.

There is also the question of the linkage of economic assistance to other goals. The G7 committed themselves to $24 billion worth of assistance to Russia over three years, though by early 1993 less than $1 billion has been approved for dispensation. In Russia the level of this aid is viewed as laughable by many: it will make little substantive difference given the magnitude of the task at hand, and should certainly not be used by the West as a tool to manage Russia's internal policies. The economic yoke of bodies like the IMF and World Bank does not fit easily on newly born nationalists' necks. Economic linkage may also backfire. For example, Ukraine has used precisely the same tactic to demand huge financial aid for the removal of nuclear weapons from its territory, and has threatened to sell its own nuclear material if it does not receive funds.[9] The West should recall that it set the precedent for this type of linkage.

This raises the issue of just how involved the West should be in the national security problems of the FSU. Until now, concern has been directed largely at the control of nuclear weapons. The US Congress approved $800 million dollars to assist in the secure transport and dismantling of nuclear weapons, and the re-employment of nuclear scientists in Russia. However, has the Western emphasis on Russia, both economically and in arms reduction negotiations, risked alienating the other nuclear states and perhaps even pushing them towards the maintenance of a nuclear potential? Policies focused on Russia will always risk exacerbating tensions between former republics in unforeseen ways if intra-FSU relations are not taken into account.

The issue of involvement in FSU regional conflicts is even more difficult. The West is already overburdened with 'humanitarian interventions' in Iraq, former Yugoslavia, and Somalia. The possibilities for these new-style military actions are limitless. As long as conflicts do not become 'internationalised' beyond FSU borders, there is probably little prospect of Western involvement in the foreseeable future, short of humanitarian intervention in a major natural disaster. Whether a policy of selective western humanitarian intervention, which excludes the FSU, can be justified is a matter open to debate.

CONCLUSION

Predictions of catastrophe in the FSU have reached the level of an art form. Thus far though, there has been no illicit use of nuclear weapons, no mass famine, no unmanageable influx of refugees into Western Europe, no hyperinflation (as yet), and no large rebellion within the Army. Most governments have even avoided military coups. On the other hand, democracy did not suddenly drift down like a snowfall on the territory of the FSU, and terrible human suffering has occurred as thousands are killed or displaced in ethnic conflicts. Communist governments still exist and where they have been replaced, nationalism may yet prove, to be an oppressive and destabilising force. Not least, the population is weary of political experiments. Still, many in the former Soviet Union would probably concur with Winston Churchill when he reflected that democracy may be the worst form of government, except for all the others that have been tried.

Notes

[1] On 7 October 1992 the Azerbaijan parliament voted against ratification of the CIS Treaty and the country is no longer considered a member of the CIS.

[2] It is noteworthy that the issue of succession was so contentious that Article 1 of the protocol declared that all four nuclear states would be considered as 'successors' of the Soviet Union.

[3] *Rossiiskaya Gazeta,* 13 November 1992.

[4] The exceptions include some international interest in the Azerbaijan-Armenian conflict; a joint Georgian-Russian effort South Ossetia; and the intention of Kazakhstan, Uzbekistan and Kyrgyzstan to contribute to Russian peacekeeping forces in Tajikistan. An agreement on the 'Groups of Military Observers and Collective Peacekeeping Forces in the CIS' was signed by 10 out of 11 CIS members on 20 March 1992.

Sergei Rogov, Yuiri Ivanov, Valeriy Mazing, Sergei Oznobistchev, Dmitriy Evstafiev, Andrei Kurasov, Irina Modnikova, and Boris Zhelezov, *Commonwealth Defense Arrangements and International Security,* Centre for Naval Analysis Occasional Paper, June 1992, p. 2.

[6] Tony Barber, 'Humiliated in their former empire', *Independent,* 16 November 1992.

[7] All other new states, including Lithuania, have been prepared to grant citizenship rights to those residing on their territory at the time citizenship laws were passed.

[8] The eight summits were held in Minsk, 8 December 1991; Alma Ata, 21 December 1991; Minsk, 30 December 1991; Minsk, 14 February 1992; Kiev, 20 March 1992; Tashkent, 15 May 1992; Moscow, 6 July, 1992; and Bishkek, 7 October 1992.

[9] The US has offered $175 million but some in Ukraine claim costs of up to 1.5 billion dollars.

9

The Creation of Russian Armed Forces

KONSTANTIN SOROKIN

Senior Researcher, Institute of Europe, Moscow

A new actor, Russia, is emerging on the world scene as the main successor of the now defunct Soviet Union. Having inherited so many of the Soviet Union's security problems, it also has security dilemmas of its own. Professing a desire to rely on peaceful means to ensure the safety of the country's borders, the present Russian leadership regards national armed forces as an indispensable instrument for protecting national interests. Plans to create an army for Russia and the first steps to implement them have drawn much attention and caused concern both among Russia's neighbours and in more distant quarters.

THE IDEA OF A RUSSIAN ARMY: AN UNEASY INCEPTION

The initial move towards establishing a degree of Russian authority in the military domain came in June 1990 at the First Congress of Russian Deputies. It was decided that the post of Defence Secretary without Portfolio should be created to 'coordinate the activities' of the Soviet Defence Ministry on the territory of Russia as a sign of growing Russian autonomy. The idea, however, did not get off the ground. But in Spring 1991, the Russian State Committee on Defence and Security, required among other things to exercise a degree of political control over the Soviet Defence Department, was established. The August coup, of course, indicated that it had failed in this initial requirement.

After the failed coup, President Boris Yeltsin somewhat unex-
pectedly supported the idea of single *edinii* Armed Forces.
There were three reasons for this. First, there were considerations of economic and military utility. Next, a single army would
help keep the republics together and, given the unchallenged
domination of Russia in such an army, could secure its leading
role in the Gorbachev-sponsored 'renovated Soviet Union', and
later in the Commonwealth of Independent States (CIS).
Besides, most middle and high ranking officers, whose opinion
is to be reckoned with, rejected the very idea of dividing the
armed forces. This official line did not enjoy unanimous support in the Russian leadership, however. In November 1991, a
month before the three Slavic Presidents signed the death warrant of the Soviet Union, the new Chairman of the Committee
on Defence and Security in the Russian Parliament – S.
Stepashin – said it was time to switch to the concept of joint
(*ob'edinennye*) armed forces (of the new Soviet Union) and to
create a fully fledged Russian Ministry of Defence (MOD).[1]
Yeltsin seemed to be in two minds on the issue. As early as
December 1991, he covertly endorsed the creation of Russia's
MOD[2] in principle and made several highly publicised gestures
to woo the military on to Russia's side.[3] The President was probably preparing the escape route, should the single army idea fall
through. Several factors combined to bring about Yeltsin's decisive swing in favour of a national army by the middle of March
1992. In the first place, several republics, notably Ukraine,
Azerbaijan and Moldova, later followed by Belarus and
Uzbekistan, pressed ahead in claiming authority over parts of
the Soviet Army on their territories to use them as a basis for
national armed forces. By early spring, this process had clearly
gone beyond the point of no return, while all attempts to create
CIS-wide joint conventional forces were stalled. Besides, the
more European republics of the former USSR were in no mood
to compromise with Russia in sharing out the treaty-limited
equipment quotas agreed under the Conventional Forces in
Europe Treaty (CFE-1). Secondly, the uncertainty reigning over
the future of the armed forces militated against moves to
reform. It also placed the defence burden almost entirely on
Russia, starving it of resources and preventing it from providing
decent living conditions for servicemen in Russia proper.[3]

Thirdly, prospects for preserving the unity of the armed forces were further soured by the Ukrainian decision in late February 1992 to suspend the transfer of tactical nuclear weapons from its territory to that of Russia for dismantling. This decision was met with 'understanding' in the Belarus Ministry (which was apparently willing to follow suit) and caused Kazakhstan's renewed insistence on retaining some access to nuclear weapons. All these developments were in sharp conflict with the collective decisions reached earlier. They indicated that Russia's partners were tending towards 'go it alone' policies which made them difficult partners with whom Russia could do business.[4] Finally, Yeltsin was preparing for a serious clash with the combined forces of neo-communist and ultra patriot groups at the 6th Congress of Peoples Deputies due to be held in April 1992. He also faced mounting problems in trying to negotiate a new federal treaty. By beginning a process of constructing a national army, the Russian leadership had hoped to do two things: to rebuff its political opponents' accusations of weak and compliant foreign policy and thus improve its chances at the Congress; and to obtain some extra political clout in the final stages of negotiations with the autonomous provinces in Russia.

On 16 March 1992, Yeltsin announced his decision to create a Ministry of Defence and to take personal control of it. On 4 April, he appointed a commission to set up the Ministry and named two First Deputy Ministers, General P Grachev and the civilian expert A Kokoshin. A month later, the President formally authorised the creation of the Russian armed forces by special decree and named Grachev as Acting Defence Minister. Grachev was finally approved in this post on 18 May. This was a circumspect way of institutionalising the original March decision. This was because it was necessary to draw a clear line between the existence of the CIS High Command (formerly the Soviet Ministry of Defence), which had often represented Russia's interests in inter-republican relations, and a future Russian military command structure. The matter could have been handled by creating a completely new Russian military establishment, or else making use of the CIS High Command setup. In the event, the latter was adopted in a more extreme version – the High Command was renamed as the Russian MOD with several hundred officers set aside to man new CIS High Command staff structures. There was also some protracted bickering behind the scenes over the role of civilians in running the Army. It was argued in some quarters that a civilian Defence Minister would help to keep the Army in check and it seemed initially as if supporters of this view (among them politicians, civil experts and 'independent generals') were gaining the upper hand. Later, however, the idea of having 'two lines of leadership', both civil and military, in the MOD seemed to prevail. Eventually, however, the military got their way, securing the defence portfolio for General Grachev by warning of unrest in the Army.

It also took time and effort to reconcile the MOD and General Staff structures, who were locked in conflict, since at least the time of the stand-off between Marshal Shaposhnikov (then Soviet Defence Minister) and General Lobov (Chief of the General Staff) in the autumn of 1991. To avoid further quarrels, it was finally decided to provide each of them with a clearly defined area of responsibility; the General Staff was made responsible for operational control of the Army, training and readiness, while the MOD was limited to political and administrative functions. Then, too, many lobby groups were jockeying for position within the Russian military hierarchy, making it more difficult for the President to make final choices.

THE THEORY BEHIND THE FORMATION OF THE RUSSIAN ARMY

As a new state, Russia must find its place in the world and is therefore looking for an adequate politico-military strategy which helps it to define its national security interests, define what or who threatens it, and how to meet existing and likely future challenges. In keeping with a long-established tradition, this will be institutionalised in a military doctrine. This doctrine is presently being developed[5] and on its completion has still to be approved by Parliament. Debates are now going on around the doctrine, however, and a certain inertia in the security mentality of Russia offers some pointers as to the shape the doctrine will eventually take.

It is easy to predict that the 'political side' of the doctrine will be largely composed of familiar concepts and ideas which have evolved from the 'new thinking' and the rules of the game played at least since the time of Mikhail Gorbachev's rise to power. That is, it will enunciate the overriding necessity to avert and deter war; the ultimate importance of arms control and security cooperation with the West; and so on. Important though these are in principle, their practical utility in defining Russia's precise course of action is questionable. We can expect to see more meaningful, though less traditional provisions in the 'military-technical side'. While Russia's foreign policy and the political side of the doctrine are being collectively defined by various state institutions, it seems certain that the elaboration of the military-technical aspects of the doctrine will remain almost entirely in the hands of the military themselves, as was the case in the former Soviet Union.[6] And the military clearly think of Russia as a superpower, having both global and regional national security interests a view increasingly shared among both the élite and the general public. This is a new variation on the conventional wisdom, which over the last few years had been strongly argued in the press and among specialists, that Russia – at that time part of a much bigger Soviet Union – given its extremely poor economic health and growing internal divisions, should be seen more as of a regional than a 'super' power. This departure from the conventional wisdom of the last few years is accompanied by another innovation which will also affect the final version of the military doctrine. This is in the definition of security challenges. When the Gorbachev policy of new thinking was blossoming, it was regarded as almost a matter of bad taste to discuss challenges emanating from abroad. The general view now, however, is less sanguine though it is far from reverting to notions that prevailed before 1985.

Challenges from abroad have been traditionally classified in one of two ways. First, they can be defined as a potential military danger (*voennaia opasnost*) meaning a state of international relations in which war cannot be ruled out but yet is not inevitable, and where the likely opponent is implied but not named. The second definition envisages an actual military threat (*voennaia ugroza*) which describes a situation in which a war (especially a general war) is probable and even imminent and the opponent is obvious. In the pre-Gorbachev era, Soviet military thinking was mainly preoccupied with multiple military threats but in the latter half of the 1980s it switched to admitting only residual military dangers whilst claiming that the threat of war was almost reduced to nil. The picture now, however, is changing once again.

In the present post-Cold War era, the threat, or even the danger, of a direct large-scale military confrontation with the West is generally viewed as unlikely for the foreseeable future.[7] On the other hand, multiple and real challenges on a lesser scale, classified as 'dangers' aggravated by the less favourable geopolitical position which Russia now occupies compared with that of the former Soviet Union, are taken very seriously. Such dangers include the general instability of a world in transformation: economic, ethnic and religious conflicts in the world; explicit and implicit territorial claims on Russia; a possible reversion to confrontation among the major states which includes the huge extant military potential of former enemies, NATO and the United States, located now in close proximity to Russia proper; and 'the existence of major states and coalitions, seeking to dominate in certain regions and in the world at large, to impose their will . . . to stir up intrastate tensions'.[8] Such 'dangers' can easily be transformed into 'threats', leaving possibilities for low-level internal armed conflicts in Russia, and the increasing incidence of local and even regional wars along Russia's borders with other CIS states. The prospects of global nuclear, and general conventional, wars are not thought to be immediate, and are pushed down the list of priorities, though they are certainly far from being disregarded.[9] The view shared, among others, by the Defence Minister and the Chief of the General Staff Military Academy, where military doctrine is largely being elaborated, is that in practical terms this comes down to the need for Russia's armed forces to be ready for any contingency ranging from low intensity to general nuclear war.[10]

A similar logic operates on the thorny issue of defensive versus offensive elements in the strategy, which will be dealt with on the military-technical side of the doctrine. Several years ago, a group of prolific civilian armchair strategists (Kokoshin, now First Deputy Defence Minister, among them) severely criticised traditional Soviet military doctrine for its exclusive reliance on offensive operations at the very beginning of hostilities, and argued instead for a more defensive concept. Their efforts, combined with those of the top political 'new thinkers' had produced a military strategy not seen before. Describing it as a 'losing strategy', the military alleged that it imposed pernicious restrictions on their operations, barring them from pre-emptive actions prior to and during hostilities, and condemning them to deliberate defensive operations at the beginning of a conflict, thereby limiting them to counter-offensives strictly within the national borders at the closing stages of any war.[11] Russian military leaders now call for a legitimate acceptance of their right to decide on any course of action dictated by the 'natural laws of armed struggle', including pre-emption and any suitable combination of strategies.[12] The military are likely to have most of their views prevail, but in at least one case they will have to fight hard. This concerns the difficult issue of no-first-use of nuclear weapons. President Yeltsin repeated a pledge that Russia will not be the first to employ nuclear weapons,[13] but the military are clamouring for the abrogation of this long-standing Soviet policy, describing it as no more than political propaganda devoid of any practical military sense, and even as downright dangerous.[14] On 1 April 1992, the statement of the Presidium of the Supreme Soviet of the Russian Federation on priorities in defence policy was not very explicit on this subject but could be taken to imply the use of nuclear weapons in the case of repelling large scale conventional aggression against the homeland.

The present situation, therefore, is one of considerable uncertainty. First, with crucial issues still to be resolved, Russia's proposed military doctrine is not likely to be accepted officially in the very near future. Second, the new doctrine will probably go beyond the traditional Soviet strategy of making ready for large scale conventional and nuclear operations and will add preparations for low- and medium-intensity conflicts as top priorities. Third, there will probably be, yet again, a gap between a more pragmatic offensive-orientated military-technical side of the doctrine and a more defensive and cooperative political side. The political side may also suffer from some internal conflicts since deterrence implies strong and effective armed forces. Fourth, under existing plans, Russia's general purpose forces are to be primarily intended for medium- to low-intensity conflicts. This does not fit easily with the emerging doctrine, which in fact calls for 'all out vigilance'. Finally, since official military doctrine is still to be formally articulated, the radical arms control policy of the Yeltsin Administration is now driven by commonsense and political ambition: both of which, even in combination, will probably turn out to provide insufficient motivation. Commonsense, rather than law, also seems to be behind plans to reconstruct and reorganise the Armed Forces, and here too it will probably prove inadequate in the absence of a clear military doctrine. Above all, once documents elaborating Russia's new military doctrine are prepared, they will almost certainly be altered and amended by the Russian Parliament, who may well try to force changes in policies relating to arms control, and the articulation of new missions for the Armed Forces.

THE RUSSIAN ARMY TODAY

The Russian Armed Forces are being created under the decree signed by President Yeltsin on 7 May 1992. They presently include all armed formations and military institutions of the former Soviet Army on Russian territory (all strategic nuclear offensive and strategic defensive forces;[15] general purpose forces, grouped in seven military districts; northern and far eastern fleets[16]) plus groups of forces, armed formations, bases, military installations and other defence institutions of the Red Army located outside Russia's territory, not claimed by other former Soviet republics and taken under Russian control. The western group of forces in Germany is due to be recalled to Russia by the end of 1994; the northern group of forces in Poland is to be fully withdrawn at approximately the same time; the north western group of forces in the Baltic region and the Kaliningrad area plus the Baltic fleet;[17] the trans-Caucasian military district;[18] and the 14th Army in Moldova are due to be withdrawn at an as yet unspecified date. The Russian Navy will return a base on the Caspian Sea, left to Russia after the division of the Caspian flotilla. Armed forces will be maintained in Central Asia;[19] as will some military bases outside the borders of the former Soviet Union.[20] All Russian forces classed as 'strategic' under the CIS agreement on strategic forces signed in Minsk on 30 December 1991 will be kept under the operational control of the CIS High Command.[21] The Black Sea fleet will be jointly owned and controlled by Russia and Ukraine outside the CIS structure until it is formally divided between the two countries in 1995.

Though the sheer size of the forces under Russian control is considerable, their readiness and combat effectiveness is generally low. First, it is mostly composed of odd parts of what was once a single army, which is not necessarily a homogenous military structure. Second, Russian-controlled forces are beset by formidable problems as described below. A well-known military reformer (a prominent member of the Russian Parliament), Major Lopatin, is very pessimistic saying that the armed forces' combat effectiveness has reached zero.[22] This is probably an exaggeration as the situation is somewhat mixed. The strategic nuclear forces, anti-ballistic missile and defence systems, are apparently at relatively effective alert status at present. Mobile ballistic missile systems, however, are retained at their bases under the Yeltsin peace initiatives, and only a tiny part of the SSBN submarine force is on patrol at any given moment, due to severe material shortages. Strategic bombers are grounded for the same reason, and air defence forces cannot function properly because of huge gaps in the radar coverage of air space over the territories of the newly independent republics. General purpose forces are evidently in much poorer shape.[23]

PROSPECTS FOR THE FUTURE

One of the greatest developments in 1992 in the field of the construction of the Russian national Army, second only to the decision in principle to go ahead with the creation of Russian armed forces, was the emergence of a consensus of authoritative ideas as to what the Army should look like. Generally, it is to be smaller, cheaper, but more modern and capable than what is presently available to Russia. So far, there is no single plan for army construction and the long-awaited military reforms, which will probably have to be ratified by Parliament, may well not square with one another. Nevertheless, it is possible to assert some of the basic principles which will underlie prospective military reform in Russia. Some are already being implemented, others are still some way from becoming reality.

1 Drastic reductions are certain in the size of the active Armed Forces. At 1 May 1992, the strength of the Russian-controlled forces totalled 2,800,000 servicemen, 2,200,000 of whom were located on Russian territory. By 1995, the Army is to be reduced to 2,100,000 troops and by the year 2000 to 1,500,000.[24] The final figure is supposedly based on a calculation that in peacetime a country spending 6–7 per cent of its GNP on defence (the target figure for Russia) cannot afford an army strength of more than 1 per cent of its population. The Russian population is estimated to be around 150,000,000. These calculations, however, are disputed both by those who believe that a smaller army will suffice,[25] and conversely by those who would like to have its size tied tightly to the task of securing national interests without imposing 'artificial ceilings'.[26] The tempo of reductions which are already underway is slower than might be expected, due to the difficulties of dismissing more than 70 to 80,000 commissioned and non-commissioned officers a year with adequate social protection and rehabilitation arrangements.

2 The Army has to manage the gradual evolution in the present mixed system of manning in which conscripts and professional officers serve together. It is assumed that the share of professionals will grow after 1993, but it is not yet clear whether conscription will survive even on a much reduced scale, or whether the Army will be made fully professional.[27]

3 There will be a heavy reliance on reserves, which should offset the progressive reductions in the active strength of the Army. It is suggested that the reserve component of the Russian Army will have a three-tier structure. The ready reserve troops will number 1,000,000 servicemen along with 1,000,000 non-military personnel employed by the MOD and 'automatically' mobilised in case of emergency. Thus, under the threat of local or regional war, the Army could be quick-

ly expanded to 3,500,000 servicemen. In the case of general war, the standby reserve (reservists up to 45 years old) and the retired reserve (reservists up to 50 years of age) can also be mobilised.[28] In a somewhat contradictory move, the present military leadership plans drastically to reduce the number of the so-called 'cadre formations' (divisions and lesser units with low manning levels but high levels of weapons and equipment).[29] It is far from clear whether such plans for mobilising massive reserves in the case of war will prove feasible. It is even more unclear how such reserves are to be sustained, given the projected ending of the draft system.

4 Defence planning is moving towards a reversal of the forward basing system, and to the withdrawal of the bulk of Russian forces from abroad (most of which will be completed by late 1994) and the adoption of a 'defence from within national borders' stance. This concept will not exclude the seeking of limited basing rights, as for the Baltic Fleet in the Baltic region, and the stationing of small contingents of Russian troops in certain CIS states.

5 Russian forces face the abandonment of the strong, echeloned layer of defence along Russian borders. This will be impossible to maintain, given the length of the frontiers, the lack of adequate material and financial resources, and the dwindling size of the Army. Instead, Russia is soon to rely on mobile defences with effective and mobile forces capable of being quickly moved to any endangered areas of the homeland.[30]

6 The territorial organisation of defence will be reappraised. The existing seven military districts (MDs) will be partially reorganised, allowing for the creation of perhaps two new districts – Smolensk MD (to form the first echelon of defence together with the Leningrad and North Caucasian MDs, and to give an extra layer of protection to the Moscow MD) and the Ural MD – over the next few years.[31] The MDs will be superseded by three or four larger administrative territorial commands. In two to three years time, the military leadership

plans to re-establish operational commands, which first appeared in the Soviet Army in the early 1980s. There will be three or four of them, probably Southern/Central, Western and Eastern.[32]

7 A smaller but more effective and flexible system of command and control is already being established, which will be closely linked to the projected structure of the Army.[33]

8 Armed forces will be restructured to give more weight to the speedy development of the 'high technology services', especially the Air Force, Navy, Space Systems Command and Air Defences,[34] while the tank-heavy land forces which have been tailored to fight a major war in Europe will be substantially reduced and reorganised.[35] Top priority will be given to mobile units, best suited to meet the more probable local conflicts. The proportion of heavy tank formations will shrink, possibly to the point of complete extinction. The future of combined arms units is still not clear at present.

9 In an attempt to erect a firebreak between conventional and nuclear operations, the future Army is to be composed of Strategic Deterrent Forces (SDF) – strategic nuclear offensive and defensive systems, to include later on strategic conventional components, and General Purpose Forces (GPF) – the Land Forces and the Navy plus, initially, the Air Force and the Air Defence Force. In fact, certain steps in this direction have already been taken following the signing by Mikhail Gorbachev of a decree on 14 November 1991 which stipulated the creation of the Soviet SDF. The net effect of this innovation will be less than the expectations, since the GPF will eventually be unable to deter or repel an attack of any considerable proportion without resorting to the help of the SDF. It is indicative, for example, that the mobile forces are to include some SDF components.

10 Within major Operational Commands, the GPF will be grouped according to their mission. This will include *covering, constant readiness forces* along borders tasked to deter or repel local aggression on a limited scale; *mobile, rapid reaction forces*

located further inland and capable of being speedily moved to a threatened area to augment the covering forces or to beat off medium-sized aggression and, if necessary, to cover the safe deployment of reserves; and *reserve forces* mobilised and deployed in a period short of war or during a war to meet a larger attack.[36] The mobile forces, which are so much a centrepiece of this arrangement, will be 'strategic-operational level large units' and will be comprised of airborne troops, marine infantry and light army formations, helicopter and army aviation squadrons, military transport aircraft, and so on.[37]

11 There will be a basic shift from the Army/Division structure of the land forces to Corps/Brigade formations in order to increase mobility.

12 In line with official Soviet policy of the previous five years, there will be an overall switch to producing fewer weapons in favour of weapons of advanced technology. Those systems most emphasised will be strategic weapons; C^3I systems; space and air defence systems; new generation aircraft; high-precision conventional weapons, particularly ballistic and cruise missiles and 'strike-reconnaissance complexes'; advanced remote mining systems and engineering equipment; air transportable weapons and equipment; and means of air and road mobility.[38] The military remain rather tight lipped about their preferences in relation to strategic nuclear weapons. One might guess that they will insist on preserving the priority of fixed and mobile land based missiles, keeping the present correlation between the three legs of the nuclear triad and resisting the American urge to de-MIRV their ballistic missiles.[39] The existing systems of organising research and development and buying weapons for the Army are to be streamlined to make the best use of scarce resources.

All these principles are to be implemented in three stages. The first is largely preparatory, laying the basis for further actions, such as creating key military bodies and establishing a legal basis for creating and operating Russia's Armed Forces, and will conclude by early 1993. The second stage will run from

1993 until the end of 1995. Plans for the new Army structure are
to be finalised and their implementation is to begin. The main
GPF groupings inside national borders are to be organised and
mobile forces are to be established. A gradual switch to the
corps/brigade system will start and the proportion of professionals in the Army will expand. The new departures in weapons
development and production strategies will, it is hoped, occur;
and troop withdrawals will by then be almost completed. The
third and final stage is due to end around the year 2000.[40] This
will result in a Russian Army whose projected shape by the turn
of the century is described in Fig 1.

The President, C-in-C		
Minister of Defence		
General Staff		
	(Armed Services)	
SDF*	**Land Forces**	**Navy**
Ballistic Missile Armies (ICBMs and SLBMs)	Combined Arms Corps (+ Armies?)	Fleets
Strategic Aviation	Military Districts (territorial commands?)	Flotillas
Operational-level Aviation	Reserve Forces	Squadrons
Front-level (tactical) Aviation	National Guard	Naval bases
Military Transport Aviation	Training Centres	
BMD Corps	Air Defence missile and radar (large) units	
Space Control Corps		
BMEW Corps		
Other Space forces		
* Will include fighter-interceptors from the disbanded Air Defence Service *(Source: Voennaia Mysl, Special edition, July 1992, p. 52)*		

Fig. 1 *The proposed shape of Russia's Armed Forces by the year 2000*

RESULTS AND EXPECTATIONS

Such proposed changes are undoubtedly drastic, though the actual results may fall well short of expectations. Two key questions arise in this respect: whether the newly-formed Russian military leadership is up to the job, and the obstacles it will have to overcome in order to implement its plans. In answer to the first question, it is important to be mindful of two conflicting sets of evidence. On the one hand, new top job holders cannot be regarded as injections of entirely new blood, as all the deputy Defence Ministers (apart from one civilian appointee), the Chief of the General Staff, and the Service Chiefs, have previously held senior positions in the Soviet Army at least in the late-1980s when military reform was hotly debated but never implemented. Practically all of them come from the Land/Airborne Forces establishment, which has traditionally been one of the seats of military conservatism. Some of them, at least, may be reluctant to go along with reform which will militate against the interests of their own service. Notable by their absence in the new leadership are representatives of the Air Force and the Navy, both of which are designed to be at the forefront of reform. On the other hand, the Grachev team does seem to have generated new ideas (even if some of them are based on earlier ideas nurtured by General Lobov during his short career as Chief of the Soviet Army General Staff) and one cannot entirely blame members of the Grachev team for the exceedingly slow pace of military reform in the last several years, since at that time they generally only held upper middle command positions in the military hierarchy and were not in a position decisively to influence the defence ministry of the time.

Finally, some of the new job holders have had combat experience in Afghanistan where they could clearly see the gaping flaws in the Soviet military machine. This experience may well be an added stimulus to the attempts at radical overhaul. Doubtless, the new team will start the process of reform.

Whether this team can carry it through, however, without the hesitations and deviations so common in the Gorbachev era, remains a major question. To begin with, the team is not homogeneous (note the unexpected and yet unexplained appointment of General B Gromov, notorious for his support of the August coup, as Deputy Defence Minister) and will be hard put to resist external pressure. Such pressures will unquestionably be high. One can imagine immediate and tough opposition to new ideas from outside interests such as the defence industry, and from within the Armed Forces. Old cadres still remain in key positions in the Armed Forces, especially in the provinces, and there are many who stand to lose their jobs as a result of reform in the service headquarters. In the extreme case of Russian democratic leaders being removed from office by an opposition grouping, the present concept of creating and reforming the Russian Armed Forces will most likely disappear with its political mentors. Alternatively, such concepts could be revised beyond recognition by an anti-democratic government, probably along traditional Soviet lines, which may cause large scale unrest and could even lead to a total disintegration of Russia and its Army.

A still more daunting task is to get to grips with the huge deficit of financial and material resources. It may seem amazing, but no serious calculations of the overall cost of Army construction and reform have yet been made.

Only one notable attempt to put figures to the task ahead is available. Speaking in Parliament on 12 May 1992, General Barinkin of the General Staff noted that there were at least seven major state programmes running up to the year 2000 linked with military reform (see Table 1). The total cost is put at around 1.2 trillion roubles (in 1992 prices) up to that year. This represents some 130 billion roubles a year from 1992. This price tag, however, primarily covers the reduction aspects of the reform and excludes the creative side which will demand at least as much expenditure again.

The overall price that Russia will have to pay for its new Army, therefore, is likely to be very high, as a result of the considerable scale of both the reorganisation and the creative tasks which lie ahead.[41] It will have to cope with real price inflation for military R&D and modern weapons and equipment, along with the widespread inefficiencies in implementing reform. An appreciable proportion of the 'reconstruction and reform money' will have to be added to the costs of a 'regular' defence budget.

It is doubtful whether the crisis-stricken nation can muster the required resources to sustain the Armed Forces that it now pos-

Table 1 *Major State/Defence reform programmes to the year 2000 (billion roubles)*

1	Troop withdrawals	346
2	Extra personnel payments annually (50% draft and 50% contract system)	59
3	Dismantling and safe storage of nuclear-powered submarines	100
4	Destruction of strategic nuclear weapons	23
5	Destruction of tactical nuclear weapons	150
6	Destruction of chemical weapons	90
7	Destruction of conventional weapons	5

sesses and still carry out a military reform programme in full. Defence expenditure has already been declining in real terms for some years and is likely to go down still further.[42] In principle there are three ways in which reform can be married to the dire economic reality. First, it might be necessary to drop some of the reform provisions altogether. Second, it may be possible to go back on some of the more expensive arms control commitments (especially unilateral commitments) in order to get extra funds for the restructuring of the Army. Third, and most likely, is the possibility of stretching the implementation of the reforms, or some key provisions, well into the 21st century.[43] All three options, however, seem unpalatable and may eventually disable the reform process.

There is also a problem with Army personnel. At present, the Army suffers from low morale, depletion of the officer corps, internal ethnic tensions, and the growing shortage and declining quality of its conscripts. Birthrates have been declining in Russia for years, causing an ever worsening shortage of Slavic conscripts. At present, the 'drafting resources' in Russia stand at 252,000 young people, which is barely one third of what is required.[44] The situation is further aggravated by the increasing 'evasion rates'. At present the greatest number of those refusing to serve live in the southern and eastern parts of European Russia. A further aggravating factor is the impending introduction of an alternative service scheme, since a law to this effect has already been passed. There is also a steep rise in the number of those eligible for exemption or deferment.[45] If these trends continue, as they probably will, the shortage of draftees will grow to insupportable proportions and to an undersized army by the year 2000. For the first time in decades, the birthrate in Russia has dropped below the death rate and is expected to fall still further since there are no real prospects for health improvement.

The demographic problem may be somewhat mitigated by the influx of refugees (estimated to number between 400,000 and 2,000,000[46]). Another mitigating factor would be the negotiation of extra supplies of 'human resources' from Central Asia and Kazakhstan, since today some 40 per cent of soldiers in Russia come from this area.[47] Yet another way out may be to lower health standards and/or to abandon deferments, prompted by Grachev's repeated criticism of his Soviet predecessor's moves to raise health standards for conscripts and to widen the spectrum of reasons for deferment. But all these measures are palliatives which may backfire in a still lower quality of conscripts, a further downward spiral in morale, and the incidence of higher ethnic tensions, all of which may sign a death warrant for military reform. The only radical solution – the transition to a fully professional army – is hardly feasible in the present century, if only for economic reasons.

The general conclusion is that by the year 2000 Russia will most likely have gone some way, but only a certain way, towards implementing its military reform goals. Its progress will depend upon socio-economic, political and demographic factors in the country, provided that the situation around Russia's borders remains largely unchanged. In any case, the future Russian Army will still be a force to be reckoned with, beset with problems but sustained by at least a residual nuclear arsenal.

Notes

1 *Krasnaia Zvezda*, 5 Nov. 1991.
2 *Krasnaia Zvezda*, 14 April 1992.
3 In late August 1991 B Yeltsin signed a decree on "social protection of servicemen' on Russian territory; on 3 December 1991 he ordered the increase of salaries of servicemen and civilians employed by the Soviet MOD at the expense of Russian Federation; in January next year the President 'sponsored' a socially-oriented budget, where some 65 per cent of resources went to alleviate the Army's social problems; and speaking at the Congress of offi-

cers' representatives he made generous social commitments to the officer corps; finally, in mid-February he issued yet another decree to increase 'social protection of servicemen'. All these moves were primarily aimed at the officer corps, whose position was crucial, and did little to improve conditions for the enlisted personnel.

[4] Speaking in mid-March in Parliament E Gaidar admitted, that Russia was practically alone in financially supporting what once was the Soviet Army, with only Ukraine paying for the armed forces on its territory.

[5] By mid-autumn 1992 the only official document dealing with the issue was 'The Statement of the Presidium of the Russian Federation Supreme Soviet on priorities in Russia's military policy', adopted on 1 April 1992. But it is a tiny, very general and rather vague document, two thirds of which are devoted to the problems of conversion and military cooperation with other CIS nations.

[6] It is indicative that it was the military who fully dominated at the highly publicised conference organised in late May 1992 to discuss the contents of a future military doctrine and ways to reform the Armed Forces. The few civilian scientists and experts present kept an extremely low profile.

[7] Some military hardliners claim, that if and when Russia gets back on its feet, the possibility of an armed conflict with the grudging West will be much greater than now. See, for example, views of general N Klokotov, chief of the military strategy department of the General Staff Military Academy: *Voennaia Mysl*, Special edition, July 1992, p. 36–37.

[8] General V Miruk. 'Voennaia doktrina Rossii: kakoi ei byt?' (Russia's military doctrine: what should it look like?). *Krasnaia Zvezda*, 25 April 1992; *Voennaia Mysl*, Special edition, July 1992, pp. 8, 9, 35–38.

[9] See, for example I Radionov (Chief of the General Staff Military Academy). 'Nekotorye podhodi k razrabotke voennoi doktrini Rossii' (On certain approaches to developing Russia's military doctrine). *Voennaia Mysl*, Special edition, July 1992, pp. 10–11.

[10] P Grachev's views expressed in *Krasnaia Zvezda*, 20 May and 26 May, 1992; I Radionov, *op. cit.*, p. 11.

[11] I Radionov, *op. cit.*, p. 11.

[12] See: V Turchenko, 'O razvitii teorii strategicheskoi oboronitelnoi operatsii' (On improving the theory of strategic defensive operation). *Voennaia Mysl*, N 4–5, 1992, pp. 3–8.

[13] *Izvestia*, 22 Feb 1992.

[14] A Vitkovski, 'Osnovi primenenia vooruzhennykh sil Rossii' (Basic principles for employing Russia's Armed Forces). *Voennaia Mysl*, Special edition, July 1992, pp. 100–101; I Rodionov. *op. cit.*, p. 13.

[15] The Russian leadership believes, that by the year 2000 strategic and tactical nuclear forces in Russia will be the only such forces in the CIS. See Yeltsin's interview in *Komsomolskaia Pravda*, 27 May 1992; Grachev's interview in *Krasnaia Zvezda*, 6 June 1992.

[16] It is estimated that some 90–92 per cent of the former Soviet Navy are based on Russian soil. *Krasnaia Zvezda*. 21 May 1992.

[17] Moscow proposes to withdraw its troops from the three Baltic republics by 1995, but the Baltic governments insist on a much earlier date (the future of Russian forces in the Kaliningrad area is still undecided).

[18] It is believed, that Russian forces in Azerbaijan will be the first to withdraw, while in Armenia and Georgia Russian troops may stay longer on request of the two republics' governments, if they manage to stop the surge of violence directed against these troops. In any case, the greatest part of their weapons and military equipment will be left to the three republics.

[19] The Uzbek government has asked Russian troops to stay on indefinitely. B Yeltsin's interview in *Komsomolskaia Pravda*, 3 July 1992.

[20] I.e., the base in Cam Ran, Vietnam. *Izvestia*, 23 July 1992.

[21] SRNF, Air Force, Navy, Air Defence, space forces, air-borne troops and related institutions; nuclear warhead guardians; strategic and operational-level intelligence. *Diplomaticheskii vestnik*, N 2–3, 1992, p. 10.

[22] *Kuranty*, 23 May 1992.

[23] As A Rutskoi, the Vice-President, put it, the existing 'armed formations can hardly be called the Army. Command and control systems as well as weapons do not come up to modern standards'. — *Voennaia Mysl*, Special edition, July 1992, p. 44.

[24] Statement by the General Staff representative General V Barinkin to Parliament on 12 May 1992.

[25] General D Volkogonov, head of the Commission charged with creating Russia's Ministry of Defence and the Armed Forces, thinks that 1200–1300 thousand servicemen will be enough. *Krasnaia Zvezda*, 11 April 1992; and General V Samoilov, who once held the position of deputy Chief of the (CIS) Armed Forces Personnel Department, mentioned the figure of 1 million troops (including 100–150 thousand officers) – *Krasnaia Zvezda*, 14 Feb 1992. As for Grachev, he originally tilted to the figure of 1.2–1.3 million (*Krasnaia Zvezda*, 1 April 1992), but later firmly switched to 1.5 million.

[26] I Rodionov, *op. cit.* p. 12.

[27] In his earlier interviews General Grachev spoke about a fully professional Army (*Moskovskii Komsomolets*, 19 May 1992), but later admitted, that for financial reasons even a combination of draft and contract for lower ranks may present too heavy a burden (*Krasnaia Zvezda*, 1 June 1992).

[28] *Voennaia Mysl*, Special edition, 21 July 1992, p. 53.

[29] *Krasnaia Zvezda*, 21 July 1992.

[30] A Kokshin (deputy Defence Minister) in: *Izvestia*, 20 July 1992. The Vice-President A Rutskoi stands for an 'impregnable shield' along the borders (*Krasnaia Zvezda*, 22 May 1992), but it looks more like a metaphor.

[31] Grachev's views expressed in *Krasnaia Zvezda*, 1 June 1992; 21 July 1992.

[32] *Voennaia Mysl*, Special edition, July 1992, p. 13, 49–50.

[33] The size of the Russian MOD and General Staff may not exceed 4–7 thousand people, which is a 3–4 times drop compared to the corresponding Soviet structures, *Krasnaia Zvezda*, 31 March 31 1992. By the year 2000 the Services Commands may be transformed into much smaller departments within the MOD. – *Krasnaia Zvezda*, 21 July 1992.

[34] A Kokoshin in *Krasnaia Zvezda*, 17 March and 23 June 1992.

[35] P Grachev stresses, that the tank-heavy land formations will no longer suit both local and large-scale conventional highly mobile wars of the future, *Krasnaia Zvezda*, 1 April 1992.

[36] *Voennaia Mysl*, Special edition, July 1992, pp. 56–57.

[37] *Krasnaia Zvezda*, 21 July 1992.

[38] *Krasnaia Zvezda*, 23 June 1992; *Voennaia Mysl*, Special edition, July 1992, p. 31–32.

[39] See: *Voennaia Mysl*, Special edition, July 1992, p. 57–60.

[40] *Krasnaia Zvezda*, 21 July 1992.

[41] For instance, only 20 per cent of the present Russian weapons stock can be called modern, the rest is up for renewal, *Krasnaia Zvezda*, 19 August 1992.

[42] By 2.5 times in 1992 compared to 1990. *Voennaia Mysl*, Special edition, July 1992, p. 47.

[43] The 'go slow' principle is already establishing itself in the crucial area of military R&D. Compared to 1991, allocations here dropped by 16.5 per cent in real terms in 1992. They are expected to fall further by 2.4 per cent in 1993 and by 1.6 per cent in 1994, and then remain steady (*Krasnaia Zvezda*, 19 Aug 1992), while the 'spirit of reform' clearly calls-for expanding the military R&D.

[44] *Kuranty*, 16 May 1992.

[45] In Moscow only 10–12 out of 100 potential conscripts are actually called up. Others have deferments or are exempt from active duty for health reasons. The share of the latter is fast growing. Health reasons accounted for 10 per cent of exemptions in 1989 and for over 20 per cent in 1991/1992 (in Russia). The most noticeable growth came in the nerve-related diseases (72 per cent rise over the last few years), mental debility and retardness included, *Krasnaia Zvezda*, 9 June 1992.

[46] *Kuranty*, 9 June 1992.

[47] *Krasnaia Zvezda*, 1 June 1992.

10

Armed Forces of Ukraine and Problems of National Security

A N HONCHARENKO AND E M LISITSYN

*Dr Alexander Honcharenko was formerly head of the National and
International Security Department of the Institute of World
Economy and International Relations, Ukraine; and Colonel
Eduard M Lisitsyn is a member of the General Staff serving in the
Ministry of Defence, Ukraine*

One of the most important tasks for Ukraine, as for any
European sovereign state, is the creation of an adequate system
of national security, in all its military, political, economic, legal
and informational aspects. The creation of such a system in the
general context of Ukraine's national interests is a vital priority
for the future of the country. The ability of Ukraine to create
such a system, however, is conditioned by the serious external
and internal threats which it faces, and which call into question
the very existence of the young state.

The most important external threat remains the potential for
imperialist ambitions on the part of Russia, and a claim to
regional domination, born of a stubborn reluctance of the right
wing and some democratic political circles in the Russian federation to recognise fully the existence of Ukraine as an
independent, equal and sovereign state. The continuing presence of military formations controlled by Moscow in the
territory of the Ukraine and the resistance of Russian military
leaders to serious talks on a phased withdrawal of these formations, along with problems involved in the division of the Black
Sea fleet and the withdrawal of Russian naval units from the
territory of Ukraine has been added to increased Russian economic pressure to involve Ukraine in the newly formed CIS
superstate. The danger is that such a superstate will represent a
post-imperialist structure, stimulating separatist movements and
ethnic conflicts from outside aimed at territorial divisions within Ukraine and embodying an ideology of pan-Slavism,

accompanied by attempts to foster socio-cultural Russian domination as an ideological basis for the recreation of the Russian Empire within the borders of the former USSR.

Threats of an internal character are mainly connected with economic factors and the successes or failures of economic reforms in Ukraine. The failure of economic reforms and a further worsening of general living standards can result in social instability, the strengthening of separatist tendencies, ethnic conflicts and, finally, can undermine the very idea of Ukrainian independence.

Finally, it should be remembered that there are also serious threats of an ecological character resulting still from the consequences of the Chernobyl catastrophe and the disastrous levels of pollution existing in significant areas of Ukrainian territory, which is a danger not only to the immediate lives and health of the population in different regions but also to the genetic reserves of the nation in general.

Such threats are complicated by the lack of a comprehensively developed system within Ukraine of national security and the lack of powerful state institutions which can guarantee observance of human rights and freedoms and the protection of the population from unfavourable internal and external influences. Nor is there any stable consensus within the Ukrainian population on the problems of national security. It is perhaps inevitable that in such a young state a public consensus has not yet had time to form, leaving a vacuum in which can flourish competing understandings of national security by various social and ethnic groups. Such a lack of consensus hinders the functioning of necessary state institutions and also significantly decreases the general level of security for all social and ethnic groups within the state.

In order to coordinate the establishment of a necessarily complex system of national security and implement it, the Council for National Security of Ukraine was formed by a decree of the President on 1 July 1992. Among the permanent members of the Council are the President of Ukraine (Chairman of the Council), the State Adviser on matters of national security (Secretary of the Council), the Prime Minister, the Defence Minister, the Chief of the Security Service, and the Minister of Foreign Affairs. The Ministers of Public Health, of Protection of the Environment, the President of the Academy of Sciences, the Ministry of Internal Affairs, the Chairman of the State Committee on Security of State Borders, and the Chairman of the Board of the National Bank of Ukraine, are also members of the Council, though possessing the right of decisive vote only in cases where matters involving their respective competences are under consideration.

The fundamental task for the Council for National Security is to provide consultation and advice to the President on all aspects of policy in the sphere of national security and its implementation. The Council is also intended to function as an interdepartmental structure, to organise the system of executive power, being entrusted with the functions of integration and coordination of all those matters relevant to national security falling in the spheres of domestic, foreign and military policies, economics, ecology, intelligence services, and so on. The Council can play an important role in stabilising the relationship between civil and military departments and aiding the democratisation of the process of building a new national army in Ukraine. This may be particularly important in conditions where there is an absence of direct civil control over the activities of such departments – particularly in relation to defence and the intelligence services. Partial control over these departments is exercised, of course, by the Parliament and by the President as Supreme Commander in Chief of the Armed Forces, but the Council provides an important legitimising device.

THE EVOLUTION OF THE ARMED FORCES
OF UKRAINE

The Supreme Council of Ukraine in 1991 adopted the concept of 'Defence and Build-up of the Armed Forces of Ukraine'. The political and military-technical aspects of this concept are based on the essentially defensive character of Ukraine's military posture. Ukraine, therefore, does not consider the use of force as a means of achieving any economic, political, or other aims. Ukraine therefore supports the recognition and adoption by all states of obligations regarding mutual non-aggression, as well as the formation of armed forces embodying such qualitative and quantitative characteristics as to allow for only defensive operations in a non-mobilised state.

Ukraine has already declared its future non-nuclear status and intends strictly to follow three non-nuclear principles: not to accept; not to produce; and not to acquire, nuclear weapons. Ukraine has also declared its non-alignment to any military blocs or alliances. The most important doctrinal stipulations of Ukrainian policy are a recognition of the priority of general human values and a comprehensive approach to ensuring the security of states. In this connection, Ukraine intends to take part – indeed is already taking part – in deploying troops for peacekeeping operations and in efforts undertaken by the world community to create an effective system of international security within the framework of the United Nations and also of the Conference on Security and Cooperation in Europe (CSCE). In this way, Ukraine regards its own security as an integral part of international security, for which purpose it will strive for the creation of such a system of interstate relations which would remove threats of war or military confrontation.

At the more particular level, provision is made for three fighting arms within the Armed Forces of Ukraine; land troops, an air force and the navy. The land troops are known as 'troops of land defence' and the air force as 'the arm of air defence', to emphasise the defensive character of Ukrainian military structures. The Armed Forces of Ukraine are manned on the mixed principle, which allows manning on a voluntary basis as well as on the basis of the law on Universal Military Obligation against territorial and extra-territorial threats. The Armed Forces of Ukraine are regular and multinational. Military personnel of more than 100 nationalities can, and do, serve the Ukrainian state in good faith.

At the present time, the establishment of two of the military arms is practically accomplished; the Land Forces and the Air Force. Anti-aircraft defence formations have been included in the Air Force. The numerical strength of the Armed Forces of Ukraine is estimated by the general headquarters of the Armed Forces of Russia as being close to 500,000.

The strategic nuclear forces located in Ukraine are subordinated to the joint General Headquarters of the Strategic Forces

(Commander in Chief General Yuf Maximov). At present these forces are under the administrative and functional management and command of the military bodies of the Russian federation. Pursuant to the Agreement on Organisation of Activities of General Headquarters (*Glavkomat*) of the Joint Armed Forces (*OVS*) of the Commonwealth of Independent States adopted at a sitting of the Council of the State Members of the CIS, the strategic forces are included in *Glavkomat OVS* of the CIS according to the principles and rights of the general headquarters. The Commander in Chief of the CIS, Marshal of Aviation Yugeny Shaposhnikov has stated that 'despite the existing disagreements, strategic missile forces located in the Ukraine are under the centralised control of Moscow, though it does not mean that they are "closed" for the leaders of the sovereign state (Ukraine)'.

Disagreements between Ukraine and Russia referred to by Marshal Shaposhnikov cover three general questions. First, there is the question of the CIS OVS. The structure of these forces is shown in Figure 1.[1] The definition of the OVS in such a complicated structure is further evidence of the striving of Russian leaders for the formation of a single military policy for the CIS. Ukraine does not intend, however, to pursue its security in such a way. At the end of August 1992, the Ministry of Foreign Affairs of Ukraine made a statement rejecting rumours that the Ministry had prepared a draft agreement between Russia and Ukraine, allowing participation of Ukraine in the OVS of the CIS – even as far as locating Russian troops on the territory of Ukraine. This statement was confirmed by Ukrainian leaders in a later meeting at Bishkek.

Secondly, there is the question of the administrative management of military formations of the strategic nuclear forces on the territory of Ukraine. As early as the beginning of July 1992, during the Moscow Summit, the Ukrainian delegation declared the intention of Ukraine to extend its administrative control over the strategic nuclear forces located on its territory. This declaration was met by observers in Moscow with 'perplexity'. This should not have perplexed anyone, however. Since Ukraine does not intend to have foreign troops on its territory, such a declaration was both understandable and natural. More recently, Russia has increased the pressure: during a meeting of

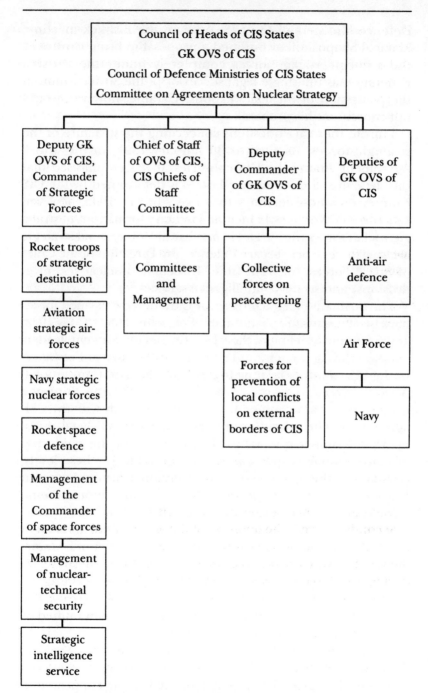

Fig. 1 *Structure of Joint Armed Forces of the CIS*

Defence Ministers of the CIS, prior to the Bishkek meeting, Marshal Shaposhnikov outlined a proposal to bring control of the strategic rocket forces completely under the Russian Federation as the single legal successor of the Soviet Union in the possession of nuclear weapons. Ukraine, however, would not consent to this proposal.

Thirdly, there are questions concerning the structure of the strategic forces. As early as 30 January 1991, in the Minsk Agreement among the CIS countries, it was emphasised that the structure of the Strategic Forces is determined by the CIS country on whose territory they exist. In July 1992, however, *Glavkomat OVS* of the CIS included military formations of strategic rocket forces, the strategic nuclear air force, naval strategic nuclear forces, rocket-space defence, the Direction of the Chief of Space Forces, the 12th Chief Direction (nuclear technical divisions) and strategic intelligence services.[2]

The qualitative characteristics of Ukraine's own armed forces have been discussed on a number of occasions. On 15 May 1992, at the Summit Meeting of the CIS countries in Tashkent, leaders adopted the Agreement on Principles and Order of Execution by the CIS countries relating to the Agreement on Conventional Armed Forces in Europe. In mid-July 1992, the Supreme Council of Ukraine ratified this agreement jointly with the CFE agreement. The adoption of these international legal documents determined quotas for Ukraine regarding the main types of conventional weapons, as set out in Table 1. These levels, pursuant to the agreement on Conventional Armed Forces in Europe and within the framework of military reforms being conducted in Ukraine, are due to be reached in 1995, that is, some 40 months after the date of ratification of the agreement by the Parliament of Ukraine. The Defence Minister of Ukraine, jointly with Ministers of Foreign Affairs of Russia, Belarus and Khazakhstan, signed a protocol in Lisbon on joining the agreement on strategic offensive weapons – the START Treaty. The agreement itself, at the time of writing, has not been ratified by the Ukrainian Parliament.

To date, disagreements over the future of the Black Sea fleet have been the main source of tension in relations between Ukraine and Russia. The problem of the fleet first appeared in January 1992 in connection with the issue of swearing an oath of

Table 1 *Maximum levels of conventional weapons in Ukraine under the terms of the Paris Agreement of 19.11.90*

Weapon System	Maximum Holding
Tanks	4080
Armoured fighting vehicles	5050
Artillery installations	4040
Combat aircraft	1090
Shock helicopters	330
Naval shore-based aircraft	80

loyalty by Ukraine military servicemen of the former Soviet Union serving in Ukraine and willing to commit themselves to its service.

Admiral Kasatonov, appointed Commander of the Navy before the disintegration of the Soviet Union, froze the process of swearing in for the Navy, using severe measures in order to do so. At the Yalta meeting in August 1992 between Presidents Kravchuk and Yeltsin, the Black Sea fleet, formerly regarded as part of the joint armed forces of the CIS, was placed under joint control of both Ukraine and Russia. Nevertheless, Admiral Kasatonov has continued to pursue Russian interests in regard to the Navy and intensively opposes any Ukrainianisation of the fleet. The problem of the Black Sea fleet, however, does not exist in a vacuum. It is one dimension of a larger problem, namely that of the Crimea, and the presence of Russia in the Black Sea and the Mediterranean. The desire of Russia to preserve its presence in these areas is both reasonable and understandable, since its presence is intimately connected with its interests in the Black Sea and the Mediterranean Basin. The methods by which it seeks to maintain this presence, however, are sometimes unacceptable. A group of deputies of the Russian Parliament, for example, headed by V Baburin, raised the question of the legal status of the original transfer of the Crimea to Ukraine by Nikita Krushchev in 1954. This sets a dangerous precedent, not only for Ukraine but for Eastern Europe in general. The problems of the Crimea and the Black Sea fleet are a mixture, in effect, of both objective and subjective factors. Among the objective factors is this: that Ukraine, pursuant to the Minsk Agreement, as well as in its capacity as a sovereign state, possesses a legal right to its own navy in the Black Sea. Ukraine also needs its own navy for the protection of its maritime borders and to safeguard its national interests in the Black Sea and the Mediterranean Basin. Within the Crimean territory of the Ukraine is located almost the whole system of the Black Sea fleet basin, including facilities for the building and repair of warships; the financial and technical maintenance of the Black Sea fleet has traditionally been carried out by Ukraine only. Moreover, when it was a structural unit of the Soviet Navy, the Black Sea fleet was devoted almost exclusively to the defence of the sea borders of Ukraine. Russia possesses a legal right to ensure the protection of its southern regions, including the Black Sea borders, and to preserve its position in the Black Sea and Mediterranean regions. The Black Sea fleet has within its order of battle, however, ships designed for deep water operations and to address tasks far beyond the frame of interests of Ukraine.

Subjective factors involved in the dispute include an awareness in the public mentality of the Russian population of a deep belief about the Black Sea fleet and the Crimea as vital outposts of Russia's southern regions and as an indivisible part of Russia. There is also a belief in the population of the Crimea that the Black Sea fleet remains the military guarantee of the protection of their national rights and interests. The loyalty of the personnel of the Black Sea fleet should also be considered, taking account of the principles on which it was founded in the era of the Russia Empire. Inevitably, there is a danger, in assessing such subjective factors, that the Russian Empire and the modern Russian federation come to be regarded as synonymous. This is not necessarily correct, but it is a dangerous belief nevertheless.

Aware of the need to address the problem of the Black Sea fleet with sufficient political will, Presidents Kravchuk and Yeltsin, first at Dagomys and then at Yalta, reached certain balanced agreements. The proposed solutions are as complicated as the problem, however, and there are both positive and negative characteristics of these solutions from the point of view of Ukraine. One of the positive characteristics is that Russia has officially agreed to the requirement that Ukraine shall establish its own navy on the basis of the Black Sea fleet. Moreover, the division of the Black Sea fleet has been officially determined; the financial and technical maintenance of the fleet shall be shared by the two states; and Ukraine has been officially recognised as one of the parties responsible for the direction and control of the fleet. The right of Ukraine to require the personnel of the Navy to swear an oath of loyalty to the people of Ukraine has been officially recognised.

The negative side of the agreements, however, must also be recognised. The agreements postpone, for more than three years, a complete solution to the problem of the Black Sea fleet and consequently postpone Ukraine's design to build its own navy within that time. This will have knock-on effects in the general scheme to create new armed forces in the immediate future. A similar postponement also applies to any consideration of the question of basing Russian naval forces within Ukrainian facilities. Consequently, payment for such basing – which is a not inconsiderable financial benefit for Ukraine – is also postponed for three years. In the context of the creation of an independent military policy for Ukraine, the formation of a joint Ukrainian/Russian Navy is something of a step backwards. For the first time since the formation of an independent Ukraine, a joint Ukrainian/Russian force has emerged – an idea which had been consistently rejected by Ukraine before the Yalta meeting of 1992. Moreover, the Yalta agreement by itself does not discharge the burden of the problem but only marks a route towards a solution. The implementation of the agreement will clearly depend on the achievements of Ukraine and Russia in overcoming the general crisis in their relationships, the formation of successful market economies, and the gradual elaboration of military policies by both parties as well as the general security situation in Eastern Europe. The possibility of interference in this problem by a third party – Georgia, for example – cannot be excluded.

The overall picture regarding the formation of the armed forces of independent Ukraine is therefore both dynamic and dramatic. Every move in this drama is being evaluated by political oppositions in both the former republics of the Soviet Union and within Russia. Thus, the results of the Yalta Summit with regard to the Black Sea fleet have been strongly criticised in several quarters. And within Ukraine, one of the most prominent leaders of the opposing Conservative Ukrainian Republican Party, Stepan Khmara, has prepared his own draft military document for Ukraine which states in relation to the Black Sea fleet that 'all warships without exception at all, based in the territory of Ukraine, are part of the property of Ukraine'.

But for Russia's confrontation with Ukraine over the question of the Black Sea fleet, Ukraine could by now have organised its own armed forces into a balanced system. Nevertheless, Ukraine has gone some way already in that direction. Once the process of establishing control over troops and naval forces on the territory of Ukraine had been completed, it was always planned to have some 400,000 to 420,000 total armed forces in Ukraine including about 200,000 in the Army, 90,000 in the Air Force and up to 50,000 or 60,000 in the Navy. This corresponds to 0.8 per cent of the total population of Ukraine, which is a favourable figure in comparison, for example, with France, with 0.9 per cent or Greece, with 1.9 per cent. Though the failure to find an immediate solution to the Black Sea fleet problem will certainly distort these figures, the strengths of the Ukrainian armed forces in the immediate future will nevertheless be close to them.

It should be stressed, however, that the figure of 420,000, does not represent a long-term goal for Ukrainian armed force strength. It is rather an intermediate one, adopted on the assumption that the Armed Forces will move down the scale to a more stable state. Constant reductions by the end of the century – assuming a condition of peace in the region – will, it is assumed, result in forces of well below 250,000, as outlined in Fig. 2. Thus a stable figure should be achieved by 1999, at which point it will have fallen to about 180,000 overall. The fact that Ukraine has the right to international guarantees of its security in exchange for its refusal to be a nuclear power and its intention constantly to reduce its armed forces in this way seems indisputable.

There are a number of further tasks to be accomplished in the building of the Ukrainian Armed Forces. One is a final resolution on the question of Ukraine's own Navy. A second is a positive solution to the problem of the administrative subordi-

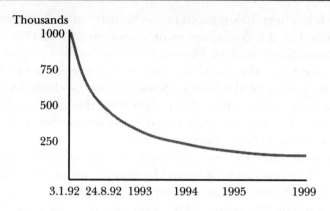

Fig. 2 *Numerical strength of the Armed Forces of Ukraine*

nation of Ukraine within the structure of the strategic rocket forces located on its territory. Third, there is a more comprehensive task regarding a qualitative reconstruction of the Armed Forces. This last task was emphasised by the Defence Minister, K Morozov, in an article published in the Army newspaper: 'What problems are connected with the qualitative reconstruction of Ukrainian armed forces?' One of the most general is the problem of democratisation. The essence of the development process that the Army is now undergoing is not so much one of the reform of structures or numerical strengths, locations or combat tasks, but rather the transformation of its non-democratic character to a more democratic one. Here the positive feature is that the appropriate legal basis for this transformation is, in general, ready. At the highest level, therefore, appropriate national laws exist. As far as service regulations go, however – regulations which dominate the day-to-day life of the Armed Forces – it must be admitted that they do not yet exist. Many undemocratic elements still prevail since the Armed Forces consist of soldiers, warrant officers and officers who were in effect brought up in the former Soviet Army, where discipline was low and non-democratic elements were very obvious. It is difficult for the Ukrainian Army to break the mould of the past. A great deal has been published and disseminated on the topic by the Head of the Officers' Union of Ukraine, G Omelchenko. The implementation of objectively grounded official methods of the selection and placing of personnel is of vital importance.

Research has been undertaken in the Ministry of Defence since 1991 aimed at the development of a concept of selection and placement. Such studies, however, are yet to be completed. There is for Ukrainians, as indeed for many other of the peoples of the Republics of the former Soviet Union, a characteristic moral vacuum in their lives. For the military, this mental state is strengthened by the absence of what in the former Soviet Army were known as 'political classes'.

In general, improvement of military discipline in the Armed Forces of Ukraine can be achieved by drawing lessons and experience from democratisation in other armies; such experience has accumulated in post-war Germany and in other countries. Experience such as this can help Ukraine to consolidate its efforts in building national statehood and, quite apart from the benefits for the Armed Forces, may help in developing a more cohesive national feeling. The problem of social adaptation of military personnel to civilian life still remains a problem. It is a problem, however, on a national scale, and concerns hundreds of thousands of military personnel who, along with their families, account for some millions of people. As yet, the state has taken few visible steps towards the provision of a solution. The problem of the military industrial complex (MIC) of Ukraine exists on the borderline between the Armed Forces and the civil sphere of Ukrainian society. The problem of the MIC for the Ukraine concerns the need to obtain almost everything that Ukraine requires for technical maintenance out of what was formerly the defence sector. Having been part of the Soviet Union, Ukraine built aircraft carriers, heavy cruisers, all types of missiles, aircraft, tanks and various forms of radio equipment, computerised control systems and many other types of weapons and military equipment. This pattern of production, however, has created a significant problem for the economy of Ukraine. First, the Soviet military industrial complex disintegrated, as did the State itself and the distribution of MIC industries has been inequitable among the territories of the former USSR. The horizontal links which existed between different industries were disrupted. Their restoration based on new principles of cooperation is virtually impossible because of the lack of finance required for the implementation of successful market economy laws and because of the political complications over the relations between newly formed states in the territories of the former USSR. It is impossible for production to function normally in the old economic 'hot spots'. Secondly, there has been some incompetent and clumsy experimentation with the conversion of military production to civilianised industry. For in Ukraine, almost all defence enterprises have to be converted. Third, it is not entirely clear what the Defence Ministry of Ukraine will require in the way of technical maintenance for its armed forces. This uncertainty significantly hinders the attempt to convert defence production and the ability to do so on the basis of a coherent blueprint. At present, Ukraine hosts about 15 per cent of the total scientific and industrial potential of the defence complex of the former Soviet Union. This amounts to some 7,000 plants, design bureaux and research and development institutes, which are fully or partly engaged in military production. These establishments employ some 1,200,000 people. The total Ukrainian output by volume was some (Rb)32bn (roubles) in January 1992 – around 40 per cent of which fell within the sphere of military production. By June 1992, however, this had been reduced to 16 per cent, thanks to the disintegration of economic links with other CIS countries.

Ukraine planned to spend around (Rb)22bn in 1992 on the conversion of military industries. The Ukrainian Minister of Engineering, MIC and Conversion, V Antonov, stated that a stocktaking of Ukrainian military industry had already been conducted. Some 5,000 different types of products had been defined and are being considered as those which may support further defence production. The Minister expressed an intention to gain assistance from the United States. This aspiration, however, has to be set against reduced expenditure in the United States as well, and it is generally accepted now that it would be a mistake to place too many hopes on Western credits. As the first Vice Prime Minister, Simonenko, has stated, Ukraine must solve its own problems using its own resources. Nevertheless, an investment in defence conversion within Ukraine represents considerable opportunity for Western businesses which should be exploited. For the Ukraine, the reference points for conversion may be stated quite simply. First, there is a law on conversion; second, the creation of an optimal structure for defence production consistent with progress towards denationalisation and demonopolisation of enterprises through the creation of small businesses. Thirdly, a determination of the direction in which conversion should go without radical changes, if possible, to existing economic trends. Fourthly, the use of scientifically based technologies and the development and maintenance of high technology wherever possible. Fifthly, the financing of conversion. Sixth, extending international cooperation on conversion. Seventh, the formation of necessary state administrative bodies for the coordination of state military, economic, scientific and other bodies concerned with Ukrainian defence interests. Finally, a social safety net is required for the employees of defence sector enterprises during the period of transition.

CONCLUSION

These problems cannot all be settled overnight. Their solutions will require commitment from society as a whole and the work of the best minds in Ukrainian society to outline the necessary steps. Even this, however, will not be sufficient for the accomplishment of the necessary tasks. The problems of building armed forces in Ukraine, as do the problems of the state as a whole, require Ukraine to learn from the extended experiences of foreign countries. In this connection, a study of the achievements of the United States and the countries of Western Europe and their procedures of policy implementation should become one of our strategic requirements for state and military development in modern Ukraine.

Notes

[1] Published by Glavkomat (GK) OVS CIS, July 1992.

[2] At the meeting in Bishkek the Commander in Chief of the CIS OVS, Marshal Shaposhnikov, significantly changed his position on the matter, having stated that the strategic forces structure should include only nuclear forces. That is, he backed up the position of the Ukrainians but only for the purpose of subordinating the strategic forces to Russia on this basis.

11

The Baltic Region in the New Europe

AUDRIUS BUTKEVICIUS

Minister of National Defence, Republic of Lithuania

The most that Europe and the rest of the world normally know about Lithuania is that the country was occupied, proclaimed its independence, is presently seeking the withdrawal of a foreign army, and is pursuing a firm policy in relation to its neighbour, Russia. This is all true, but neither the restoration of an independent state nor the withdrawal of the foreign army constitute the main goals of Lithuanian external policy; rather they are the precondition for the preservation of the Lithuanian way of life and the welfare of its citizens.

Let us consider Lithuania's geopolitical situation in contemporary Europe, as it is seen by the people of the country. Lithuania is at the geographical centre of the Europe which ends at the Ural Mountains. At the same time it is the shortest route between the countries of North-East and West Europe. Lithuania is at the crossroads between East, North and Central Europe. Many of its historical and cultural characteristics are therefore the result of this unique geopolitical position. After the decline of the Roman Empire, and given the spread of Christianity in Europe from both Rome and Byzantium, European religion and culture began to concentrate at the centre. Traditional European gods at that time were described as 'devilish', but they were still alive in Lithuania until the end of the 16th century; and this influenced significant peculiarities in Lithuanian culture. The late arrival of Christianity – in the form of Roman Catholicism – demanded much more tolerance in Lithuania than in many other European countries. The country witnessed no inquisition fires nor the pogroms against those of another faith. The fact that Lithuania was on the route from West to East and possessed good waterways enabled the establishment of links between the main rivers in East and West, thus attracting numerous foreigners, merchants and manufacturers. Since such people were obviously useful to Lithuania, their rights were protected by law and tolerance towards different faiths was encouraged. All this was established in the oldest written East European legislative document – the Lithuanian Statute.

Merchants and scientists also made their way to Lithuania. There is ample evidence of this in the baroque architecture of Vilnius, created by the Italian masters, and in one of the oldest East European universities, also in the capital. Thus Lithuania's geopolitical situation in peacetime was decisive for the rapid development and prosperity of the country. Most of Lithuania's history, however, was characterised by devastating wars and crises, due in part to its geopolitical position. Up to the 12th century, Lithuania had to resist the Slavonic tribes advancing westwards (and similar Tartar-Mongol pressures later), followed at the beginning of the 13th century by the pressure of German knights advancing eastwards.

The Lithuanian tribes also had to resist strong Czech/Polish/Hungarian pressure and finally with the growth of Swedish power in the early 18th century, Swedish marches to the East.

Such attempts to survive and defend Lithuania's way of life promoted the early development of a centralised Lithuanian state and the evolution of distinctive domestic policy influences – influences that were also peculiarly Eastern – which are still present. In the 19th and 20th centuries, with the development of a greater polarisation between East and West, parts of Lithuania, tended to become border territories of the Russian and German Empires. Peter the Great of Russia had always referred to Lithuania as Russia's window to the West and the country remained of prime importance for Russia, which constantly sought to modernise its backward economy to create a more Europeanised state. For Germany and other Western countries it was the road to the underdeveloped Eastern market and the natural resources that they sought.

Today, with relatively minor changes, the situation is quite similar. The status of the near-border territories of the Russian

or German Empires or, in other words, the status of the unprotected territories, resulted in an intensive militarisation of
Lithuania, which significantly reduced the possibilities of economic development. This situation prevailed until the end of
the Cold War. A genuine internal European border, dividing the
continent into East and West, still runs across Lithuania along
the Nemunas River. In a sense this was also a cultural boundary
which even now influences Lithuanian domestic policy.
Regardless of a relatively high percentage of other nationalities
making up some 20 per cent of the residents of the country,
Lithuania has no significant ethnic minority problems.

The result of this, we may well say, is that the geopolitical
position of Lithuania promotes dramatically different influences
in the country according to the prevailing international situation. In peacetime its geographical position ensures rapid
development, utilising the opportunities provided by Lithuania
in its role as a mediator; at times of crisis or conflict, however,
Lithuania is highly vulnerable. Loss of political control over
Lithuanian territory blocks economic development for the population of Lithuania and turns the country into the front line of
defence, as described, for example, in the defence doctrine of
the Soviet Union.

Thus, Lithuania lives under the constant influence of both
East and West. It is therefore very much in Lithuania's interests
to promote a situation in which neither Eastern nor Western
powers are dominant. This may be regarded as the main objective of Lithuanian external policy. It is not only a central tenet of
security policy but is also a prerequisite to economic and cultural development. How, therefore, can Lithuania realise this
goal in the articulation of its security policy?

THREATS TO LITHUANIAN SECURITY

The possible threats to the Lithuanian state can be divided into
three groups.

First are those threats connected to the growing instability
within the territories of the former Soviet Union; inter-regional
conflicts, inter-religious conflicts, and the social conflicts pro-
voked by a declining economy.

Secondly, there are those threats arising from growing tendencies towards authoritarianism and nationalism within the former Soviet Union's territory, primarily within the Russian Federation. The quintessence of this threat is encapsulated in the ideas presented – for whatever reason – by the Russian Minister for Foreign Affairs, Andre Kozyrev, in his famous speech delivered in Stockholm on 14 December 1992, where he tried to show what an aggressive nationalist Russia might demand.

Thirdly, a group of essentially internal threats has evolved which may be regarded as security matters, such as the growth in the crime rate within Lithuania and security problems following potential disasters arising from failures in industrial and energy facilities. Such problems encapsulate a host of social ills such as the smuggling of drugs, guns and radioactive materials; the illegal transport of other goods, and the growth of organised crime in connection with all of the above. There is a large number of people from the territory of the former Soviet Union, who attempt illegally to emigrate to Western countries and from whom are drawn many recruits to criminal organisations. The transport of dangerous materials through the territory of Lithuania is also a considerable problem, over which the government does not have total control.

Potential threats such as these can be neutralised by developing a security policy which proceeds in a number of directions simultaneously.

The international relations of Lithuania

The main goal of Lithuanian security policy must be to increase the political and economic stability of the territory of all the Baltic states by working to achieve a stable balance of influences between East and West. In particular, Lithuania is in a position to participate in the European integration process in economic, political and security spheres. Having long been territories in which there was constant confrontation, Lithuania and the other Baltic states are now in a position to become instead territories of intensive cooperation. The geopolitical situation, their economic relations, their transport system orientated towards the East, as well as their industrial infrastructure, enable the Baltic states to assist the integration of Russia and other states of the former Soviet Union into the integration process of Western Europe. The successor states of the Soviet Union are breaking down their isolation and can help reduce tension within central Europe and support democratic processes and economic reforms in the region. In this situation, the Baltic countries could play an important role as the buffer zone necessary in a transitional stage of European international relations by minimising differences in economic, cultural and security spheres.

The most crucial elements in Lithuania's attempts to neutralise the threats that it faces are likely to be common European mechanisms designed to increase security and stability, and in particular the activities of NATO in its role as a transatlantic organisation. Lithuania's participation in the North Atlantic Cooperation Council (NACC) is therefore both desirable and necessary. Lithuania would also benefit from associate membership of the West European Union (WEU). As well as being an active participant in the Conference on Security and Cooperation in Europe (CSCE) in Vienna, a process charged with conflict prevention and the creation of confidence-building measures, Lithuania also plans to participate in peacekeeping actions in the future.

Lithuania must also concentrate on the establishment of good bilateral relations with the countries on its borders. Lithuanian relations with Poland are enshrined in the Lithuanian/Polish declaration, which proclaims the principle of the inviolability of international borders. An agreement was signed on the functioning of border control points and on customs procedures, and a treaty between the defence ministries of Lithuania and Poland is in preparation. Both countries have a joint programme on the construction of *via Balticum* which is of international importance. Since Poland provides the link to Central and Western Europe, it represents for Lithuania a crucial determinant of its security policy. Good Lithuanian/Polish relations are a major contribution in any attempt to increase stability within the region.

With respect to Belarus, Lithuania is in the process of negotiations on the establishment of diplomatic relations, border demarcation, and border controls. The border with Belarus is the longest border of the Lithuanian Republic, stretching for some 740 kilometres, and has never been precisely delineated. Neither country has any territorial claims on the other, and both share common interests in economic and transit issues. For Lithuania, Belarus provides access to Russia and the countries of the Black Sea region, and is therefore of great significance to Lithuanian security policy. The Belarusian road system connects Lithuania with the Trans-Siberia route, and it is therefore necessary to encourage common mechanisms of increased security between the two countries.

Most significant of all are relations with Russia. Lithuanian and Russian relations are regulated by the Lithuanian/Russian state agreement, and a special agreement on the Kaliningrad region which tackles matters relating to civilian transit. The withdrawal of the Russian Army from Lithuanian territory is regulated by the agreement of 8 September 1992 and the timetable of withdrawal set out in that document. Neither country has any territorial claims on the other. Russia is presently proposing negotiations with Lithuania on matters concerning the coordination of military transit to the Kaliningrad region through Lithuanian territory. Lithuania's position, however, is that negotiations on this kind of an agreement as well as on other matters which are germane to security policy can only be possible following the complete withdrawal of the Russian Army from all three Baltic states.

Within the area of the Baltic states themselves, Lithuanian/ Latvian relations are based on common experiences of a friendly nature of many years standing. They are also regulated by several treaties and common policies, which also include Estonia and are coordinated within the Council of the Baltic States. The *via Balticum* is one of the main joint projects discussed in the Council. The work of the three defence ministries is regulated by the Parnu Treaty of 1992.

Baltic regional approaches to security

There are three particular priorities in the way in which Lithuania has tackled its regional security problems since its new-found independence.

First, there has been a concerted effort to coordinate the foreign and economic policies of Lithuania, Latvia and Estonia, and to consolidate relations with the Scandinavian countries and members of the Nordic Council. In particular, there has been an active search to establish mechanisms of increased stability and security in the Baltic Sea region. Secondly, Lithuania, possibly also embracing Latvia and Estonia, has tried to expand relations with the countries of Central Europe: Poland, Hungary, the Czech and Slovak states, in fostering economic cooperation, coordinating their attempts to integrate themselves into European structures and in strengthening stability and security in Central Europe. Thirdly, the promotion of economic relations between Lithuania – and possibly Latvia and Estonia too – with Belarus and the Ukraine, also constitutes an important element in the search for regional stability.

Such initiatives, however, have to be set against the prospects for the development of East Prussia – the Kaliningrad region – which could pose severe regional problems for Lithuania. The Lithuanian Republic is greatly concerned about the presence and reinforcement of enormous Russian military contingents on the territory of Kaliningrad which far surpass the defence needs of Russia and hinder the peaceful development of that territory. The Lithuanian Republic, as well as other neighbouring countries, is vitally interested in the growth of economic relations, and in new possibilities for the promotion of stability in and around this Russian territory.

Lithuanian defence policy

Lithuania's defence policy is directly related to the development of its defence system. Historical experience and an analysis of the dangers shows that Lithuania can be most vulnerable in a crisis. The most dangerous putative crises are within our own region, the preconditions for which arise in the instability of Lithuania's domestic political situation, in particular through dangers of internal political confrontation, the effects of a long economic depression, a rising crime rate, and insufficient territorial control. Seeking to minimise such threats, the Lithuania Republic has undertaken a number of initiatives. One concerns a system of border controls which at present consists of the customs and military border protection forces of about 5,200 personnel. Until now Lithuania has had no agreement-based border control proceedings with other countries. The border with Poland is controlled by Lithuanian border guards following procedures similar to those which existed on the border of the former Soviet Union and Poland. The border procedures in particular locations have been established by temporary agreement between Lithuanian and Polish governments. Other Lithuanian borders are guarded in conformity with a unilateral regime established by the republic, which suits its economic needs.

In order to ensure the protection of Lithuanian territorial integrity, and of key facilities and natural resources, territorial guard units and groups of volunteers for national defence which act on principles similar to those of the Scandinavia 'Home Guard' groups, have been set up. The territorial guard force is some 3,000 strong with 12,000 in the Home Guard.

On 19 November 1992, the armed forces of the Lithuanian republic were reestablished by a special Act. At present the armed forces consist of: land forces, made up of one rapid reaction brigade, 5,000 strong, formed with a mixture of both professional and conscripted personnel; coastal guards, consisting of one coastal guard fleet, two light coastal guard frigates and four seaport security boats; and an air control force which has just begun to form. Civil defence forces are to guarantee security of Lithuanian citizens in cases of natural disasters and peacetime emergencies. They consist of a department of administrative control of dangerous facilities, dangerous transportation and special rescue, acting on a territorial basis. Lithuania is striving to integrate its civil security system into similar systems operated in other European countries. At the present time, agreements with Germany and Poland are being prepared. Lithuania is also hoping to sign agreements between Lithuanian civil defence forces and those of Scandinavian countries. The national security service operating with the Ministry of Home Affairs is responsible for dealing with organised crime.

The most immediate priority for Lithuanian security, however, remains the complete and orderly withdrawal of the Russian Army, not only from Lithuanian territory but also from that of Latvia and Estonia. The presence of such foreign forces hampers the economic development of the Baltic states, not to mention the development of good relations with the Russian Federation. It also hinders the region's integration into European economic and security structures. The Lithuanian government is concerned about Russian attempts to link the issue of troop withdrawals with the rights of ethnic minorities and what it calls the violation of human rights in Latvia and Estonia. The statements of Russian military authorities regarding Russia's defence interests in the Baltic States and the tolerant attitude of some Russian authorities toward Russian officers' statements about their possible refusal to obey commands also cause great concern.

A similar problem of no less importance is the widescale and informal sale of Russian army property – particularly the weapons, ammunition and other forms of military technology – to civilians, and the illegal transportation of goods using Russian military vehicles. An orderly takeover of the facilities left by the Russian Army presents yet another problem, since these facilities are handed over to Lithuanian forces after they have been devastated and plundered in ways that are ecologically dangerous.

Prospects

Among the republics of the former Soviet Union, Lithuania was the first to proclaim independence. Many of the democratic reforms that have characterised the new Europe started in Lithuania and later spread to other territories. It is not surprising, therefore, that the outcome of the recent elections to the Lithuanian parliament, the Seimas, which produced some unexpected results, raised the possibility in many of our minds of a reversal of the democratic process; indeed a return of former Communist leaders and of a pro-Moscow policy. Does this situation imply a shift backwards for Lithuania or, on the contrary, a new stage in its democratic development? In my opinion, the fact that Lithuania is able to live calmly through a period in which political power is changing following existing legislation, and that Lithuanians are able to continue working together shows that the country has made a step forward toward democracy. Lithuania's security policy, however, does not change. It will continue to seek to join common European security and defence systems in the future and integrate itself in the most appropriate way with an emerging European security order.

12

The Future of Peacekeeping in the Yugoslav Region

JAMES GOW

Research Officer, Centre for Defence Studies

New instruments of peacekeeping were being forged in the Yugoslav crucible during 1992. UN peacekeeping there and elsewhere crossed new frontiers and, in the Yugoslav region in particular, a number of precedents were being set with regard to UN activity. The peacekeeping forces committed in Yugoslavia constituted the first UN peacekeeping mission in continental Europe. By the end of 1992, it had become the largest ever, with over 22,000 troops deployed in Croatia and in Bosnia and Hercegovina, with their numbers seeming set to increase. This reflected the comment made by the British Foreign Secretary Douglas Hurd that peacekeeping was a 'growth industry' as international organisations would increasingly have to look at the possibility of intervening in countries to prevent unacceptable crises developing. He added that peacekeeping would become 'a regular option,' – although countries would keep the right to choose whether or not to participate in particular missions.[1]

Whilst the UN's major involvement in Cambodia during 1992 was also shaping the future of UN activity, the expanding size and scope of the force in Yugoslavia was likely to continue to shape the international agenda as both war in the Yugoslav region and the UN's responsibilities spread. The problems in Cambodia were numerous, but there were unlikely to be new ones. This was not the case with Yugoslavia which seemed likely to expand the demands being made on the UN both practically and conceptually.

The future of peacekeeping in the Yugoslav region was uncertain, experimental and ineluctably intertwined with issues of peacemaking. Both these have become barely separable from issues of enforcement. The course of events on the territory of the late-Socialist Federative Republic of Yugoslavia have increased the challenge to the representatives and capabilities of the international community at each turn. There will be no shortage of further challenges and these will make demands requiring further improvisation and innovation.

UNPROFOR IN CROATIA

UNPROFOR (the United Nations Protection Force), came into being on 21 February 1992 for an initial period of 12 months (six months longer than the customary initial period for UN peacekeeping forces). It was created to underpin the ceasefire between Serbian and Croatian forces in Croatia. Although its primary aim was to strengthen the 2 January ceasefire agreement negotiated by the UN Secretary General's Special Envoy, Cyrus Vance, it also had the secondary aim of providing a symbolic presence in neighbouring Bosnia and Hercegovina which, it was hoped, would be sufficient to prevent the outbreak of armed hostility there.

The 15,000 strong force, with contributions from 26 countries, deployed in four sectors in Croatia – North, South, East and West, with Headquarters in the capital, Zagreb. The bulk of the force comprised military personnel, although there were also small police and civilian components, all under the command of the United Nations. UNPROFOR's mission was to provide United Nations Protected Areas (UNPAs), defined as areas in which Serbs constituted the majority, or a substantial minority of the population, and in which 'inter-communal tensions' had 'led to armed conflict in the recent past'.[2]

The UNPROFOR mandate was set out in four reports by the UN Secretary General.[3] It was consistently emphasised that all arrangements were to be of an interim nature, pending the successful negotiation of a political settlement. Members of UNPROFOR were placed under the command of the Secretary General and not 'permitted to receive operational orders from the national authorities'. They were to remain impartial and 'normally' to use only minimum force when required in self-defence. (The use of the word 'normally' is important, as it implied that there could be situations in which UNPROFOR might be called upon to intervene to separate the belligerents.)

There was to be full demilitarisation of the UNPAs, with full withdrawal of Yugoslav Army forces from Croatia and local irregular units and other military personnel in UNPAs being 'disbanded and demobilised'. Demobilisation meant that the personnel concerned would 'cease to wear any uniform or carry any weapons'.[4] Weapons from such forces were to be handed over to the UN force for safekeeping. After discussions with the parties, it was decided that the most practicable way to effect this latter activity required the placement of arms 'in secure storage under a two-lock system'. One lock would be controlled by UN forces, and the other by the president of the council of the *opstina* concerned.

In addition, UNPROFOR was to identify existing arrangements for local administration and to confirm that the composition of these arrangements (including police forces) reflected the 'national composition of the population which lived in the area concerned before the recent hostilities'. Where this was not the case, UN forces were to arrange, in conjunction with existing local authorities, the necessary changes. Beyond these functions, UN forces were to monitor the work of local police forces and use their good offices to ensure that 'any changes to the status quo as regards other aspects of local administration are consistent with the spirit of the plan and pose no threat to public order'.[5]

The role of UN forces was to ensure that the areas remained demilitarised, to protect the indigenous population from 'fear of armed attack', and to aid in returning 'displaced persons' to their homes.[6] The UN High Commissioner for Refugees (UNHCR) was asked to assume responsibility for designing and implementing a practicable scheme through which this could be achieved. Confirmed violations would be taken up with the offending party and would, if necessary, be reported by the Secretary General to the Security Council. The plan clearly indicated that under no circumstances would serious violations be tolerated: 'If serious tension were to develop between nationalities in a UNPA, the United Nations Force would inter-pose itself between the two sides in order to prevent hostilities'.[7]

Fulfilment of the mandate proved problematic in several regards. Although the peacekeeping force was able to deploy and by doing so give a reasonable degree of interim security to the ceasefire, it was not able fully and wholly successfully to ensure that the provisions of the mandate were carried through in practice. As a result, there is scope for fighting to begin again in Croatia.

In general, demilitarisation has not been accomplished. Although much weaponry was placed in store under the dual key system, some was not. Certain items of materiel, including armour, were painted blue and 'transferred' to the local police force. Indeed, many members of the former Yugoslav military, as well as the irregulars who were supposed to be disbanded, were transferred to these police forces. As this process occurred, the prolonged withdrawal of the Yugoslav Army also proved to be an obstacle, although the eventual supplanting of the army with the new military-style police force meant that local radicals were able to accept the army's formal withdrawal. However, full demilitarisation was not forthcoming – and would not be, according to the Serbian leaders, until tension was reduced.

Tension was linked with the non-implementation of other features of the UNPROFOR mandate, particularly with regard to the issue of displaced persons – the 275,000 Croats and oth-ers who had lived in the UNPAs before the war. The UNHCR insisted that conditions would not be appropriate for the return of populations until demilitarisation had been completed. In the meantime, the practice of expelling populations known as 'ethnic cleansing' continued with UNPROFOR impotent to stop the process. Incidents could be reported to local authorities and were constantly investigated by the civilian police members of UNPROFOR, particularly in the Baranja region in Sector East. This activity and the UN presence perhaps tempered attacks on non-Serbian inhabitants refusing to leave, but did not prevent them.

Although UNPROFOR could report cases to the local author-ities, the responsibility for dealing with them lay with those authorities. Local administrations, formed by representatives of the Serbian political-military machine which had undertaken the war in Croatia, were not too sympathetic (although former Army officers were reported to take up matters in a serious way, whereas their irregular and civilian colleagues did not). That the local police force was composed of Serbs ran against the provision in the mandate to ensure that the police force and other parts of the local administration should reflect the region's ethnic composition prior to the war. Of course, for this to be possible, among other things, the return of non-Serb populations was necessary. Therefore, in a somewhat absurd circle: return of populations required demilitarisation, demilitarisation required reduced tension, reduced tension required an end to attacks on non-Serbs, action to stop these required de-Serbianisation of the local authorities and police force – which required the return of non-Serb populations. Yet, the UN representatives had no mandate to enforce the terms of the agreement to their deployment.

The failure to accomplish these aspects of the mandate fuelled growing frustration in Croatia and added to the fear that, whatever the formal agreements being made in the Hague, Brussels, London and Geneva, events were developing in a way which would, in reality, mean that the 'occupied territories' would be lost to Zagreb for good. The Croatian reaction to this situation was to make their own contributions to continuing tension. Regular night-time hit and run attacks by small units in the UNPAs made no contribution to the reduction of tension. Nor did sweeps by Croatian forces in the 'Pink Zones' containing significant Serb communities and bordering on UNPAs, but not part of them, which were supposed also to be demilitarised. This resulted in protests to the Zagreb government by the UN and threats that sanctions could be imposed against Croatia if it did not stop.

Finally, Croatia made attempts peacefully to return populations, in spite of warnings from the UNHCR not to do so. UNPROFOR was mobilised to prevent this happening. That action added to Croatian perceptions of UNPROFOR as something not only ineffectually confirming territorial losses through default, but actually acting against Croatia's interest. This kindled feelings both at popular and élite levels that raised question marks about UNPROFOR's presence.

In the summer and autumn of 1992, there was a groundswell

of opinion in Croatia that UNPROFOR's one year mandate meant that it would only remain for one year, unless Croatia invited it to stay. This was driven by a desire to see Zagreb's authority restored in the occupied areas. UN representatives made it clear that the one year initial mandate was intended to be renewed. However, renewal of the mandate looked likely to be problematic. The Tudjman government, irrespective of its real desire, or its judgement, appeared trapped by the ordinary citizen's expectation that control of Serb-held territories would be restored after the mandate expired and UNPROFOR troops were withdrawn somewhere between February and May 1993. If control were not to be reestablished, any government in Zagreb seemed likely to find itself in a crisis.

Therefore, talk spread in Croatia about a military move to end Serb control. The Croatian Army, apart from action in the 'Pink Zones', also quickly moved into parts of the Prevlaka Peninsula after EC and UN Special Envoys Lord Owen and Cyrus Vance had negotiated the withdrawal of the Yugoslav Army and demilitarisation. Croatia could claim with a little justice that this was necessary in order to respond to Serbian bombardments of southern Croatia from Trebinje in eastern Hercegovina (perhaps using weaponry 'withdrawn' by the Yugoslav Army). However, the action was nonetheless a clear violation of the agreement – as the President of the Federal Republic of Yugoslavia, Dobrica Cosic, was only too keen to remind the UN Secretary General and the two Special Envoys, complicating their dealings with the Yugoslav leadership.

Whether or not Croatia would refuse to give its agreement to renewal of UNPROFOR, or whether Zagreb would take moves to restore its control of the UNPAs if UNPROFOR remained, was a subject of debate. Many in Croatia believed that the matter was only bluster and that President Tudjman would not act when the time came. On the other hand, security planners in autumn 1992 were expressing the view that only a short campaign would be required to impose control and that the UN and other representatives of international opinion had demonstrated through their 'appeasement' of the Serbian camp in numerous instances and their failure to enforce agreements that such a move would be accepted, albeit, perhaps, with complaints. It was assumed that, if this happened, UNPROFOR would not commit the ultimate 'injustice' of resisting Croatian forces after having allowed Serbian ones to get away with murder – often quite literally.

The viability of UNPROFOR in Croatia was being brought into question even if renewed fighting could be averted in the spring-summer of 1993. There was a clear prospect that UNPROFOR could be caught in the cross-fire and faced with additional awkward problems to the difficulties experienced in its first year of efforts to carry out its mandate – which difficulties showed little sign of being removed. Indeed, their removal and the avoidance of renewed fighting depended on developments elsewhere – in Geneva, at the International Conference on Yugoslavia, in Bosnia and Hercegovina and, perhaps, most of all, at the nexus of the conflicts in the Yugoslav lands, in Belgrade.

UNPROFOR: BOSNIA AND HERCEGOVINA

Although the UNPROFOR mandate was restricted to Croatia, the mission's Headquarters were initially placed in the Bosnian capital, Sarajevo. Even when the Serbian assault on the city forced the UN to remove the Headquarters to Croatia, an UNPROFOR presence was maintained in Sarajevo with the mission's Chief of Staff, Canadian Brigadier (later Major General) Lewis MacKenzie attempting to act as a mediator. However, as events unfolded in Bosnia and Hercegovina, the UN role grew. As the extent of the Serbian campaign of terror became clear,[8] the UN Security Council found itself issuing a series of resolutions aimed at ending the violence there and facing calls to increase UN activity in Bosnia, up to and including an armed intervention.

UN Security Council Resolution 752 demanded that the Yugoslav Army and its equipment be withdrawn from Bosnia and Hercegovina, placed under international control, or put under the command of the Sarajevo government. When this had not happened, the Security Council invoked Chapter VII of its charter for the second time in the Yugoslav crisis (the first was to impose an arms embargo on Yugoslavia in November 1991) to impose comprehensive sanctions against Serbia and

Montenegro which had reconstituted themselves in a new state, the Federal Republic of Yugoslavia. Later measures included naval monitoring of the embargo (carried out by a combined NATO-WEU force), a ban on non-UN military flights over Bosnia and Hercegovina and creation of a second element of UNPROFOR to escort humanitarian aid missions in Bosnia and Hercegovina.

All these measures were adopted by the Security Council in response to the growing evidence that the Serbian forces in Bosnia were carrying out a campaign of violent expulsion of non-Serb populations which included the presence of camps in which ethnic Muslims were concentrated. This process by the summer of 1992 had already produced almost two million deportees and refugees from Bosnia and Hercegovina in addition to the near million spawned by war in Croatia the previous year. The international responses were a mixture of earnest moral outrage and cynical efforts made in response to television-generated public pressure. Whatever the prompts, they constituted a confused, but somewhat radical response to events. This was particularly true of UNPROFOR 2 and its humanitarian mission.

Attempts to conduct an airlift of relief to Sarajevo were intermittent and, in any case, insufficient to meet the need there – and were not available in other parts of the country.[9] Representatives of the United Nations High Commissioner for Refugees had made several efforts to get convoys of food and medicine to besieged communities in various parts of Bosnia and Hercegovina, but had run into difficulties, even when the assistance of troops drawn (beyond their mandate) from the 1,500 force based in Sarajevo was available. Those framing policy felt unable, both for practical reasons and because of the limits imposed by both the UN Charter and the conventions of international relations,[10] to undertake more decisive military action. But, they wished to do something which would both send signals to Belgrade and Banja Luka (the Bosnian Serbs' 'capital') and which would also make a positive contribution to the welfare of those suffering around the country. The answer seemed to lie in some form of 'humanitarian intervention' supported by armed force.[11]

On 13 August, the UN Security Council empowered 'states to

use any measures necessary for the delivery of humanitarian relief, including military measures.' But, it 'did not prescribe the use of force',[12] the use of which was deemed not to be desirable, but might prove necessary. Discussion of the use of force made UN Secretary General Boutros Boutros Ghali nervous. He expressed fears in a letter to the Security Council, arguing that the use-of-force resolution could endanger UN peacekeepers already operating in Bosnia and Hercegovina – and even those in Croatia; and he hinted at their withdrawal by demanding 'adequate' advance warning of military intervention so that threat to UN peacekeepers could be minimised. Those discussing the sending of armed escorts for the food and medicine convoys allayed some of his fears, however, by moving cautiously.

The nature of the problems involved in the mission in Bosnia and Hercegovina, difficulties already experienced and, not least NATO's need to establish a new role for itself, all contributed to NATO's planning and organising UNPROFOR 2, although most of the relevant contributions were initially offered through the WEU at the end of the London Conference on Yugoslavia in August 1992. Under a French commanding officer, General Phillipe Morillon, the UN Headquarters for the 7,000-strong UNPROFOR 2 was provided by NATO, which lifted large parts of the Northern Army Group Headquarters in Germany and based them in Zagreb, with forward elements at Kiseljak.[13] The use of NATO facilities overcame certain operational problems, but not all of them: communications difficulties remained between British and Belgian units operating together.[14]

The first of these was widespread concern at the lack of communications between elements of the multinational peacekeeping force. Though less of a problem in Croatia, where the operation more closely resembled traditional peacekeeping efforts, matters were altogether more complex and basic questions of communication, especially between Egyptians and Ukrainians in Sarajevo, had led the embryo of UNPROFOR 2 into unnecessary difficulties. An integrated, well-practised C^3 function, based on NATO procedures, would overcome the kind of problems experienced in and around Sarajevo and on convoys from the Bosnian capital to towns in the south.

This was a significant development in terms of peacekeeping, carrying with it two implications. The first was that 'complicated' peacekeeping or 'peacekeeping plus' operations, which seemed set to expand in number and scope in the future, required the kind of military organisation not usually associated with peacekeeping missions. The second was the possibility that the traditional peacekeeping practices of open communication and using 'information' shared with all parties, rather than 'intelligence' might be altered in certain circumstances. In this respect, a further advantage of transposing a NATO Head-quarters to run UNPROFOR 2 was the presence of Americans in the Staff with access to US intelligence and logistics resources.

UNPROFOR 2 was not charged with 'blasting its way through' to its point of destination. Instead, it was to escort the convoys in 'benign' ways, only using its armaments in self-defence, if fired upon first (although the French force at Bihac was far more assertive, given the scope Paris allowed it, than the British con-tingent at Vitez which had very restrictive rules of engagement imposed by London). This avoided the obvious difficulties that could be envisaged if convoys got into frequent firefights. However, it also meant that there were continuing problems ensuring the passage of aid where the way was blocked by com-batants. Although the Serbian camp, as in most other matters, was easily the worst offender in this respect, the UN Civilian Affairs representative, Cedric Thornberry, made it clear that all parties had frustrated the work of those attempting to deliver aid.[15]

In addition, over one month after Cyrus Vance had criticised the delay in deployment of the new forces and three months after their role had been authorised by the UN Security Council, when the detachments began their work, others were some way short of beginning operations. Whereas the British-Dutch-Belgian element of UNPROFOR 2 based at Vitez was functioning towards the end of November and beginning to use means such as the diplomatic skills of its commanding offi-cer, Lieutenant-Colonel Bob Stewart, to negotiate the passage of convoys, the Canadian-Dutch element supposed to operate from Serb-controlled Banja Luka had not reached first base. The Canadians, in an effort, presumably, to use 'all necessary means' had even reluctantly carried out the UN's wish to com-ply with Serbian extortion: at the instruction of the UN, on 9 November, Canadians paid the Serbian authorities in Banja

Luka, $49,000 of a demanded $250,000, ostensibly to defray 'administrative costs'. However, Canadian delegations going each day to the outskirts of Banja Luka were still not allowed to enter the town to prepare for the deployment of UNPROFOR in this area. In the meantime, there was powerful evidence that large-scale, systematic 'ethnic cleansing' was being executed in the region.[16]

In this instance, the Canadians found themselves at the crux of the problem faced by all those trying to deal with the Serbian political-military machine in the Yugoslav wars. This was that unless the Serbian leadership could be coerced into accommodating the demands of others, or forced to keep to agreements, it did not do so. Yet, with regard to UNPROFOR 2, there would be unwelcome risks in attempting to force through the passage of aid: it would compromise the force's impartiality (although of course no humanitarian intervention can be free from some degree of partiality simply because, for example, breaking sieges offers support to the besieged); and it would put relatively small forces in potentially disadvantageous military circumstances.

The same dilemma was present in discussions about the 'air-exclusion zone' ordered by the UN Security Council in September. This banned military flights over Bosnia and Hercegovina. At first, Serbian aircraft simply ignored it; later under pressure from Owen and Vance at the Conference in Geneva, they agreed not to fly the aircraft and, indeed, to transfer them for safe-keeping to the territory of the Federated Republics of Yugoslavia. However, this did not happen and sorties continued to be flown. The problem here was that the air-exclusion zone was ordered, but there was deliberately no provision for its enforcement – it was judged by Britain and France that their 'neutral' troops on the ground would be vulnerable to reprisals if Serbian aircraft were shot down. A valid concern, this therefore left Serbian aircraft free to continue their missions as there was no chance that the 'no-fly' regime would be enforced. Indeed, UN representatives reported in November that it had been broken over 100 times; those violations included flights from bases in Serbia, among them, helicopters carrying troops.

Thus, although there was growing impatience with the situation, there was still not the will among those involved on the ground to accept a shift towards enforcement. Some countries, such as the US, which had favoured provision for enforcement in the original resolution, continued to believe that this was desirable. Indeed, the US was prepared to use the air element of the 6th Fleet based in the Adriatic. But without troops engaged on the ground in Bosnia and Hercegovina, it found itself in a relatively weak position in negotiations. Meanwhile, this feature, like so many other aspects of international involvement, including UNPROFOR, was undermined by the inability to make the Serbian camp believe that it had to comply with international demands, or with agreements it had made.

UNPROFOR 2 was undoubtedly allieviating some of Bosnia's misery and probably acting as, if not a deterrent, a presence which meant the level of violence was less than it might have been otherwise. However, neither it, nor the UNHCR and the International Red Cross with both of which it was working, could be expected to handle the scale of the problem present- ed by hundreds of thousands of deportees and refugees without food, shelter and medicines as winter approached – and with nowhere to go, given the growing reluctance of other countries, including oversaturated neighbours,[17] to accept them.

The question of creating 'safe havens' in areas still under control of Bosnian government forces which would require the stopping of Serbian land seizure, was raised by UN representa- tives in Bosnia and Hercegovina. It had been rejected already in various quarters. But, with Bosnian forces unable adequately to defend them, exits being closed by a coordinated international policy based on keeping the refugees as close to their homes as possible, there being no accommodation for several hundred thousand people in Bosnia and Hercegovina and the prospect that a quarter of a million deaths were being predicted in the course of the winter, if not through armed action, then through disease and cold, the possibility was increasing that action simi- lar to that taken on behalf of the Kurds in northern Iraq might have to be repeated, but in worse conditions. However, the cre- ation of such protected areas could only be accomplished if the enforcement barrier were crossed – a move that would pose many questions for peacekeeping missions in the future.

In addition to the problems already faced by the UN in

Bosnia and Hercegovina, there was no doubt that there was a long future, riddled with difficulties, for peacekeeping in Bosnia and Hercegovina. There was little prospect that having committed so much already, there would not, at some stage, be a more traditional peacekeeping force deployed in Bosnia and Hercegovina – as well, perhaps, as a Cambodian-type temporary administration, or a UN trusteeship . This was something generally overlooked in debates on the sending of major armed contingents on combat missions in the country, in which it was frequently suggested that to do so would be to engage in a long-term commitment. In truth, the UN (and, in reality, the West's) long-term commitment was already determined. The relevant questions concerned when the long-term peacekeeping commitment would begin and on whose terms. The reality of 128,000 dead or missing-presumed-dead in December and more expected, and the realisation that only a decisive step backed by military force would shake the Serbian leadership, was pushing the international community towards bolder measures. Even the UN Commanding Officer in Sarajevo, Egyptian General Adnan Abdelrazek, took the unprecedented step for a UN representative of calling the mission in Bosnia and Hercegovina a 'failure' and calling on the UN to 'intervene by force to put an end to the war and save the population'.[18] Moreover, there was alarm that the southern part of the former Yugoslavia would present even bigger and graver problems.

UNPROFORS GALORE?: THE 'SOUTHERN FRONT' AND THE FUTURE

In November 1991, there were calls from the Bosnian President Alija Izetbegovic for the deployment of a preventative peacekeeping force to avert the outbreak of violence in his republic. It is possible to imagine that if the UN had been prepared to take this unprecedented step, the Bosnian catastrophe might have been avoided. With this in mind and Cassandra foreseeing war in the southern parts of the old Yugoslavia, the UN Secretary General undertook to broach the virgin territory of preventative peacekeeping.

At the end of November, Boutros Boutros Ghali sent 12

peacekeepers to Macedonia. Their mission was to assess the possibility of deploying a larger peacekeeping force there, particularly along the borders with Albania and southern Serbia. This reflected the high degree of international concern about the prospects of war in the southern parts of the old Yugoslavia, of which there were plenty, which threatened to spread beyond the borders of the old state. However, whilst representing a welcome effort to learn the lessons of earlier international failures to take preventative measures, sending peacekeepers to Macedonia was, at least in isolation, a questionable move.

There were three regions of crucial concern: the Sandzak region, straddling the border between Macedonia and Serbia, with its large Slav Muslim population; the southern Serbian Province of Kosovo, with a 90 per cent ethnic Albanian population living in repressive conditions; and the old Republic of Macedonia. Sandzak was slightly less of a problem in that it did not pose an immediate threat at the international level as the immediate consequences would not be felt across the old international frontiers. In addition to this, there had been the welcome development of Montenegrin Interior Ministry troops and local units of the Yugoslavian Army restoring order around the town of Pljevlja and giving protection to Muslims coming under attack from Serbian paramilitary groups crossing the border. These developments, however, contributed to the growing divisions between Montenegro and the Federation, on one side, and Serbia on the other.

The situation in Kosovo was both more straightforward and more obviously dangerous. It warranted the agreement at the London Conference to place CSCE monitors in Kosovo, although the Serbian régime made it difficult to do this, as well as a call by outgoing US President George Bush at the end of November 1992 for the stationing of as many civilian international monitors there as possible. The situation contained three dangers. The first (and least likely) was that the repressed Albanian majority would give up its passive resistance to repression and begin a suicidal uprising. The second was that elements of the Serbian paramilitary network organised in Kosovo could become a loose cannon, setting off a wider conflict through impatience or accident.

The last (and most likely) was that the paramilitaries and

Serbian Interior Ministry Forces would begin the campaign for which the Serbian authorities had placed them in Kosovo – to 'cleanse' it of Albanians. Any attack on the Albanians in Kosovo would inevitably draw support from Albania and the Albanians in western Macedonia, whilst refugees fled there. That involved the risk that Serbian forces would have to carry operations into those countries. Although Albania's being dragged into armed conflict would be a major concern for the international community, Macedonia's being sucked in presented real threats of a general Balkan war involving Greece, Turkey, and possibly others.

The threat inherent in the Kosovo situation for Macedonia was accentuated by the disintegration within the republic engendered by Macedonia's year in limbo. Unrecognised by most countries as having independent international personality because of a Greek objection to the republic's name, Macedonia's economy, the weakest in the old Yugoslavia, had been exhausted both by the inability to secure external investment and by the burden of UN sanctions on the Federal Republic of Yugoslavia. In addition, tensions had been growing within the republic between the ethnic Albanian population in western Macedonia and elements of the ethnic Macedonian population. Greece and Serbia were seeking to destabilise Macedonia by apparently providing arms to the Albanians (although, from the Serbian point of view, arming Albanians had implications for the situation in Kosovo, as well); radical elements of the Internal Macedonian Revolutionary Movement (VMRO) were returning to the movement's historic terroristic roots and training paramilitary groups, creating the conditions for a split with the democratic wing – which was anyway drawing support away from the moderate government as a result of the republic's parlous position.

Thus, the idea of deploying an experimental, precedent-setting pre-emptive peacekeeping force in Macedonia was questionable. Were such a force to be deployed it would either have to hope that its presence would be a sufficient symbolic gesture to deter the twin threats inherent in the Macedonian case, or its mandate would have to give it the authority both to become a defensive force in the event of war racing across the border from Kosovo and, within Macedonia, to take on a role in

the maintenance of law and order. Whilst the UN's Congo experience provides a problematic but successful precedent for the
latter, the creation of a defensive role mandate would increase
the precedent-setting quality of a pre-emptive deployment in
Macedonia. An additional problem was Macedonia's limbo status: with only three countries having granted international
recognition to the republic (Russia, Bulgaria and Turkey), a
peacekeeping force with a mandate to defend Macedonia's borders would be in the quite curious position of defending the
borders of an entity which was not one of the UN's member
states.

At the time of writing, these were unresolved questions, but
pressure was growing to break the Greek block on recognition,
although this seemed unlikely to produce results unless the EC
broke its Common Foreign and Security Policy only a year after
its inception; other, more radical, steps were either for the UN
to take further extraordinary measures, including the placing of
Macedonia under some kind of international authority, further
increasing its responsibilities in the republic, or to move towards
deployment on a legally unclear basis – as had already become
the case with the envoy of the initial exploratory mission. Apart
from all this, there was the option of foregoing the experiment
in Macedonia.

It was certainly important to be aware of the particular difficulties of the situation and to avoid making the mistake of
thinking that it was the same as had been the case in Bosnia and
Hercegovina. Deployment of a pre-emptive peacekeeping force
in Bosnia and Hercegovina would have very likely helped to
avert war there – it would certainly have created a physical
impediment to the wave of Serbian incursions across the River
Drina (the border between Serbia and Bosnia and Hercegovina)
in the first week of April 1992 which were the vanguard moves of
what, despite strong civil elements, has essentially been a war of
annexation.

Violence in Macedonia, however, would have a different character: Serbo-Yugoslav forces would carry the war across the
border not to annex territory (although the attempt to incorporate the small Serb-populated area near Kumanovo in
northern Macedonian could not be excluded) but to suppress
Albanian resistance which would inevitably have bases in

Macedonia; the tensions between ethnic-Albanians and Macedonians, on the other hand, whilst predicated on the desire of large elements in the Albanian community for unification with the Albanian state, would primarily be a low-intensity civil conflict. Thus, whilst preventative peacekeeping in itself was an idea which contained many virtues and could be appropriate in certain circumstances, of which Bosnia and Hercegovina might have been one, the deployment of a classical peacekeeping force in Macedonia faced the strong prospect of failure, unless there were adequate complementary measures. A deployment in the republic, to be successful and safe, would require more than the traditional peacekeeping mandate.

CONCLUSIONS

Two big issues arise from the UN's peacekeeping involvement in the former Yugoslavia, although they are not exclusive to the Yugoslav case. These are the budgetary implications of the expanding number and type of missions, and the growing tension between Chapter VI and Chapter VII UN operations as peacekeeping moves beyond its traditional scope into the 'Chapter VI and a half' domain of peacekeeping with enforcement characteristics. The discussions at the end of 1992 about an armed intervention in Bosnia and Hercegovina seemed to be pushing the boundaries of peacekeeping further, whilst the way in which UNPROFOR 2 was funded was setting further precedents.

The greatest restriction on UNPROFOR was its cost. For the first year of UNPROFOR in Croatia the budget was likely to exceed the minimum US $607.5m agreed at the time of its deployment. With member states already heavily in debt to the UN with regard to contributions for peacekeeping, it seemed unlikely that the UN would be able to finance the operation in Croatia either successfully or indefinitely. The UN, in addition, estimated that emergency winter relief programmes in Bosnia and Hercegovina were likely to reach $1bn by March 1993. In December 1992, less than half that sum had been paid and, of the materials and money provided up to that point, half had come from the EC alone. Some relief on the UN's financial resources had come, however, in the decision by the governments committing forces to UNPROFOR 2 to accept the costs of their engagement. This seemed likely to be a precedent for future peacekeeping – certainly 'peacekeeping plus' – missions. That, in turn, however, would leave the UN even more hostage to the wishes of the governments of its member states, particularly of the Permanent Five.

The tension between Chapter VI operations and Chapter VII measures was evident in Bosnia and Hercegovina in various ways, such as the non-enforcement of the air-exclusion zone over the country because of fears that this would leave troops on the ground, deployed formally as peacekeepers, vulnerable to reprisals. It was clear that, by becoming involved in situations where agreement was achieved on various matters, such as ceasefires and the deployment of a UN force, but where agreements were not always implemented or respected, the UN would find itself either having to withdraw ignominiously or resort to measures designed to enforce.

This tension reflected the experience of UN deployments in the former Yugoslavia and of the problems that UN forces were likely to face. Whilst the UN's presence may have helped to stabilise the situation in Croatia temporarily, UNPROFOR clearly faced problems there, and although involvement had some limiting effect on the war in Bosnia and Hercegovina, this was clearly insufficient. At the end of 1992, it seemed likely that the UN would be required to do more. It also seemed likely that the size, scope and nature of the UN's involvement in the Yugoslav region would be expanded as particular problems of the post-Yugoslav nightmare and the conceptual framework for future UN peacekeeping activities (linked to peacemaking and enforcement questions) were addressed simultaneously.

Notes

[1] Douglas Hurd, quoted in *The Guardian*, 14 October 1992.
[2] UN doc. S/23280, 11 December 1991.
[3] Annex III, UN doc. S/23280, 11 December 1991; UN doc. S/23592, 15 February 1992; UN doc. S/23777, 2 April 1992; and UN doc. S/23844, 24 April 1992.
[4] Annex III, UN doc. S/23280, 11 December 1991.

[5] UN doc. S/23592, 15 February 1992.

[6] UN doc. S/23280, 11 December 1991.

[7] *Ibid.*

[8] It is of note that members of UNPROFOR were reporting acts of 'ethnic cleansing' in Bosnia at an early stage, some two months before the scale of what had happened became widely known.

[9] It remained a mystery that Tuzla airport in north-eastern Bosnia, lying within a region securely controlled by Bosnian government forces, was not used for airlifts into that region, which otherwise presented problems for those trying to approach by land, as it could only be reached with great difficulty by road.

[10] On these limitations and the ways in which various crises in the early 1990s were leading to 'inventions' and 'innovations', which whilst apparently meagre in terms of the problems they sought to address, were radical departures which could only be made after serious consideration, see Paul Fifoot, 'Functions and powers and inventions: UN action in respect of human rights and humanitarian intervention', in Nigel Rodley, ed., *To Loose the Bands of Wickedness: International Intervention in Defence of Human Rights,* Brassey's in association with the David Davies Memorial Institute, London, 1992, pp 133–164.

[11] On the issue of humanitarian intervention, see generally Rodley, ed., *op. cit.,*.

[12] Sir David Hannay, UK Ambassador to the UN, quoted in *The Daily Telegraph,* 14 August 1992.

[13] In terms of the history of NATO, it was an interesting development that French troops were taking part. Although this was a NATO organised operation, because it was beyond the Alliance's charter, German participation was not possible. The places of German staff officers were taken by the French. This represented a small step towards the already signalled moves towards re-integration into the military structures of NATO but was consistent with traditional French practice because this *de facto* NATO operation was *de jure* NATO by another name – the UN. The appointment of General Morillon was undoubtedly due not only to his experience in Yugoslavia as Deputy-Commander of UNPROFOR, but also to the benefit of sweetening French participation in NATO.

[14] See *The Daily Telegraph,* 7 December 1992.

[15] *The Guardian,* 24 November 1992.

[16] On 1 December 1992, the UN Human Rights Commission met for only the second time in its history to vote to condemn the 'crimes against humanity' in Bosnia and Hercegovina, with the US Secretary of State Lawrence Eagleburger in the forefront, naming a number of senior figures in the Serbian camp with cases to answer. These included the Serbian President Sobodan Milosevic, the Serbian leader in Bosnia, Radovan Karadzic and the commander of the Serbian Army in Bosnia, Col.Gen. Ratko Mladic.

[17] The proportion of refugees to population in Croatia, for example, which had its refugee policy criticised by others reluctant to take refugees themselves, represented the equivalent of an influx of 12 million people to the UK.

[18] Quoted in *The Guardian*, 7 December 1992.

ARMS CONTROL

13

The Lessons of Intrusive
Verification in Iraq

DAVID KAY

*Secretary General of the Uranium Institute, formerly an
inspection team leader for the UN Special Commission in Iraq*

As of the end of 1992 there have been more than 40 inspections
in Iraq carried out by United Nations teams under the authority of UN Security Council Resolution 687 (3 April 1991), the
cease-fire resolution which ended the Gulf War. This resolution
requires that all chemical and biological weapons, nuclear
weapons material and ballistic missiles with a range greater than
150 kilometres be identified and destroyed, removed or rendered harmless. The resolution further directs that this same
process should apply to all subsystems or components and any
research, development, support or manufacturing facilities for
such nuclear material or prohibited weapons and that Iraq's
undertaking not to use, develop, construct or acquire such
weapons in the future shall be the subject of an ongoing monitoring and verification régime.

These inspections in terms of their intrusiveness have been
quite unlike any others previously conducted or contemplated
as part of arms limitation arrangements, such as in the
Intermediate Nuclear Forces, Conventional Forces in Europe,
and Strategic Arms Reduction Treaties. There have been four
unique aspects to this set of UN-directed inspections.

First, the inspections began on the basis of what was in many
ways a coerced acceptance of the inspection arrangements by
Iraq and only a partial and very misleading declaration by Iraq
of the weapons and material in its possession that were to be covered by the inspection régime. In its letter of 6 April 1991 to the
President of the Security Council, Iraq, after listing seven pages

of objections, noted that it had 'no choice but to accept this resolution'.[1] While the President of the Security Council in a letter
of 11 April to the Permanent Representative of Iraq noted that
the Iraqi Ambassador in a meeting on 8 April had confirmed
that Iraq's letter constituted its 'irrevocable and unqualified
acceptance' of Resolution 687, the actual letter and rhetoric
from Baghdad left little doubt in anyone's mind that Iraq was
not a willing party to this arms control régime.[2]

On 18 April, Iraq submitted details of the quantities and locations of its chemical, biological, ballistic missile and nuclear
material stocks. This listing which was required by the terms of
Resolution 687 and was to provide the baseline for the inspection activities was signed by no less than President Saddam
Hussein and accompanied by a letter from Iraq's Foreign
Minister, Ahmed Hussein. This declaration acknowledged nearly 10,000 nerve-gas warheads, 1,000 tons of nerve and mustard
gas, 1,500 chemical weapon bombs and shells, 52 Scud missiles
with 30 chemical and 23 conventional high explosive warheads.
Iraq, however, denied that it had any nuclear materials that fell
under the resolution or any biological weapons. While this declaration was eye-opening with regard to the Iraqi chemical
weapons stockpile and its acknowledgment of chemical warheads for Scuds, it was widely acknowledged at the time – and
subsequently confirmed by on-site inspection – to be seriously
misleading in the nuclear, biological and missile fields. It also
turned out to have been a serious misstatement of the size of the
Iraqi chemical weapons arsenal as well. The Chairman of the
Special Commission, Rolf Ekeus, informed the Security Council
on 30 July 1991 that inspectors had already found four times
more chemical weapons than Baghdad had declared (46,000
chemical shells as compared to 11,500 and 3,000 tons of chemical agents as compared to 650 tons declared). By October 1991,
inspectors had found 100,000 chemical shells and bombs –
almost ten times the number initially declared.

With inspection still on-going, the extent of the deception
involved in the initial Iraqi declarations is still not fully known,
but one measure can be provided by a comparison of the Iraqi
nuclear programme as initially declared with what has been
found to date. Iraq's initial declaration of 19 April avowed that it
had no proscribed nuclear materials, but this was amended on

27 April to acknowledge that it did have what had been reported to the IAEA before the war, including 27.6 pounds of high enriched uranium and 22 pounds of low enriched uranium and a peaceful research programme centred on the Tuwaitha Nuclear Research Centre. Inspections have subsequently found that instead of this strictly peaceful research programme, Iraq in fact had, beginning in 1981, embarked on a clandestine uranium enrichment programme using three different methods; (electromagnetic isotope separation, the so-called Calutron method; chemical enrichment; and gaseous centrifuge enrichment). At the time of the war, it had begun the start-up for industrial-scale enrichment using Calutrons on two major sites and had acquired the material, designs and equipment for 20,000 modern centrifuges. Design, testing and the constructing of manufacturing facilities for actual bomb production was well advanced and the Iraqis had calculated the yield of one of their designs as 20 kilotons. Preliminary research was underway to develop the technology to provide fusion boosting of fission warheads using the lithium-6 route. Over 20,000 people were determined to have been employed in this clandestine nuclear weapons programme.

The fact that inspections had to begin in Iraq on the basis of very incomplete declarations of amounts and locations of material to be inspected and a clear statement from Iraq that it found the basis of the inspection to be seriously inequitable, represented a significant break with previous arms control arrangements. In earlier arrangements, the diplomats and arms control experts had fought the battle of desirability and extent of coverage prior to the signing of agreements. In Iraq, the inspectors had to find in the field what was to be covered and to deal on a day-to-day basis with an Iraqi unhappiness that there was any inspection at all.

Secondly, the UN inspectors have had to cope with an unparalleled level of deception, fraud, cheating and intimidation. The record of Iraqi activities designed to deceive and mislead inspectors runs from the subtle to the outrageous and began even before the first inspection team arrived. Prior to the first inspection team – a nuclear inspection, under Resolution 687 arriving in Iraq on 15 May – aerial and space-based surveillance observed extensive clearing activities, involving the burying of what was first believed to be debris from the bombing, underway at several sites, including the Tuwaitha Nuclear Research Centre and a large industrial complex that was a suspect nuclear site north of Baghdad, known as Tarmiya. When the first group of on-site inspectors arrived at Tuwaitha, they discovered that much of the clean-up activities was unrelated to bombing but appeared to be the result of Iraqi destruction and removal of undamaged or lightly damaged buildings. Immediately after the departure of the team, the same observation methods recorded the Iraqis unearthing previously buried material and moving it to other locations. A combination of luck and information brought out by the first inspection team allowed some of this material to be unambiguously identified as part of a Calutron uranium enrichment facility.

During subsequent inspection activities by another team of inspectors to gain access to these Calutron parts, shots were fired over their heads by Iraqi troops, 40 garbage trucks loaded with unrelated debris were offered up for inspection, and completely unrelated equipment was brought forth and attested by the Chairman of the Iraqi Atomic Energy Commission to be the exact material in the photographs and that observed by the inspectors being spirited away. After strong international pressure, the Iraqis admitted that they had indeed had a Calutron programme and described with some glee how they had kept both the pre-war IAEA inspections under the Non-Proliferation Treaty (NPT) away from this equipment and had misled the first group of inspectors under Resolution 687.

In one of the most dangerous deception activities, the Iraqis, during the course of three inspections, moved two clandestinely irradiated fuel elements around the Tuwaitha Centre on the back of an unprotected truck just out of sight of the inspectors. These highly radioactive elements posed a serious radiation hazard to both the Iraqi staff and inspectors during this deception operation. Iraq subsequently admitted that these two fuel elements were part of a secret plutonium production effort in clear violation of the NPT.

On 24 September 1991, when a group of inspectors finally gained access to part of the archives of the Iraqi nuclear weapons programme, the Iraqi authorities held the inspectors hostage in a downtown Baghdad parking lot for four days before relenting and allowing the team to depart with the documents.

In July 1992, another team of inspectors was denied entry for three weeks to a suspect site in the Ministry of Agriculture building and finally left Baghdad after the level of physical threats led the UN to fear that actual violence was imminent.

In late December, a high ranking Iraqi official was quoted as telling the chief inspector of a UN arms team that Iraqis would 'like to drink the blood' of the UN inspectors and that he would personally break the neck of any Iraqi that cooperated with the arms inspections. Attempts at intimidation have become part of the daily routine of arms verification in Iraq.

In contrast with many arms limitation agreements, where verification has been solely or mostly based on non-intrusive National Technical Means (NTM) for verification, the effort in Iraq would not have been possible without intrusive on-site inspection. Even those recent arms limitation agreements that have resorted to on-site inspectors have done so in a non-confrontational, record keeping and observer role. The Iraqi experience is quite distinctly different, with a great emphasis on unearthing a programme that is being actively shielded from inspection and verification.

Third, many of the techniques and approaches available to the inspectors have never before been used in an arms control environment. These include zero-notice inspections, 'go anytime, anyplace, with anyone and anything' authority, right of unlimited aerial photography, the right to bring in all necessary inspection equipment without prior notice or the right of Iraqi inspection of it, unlimited sampling authority, freedom to mount helicopter flights for observation and movement and the right to operate without restriction open and encrypted communications. The UN Special Commission has been able to lease from the US Government a U-2 reconnaissance aircraft for regular flights over Iraq and to obtain the trained photo interpretation services to make use of this asset.

While this degree of intrusiveness may seem ideal from an arms control perspective, it should be noted that even after 20 months of such inspection much of the Iraq weapons programme still remains obscure and the Special Commission admits that it is uncertain how much of the Iraqi programme has been found and eliminated. This is powerful testimony to the advantages of interior lines – Saddam still controls the country (a fact that no inspector has ever been left in doubt about) and the difficulty of discovery in the face of active deception measures. The post-war experience with Iraq must clearly indicate the limits of what can be expected of coercive arms control arrangements where one of the parties calculates that the arrangements are not in his interest. This has broader relevance than Iraq, particularly in other areas of the Middle East, North and South Asia.

Inspectors in Iraq have also been charged with carrying out, according to plans approved by the Security council, the 'destruction, removal, or rendering harmless' of the prescribed weapons, sub-systems, components and facilities. This has been the source of some of the most serious confrontations with the Iraqis who have been obligated to participate in or observe the destruction of facilities and equipment worth hundreds of millions of dollars. In other arms control arrangements, such as INF, where weapons have been destroyed, both a reciprocal parity of weapons eliminations between treaty partners and an agreed destruction procedure was negotiated prior to any inspections, and the inspectors were simply observers to confirm that the agreed destruction took place. This has not been the case in Iraq. Only Iraqi weapons are being eliminated and the inspectors – faced with an Iraqi refusal to co-operate – are playing a much more military role of 'locate, fix, eliminate' than the traditional arms control doctrine ever contemplated.

Fourth, inspection activities in Iraq were placed in the hands of a body created for just this purpose, the United Nations Special Commission, a subsidiary organ of the Security Council. The Special Commission, headed by a Swedish diplomat, Rolf Ekeus, was able to tap over twenty governments to build a full-time staff that grew at its peak to more than 50 staff in its New York headquarters and an almost equal number based in Bahrain, its forward deployment base, and Baghdad. Most importantly this Special Commission became the vehicle through which national governments could pass intelligence information to the international inspection effort and an institution with a commitment to keep the Iraqi issue before the Security Council and before governments. While the Iraqi authorities have no doubt come to view the Special Commission as just an agent of the Coalition powers, and particularly the

United States, from the inside its role has been much more complex. First, of all the Commission, and this really means its Chairman, has had the necessary but unenviable task of vetting and maintaining a sense of proportion in the face of intelligence reports that often overstate what is known as opposed to what is simply suspected, or judged possible. In the face of the highly efficient Iraqi deception activities, the inspections could not have gone forward without accurate intelligence. On the other hand, if every intelligence lead had been chased down by an inspection team, the operation would have come to a grinding halt in its first few months. National governments have developed various means for coping with the well known propensity of their intelligence services to overstate the capabilities of opponents – the most common method on both sides of the Atlantic is to operate competing national intelligence services within a single government in order that through competition they will keep each other honest. International arms control arrangements have never had to come to terms before with the problem of vetting intelligence estimates.

A second vital function performed by the Special Commission has been legitimising the passage of national intelligence information to an international activity. In the early days of the Iraqi inspections, I often wondered which would force us to grind to a halt first: the fear of national intelligence services that sources and methods would be irreversibly compromised if valuable intelligence passed into the hands of a group of international inspectors or the fear of my superiors in the International Atomic Energy Agency and the United Nations that their moral purity would be forever ruined if they allowed those of us engaged in the inspection effort to have access to intelligence gathered by national intelligence communities and in turn to provide these services with an assessment, based on our inspections, of the accuracy of this information. That these mutual barriers have largely been overcome is due principally to the tact and intelligence of Rolf Ekeus and his colleagues on the Special Commission.

It is too early to say definitively what has been accomplished by the United Nations inspections in Iraq and what the implications of these might be for future arms control activities. The task of rooting out the Iraqi weapons of mass destruction is certainly not complete even though much has been accomplished. For example, it is of more than idle interest to note that international inspectors have identified and destroyed more of the Iraqi nuclear and missile programmes than Coalition military power did before the cease fire.

The long term monitoring and verification effort needed to ensure that the Iraqi programme is not restarted has barely begun. If the government of Saddam Hussein remains in power, with all that implies for its neighbours and for inspection activities, one must have the gravest doubts as to whether the international community will be able to maintain sufficient pressure on Iraq to allow such a long term, intrusive inspection régime to work. On at least seven occasions since the end of the Gulf War, the inspection process has ground to a halt in the face of Iraqi intransigence and only the threat of resumed military action overcame these roadblocks. This is certainly a shaky – and dangerous – basis on which to rest an arms control agreement.

IMPLICATIONS FOR THE FUTURE

As to the implications of this experience for other arms control arrangements, one must also be cautious. The initial reaction of the traditional arms control community has certainly been largely to dismiss this experience. They may be correct at least as regards to the total approach employed in the case of Iraq. It would be impossible to imagine operating an arms control arrangement in Russia or China in the fashion that the Special commission has in Iraq. This dismissive attitude is, however, probably wrong with regard to important aspects of the intrusive approach taken in Iraq.

The critical aspects that I believe will have continued importance and relevance to the arms control community include the recognition of the impact that can be had by coupling national intelligence information to an international inspectorate; a resounding message that knowledgeable and determined deception can defeat NTM and consequently a recognition that NTM must be quickly pushed beyond simply seeking better resolution photography if it is really to support arms control; a new appreciation for what vigorous, intrusive on-site inspection can accomplish even in a hostile environment; and a recognition that much more work needs to be done to understand how best to support on-site inspection. Much greater research support is now required to develop technologies that can support intrusive on-site inspections. These include detection technologies that can be used in the field and give immediate results to guide on-site inspection activities, secure communication, facilities that can dependably link inspectors to their support bases and 'tagging' technology that can confidently ensure that an item once inspected is not removed or misused.

There are, in my view, at least four probable situations in which intrusive inspection régimes will be likely in the coming few years. The first situation would involve regional peace settlements or arms limitations arrangements in places such as India/Pakistan, the Middle East or the Korean peninsula. In such areas of deep distrust, arms limitations are unlikely to be entered into unless inspections procedures can be agreed which give all parties confidence in their effectiveness and honesty. The Iraqi inspection effort, if it is finally carried to a successful conclusion, may well give the required confidence to those very sceptical states, such as Israel and India, who find themselves caught in difficult regional power struggles and who are now being urged to undertake regional arms control arrangements as part of over-all political settlements. In the past, Israel and India certainly had every right to doubt whether traditional IAEA-type NPT inspections would have provided them with any security at all. Now there is at least another model which can be brought forth and discussed as a workable, credible alternative.

A second general situation likely to require intrusive inspections will be one in which an existing nuclear programme is being dismantled or sharply curtailed. The most likely venue of such a situation is the former Soviet Union, where the political and economic conditions and mistrust among republics will exert strong pressure for more intrusive inspection requirements to ensure that weapons are actually dismantled and that the resulting fissile material is adequately controlled. The various republics, Moscow, and the international community share an interest in having positive assurances that weapons agreed to be removed and dismantled are, in fact, actually removed and dismantled. The withdrawn weapons and fissile nuclear material that will result from weapon dismantlement will continue to represent a threat to international security for many years, the more so in the uncertain conditions of the former soviet Union. The assurance that can be gained from intrusive international inspection, rather than simple unilateral assertions of good intentions, of such weapons and material will likely become an overriding objective in the next few years.

A third situation likely to require intrusive inspection mechanisms will be a relatively few cases in which new governments may request help in conducting intrusive inspections to root out suspected secret weapons programmes. One can imagine such a situation developing if an ANC-led government came to power in South Africa or unification were to suddenly occur on the Korean peninsula as a result of the collapse of the North. In such situations the new government, or its neighbours, may doubt the ability of the government to discover fully a clandestine programme and turn to intrusive international inspection procedures to provide added confidence that everything has been discovered and eliminated.

And finally, intrusive inspections may well be required to give the international community confidence that exports of dual-use equipment are not being misused. At present, dual-use equipment is exported under national licensing procedures that rely on the exporter and recipient country to provide an end use certificate that purports to give the final user and declared use of the equipment. This has been found, most recently in the case of Iraq, to be an almost meaningless control procedure. It is very likely that some form of inspection during use will soon become standard for the most sensitive type of dual-use exports. Unless this is done, it is hard to see how exporting states will avoid bitter disputes among themselves about exports to 'untrustworthy' states or how they will be able to protect themselves from the security problems that can arise from clandestine programmes or the embarrassing political problems of the future 'Iraqgates'.

Notes:

[1] United Nations Doc S/22456, 6 April 1991, pp. 1–7.
[2] United Nations Doc S/22485, 11 April, p. 1.

14

Nuclear Non-Proliferation: The Evolving Contest[1]

JOHN SIMPSON

Professor of International Relations and Director of the Mountbatten Centre for International Studies, University of Southampton

Revolutionary changes have been taking place in the nuclear non-proliferation scene. Several can be related directly to the 'end of the Cold War', but the majority arise from pressures generated autonomously by the nuclear non-proliferation system itself and the state of the international nuclear technology and materials markets. Despite these changes, the prospects for preventing proliferation are probably as positive now as at any time since 1945.

The main strands of these changes in the international non-proliferation context can be summarised through five general propositions. First, the advanced industrialised states are now much more united in their policies against nuclear proliferation than was the case in the 1970s. Secondly, there has been a discernible shift in public expectations and institutional activity away from a minimalist nuclear non-proliferation verification régime based upon the International Atomic Energy Agency, towards an imposed one, centred upon export controls and UN Security Council action. Thirdly, regional solutions to non-proliferation problems have now been accepted as an effective way forward in several regions of long-standing proliferation concern. Fourthly, a new class of proliferation problem has been created by the dismantling of the Soviet Union. Finally, the outcome of the international conference in 1995 to extend the Nuclear Non-Proliferation Treaty (NPT), the legal cornerstone of the nuclear non-proliferation régime, will be crucial for its future. The outcome will almost certainly be positive, but the nature of the ongoing debate will illuminate a totally new set of disagreements and diplomatic alliances that is slowly emerging over the objectives of the régime and the means by which they might be obtained.

NUCLEAR HARMONY AMONG
THE INDUSTRIALISED DEMOCRACIES

In the 1970s, acute divisions existed between the nuclear industry and the nuclear non-proliferation community, and between the United States government and its allies in Western Europe, over non-proliferation policies. In 1992, nuclear non-proliferation is probably higher on the international political agenda than it was in the late 1970s, yet it generates less conflict among developed states. Why is this so?

The most obvious general explanation is that the expectations of state officials and those working in the nuclear energy field are totally different in 1992 from 1979, as is the objective situation. In the latter year, nuclear energy was still regarded by the advanced industrial states as the spearhead technology, with access to it essential for economic development. Global nuclear power capacity was expected to grow rapidly as the century progressed, providing a steady home and export market for national nuclear industries. Export deals with states such as Brazil, Argentina, Iran and Pakistan involved huge contracts and sharp commercial competition. And uranium availability and prices were expected to remain at levels which would justify reprocessing of used nuclear fuel, the building of commercial fast breeder reactors and the creation of a 'plutonium economy', thus precipitating the proliferation concerns that found their expression in the Carter administration's 'war on plutonium' and the International Nuclear Fuel Cycle Evaluation programme.

The situation in 1992 is totally different. The size, global spread and profitability of nuclear power programmes has been limited to a point where commercial competition is muted and nuclear energy is no longer regarded as an essential technology for national economic development. The sole exception to this is the attempt by China to open up an export market for its nuclear technology. Companies in the nuclear industry and their parent states have been forced to accept cross-national mergers, with their attendant need to harmonise non-proliferation policies between states. Meanwhile the bottom has fallen out of the uranium market, the existence of significant military stocks which could be released on to the market seems likely to keep it depressed for some years, if not decades, and the economic and energy security rationales for nuclear fuel reprocessing have – perhaps temporarily – dissolved.

A second general explanation is that although East-West cooperation on nuclear non-proliferation developed strongly from 1968 onwards, it was only after 1990 that concerns in the former East over self-policing by Western European states, especially Germany, and subsequent disagreements arising from these concerns, have abated. The impact of this can be seen in particular in the evolution of International Atomic Energy Authority (IAEA) safeguards, where a partnership arrangement is emerging with EURATOM that would have been unthinkable two years ago.

A third general explanation is that the European Community states have evolved common positions over nuclear non-proliferation through the mechanisms provided by the European Political Cooperation (EPC) structure. The specifics of this start with the changed attitude of France. The French accession to the NPT on 3 August 1992 was the logical conclusion of a series of moves bringing its non-proliferation policies into line with its Western European neighbours. The start of this may be detected in the industrial alliances forged between French companies and their European counterparts in reactor construction, fuel reprocessing and uranium enrichment. This created a situation where there were no obvious future commercial benefits to be gained from remaining outside the formal non-proliferation system.

In August 1990, the Foreign Minister of the Federal Republic of Germany announced that IAEA safeguards on all nuclear materials and operating facilities within a non-NPT party [Full-Scope Safeguards or FSS] would be a condition for future supply of nuclear technology. This followed closely upon a similar decision by Japan. One consequence was to facilitate Britain and France announcing in September 1991 that both would insist on FSS as a condition of nuclear supply in future. Given their lead, those other European states which had strongly resisted making FSS a condition of nuclear supply for twenty years rapidly fell into line behind their neighbours. These and other developments have left China as the only major nuclear supplier not insisting on FSS as a condition of supply.

Changes in the global nuclear energy industry, the end of the East/West divide and the increased cohesiveness of West European policies have thus created an unprecedented situation of harmony between the industrialised democracies over nuclear non-proliferation issues. This has led to developments which were inconceivable three years ago. Perhaps its most positive manifestation, however, is found in the statement by the Group of Seven that their objective at the 1995 conference to extend the NPT will be an unconditional extension of the Treaty. The full significance of this can only be appreciated by recalling the reluctance of the Federal Republic of Germany and Japan to commit themselves to the Treaty in the early 1970s.

There does remain, however, one very sensitive issue which seems destined to continue to generate disharmony among the industrialised states. This is the difference that manifested itself in the 1970s between groups in the United States on the one hand, and the governments of Japan, France, the United Kingdom and some other European countries on the other, over the separation and use of plutonium in the civil fuel cycle. The 1970s dispute was settled by an agreement to differ; by the United States administration accepting Japanese concerns over energy security and by it choosing not to exercise its right to veto Japan's reprocessing of US supplied fuel. Britain, France and Japan went ahead with arrangements for recycling Japanese fuel in facilities in Europe, and returning the plutonium to Japan for use in fast-breeder reactor research and in mixed-oxide (MOX) fuel. These facilities are now in the process of becoming fully operational, and the movement of plutonium from Europe to Japan has started.

Two new elements have entered the picture since the 1970s, however. One is that the price of uranium has slumped and inventories and stockpiles are high, throwing doubt on the contemporary relevance of Japan's concerns over energy security. Second, it seems certain that enriched uranium and plutonium will enter the market from the United States and former USSR military stockpiles. Since military plutonium is easier to use as fuel in reactors than recycled, high-burn up material from light water reactors (LWRs), and since such use removes most of its military explosive potential, the technical, energy security and economic logic of continuing with recycling is weakening. Yet Britain, France and Japan have made significant financial and resource investments in these arrangements, and suspending or terminating them at this stage appears commercially and politically impossible.

The stage thus seems set for a resumption of the 1970s United States 'war on plutonium' to prevent commerce in plutonium; routine shipments of the material around the globe; and any further increase in stockpiles of separated potential nuclear weapons materials. Given the adverse commercial, and political, implications for France, Japan and the United Kingdom of suspending these arrangements, the potential for disharmony arising from this situation is great, and might even undermine the improvements in relations over non-proliferation policies that have taken place over the last few years. The situation is made even more complex by the United States having the theoretical right to veto such reprocessing, and to prevent the shipment of plutonium to Japan, but having chosen so far not to exercise these rights.

EVOLUTION OF THE NUCLEAR NON-PROLIFERATION VERIFICATION SYSTEM

Two control and verification systems are linked to the global nuclear non-proliferation system: national systems of export controls based upon agreed international guidelines and the IAEA safeguards system covering fissile materials. Both have been subjected to criticism and significant revision since 1990.

Prior to 1991, the system of export controls applied by states which were nuclear technology and materials suppliers was based on guidelines over what should be exported which were agreed in the mid-1970s. These guidelines covered complete nuclear plants and sub-assemblies for such plants, but not 'dual-use' technologies [i.e. those that could have both nuclear and non-nuclear applications]. When the first meeting for over a decade of the 26 states accepting the 'Nuclear Supplier Guidelines' (NSG) was convened by the Dutch Government in the Hague in March 1991, it was decided to set up a working group to make proposals for the control of 'dual-use' technologies and materials, in order to produce a more comprehensive nuclear export system.

The relevance of this move became apparent when it emerged that Iraq had purchased much of the equipment and materials for its clandestine nuclear weapon programme from suppliers in advanced industrial states unconnected with national nuclear industries. In March/April 1992, the NSG states met in Warsaw and agreed to export guidelines covering 64 types of 'dual-use' equipment and materials. They also initiated a consultative mechanism on requests for export sales of dual-use items, and agreed to make FSS a condition of supply for all nuclear related items.

The NPT, which came into force in 1970, made it mandatory for all non-nuclear weapon parties to the Treaty to sign a safeguards agreement with the IAEA covering all fissile and other special nuclear materials within their territory. The standard agreement for this purpose is known as an INFCIRC/153. INFCIRC/153 involves a non-nuclear weapon state making an initial declaration to the IAEA of the fissile materials within its territory, and the IAEA then monitoring any changes in that inventory. In its annual safeguards reports, the IAEA has always indicated that material *declared* to it has remained in known uses and locations, but has never stated that undeclared material and facilities do not exist within a state.

INFCIRC/153 was drafted in the context of a specific set of circumstances.[2] The potential proliferators of the 1960s were Western advanced industrial states. The prime aim of the safeguards system was perceived as preventing them clandestinely diverting fissile materials from their nuclear power programmes and fuel cycles to use in military explosives. The USSR wished to see as intrusive a system as possible operate in the Federal Republic of Germany (FRG) to prevent it acquiring nuclear weapons: they were adamant that Western Europe had to be subject to a parallel system of IAEA and EURATOM safeguards to prevent self-policing. The FRG and Japan wished to minimise intrusive safeguards which would, in their eyes, unfairly advantage the nuclear industries of nuclear weapon states such as the United States. Other Western states were prepared to implement a less than perfect safeguards system if this would facilitate the FRG and Japan signing the NPT. The consequence was that the implementation of IAEA safeguards concentrated upon providing assurances of non-diversion, and early warning of possible diversion, from industrialised states with extensive nuclear power programmes. The inspectorate was not tasked by the governments of the day with aggressively seeking out clandestine programmes and activities, while developing states with small nuclear programmes and research reactors were subject to much less intrusive inspection than developed ones. Yet the image developed among publics and politicians that the IAEA was acting as a policeman to ensure that states covered by its safeguards did not develop nuclear weapons. The operational reality involved a much more restricted conception of tasks and capabilities. The point at which the difference between image and reality became painfully apparent was in mid-1991, when the existence of a clandestine programme for producing fissile materials for weapons was uncovered in Iraq.

In parallel with the Iraqi 'proliferation shock', the wider context in which IAEA safeguards operated was also changing. The USSR had dissolved, and Russia and the other republics of the Commonwealth of Independent States (CIS) no longer opposed the removal of duplication between the two safeguards systems in Western Europe. At the end of April 1992, the IAEA and EURATOM agreed to a new partnership approach to reduce duplication of tasks and release some of the IAEA's annual $60 million safeguards budget for other purposes. The need to release such resources was necessitated by the reluctance of member states, despite the experience of Iraq, to find additional finance to allow the Agency to increase its safeguards expenditure. At the same time the constraints imposed by the industrialised states upon the implementation of a more intrusive safeguards régime have been reduced by a mixture of a lessening of the political leverage enjoyed by national nuclear industries and the demands for a strengthened IAEA safeguards régime following the revelations about Iraq .

The concern since mid-1991 has been to enhance the IAEA's

ability to detect clandestine nuclear programmes in states with emerging nuclear capabilities. The IAEA safeguards system is now expected actively to seek out and aggressively prevent proliferation, rather than merely providing reassuring evidence that it is not occurring. Although the IAEA's 'any time, any place' inspection work on behalf of the UN Special Commission disarming Iraq under UN Security Council Resolution 687 is a special case, it has served to create further unrealistic expectations about future IAEA safeguarding activities. Proving a negative conclusively is almost impossible, and 'surprise' special inspections are logistically difficult to mount. But these developments, among others, have led to the slow emergence of a revised concept of IAEA safeguards, encapsulated in the phrase 'transparency and early warning'. This revised concept would involve total openness about all nuclear activities within a state; the integration of relevant knowledge by the IAEA; and the advance acceptance of special inspections in the event of accusations of clandestine weapons activity.

The IAEA secretariat has attempted to move the safeguards system towards greater transparency in several ways. The starting point for these changes was to create mechanisms to implement special inspections. This involved the Board of Governors agreeing that it was legitimate to invoke such inspections; the setting up of a unit within the IAEA Secretariat to receive, collect and analyse information from all sources on possible clandestine activities; and encouraging Safeguards Inspectors to be more inquisitive in relation to facilities at nuclear sites other than those declared to contain fissile materials.

A second element of the revised concept is early submission of design information on all new nuclear facilities being planned and constructed within a state. In the case of Iraq, its construction of large Calutron plants to enrich uranium did not constitute a violation of existing safeguards practice, as the provisions in INFCIRC/153 on supply of design information had been interpreted as meaning its provision 180 days prior to the introduction of nuclear materials into a plant. In February 1992, however, the Board of Governors of the IAEA endorsed the secretariat's proposal that design information on nuclear facilities should be transmitted to the Agency at the time of the decision to build, or authorise building, of any nuclear plant, or to adapt an existing plant. This would also give inspectors the right to visit the plant at an early stage of construction.

The third element of the revised concept is universal reporting. This implies the ability of the IAEA to compile an ongoing inventory of all exports, imports, production and inventory associated with each state, and thus develop a comprehensive global picture of all peaceful nuclear activities. Again, this would close a loophole uncovered by the Iraqi case. Proposals on this were submitted to the IAEA Board of Governors in February and June 1992, the later submission having the reporting of production of nuclear material or equipment and the routine verification of reports omitted. In June 1992, the IAEA Board agreed to encourage voluntary reporting to the Agency by those states willing to do so as an interim measure. It seems probable, however, that eventually the Board will agree to mandatory reporting of the export and import of nuclear materials. The problems involved in agreeing this proposal concern reporting of inventories of nuclear materials, such as ores and ore concentrates, and possible overlaps with the existing supplier state export control system, and do not appear to be heavily political in nature.

The IAEA Board has yet to address two other significant issues of safeguards practice: the need to reconsider the 'significant quantities' of fissile materials that determine the frequency of routine safeguards inspections and the need to make safeguards state and facility, rather than 'Material Balance Area' (MBA) orientated. The figures for 'significant quantities' originated in a report on nuclear weapons published in 1967 by the UN. They were based on the minimum quantities of these materials that was then publicly believed to be required to make a nuclear weapon, but these figures are now generally regarded as overestimates. The problem is to find an alternative set of lower figures around which consensus might be built.

The need to make safeguards state and facility, rather than MBA, orientated, was demonstrated when it was revealed that there had been sufficient safeguarded enriched uranium in Iraq to make a bomb. However, it was divided between several MBAs in the same facility, each of which contained less than a significant quantity. The quantities of material in the MBAs determined the frequency of routine inspections, not the total amount present in the facility or state. Yet all states remain wary of changes that would impose additional administrative or financial demands upon them, or bear upon them in a discriminatory fashion, and it remains to be seen whether the Secretariat's attempt to revise this and other IAEA safeguards practices will continue to receive the political support it requires.

Prior to 1991, an imposed nuclear non-proliferation régime was an unrealistic option because the basic antagonisms between the five permanent members of the UN Security Council made a consensus on such issues unthinkable. But the events of 1991 demonstrated that, for the first time, the political conditions existed to enable the permanent members of the UN Security Council to play the executive role of the 'five policemen of the world' originally assigned to them in 1945. Moreover, UN Security Council Resolution 687 set up the Special Commission to oversee the liquidation of Iraq's capabilities to make, and inventories of, weapons of mass destruction. The Special Commission used the IAEA as their agents in the nuclear area: in doing so they gave the IAEA inspectors enhanced powers which may not apply in any other set of circumstances.

The emergence of the UN as a new actor on the non-proliferation scene through the Iraq episode led to considerable debate over the future roles of the UN Security Council and the IAEA in this area. In practice it has always been clear that the IAEA itself could never act decisively if it discovered evidence of clandestine nuclear activity: it could merely report the matter to the UN Security Council for further action, as it did when it uncovered evidence of the unreported manufacture of enriched uranium and plutonium by Iraq. Enforcement action against proven proliferators has always been the province of the Security Council: the big change in 1991 was that it was demonstrated that the international community, led by the United States, now had the will and ability to act in this matter, and to serve as a significant deterrent against clandestine proliferation.

This was underlined on 31 January 1992 when United Kingdom Prime Minister John Major, as Chairman of the Security Council, stated that 'The proliferation of all weapons of mass destruction constitutes a threat to international peace and security'. This was the first occasion upon which it had been clearly indicated by the Council that proliferation itself would necessitate an active response under Chapter VII of the UN Charter. The effect of this was to place future nuclear prolifera- tors on warning that the international community would probably intervene to prevent any further nuclear proliferation – if the existing international consensus among the permanent members of the Security Council could be sustained. It also strongly reinforced the existing international norm, contained in the NPT, outlawing nuclear proliferation.

The rise of the UN Security Council as an active force pre- venting proliferation did have some significant side effects. There was seen to be a clash of operational philosophies between the IAEA's more collaborative, less aggressive, approach to verification based upon professional respect, and the confrontational consequences of the activities of the UN Special Commission. This led to proposals to abandon the IAEA and create a new, more interventionist, verification organisa- tion, as well as a realisation that a 'hard man-soft man' partnership between the IAEA and a permanent UN Special Commission on Weapons of Mass Destruction might also be very effective in combatting proliferation. In practice the root of this tension was over access to intelligence information. Such material was more likely to be entrusted to a US dominated UN Special Commission in New York than to the more multina- tional IAEA secretariat in Vienna. And as the intelligence failure that lay at the heart of the Iraqi experience indicated, without access to effective intelligence neither the IAEA nor the UN could mount any-place, any-time inspections.

The new supplier controls on dual use items, the attempt to reinforce the application of IAEA safeguards system around the concept of transparency, the operations of the IAEA and UN Special Commission in Iraq and the declaration of the UN Security Council that proliferation is a threat to the peace, have all combined to create a new non-proliferation climate. This climate suggests that, within the non-proliferation context, and even within that of the NPT itself, measures to prevent prolifer- ation may now be given priority over concerns to prevent discrimination and allow unconstrained transfers of nuclear technology to developing states. In its extreme form, this may result in nuclear energy being positively denied to developing states if this gives greater assurance that it will not be misused. The underlying mechanism of the non-proliferation system may be moving in the direction of imposition of rules by the industrialised states in the interests of all, rather than consensus. While this may offer benefits to smaller states, it seems unlikely to endear itself to many of the aspiring regional powers in the developing world.

REGIONAL SOLUTIONS FOR NUCLEAR NON-PROLIFERATION CONCERNS

From 1945 onwards, successive United States governments have sought to create a universal and global nuclear non-proliferation régime. One significant change in the 1990s has been the development and application of the concept that regional non-proliferation agreements, particularly those creating nuclear-weapon-free zones, might have a valuable role to play in reinforcing, and in some cases even substituting for, global non-proliferation policies. This change is related to the recognition that among the strongest perceived motives for nuclear proliferation are the acquisition of regional prestige and status and to solve national security problems. These motivations have appeared to become even more relevant as some of the nuclear security structures associated with the East/West conflicts have been liquidated, and the global political system has become less centralised.

Three broad types of regional arrangement have been developed to prevent nuclear proliferation and nuclear war: nuclear-weapon or nuclear-free zones (N[W]FZ); bilateral or multilateral regional safeguards and confidence-building arrangements; and agreements not to reprocess nuclear fuel or enrich uranium. The three NWFZs that have been negotiated cover Latin America (The Treaty of Tlatelolco); the South Pacific (The Treaty of Raratonga) and the Antarctic. One recent development is that the Treaty of Tlatelolco may be fully implemented after 25 years of existence, following changes to it requested by Argentina and Brazil. In addition, discussions are now taking place on a NWFZ covering the whole of Africa, following the accession of a former nuclear proliferation suspect, South Africa, to the NPT. Ideas exist also for a similar zone in Europe and a zone free from all weapons of mass destruction in the Middle East.

The really significant developments in regional arrangements, however, have been in the area of bi-lateral arrangements. The decision of the Federal Republic of Germany to make FSS a condition of supply for nuclear commerce in mid-1990 threatened to have its greatest effects upon Argentina and Brazil, long-time customers for its nuclear technology. This, in part, stimulated decisions at the highest levels in both countries to strengthen their non-proliferation credentials by a mutual process of accepting FSS. Their nuclear facilities were opened up to each other, and a bi-lateral nuclear verification organisation was created, the Argentine-Brazilian Agency for Accounting and Control of Nuclear Materials [ABAAC]. This arrangement has some similarities to the EURATOM safeguards system. Both states and ABAAC have signed a full-scope safeguards agreement with the IAEA, and its effect is to open all nuclear facilities in Argentina and Brazil to both mutual and international inspection, effectively removing both states from the list of proliferation suspects.

The Korean peninsula is a second area where a bi-lateral verification agreement appears likely to play a key role in reinforcing the non-proliferation situation. South Korea had a plutonium separation plant under construction in the early 1970s, but abandoned it when it became an NPT party in 1975 and completed its safeguards agreement with the IAEA. North Korea acceded to the NPT in 1985, but made little attempt to sign rapidly its mandatory safeguards agreement with the IAEA. Information then emerged that North Korea was constructing a series of gas/graphite reactors, similar to the British Calder Hall type, and allegations were made that it was building a reprocessing plant also.

North Korea linked its acceptance of its IAEA safeguards agreement with the withdrawal of US nuclear weapons from bases in South Korea. When this withdrawal occurred as part of global redeployment and reductions in its nuclear weapons, it opened the way to the North accepting and ratifying its IAEA safeguards agreement. However, to stabilise the nuclear situation in the peninsula further, this has been linked to a mutual inspection régime encompassing nuclear facilities and military bases which formerly held nuclear weapons. Although an outline agreement on this has been signed, negotiations are still proceeding on its implementation. In addition, it has been proposed that both states should refrain from reprocessing and enrichment activities, though North Korea appears to have linked this with external assistance in building and operating light-water reactors. Such an agreement may have some significance also for Japan's programme to reprocess and utilise plutonium in its fuel cycle.

There have been suggestions that similar regional fuel cycle and safeguarding arrangements may offer a means of meeting nuclear non-proliferation concerns involving India and Pakistan. Pakistan has made a series of such proposals. However, the nuclear-weapon status of China makes it unlikely that there can be significant progress on such arrangements in this region until a method can be found to resolve or evade this problem.

The development of regional non-proliferation arrangements has thus been a strategy utilised in several instances over the last three years to deal with proliferation concerns. It remains to be seen whether additional regions could use the same strategy to reduce their nuclear proliferation problems.

THE CONSEQUENCES OF THE DISSOLUTION OF THE SOVIET UNION

The break-up of the former Soviet Union into 15 republics has generated new challenges for the nuclear non-proliferation régime. At least four issues relevant to nuclear non-proliferation have arisen since the Union was dissolved at the end of 1991: the security of nuclear warheads; NPT membership and IAEA safeguards; export controls and the dissemination of nuclear knowledge; and the disposal of nuclear warheads.

Nuclear weapons, particularly small, easily transportable tactical ones, were present in most Soviet republics in 1991. Ensuring that only one of the republics, Russia, remained a nuclear weapon state at the end of the process of dissolution,

while the others all acceded to the NPT as non-nuclear weapon
states, was the immediate non-proliferation objective in 1992.
The Alma-Ata Declaration and the Minsk Agreement of
December 1991 provided a constructive basis for achieving this
objective.[3] During the early part of 1992, intensive activity
occurred to transfer the tactical nuclear warheads to Russia.

By mid-1992, nuclear warheads remained in only four
republics Russia: Belarus; Kazakhstan; and the Ukraine. Those
in the latter three republics were all for strategic systems. These
warheads do not have to be removed to Russia before 1999,
however, under the terms of a protocol to the START agreement between Russia and the United States in May 1992.
Custody over these warheads is held nominally by the
Commonwealth of Independent States (CIS), a unique legal
and semi-state entity, with the final decision over their use
retained by the President of Russia.

By any calculation, the world has been very fortunate that
the break-up of a nuclear weapon state with its arsenal of 25,000
plus warheads has not yet produced situations where some of
these warheads have moved outside central control. The danger
of loss of central control over tactical weapons appears to have
passed, but hundreds of strategic weapons are likely to remain
outside Russia and nominally under the control of the CIS for
some years to come. At the same time, any fission of Russia
would generate a fresh set of concerns similar to those that
existed at the time the Union dissolved.

The existence of the CIS has given its member republics other
than Russia the legal ability to accede to the NPT as non-nuclear
weapon states. Although the Ukraine promised to accede to the
NPT by September 1992, it did not do so. Belarus and
Kazakhstan were similarly committed to accede 'as soon as possible', Azerbaijan, Estonia, Latvia, Lithuania and Uzbekistan
had acceded to the NPT by November 1992, while Russia
acquired the Soviet Union's depository and nuclear weapon status by succession. However, these commitments mask two
significant causes for concern. One is that strategic nuclear
weapons in republics other than Russia may be perceived to
enhance state security against the nuclear-weapon Russian state
and to provide political leverage in the search for economic
assistance from the industrialised democracies. The second is

that the Ukraine, and possibly some of the other republics, have sought to lay claims to a proportion of the value of the *fissile materials* in all the former Soviet weapons, in the light of their claims to be successor states to the USSR. The agreement between Russia and the Ukraine dealing with Ukrainian access to the weapon dismantling process may also relate to rights of ownership over materials contained within retired weapons.

Although the IAEA had been given the opportunity to place under its safeguards all civil nuclear facilities or materials within the boundaries of the former Soviet Union under the terms of the IAEA-USSR nuclear-weapon state voluntary safeguards agreement, the IAEA had actually applied safeguards to very few of them. The accession of the non-nuclear weapon republics of the CIS to the NPT has and will generate a priority to have them negotiate an INFCIRC/153 safeguards agreement with the IAEA. The Agency will then be faced with the need to expand its safeguards activities to nuclear power plants and other facilities in several of the republics, particularly the Ukraine. This will involve a heavy workload, including the need to verify the initial inventory of nuclear materials in these states, in a situation where the financial resources available to the Agency are likely to be stretched. It also poses the question of whether there may be merit in encouraging a CISATOM system of transnational ownership, control and safeguarding of peaceful nuclear activities in these states, along the lines of EURATOM.

The collapse of the Soviet Union has created a need to replace its centralised nuclear export control system with one based on the individual republics and geared to free market conditions. Similar needs exist in some Eastern European states. Attempts have been made by the Nuclear Suppliers Group and the Group of Seven to assist in this process by supplying information and expertise. In addition, the setting up of science and technology centres in Moscow and Kiev may help to alleviate this latter problem. Specialists will also be retained in Russia if the nuclear complexes continue to function, and can be funded by preferential treatment over exports of natural and enriched uranium, and enrichment and other fuel cycle services. But there remains a long term risk that, without such an export control framework and continuing support for Russian and other CIS nuclear energy activities, nuclear materials, technology and specialists may leave the area in return for hard currency.

This issue has close links to the fate of the warheads retired from the former Soviet arsenal. The initial Russian policy appeared to involve storing them indefinitely in a disabled, but relatively intact form, in a new facility to be built at Tomsk, so long as high explosive safety considerations allowed this. This was seen to offer two non-proliferation advantages: it allowed Russia to earn hard currency for current production of uranium and for fuel cycle services and it prevented the nuclear fuel market being flooded by fissile materials released from weapons. Such a policy would have served also to sustain the Russian nuclear complex and made it easier to verify that no materials from weapons were unaccounted for, especially crucial non-nuclear components.

The process of dismantling warheads in Russia will take many years, if not decades to accomplish, and involve a considerable input of resources. In September 1992, Russia and the United States reached an agreement under which the former was to supply to the latter high enriched uranium to be fed into United States plants enriching uranium for civil fuel applications. This would serve the dual ends of diluting the Russian material down to 4 per cent enriched and reducing the cost of the United States output. Some 500 tons of weapon grade High Enriched Uranium [HEU] will be disposed of under this arrangement, if it was ever to be fully implemented. It is assumed that the majority of the material will come from the dismantling of nuclear warheads within Russia.

The weapon-grade plutonium from these warheads is likely to be stored initially, as its disposal poses an intrinsically more difficult problem than HEU. Three methods are potentially available for its disposal: burning in specially constructed fast reactors or as MOX fuel in existing thermal power reactors; permanent disposal deep underground, either separated from weapons and mixed with high active waste or through nuclear explosive techniques; or long-term secure storage in a similar manner to separated plutonium from civil reactors. Japan is probably the state most interested in assisting the USSR developing techniques for disposing of the plutonium in power reactors.

In all these options, arguments among the CIS states over the ownership of the materials seem likely to play a major role. The IAEA may also be called upon to apply safeguards if the material is designated for peaceful use. But the central dilemma that is now presenting itself is that arguments for indefinite storage in disabled form appear to be increasingly persuasive on cost, verification and risks of component and fissile materials proliferation grounds. Yet such storage will be seen to allow the warheads to be reactivated with a minimum of effort, and could have significant adverse security implications, as well as raising concerns over 'phoney' disarmament. It also provides no opportunities to sell materials from the warheads for legitimate purposes, which in turn would provide resources to sustain the dismantling and safeguarding processes and maintain the nuclear complex intact.

The non-proliferation problems posed by the collapse of the Soviet Union will require major policy initiatives and large injections of resources from the advanced industrial states if they are to be resolved. They will also require a significant expansion of the $60 million safeguards budget of the IAEA. The positive side of these developments, however, is that by the time the NPT Extension Conference assembles in 1995, the issue which contributed to the failure of the 1990 Review Conference, demands for a Comprehensive Test Ban Treaty (CTBT), may appear relatively less significant in the light of the nuclear weapon reductions being implemented by Russia and the United States.

THE CHANGED NUCLEAR NON-PROLIFERATION CONTEXT: EXTENSION OF THE NPT IN 1995

The basis of the current global nuclear non-proliferation system is the NPT, the only global legal instrument through which states can renounce formally their possession of nuclear weapons.[4] The Treaty stipulates that in 1995 a conference will convene to decide on the period that the NPT should be extended beyond that date. This extension conference presents something of a procedural nightmare as the Treaty itself, and general treaty law, offer few guides in that regard for its conduct.[5] What is clear, however, is that the Iraqi experience has assisted in creating a situation where the United States and its industrialised allies could probably vote through an indefinite extension of the Treaty despite opposition from any vocal minority of developing states.

There are good grounds for arguing, however, that a consensus decision would serve to strengthen the non-proliferation régime whereas voting might weaken it by appearing to demonstrate the existence of irreconcilable differences. A consensus decision, however, will necessitate agreement on three of the key agenda issues at past NPT review conferences: the nuclear disarmament provisions of Article VI; security assurances to non-nuclear weapon states; and the provisions for access by the developing world to nuclear energy under Article IV.

Article VI of the NPT commits *all* parties, 'to pursue negotiations in good faith on effective measures relating to cessation of the nuclear arms race at an early date and to nuclear disarmament, and on a treaty on general and complete disarmament under strict and effective international control.' Its political and symbolic significance is that it serves to ameliorate what would otherwise be a discriminatory treaty which denies nuclear weapons to all but five states. Debate in 1995 over this matter will take place in a radically changed context. All five declared nuclear weapon states will be present for the first time at an NPT conference. Moreover, it will be difficult to argue that 'the nuclear arms race', which was traditionally interpreted by the non-aligned movement as the United States-Soviet Union nuclear relationship, is still continuing, if only because the Soviet Union no longer exists. Third, unlike the situation in 1990, France, Russia, the United Kingdom and the United States will be able to point to reductions in their nuclear weapon stockpiles, and will undoubtedly argue that they have more than fulfilled their obligations under the Treaty.

Notes of discord seem likely to emerge from three quarters. One is the issue of a ban on nuclear testing. France, Russia and the United States have suspended testing to the end of 1992, and the US Congress has voted through a plan to terminate testing by the United States after 1996, and in the meantime limit testing to a small annual quota for safety purposes only. However, it remains uncertain whether a serious attempt will be made to negotiate CTBT before 1995, despite the technical and political arguments for and against a testing ban being more finely balanced than in the past.[6] Thus although this measure is likely to have only a limited impact on 'the nuclear arms race . . . and nuclear disarmament' it seems inevitable that it will remain the centre of the political argument over this Article.

A second area of discord may be over a cut-off in production of fissile materials for military purposes by the five nuclear-weapon states. The implication of this is that it would permit them to accept the application of IAEA safeguards over all of the reactors and enrichment plants on their territories [procedures already exist for dealing with nuclear submarine fuel in this context], and thus strengthen the attempts of the IAEA to foster greater transparency in nuclear activities, as well as placing an upper limit on the future nuclear weapon stockpiles of the five states. While the United States and France appear to be in a position to accept an international agreement binding themselves to such a policy, and the Russian Foreign Ministry also appears to favour it, the position of the Russian Ministry of Atomic Energy, the United Kingdom and China remains unclear. Making an agreement on this issue to ameliorate any possible criticism over the lack of progress on a testing ban may be a very attractive option for France, Russia and the United States, and thus leave the United Kingdom in a very exposed position.

A third area of new debate seems likely to be the issue of a 'treaty on general and complete disarmament'. The European states will doubtless point to the reduction in nuclear and conventional disarmament levels in Europe and demand similar reductions in other regions. But the more divisive issue likely to emerge around this phrase may be a demand by many NPT parties for a clear commitment by the nuclear weapon states to a timetable for their nuclear disarmament. This issue could also become merged with debates on a CTBT, as one key argument against a testing ban is the need to maintain indefinitely nuclear weapon stockpiles.

Two totally novel developments could occur over this issue. One relates to possible pressures on Russia from the other CIS republics to commit itself to nuclear disarmament in order to remove threats to themselves which might otherwise force them in the direction of nuclear proliferation. A second is a possible overt demand by Japan, Germany and other Western European states, Ukraine and Kazakhstan for a timetable for disarmament arising from the radically changed security environment. Since the latter two portray themselves as the third and fourth nuclear weapons states in size in 1992, yet are committed to nuclear disarmament, this could generate a totally new set of political alignments over this issue, with unpredictable consequences. In addition, there may even be a return to the debates of the 1950s over whether it would be desirable for the UN Security Council to have access to nuclear weapons in any eventual nuclear disarmed world. This suggests that the debate on Article VI is likely to focus more on the long term aspects of nuclear disarmament than the short term question of a CTBT.

Although the NPT contains no security assurances, they have always been seen as an important element of the nuclear non-proliferation régime pending the achievement of global nuclear disarmament. Such assurances have been of two types: positive assurances that the nuclear weapon states would intervene in the event of an attack with nuclear weapons upon a non-nuclear weapon state; and negative assurances by the nuclear weapon states, guaranteeing that they would not use nuclear weapons against non-nuclear weapon parties. Positive assurances have been made via a UN Security Council Resolution of 1968, which covered the position of the three NPT depositary states. Negative declarations have been made through unilateral statements at the First United Nations Special Session on Disarmament (UNSSOD I) in 1978 and the Second Special Session (UNSSOD II) in 1982. Only China's negative security declaration is unconditional, due to complications arising from, among other things, the nature of pre-1991 military doctrines for the defence of Western Europe and South Korea.

The changed international context makes it possible to contemplate further security assurances to strengthen the nuclear non-proliferation régime. The accession of China and France to the NPT clears the way for a new UN Security Council Resolution on positive assurances subscribed to by all the nuclear weapon states, not just the NPT depositaries. This might be linked to a strengthened statement defining proliferation as a threat to the peace. Moreover, it now seems possible for all the nuclear weapon states to subscribe to an unconditional collective negative security assurance to replace the five unilateral ones. Given existing requests for security assurances from many CIS and Eastern European states, such innovations could be an issue generating very wide international support. All of this should contribute to perceptions of the substantive security value of being an NPT non-nuclear weapon state party.

One core assumption underpinning the NPT has always been that peaceful and military nuclear activities can be clearly distinguished, and that international arrangements can be devised to provide assurances of the peaceful use of all nuclear materials within a non-nuclear weapon state. In theory, this should leave parties free to transfer all types of nuclear technology and materials to others. In practice, this right has been constrained both by the cost of nuclear power programmes and the conscious decision of supplier states to refrain from exporting 'sensitive' technologies, such as uranium enrichment and plutonium separation plants or their components.

To date, this has been more of an irritant than an issue, as perceptions of nuclear energy as an economic and safe source of electricity have declined in the industrialised world. The recent agreement to constrain dual-use technologies may serve to enhance sensitivities to the political symbolism attached to this matter, however, and marshal support for viewing the implementation of Article IV as a prime example of discrimination against the developing world. The degree to which this becomes an issue could be affected by two developments: the evolution of UN Security Council constraints upon Iraq; and of the re-emergence of a 'war on plutonium'. The UN Security Council has denied to Iraq, an NPT party which has breached its obligations under the Treaty, all rights to develop and use nuclear energy for other than medical and agricultural purposes. Iraq is already seeking to have these constraints removed on the grounds that they are unduly discriminatory.

This complaint may find resonances in other areas of the developing world if the suspicion grows that the industrialised states consider the most effective non-proliferation policy is to deny access to nuclear energy to developing states. A sensitive test-case is likely to be Iran's attempts to revive the ambitious programme of nuclear power reactors which were under construction in the 1970s. Iran is currently engaged in arbitration against German firms who are refusing to finish the construction of nuclear reactors started in the pre-revolutionary era. Policy-makers in industrialised states are reluctant to accept the risk that, despite IAEA safeguards, a future Iranian government might divert large quantities of fissile material from its power reactor programme to weapon use. Thus the conflict between the rights of developing states to have unconstrained access to the technologies they may feel are necessary for their economic development, and the desire of industrialised states never again to provide assistance for clandestine nuclear weapon programmes in such states, may prove very divisive. A further complication is that both Russia and China are now engaged in negotiations to build safeguarded reactors in Iran, and in several other states suspected of having proliferation aspirations, and thus their position on the tacit denial of nuclear energy facilities to potential proliferators is uncertain.

The re-emergence of a new Western 'war on plutonium', following the one inspired by the Carter Administration in the late 1970s, rests on the technical argument that the non-proliferation situation would be strengthened if a universal ban on all plutonium reprocessing technology and operations was agreed, with irradiated nuclear fuel being stored indefinitely and not reprocessed. Constraints on indigenous reprocessing may be a means of strengthening security in the Korean Peninsula, but contrast starkly with Japan's policy of sending fuel to Europe for reprocessing and for repatriation of its plutonium content to use in fast-breeder development and in MOX fuel. The original aim of this programme was to enhance the energy security of Japan. But the current price of uranium ore means this could now be achieved more cheaply by purchasing this raw material and placing it in a strategic stockpile. However, large investments in plant have been made in pursuit of the plutonium recycling policy and changing direction will be difficult, even though transportation of plutonium by sea between Europe and Japan will be politically very sensitive.

A development that could be linked to this issue is the disposal of fissile materials arising from the military stockpile in Russia. This process may require methods for neutralising and disposing of several tens of tons of weapon-grade plutonium.

Japan has already proposed that it should build a fast reactor to burn Russia's surplus plutonium, while Russia itself is proposing to complete a MOX fuel plant to allow recycling of plutonium from its own civil fuel. The interaction of all these developments could generate significant friction among industrialised states, which may spill over into the 1995 conference. Conversely, it may serve the positive role of stimulating a new evaluation of the merits of International Plutonium Storage (IPS), whereby the material would be transferred into the custody of the IAEA and only released to the state owning it for agreed purposes.

Finally, two debates over the objectives and instruments of the non-proliferation system that started in the 1970s seem destined to dominate the NPT conference in 1995, even if the context for them and the diplomatic alignments around them are new. The first is whether the ultimate and logical object of the Treaty, and the non-proliferation system, is to disarm the existing nuclear weapon states down to the level of the existing industrialised non-nuclear weapon states, such as Japan and Germany. The new feature of this debate may be that released from the security bonds of the East-West security confrontation, Germany and Japan, as well as Ukraine, Kazakhstan and Belarus may be in the front rank of those pressing the nuclear weapon states for such a long term commitment, rather than, as in the past, developing states such as Mexico.

The second debate is whether the conceptual basis of the non-proliferation régime should remain the twin distinctions between explosive and non-explosive uses of nuclear energy and its peaceful and military applications. Pressures are now arising to move the basis of the régime to include the outlawing of all reprocessing and production of plutonium and highly enriched uranium (HEU), in order to overcome the lack of a technical guarantee that such fissile materials will not be used for military purposes.

CONCLUSIONS

Does the changed context spelt out above represent a better prospect for non-proliferation than prior to 1990? The answer appears to be yes. The end of the Cold War, the consequences of Iraq's attack on Kuwait and the newly discovered harmony among nuclear supplier nations facilitated by the changed French position have combined to produce a much-needed stimulus to the global non-proliferation system. The IAEA safeguards system is being overhauled and modified to meet the challenges of the 1990s, a full spectrum of nuclear export controls is now in place and FSS is an almost universally accepted condition for nuclear supply. More specifically France and China are now formally part of the NPT non-proliferation régime, while Argentina, Brazil and South Africa have also removed themselves from the list of states with significant nuclear activities which do not accept full scope safeguards, leaving only India, Israel and Pakistan on that list. Problems still remain on the Korean peninsula, but they too may be susceptible to a regional solution. Finally, despite the Iraqi case, it appears that the list of states which might mount a similar clandestine nuclear programme over the next decade is very short, if it exists at all.

Unfortunately, while the old proliferation agenda may be well on its way to being liquidated, a new one is appearing. The most obvious items on this are the future of the nuclear warheads, materials and industry in the former USSR. While the more immediate concerns over this have been ameliorated, longer term problems still remain in terms of the security relations between the republics formerly comprising the USSR, and the action to be taken to implement nuclear disarmament and to dispose of retired nuclear weapons and the components and materials in them. Of wider concern, however, may be the three more conceptual choices and issues that could complicate the process of arriving at a satisfactory outcome to the NPT extension conference in 1995: an imposed non-proliferation régime rather than a consensual one; an aim of total nuclear disarmament rather than just preventing proliferation; and the attempt to limit the technical risks of proliferation by denying nuclear capabilities, or certain specific ones such as plutonium separation facilities, to all or some states.

Notes

1 This is a revised version of a paper first presented to the Annual Symposium of the Uranium Institute of London in September 1992. The papers from this symposium will be reproduced in *Proceedings of the Seventeenth International Symposium held by the Uranium Institute, September 1992* [London: Uranium Institute, 1993.

2 The remainder of this section relies heavily upon information contained in D Fischer, B Sanders, L Scheinman and G Bunn *A New Nuclear Triad: The Non-Proliferation of Nuclear Weapons, International Verification and the International Atomic Energy Agency*, PPNN Study 3, September 1992 [Southampton: The Mountbatten Centre for International Studies for the Programme for Promoting Nuclear Non-Proliferation].

3 For translations of the texts of these agreements, see *PPNN Newsbrief 16*, Winter 1991/92, pp. 15–16.

4 155 states are currently party to the NPT. Accessions since January 1992 include Azerbaijan, China, Estonia, France, Latvia, Namibia, Niger, Slovenia and Uzbekistan.

5 For an overview of the issues related to the NPT's extension in 1995 see, G. Bunn, C.N. Van Doren and D. Fischer, 'Options & Opportunities: The NPT Extension Conference of 1995,' *PPNN Study 2*, November 1991, [Southampton: The Mountbatten Centre for International Studies for the Programme for Promoting Nuclear Non-Proliferation].

6 For an overview to the nuclear testing debate see, D. Howlett and J. Simpson, 'The NPT and the CTBT: an Inextricable Relationship?', *Issue Review*, No. 1, March 1992, [Southampton: The Mountbatten Centre for International Studies for Programme for Promoting Nuclear Non-Proliferation].

15

A New Era in Arms Control Verification?

PATRICIA M LEWIS

Director, Verification Technology Information Centre, London

The world of arms control is in a state of flux. Although it has never been more needed, there is a school of thought which believes that because the Cold War is over, arms control is dead and if arms control is dead, do we really need all this verification business? This line of thinking is erroneous and if it is not challenged, it will lead us into trouble. It is inhibiting the development of new ideas and turning government ministries and funding bodies away from putting resources into the field of arms control and verification. This chapter explores the reasoning behind the myth and looks at ways to counter it.

The chapter sets out the current status of arms control verification. It investigates the reasons for the move away from a thorough inspection régime for the Chemical Weapons Convention (despite the lessons of the UN Special Commission inspection teams in Iraq) and it looks at the future for verification and monitoring in arms control.

WHAT IS VERIFICATION?

Verification is '. . . a process which establishes whether the States parties are complying with their obligations under an agreement. The process includes the collection of information relevant to obligations under arms limitation and disarmament agreements; analysis of the information; and reaching a judgement as to whether the specific terms of an agreement are being met.'[1]

There is no such thing as 100 per cent certainty in verification. It is not possible to say without any doubt that a particular activity is not occurring anywhere. The important role of verification is to ensure that a party contemplating cheating on a treaty cannot do so without running a substantial risk of being discovered.

Verification serves to deter cheating. It does this by employing strict measures which are designed to catch an evader within sufficient time to be able to respond appropriately. It also serves to build confidence in an agreement, which is achieved by allowing states actively to demonstrate their compliance with it. This in turn strengthens the agreement and can encourage other states to sign up as they see it working. The third function of verification is to increase the security of states party to the agreement. This is achieved by cooperation between the parties and increased transparency, leading to increased knowledge of other states capabilities and intentions.

Verification is contingent upon treaties and agreements. For every treaty entered into with a verification régime, that régime is tailored to it. Thus verification régimes reflect the structure of the treaties by which they are governed. A multinational agreement is verified either by a multilateral agency (as in the case of the Non-Proliferation Treaty (NPT)) or by the states party to the agreement acting as individuals, as, for example, the Stockholm Accord on Confidence and Security Building measures in Europe. A bilateral treaty, as its name implies, is verified by two states only, as in the Strategic Arms Limitations Treaties (SALT) and the Intermediate Nuclear Forces Treaty (INF).

Although there is a difference between verification and monitoring, this difference is increasingly obscure. Monitoring – the open collection of information – can be part of the verification process or it can be quite separate. For example, the 1992 multilateral Open Skies agreement is an accord which deals solely in monitoring (details of this treaty are given below). The trend for verification is likely to be an increase in agreements set up purely for monitoring for its own sake rather than to verify a set of numbers and reductions. For example, the proposal for an international arms register[2] is a measure to monitor the transfer of arms world-wide. The register does not seek to restrict or control the arms trade[3;] rather it would increase the low level of transparency and provide a warning of dangerous military build-ups.

CURRENT STATUS

There are a number of treaties which are currently in effect with verification regimes. There are also treaties which have been negotiated but have yet to take effect and there are those still in negotiation. In addition there are a number of unilateral declarations and measures which need some form of checking. A summary of these agreements, negotiations and measures is given in the tables on pages 240 and 241.

LESSONS FROM IRAQ

Following the 1991 Gulf War, it became clear that not only had Iraq developed chemical weapons (used in the Iraq-Iran war against the Kurds) and ballistic missiles (used in the 1991 war) but it had biological and nuclear weapons programmes far in advance of previous predictions. In April 1991, the UN Security Council, in Resolution 687, demanded the destruction of all Iraq's nuclear capability and of all its other weapons of mass destruction. In order to find all of the weaponry and related facilities and material, the UN set up a Special Commission (UNSCOM) of inspectors who visited Iraq throughout 1991 and 1992. The inspections of nuclear facilities were carried out by IAEA inspectors.

The inspections encountered a varying degree of compliance with Resolution 687. On some sorties inspectors were well received and Iraqi personnel relatively helpful. On other occasions the inspectors were met with hostility and were denied access to facilities, buildings and information. On one spectacular occasion IAEA inspectors were fired on when, on being denied access to Al-Fallujah, they followed a convoy of trucks which had been seen leaving via a back exit. On another occasion IAEA inspectors were detained in a car-park for four days whilst Iraq denied their right to leave with documents they had copied.

Table 15.1 *Current Agreement/Measure Verification*

	Treaty means	Verification
1925	Geneva Protocol	None – but UN Sec Gen Fact-Finding Missions
1963	Partial Test Ban	None – but NTM & Radiation Network Monitor
1968	Non-Proliferation	IAEA Safeguards
1972	Biological WPNS	None – but to be remedied
1972	Strategic Arms Limit – 1	National Tech Means
1972	Anti Ballistic Missile	NTM
1974	Threshold Test Ban (ratified 1990)	NTM OSI
1976	Peaceful Nuclear Explosions	NTM OSI (ratified 1990)
1979	Strategic Arms Limit – 2	NTM
1986	Stockholm Accord	OSI
1987	Intermediate Nuclear Forces Monitoring (PPM)	NTM & OSI Portal Perimeter
1990	Conventional Forces in Europe	NTM, MTM, OSI, AERIAL
1991	Strategic Arms Reduction (Start)	OSI, NTM, PPM
1991/2	Short Range Nuclear Forces	OSI, NTM
1992	Open Skies	Aerial Overflights

Notes: NTM = National Technical Means, MTM = Multinational Technical Means, OSI = On-Site Inspections, PPM = Portal Perimeter Monitoring, IAEA = International Atomic Energy Agency.

Table 15.2 *Future Agreement/Measure Verification*

	Treaty means	Verification
1993	Strategic Arms Reduction II *Bi-, Multilateral*	NTM, MTM, OSI
1993?	Chemical Weapons Conventional *Multilateral*	OSI, NTN
1994?	Conventional forces *Multilateral*	NTM, MTM, OSI, PPM
1994–6?	Comprehensive Test Ban *Multilateral*	NTM, OSI, AERIAL, Seismic & Radiation Networks

Notes: NTM = National Technical Means, MTM = Multinational Technical Means, OSI = On-Site Inspections, PPM = Portal Perimeter Monitoring.

Because of such disputes, the United States made various threats throughout 1991 and 1992 to attack Iraq unless it complied fully with Resolution 687. These threats were taken seriously by the Western media and seemingly by Iraq which backed down on each occasion and provided UNSCOM with the material required. The threatened use of force reached its height in March 1992 when the US sent the carrier USS *America* into the Gulf, escorted by the Aegis-class cruiser *Normandy* both carrying Tomahawk cruise missiles (several other US warships were also in the region)[4]. In addition to the 140 planes still in Saudi Arabia, the US sent an additional six B52 bombers to Britain. The Pentagon then let it be known that they had presented President Bush with a set of military options for a graduated bombing campaign to force Iraq to comply with the destruction of all its nuclear, chemical and ballistic missile facilities.[5] Several non-military options were also considered, including the seizure of Iraqi assets frozen on the invasion of Kuwait.[6] Iraq soon capitulated. However, it should be noted that General Colin Powell opposed the use of force as did other military planners. A senior British officer said 'The UN may get a report that trucks are going into a building late at night and it takes a month for that report to reach us. By the time we have checked it out, it may still be a plant for chemical weapons or it may have turned into a food warehouse. We simply do not have the real-time intelligence to avoid making a terrible mistake'.[7]

The threatened use of force is a dangerous precedent to set in the world of arms control. In the case of Iraq, the threats, although ostensibly made because of failure to comply with Resolution 687 and the UNSCOM inspections, were probably more connected to the unfinished business of the Gulf war which left Saddam Hussein in power. Nonetheless, such threats could only be made against a nation which was incapable of retaliation. For example, during the height of the Cold War the US would never have threatened to bomb the Krasnoyarsk radar which was in breach of the ABM treaty however flagrantly the Soviet Union refused to comply with the treaty. To have made such threats would have been folly. This leaves us with the uncomfortable conclusion that a large, well-armed nation would not be subjected to the same pressures as a smaller vanquished nation if it decides to cheat on a treaty. Such a situation could lead to further resentments from countries which are already sensitive to discrimination in the non-proliferation treaty and it could lead to a further reluctance to participate in multilateral treaties.

The most significant lessons to be learned from the UNSCOM inspections of Iraq, however, are the clear failure of the NPT in Iraq and the highly intrusive and intensive inspection effort which is needed to root out clandestine weapon development.

Iraq has been a signatory to the NPT since 1969 and has always complied with the declarations and inspection requests required of it by the IAEA. Prior to the Gulf War, the IAEA sent a team of inspectors to Iraq who found that Iraq was in compliance. In reality, however, even before the full extent of the Iraqi nuclear weapon programme was discovered, most analysts believed that Iraq was on the road to developing a nuclear bomb. In other words NPT-watchers were aware that the IAEA safeguards did not protect against a nation intent on developing a clandestine weapon. In the end, the safeguarded nuclear material was not the key factor in the weapons programme and the type of separation technology which Iraq had developed was a type long since discarded by the main nuclear powers because of its inefficiency. In this way, and with the help of governments and industries which had a vested in turning a blind eye, Iraq was able to go much further than the safeguards régime of the IAEA (as it stood then) could be expected to detect.

The extent of the Iraqi nuclear programme and its chemical, biological weapons and ballistic missiles development came as a shock to the world: not so much that they existed but that they were so far advanced. The state of the military programmes would never have been discovered if the UNSCOM and IAEA inspectors had not been able to visit Iraq extensively at very short notice with the powers to inspect wherever they wished. That the UN/IAEA inspectors had such rights allowed them (eventually) access to ministry buildings and suspect sites all over the country. Because the Iraqi leaders were clearly intent upon hiding as much as they could get away with, the inspectors would never have discovered the true state of the programmes, had they not had those rights. In addition UNSCOM and the IAEA were given information from intelligence sources so that they were able to target their inspection effort effectively. This intelligence allowed the inspections to focus on key facilities and enabled the timing of inspections to be well planned. Although future inspection régimes will not be able to have the same *carte blanche*, the experience will be applicable. One of the main lessons from the post-Gulf war experience in Iraq is that, if we are ever to discover clandestine activities, on-site inspections must be as truly comprehensive and as intrusive as possible. Inspection régimes must also be coupled with good intelligence gleaned from a variety of sources (satellite remote sensing, signals intelligence, human intelligence etc.).

THE IAEA AND THE NPT

Confidence in the NPT and the ability of the IAEA safeguards to detect non-compliance took a severe blow not only from the post-war discovery of Iraq's activities but also from North Korea's steadfast refusals to submit to IAEA inspections.[8] North Korea eventually signed a safeguards agreement with the IAEA in January 1992, ratified the agreement in April 1992 and the first inspection took place in June. This was after strong pressure from the USA, South Korea and Japan. It remains to be seen how effective these inspections will prove at preventing a nuclear arms race in the region.

Although the IAEA safeguards were not designed to prevent the type of clandestine activity carried out by Iraq, the IAEA nonetheless acted as though they could adequately verify the NPT. Since the UNSCOM operation, there have been calls to relieve the IAEA of the responsibility for verification of the NPT but others point out that such action would be *'throwing the baby out with the bath water'*. However the IAEA safeguards régime clearly needs a complete overhaul.

Recent work[9] by Owen Greene makes proposals for the way in which the IAEA can be substantially reformed to create an enhanced full-scope safeguards system and effective special inspections arrangements. Greene's proposals include: the requirement that preliminary information on new nuclear facilities or modifications to existing facilities should be provided to the IAEA as soon as a decision to authorise construction has been made (this proposal has been taken up by the IAEA since February 1992[10]); the establishment of improved transparency and a universal system of reporting imports, exports and production of all nuclear materials (including ore concentrates) and of sensitive non-nuclear material and equipment; increasing the capacity frequent inspections at declared facilities; reduction by approximately 50 per cent in the amount of material deemed to constitute a 'significant quantity' of fissile material; changes in the inspection guidelines, so that a nation's overall nuclear programme is monitored; the establishment of a special unit in the IAEA which can receive intelligence reports; special inspection procedures which ensure that the inspections are carried out quickly under the instruction of the IAEA Director-General; substantially increasing the IAEA safeguards budget; and reforming the *'Diplomatic Culture'* at the IAEA.

The NPT reaches a cross-roads in 1995. This is the point at which it has to be decided for how long the treaty should be extended. Not only will the safeguards régime have to be significantly strengthened by then but progress on Article VI – which requires the nuclear-weapons states party to the NPT (which now include France and China) to end the nuclear arms race – must have been made. Traditionally this article is linked to progress on a Comprehensive Test Ban Treaty (CTBT). As discussed below, recent moves in France, Russia and the USA mean that this is more likely than it has been for some years. If progress in the IAEA and on the issue of a CTBT continues, then the future of the NPT starts to look more secure.

A COMPREHENSIVE TEST BAN TREATY

Over the years, there have been many attempts to negotiate a CTBT. In 1963, after a meeting in Moscow lasting ten days, Britain, the United States and the Soviet Union concluded a treaty banning all tests above ground. That Partial Test Ban Treaty has now been ratified by 119 countries and, although not parties to it, France and China also observe its conditions. Since that time, there have been a number of abortive attempts at negotiating a CTBT. From 1977 to 1980, the US, Britain and the USSR tried yet again to negotiate a test ban but, in 1982, the US broke off the negotiations. For 19 months, from August 1985, the Soviet Union, in an attempt to stimulate talks for a CTB, placed a unilateral moratorium on nuclear testing but it was never reciprocated by the US or Britain.

In addition to the trilateral attempts, there has been a continuing battle at the 40-nation Conference on Disarmament in Geneva to achieve a negotiating mandate for a CTBT and since 1990 the Conference has a 'non-negotiating' mandate to address the possibility of a CTBT.

In 1989, frustrated by the outcome of these various fora, a group of states party to the 1963 Partial Test Ban, decided to exploit a clause in that treaty and to call for a conference to amend the 1963 treaty into a CTBT. The three Depository States (Britain, USA and USSR) were mandated to hold this conference, which took place in January 1991. There was no outcome from that conference other than to leave it open to be reconvened at a later date (the conference occurred at about the same time as the UN deadline for the withdrawal of Iraqi forces from Kuwait).

However in 1991–2, there were several moves which give rise

to the prediction that there will be a CTBT in the near future. In 1991, President Yeltsin announced a moratorium on nuclear testing in Russia. The testing site in Russia is the Arctic island, Novaya Zemlya (the previous USSR main test site is in Kazakhstan and is no longer available to Russia) and although the military have been allowed to start preparing the test site, the moratorium was further extended in 1992. In a surprise move, France announced a nuclear testing moratorium in April 1992 until the end of the year in order to 'inspire other countries to deal with nuclear proliferation'.[11]

The most significant move, however, came from the US Senate in September 1992, when President Bush, against his inclinations, signed the Energy and Water Development Appropriations Bill.[12] The legislation starts an immediate testing moratorium lasting until July 1 1993. After that date and up to 30 September 1996, the US can only conduct up to 15 safety-related tests, and a maximum of one reliability test per year if the President fulfils obligations such as starting CTBT negotiation. After 30 September 1996, the USA will not test again unless a foreign state conducts a test after this date. This legislation also affects Britain. Britain will only be allowed one test per year to be taken from the safety test quota and is not allowed to test during the 92/93 moratorium.

In addition, the election of President Clinton, who strongly supports a CTBT, ensures that the legislation will be carried out. Significantly, although Britain is directly affected by the legislation, the government seems to be taking the attitude of pretending that it will never happen.[13] In fact, sources in the Ministry of Defence have let it be known that they are actively working against the legislation. The MOD would be well advised to start actively working on the verification provisions required for a CTBT[14] and the restructuring of Aldermaston and retraining of Aldermaston scientists.

THE CHEMICAL WEAPONS AND BIOLOGICAL WEAPONS CONVENTIONS (CWC AND BWC)

1992 saw a breakthrough at the Geneva Conference on Disarmament (CD) when the participants adopted the CWC draft text. The text was to be voted on at the UN General Assembly in December 1992 and opened for signature in Paris in January 1993. The CD had been working on a Chemical Weapons Ban since 1980 although multilateral negotiations had been going on since 1968. Since the 1980s, when the USA had proposed the 'anytime, anywhere' standard for challenge on-site inspections, there have been major, shifts in position: so much so that it was the USA in 1991 along with Britain, Australia and Japan which put forward inspection proposals which fundamentally weakened the challenge inspection régime. The proposal was so complicated with respect to the agreements on the designation of a perimeter around the inspected site that a number of CD delegates devised a board game in order to explain the procedures to newcomers. More importantly, the changes to challenge inspections mean that the current delay between announcement of an inspection and the start of the actual inspection can be as much as seven days.[15]

It is hard to reconcile this softening in the approach to challenge inspections with the lessons learned from the UNSCOM in Iraq. As discussed above, time is of the essence when carrying out challenge inspections. Nevertheless, a CWC with a weaker verification régime is better than no CWC at all. However, it is difficult to reconcile why this weakening occurred at a time when the world has already seen the effect of a weak safeguards régime for the NPT and when the lack of a verification régime for BWC is being addressed.

Since the 1991 BWC Third Review Conference, the convention was strengthened with a series of Confidence-Building Measures (CBMs) and is currently undergoing a series of meetings; an 'Ad Hoc Group of Governmental Experts' to look at verification measures. The CBMs include detailed declarations, reports of disease outbreaks, publication of research and information on visits to research centres. The USA's position on the difficult issue of BWC verification has been that 'bad verification is worse than no verification'.[16] Such statements hardly concur with their attitude to CWC verification, or for that matter to the amount of money the US has been prepared to put into the United Nations and the IAEA.

UNILATERAL MEASURES

The progress of arms reductions is no longer characterised only by negotiations and treaties but also by unilateral measures. Unilateral moves (which may or may not be reciprocated) are the quickest and most effective way to achieve reductions.

Many such steps can be monitored adequately, by satellites (such as withdrawals of conventional forces and cuts in ballistic missile launchers) or other technical means (for example the 1985-88 Soviet unilateral moratorium was monitored by both satellites and by seismic detectors), but many cannot (such as the non-production of biological weapons).

Unilateral steps can often be part of, or a precursor to, or be related to negotiated agreements (for example the Czechoslovak moratorium on tank production and the USSR withdrawal of troops from Eastern Europe were both preliminary steps towards the Conventional Forces in Europe (CFE) treaty) in which case they can be monitored as part of the monitoring procedures for the agreement.

Another approach, which has many pitfalls but is better than no monitoring at all, is to declare unilateral reductions or to declare levels of stocks and allow other states to carry out ad hoc ground inspections as a token of good faith. These moves could be checked on a voluntary invitation basis, if the exact nature of the changes is declared in detail. For example, prior to the CFE agreement, the USSR started withdrawing troops from Eastern Europe and the USA also began similar action. Neither of these moves was verified, but President Gorbachev invited the West to send observers in order to witness the withdrawals and the Western media were in full attendance for the first phase of Soviet tank divisions leaving Eastern Germany.

This gesture was never put to the test however, because the USA's response was that such a proposal was old and diversionary.[17] There could be several reasons for this negative reaction. One reason could be the nature of the inspections. In 1987, representatives from states participating in the Chemical Weapons Convention negotiations in Geneva visited the Soviet Chemical Weapons Research Station at Shikhany.[18] Although the visit was successful, in that the USSR was encouraged further in openness, there were several problems arising from the visit, such as the absence of any modern chemical munitions on display.[19] Later Britain was invited by the USSR to visit the Shikhany facilities as part of an exchange of visits between the experts from Shikhany and from the British Chemical Defence Establishment at Porton Down. The British visit was treated in a similar way to an on-site inspection and included an overflight of the area and visits to requested buildings.[20] However, one incident marred the visit and brought into stark relief the type of problems which can occur on invited visits (and on bone fide on-site inspections for that matter). British delegates requested that they be allowed to visit a complex which was linked by road to the Shikhany site and showed a satellite photograph (taken by the French commercial satellite SPOT) clearly depicting the complex and linkage.[21] Their request was refused and the outcome has been used by the British government as a example of why it is not particularly wise to visit facilities by invitation, rather than as part of an inspection to verify compliance with a treaty, ever since. But perhaps invitation is better than nothing at all.

Obviously in these circumstances there is no form of redress; the former USSR was not demonstrating compliance with a treaty neither was it demonstrating compliance with its own figures.

However, on the positive side, the 1985–87 Soviet unilateral moratorium on nuclear testing was monitored and subsequently verified to have been adhered to. It was not reciprocated by the other nuclear states but it did show that it was possible to monitor such a moratorium at a distance. With in-country networks[22] and other non-seismic techniques (remote sensing satellites, aircraft, on-site inspections, radiation monitoring) the long-term unilateral absence of nuclear tests in the territory of what was the USSR would be verifiable to a very high degree.[23]

Declarations of, say, equipment levels or arms transfers deposited with other states or with the United Nations[24] could have provision for verification measures included in them, as integral parts of the declarations. For example, imagine that Russia decides to reduce the size of the post-Soviet nuclear arsenal by, say, 75 per cent or even reduce to zero. It could make that declaration to the world press and deposit details of the numbers, sites and destruction plans with the USA, Britain, France and China. The four nations would, as always, be able to monitor the reductions and deployments by NTM (and, for all but China, by Open Skies) but the republics could also include the rights of short notice inspection to deployment sites, production facilities and storage depots. They could also notify the dates, times and places of destruction and invite inspectors from the other four nuclear countries to witness the elimination of the missiles. In this way the declaration is treated as though it were a legal document and akin to a treaty and compliance with the declaration can be verified.

The Strategic Arms Reduction Treaty verification régime could also do some of the monitoring of the unilateral reductions but not all (for example short range nuclear forces or sea-launched cruise missiles would not automatically be included in the inspection). The inclusion of the other nuclear weapons states in the monitoring process could also encourage their participation in future negotiations.

In making the declaration and in inviting inspections, the state making unilateral cuts would be held to account by the states enabled to monitor the declaration.

In this way a unilateral measure takes some of the status of an international agreement. Of course, it could be that the verification provisions contained in the unilateral declaration are not sufficient for the task. In this case the inspecting states could make the point strongly to the declaring state and hope that international opinion persuades it to become more open. Otherwise the states would probably accept that, although far from perfect, a small amount of intrusive verification provision is better than none at all and carry out the inspections as invited. It would be important to remember, however, that this level of OSI is primarily for confidence-building and cannot be classed as high-security verification.

DRASTIC NUCLEAR REDUCTIONS

Given that there is now no justification for the declared nuclear weapon states to go developing newer and more sophisticated weapons and that there is political and financial pressure to reduce defence spending, it seems likely that deep cuts in the arsenals of the USA and Russia will now occur within the next few years.

Deep cuts in nuclear weapons will continue as a process of negotiated treaties and unilateral national or alliance decisions on defence needs. Before we ever get to zero however, there could be a period of very low levels of nuclear weapons which belong to a number of states (USA, Russia, Britain, France, China and others). At this point, all those weapons will have to be declared if verification can be effective for a global reduction. The problem is that these low levels (50–500 weapons per nuclear weapon state?) are very vulnerable to small increases because a small clandestine store of extra nuclear weapons possessed by one of the countries would drastically alter the balance. Now it could be that this would be irrelevant strategically – if the numbers of nuclear missiles already held are more than sufficient to destroy the enemy – but politically it would be very important. Imagine that a nation which has agreed to have the same number as another nation has an extra 50 weapons hidden away on land or sea platforms. If the numbers agreed to were high (a few thousand) then an extra 50 would not be very significant. If however, the numbers agreed to were 50 each, then a hidden 50 would double the force of the cheating nation with respect to the complying nation. As a result, verification of these low levels must be extremely stringent and costly. This could be achieved the 'traditional' way by monitoring production plants, maintenance facilities, ports, ships and deployment sites using NTM, OSI, portal perimeter monitoring and so on. The verification scheme would then be the same as for START–I and START–II but even more rigorous, certainly involving more countries. At this point the question would be asked: 'Why are we spending so much money and putting so much effort into monitoring the whereabouts of so few missiles'? It could be that the point of stringent verification and its attendant costs would by then be so well-understood by the public and legislators that the question would be quickly answered by 'we need to spend this money on verification for our security'. Certainly similar answers have worked in the past when the public and politicians have been debating very expensive new weapon systems.

Another way to solve the verification problem at low levels would be to close down all but one or two nuclear weapon deployment areas in each country, which could then be safeguarded. In this situation no nuclear weapons could ever be taken out of their designated deployment sites (these sites could be quite large for mobile missiles). If inspectors or satellites or aerial overflights ever spotted a nuclear missile out of area, that would be an obvious violation. The problem with this approach is that unless they were highly mobile, which could defeat the verification objective anyway, the weapons would be vulnerable to attack. There is, however, a technical solution to the problem in the use of tags which can store data from the Satellite Global Positioning System. That data can then be read at a later date, thus not giving real-time information, and the positions checked to ensure that they had not been out of their allocated areas. Any untagged missile would be an immediately obvious violation.

Yet another idea, which could provide a route to zero nuclear weapons at a later date, would be to close down nuclear weapon facilities in all countries and allow the nuclear nations to keep mobile nuclear missiles and warheads in a 'bank'[25] in order to protect against 'breakout' (a state clandestinely developing a cachet of nuclear weapons and then announcing the threat). The missiles and warheads would be deposited in the 'bank' by the owning states and kept under safeguards. The 'bank' could exist in several places. At any point in the future, a nation could remove its missiles and warheads but that action would be open and made known to the world. The 'bank' would have no operational control over the weapons, it would act the same way as a safe deposit, guarding the weapons only.

From the verification point of view, this is very much the easiest option for such low numbers of missiles. There would be no legally allowed missiles anywhere else. If any nuclear weapon facility or any nuclear missiles were ever to be spotted by remote-sensing satellites then that would be immediate grounds for suspicion and for a challenge inspection. The 'banked' weapons under safeguards would also act as an insurance for their owners in case a clandestine force were ever to be discovered or used as blackmail in the future. Any potential nuclear blackmailer would be quite aware that other states had fast access to the 'bank', so threats in order to gain leverage could be quite useless, particularly if all the other nuclear nations acted in concert against any threat. For this reason it is unlikely that any of the states keeping missiles in the 'bank' would feel the need to develop a clandestine stockpile. If any of those states ever wished to play nuclear blackmail, they could more easily withdraw their weapons from the 'bank' than build a secret force with all the attendant risks of being caught. A near-nuclear nation could also decide to develop nuclear missiles for deposit in the 'bank' as an insurance policy against any of its regional adversaries developing a clandestine force.

There are problems with such an approach.

☐ In which countries would such a bank be situated?
☐ Would the host countries be in a position to prevent the removal of the weapons by their owners in a time of crisis?
☐ How could a hostile force be prevented from attacking the bank?
☐ How vulnerable to attack would missiles be in transit, once removed?
☐ How strong would be the protection from terrorists?

The difficulty of verifying such low levels, with all the inherent dangers, contrasts strongly with the ease of verifying zero levels. From the verification point of view it is much better to go to zero than to have a few hundred nuclear weapons scattered around the world which require continual monitoring and vast areas where missiles could be deployed or stored, perhaps legally perhaps illegally, which also require monitoring. A great deal of effort, expense and resources, would have to go into the monitoring of a small number of missiles. A dramatic reduction from a few thousand weapons to zero would be much easier and cheaper to verify.

The infrastructure for the missiles and warheads would be dismantled. There would be no more production of nuclear missiles, no more testing of warheads or nuclear-tipped ballistic missiles. Weapons-grade plutonium and highly enriched uranium would no longer be needed and any missile seen, or warhead observed, would be an immediate sign of a violation. Verification would be carried out by remote-sensing aircraft and satellites. The right to challenge on-site inspections would have to exist for all areas within the states parties. In order to achieve this, for many countries verification procedures would have to be institutionalised into some sort of international inspectorate for the agreements.

CONCLUSIONS

Arms control is far from dead but it is in a period of metamorphosis. We are witnessing the transition from tight, adversarial bilateral arms control agreements to multilateral and unilateral measures with associated monitoring and verification. We need to find ways to deal with present and future regional conflicts, with the escalating arms trade, with the threatened spread of nuclear weapons and with tensions over increasingly scarce resources.

The experiences in arms control negotiation and in the practicalities of verification have the most potential for adaptation. Negotiators in multilateral and bilateral forums have developed a bank of experience in establishing priorities, balancing trade-offs and dealing with the trivial but crucial delicacies of negotiation language. Many of the these negotiators are now out of work, thanks to changing administrations in the ex-USSR and Central European states. It is, however, the practicalities of verification which possess the most potential for tension and conflict resolution.

Conflicts and threatened wars in the region of Central and Eastern Europe and in the ex-Soviet states could be avoided if preventative measures were now taken. Included in these measures could be various confidence-building ones such as the inspection of neighbouring states' armies, military exercises (as in the Stockholm Accord) and information exchange. These would have to be coupled with mediation and reconciliation through the CSCE. The work of the CSCE and the Conflict Prevention Centre Secretariats should be funded so that these functions could be adequately performed. Mechanisms should also be established to enable representatives of different ethnic and cultural groupings within states to use the mediation and CBMs open to nation states.

The NPT has never been more important than it is today and every measure possible should be undertaken to strengthen it. The concerns over terrorists capturing ex-Soviet nuclear warheads, over regional nuclear arms races, the trade in disenfranchised nuclear scientists and the increase of neo-nuclear weapons states are very real. More funding and resources must be put into preventing the spread of nuclear weapon technology and materials and the current nuclear powers must address the role that their nuclear weapons play in encouraging others to aspire to a permanent seat on the UN Security Council.

It must be recognised that verification and monitoring can provide security in themselves. If we could achieve more openness and transparency, the degree of security would be far higher than, it is today. It is not only the possession of information that is required, however, but also the act of going to inspect facilities to check compliance with agreements and declarations which ensures that states are open to foreign military experts and that they run a very high risk of being caught if they should decide to build prohibited weapons.

Such a situation is different from that of intelligence gathering. Verification and monitoring are explicitly linked with treaties or declarations. It is the act of monitoring by inspection providing interaction between military personnel of previously hostile countries and providing opportunities to assess capabilities and intents with a much greater degree of confidence, which increases the trust between states.

Looking at verification/monitoring from this point of view, the confidence-building aspects could eventually be its single and most important role. If the high defence spending states, in moving from a position of large numbers of weapons to a position of low numbers could spend a small fraction of their defence budgets on verification requirements then verification could become one of the chief – if not the chief – mechanisms of international security.

Notes

[1] *A Report of the Group of Governmental Experts on the Role of the UN in Verification,* A/45/372, 28 August 1990, UN General assembly.

[2] On 15 November the First Committee of the UN General Assembly voted 106–1 (8) to establish an international arms register.

[3] *Report of the Group of Governmental Experts to Carry out a Study on Ways and Means of Promoting Transparency in International Transfers of Conventional Arms,* A/46/301, UN General Assembly, December 1991.

[4] Jamie Dettmer, *The Times,* 20 March 1992.

[5] Paul Lewis, *International Herald Tribune,* 19 March 1992 and Patrick Tyler and Eric Schmitt, *The Guardian,* 20 March 1992.

[6] Op cit note 4.

[7] *Arms Control Reporter,* 19 March 1992, 453.B.132.11.

[8] North Korea has been a signatory to the NPT since December 1985 but there has been increasing evidence that it had intentions and capabilities to develop nuclear weapons within the near future. During 1990–92 pressure was exerted on North Korea to conclude the outstanding safeguards agreement with the IAEA.

[9] Owen Greene, Verifying the non-proliferation Treaty – Challenges for the 1990s, *Verification Technology Information Centre Report,* October 1992.

[10] *Arms Control Reporter,* 24–26 February 1992, 602.B.216–7.

[11] *Arms Control Reporter,* 8 April 1992, 608.B.228.

[12] *Trust and Verify,* Number 32, October 1992.

[13] Hansard Columns 403–408, 23 October and Columns WA 113–114 and 25, 2 November 1992.

[14] *Scientific and Technical Aspects of the Verification of a Comprehensive Test Ban Treaty,* A Study by the Verification Technology Information Centre, April 1990.

[15] *Trust and Verify,* No. 22, September 1991.

[16] *Arms Control Reporter,* 5 October 1992, 701.B.102.

[17] *The Times,* 18 July 1988.

[18] *Arms Control Reporter,* 704.B.244, October 3–4 1987.

[19] *Arms Control Reporter,* 704.B.325, December 1 1988.

[20] *Arms Control Reporter,* 704.B.295, 29 June 1988.

[21] *Statement on the Defence Estimates 1989* Volume 1, p. 10 HMSO, London.

[22] The Joint US–USSR (unofficial) seismic verification project, set up in 1987 by the Natural Resources Defence Council in Washington D.C. and the Soviet Academy of Sciences installed several seismic stations in the USSR and monitored the latter part of the unilateral moratorium in-country.

[23] *Scientific and Technical Aspects of Verifying a Comprehensive Test Ban,* The Verification Technology Information Centre, London, April 1990.

[24] Notes 2 & 3 Op cit.

[25] There have been a number of similar proposals over the years but this one should not be confused with the numerous proposals to make the United Nations the custodian of nuclear weapons and of the means of delivery, in short to turn the United Nations into a nuclear force. For a recent illustration of such proposals see J. Rotblat, Time to Think Again About General and Complete Disarmament, in *Ways Out of the Arms Race* J Hassard, T Kibble and P Lewis, (eds.) World Scientific 1989, p. 198.

16

Economic Incentives to Export Arms: Russia and Ukraine

SUSAN WILLETT

Research Officer, Centre for Defence Studies

In 1990, following the end of the Cold War, the former Soviet Union committed itself to reducing conventional arms exports as a gesture towards reducing global conflict. Referring to the improved international climate, Soviet officials promised reductions of from 25 to 65 per cent in arms exports, and proposed an international registry of arms sales. The government also announced that, from January 1991, all Soviet foreign trade, including arms exports, was to be conducted in foreign currency. These new policies had a dramatic effect on total sales. One Russian estimate placed 1991 earnings from arms sales at just US$4bn, compared with a SIPRI estimate of US$17.7bn in sales for 1987.[1]

However, within two years, the successor states of Russia and the Ukraine had reversed the policy of arms export restraint and are now actively engaged in recapturing their share of the global arms market. This paper examines the causes and consequences of this policy reversal.

ARMS EXPORT TRENDS

The problems in evaluating the scale of Soviet arms sales are twofold. First, the Soviets were reticent in publishing data on the value or volume of their arms transfers. And secondly, what information is available was often manipulated as writers have attempted to prove that the Soviet Union was the dominant supplier to the Third World and a source of most destabilising military technology transfers.

In the absence of all but the most ambiguous of statistics on Soviet arms transfers, the most satisfactory approach to assessing

Table 16.1 *Indices of Soviet Arms Transfers 1980–89*

	1980	1981	1982	1983	1984	1985	1986	1987	1988	1989
1.	23344	18094	26153	8118	24868	18705	17997	23187	14654	11230
2.	20506	18924	19352	19747	18906	15177	18119	29206	19625	17370
3.	12359	12787	11041	10961	10585	12796	14579	14718	12464	11652
4.	9277	8370	7565	7578	7537	8563	10327	10759	8238	8515
5.	24045	23097	23152	22547	21734	18689	22388	23037	21400	—

Source: K. Krause, Arms and the State Pattern of Military Production and Trade, Cambridge University Press 1992, p. 113.

Notes:
1 Agreement with Third World, constant 1989 US dollars. Grimmett, *Trends in Conventional Arms Transfers.*
2 Deliveries to Third World, constant 1989 US dollars. Grimmett, *Trends in Conventional Arms Transfers.*
3 Deliveries worldwide, constant 1985 US dollars, major weapons only. Stockholm International Peace Research Institute, *SIPRI Yearbook 1990,* 221 Figures for 1980–83 from SIPRI data base.
4 Deliveries to Third World, constant 1985 US dollars, major weapons only, *SIPRI Yearbook 1990,* p. 252.
5 Deliveries worldwide, constant 1988 US dollars, *ACDA, WMEAT,* various years.

the scale and trends in the Soviet arms trade is to present a number of estimates from which to glean general trends.

The measures shown in Table 16.1 differ in several ways, some count agreements, others deliveries, all employ different definitions of what is considered a military technology transfer. It may also be the case that the methods employed to convert roubles into dollars may seriously underestimate the value of Soviet arms transfers. The general trend however that these statistics indicate with both agreements and deliveries is that they appear to have levelled off or even declined somewhat from the peak levels in the early 1980s.

In the five year period 1986–1990, official Soviet arms exports were valued at 56,700 million roubles, with a 1990 figure of 9,700 million roubles.[2]

Another method of measuring military equipment exports is to count the number of weapons delivered by type.

Table 16.2 *Weapons Delivered to the Developing World: Major Categories 1982–89*

Weapon	US	USSR	Western Europe
Tanks and self propelled guns	2,849	7,265	690
Artillery	2,265	13,730	4,875
APCs and armoured cars	4,866	13,060	2,040
Major naval combatants	7	41	51
Minor naval combatants	31	150	219
Submarines	0	17	15
Supersonic aircraft	500	1,955	385
Subsonic aircraft	190	205	150
Other aircraft	350	750	458
Helicopters	280	1,490	550
Guided missile boats	0	21	12
SAMs	3,820	26,380	3,695

Source: K. Krause, ibid, p. 114

The ebb and flow of Soviet arms transfers in the 1970s and 1980s followed a similar pattern to other major arms suppliers, and mirrored Soviet foreign policy concerns. The Middle East was the greatest regional market with Iraq, Syria and Iran the largest recipients. Other major clients included Angola, Afghanistan and Vietnam. In 1989 the Soviet Union accounted for 37 per cent of the global market for conventional weapons and exported to 53 countries, including 22 customers in Africa, 6 in East Asia, 3 in Latin America, 8 in the Middle East, 4 in South Asia and even one NATO member, Greece. Arms sales accounted for roughly 20 per cent of the Soviet Union's total exports.

  · During the Cold War, the rationale for Soviet arms exports was predominantly political. The near total absence of economic assistance to, and political and cultural ties with, Third World client states meant that the Soviet Union relied on arms transfer relationships to achieve its foreign policy objectives. Little, if any, economic gain was made from transfers as the majority of sales were funded through Soviet credits. Before 1973, all sales were made through credits, which were provided on a 2.5 to 3 per cent rate of interest, generally with a grace period of several years and a 10-12 year amortisation period. After 1973, the Soviets attempted to make sales in hard currency, but with little real success, for as Belousov, the Deputy Chairman of the Council of Ministers explained in an interview in February 1992 'we were virtually buying the weapons from ourselves'.[3]

By the end of the 1980s, however, deliveries to Third World clients dropped significantly, largely due to the end of the Iran-Iraq war. Two parallel developments also took place: a shift towards supplying the most sophisticated Soviet arms to Third World clients, and a growing concern with controlling the flow of weapon systems to the Third world, in particular, the diffusion of specific military technologies, such as ballistic missiles. Such concerns were manifest in the Soviet agreement to suspend arms transfers to Iraq in the wake of the invasion of Kuwait.

The collapse of the Soviet system and the emergence of more pro-Western governments in the Ukraine and Russia promised a continuation of the policy of export restraint. But despite demonstrating a more cooperative face to the world, particularly in arms control negotiations, the new governments of Russia and Ukraine have been mounting aggressive campaigns to regain market shares and have been attempting to penetrate new markets.

Concern has been expressed in the West that many of the transfer agreements now being entered are highly destabilising. For instance, Syria is said to have concluded a huge deal with Russia for extra Mig-29 fighters and Su-24 interdiction bombers. In 1991, Iranian purchases included 25 Su-24 bombers, 50 Mig-29s, a number of Mig-31, Su-27s and 200 T-72 main battle tanks. Most alarming to Western navies operating in the Gulf has been the purchase of Russian submarines.

The Chilean government is believed to be considering the replacement of some of its ageing frontline aircraft with the Mig-29 'Fulcrum'. It is also interested in acquiring attack helicopters - a possible candidate being the Soviet Mi-8 'Hip'.[4] China has also stepped up its acquisition of Russian Su-27 'Flanker' fighter aircraft, surface-to-air missiles and naval weapons.[5]

Russian aircraft were marketed vigorously in 1992 at air shows in Paris, Dubai, Moscow and Farnborough, where several new fighter aircraft – the Su-35 and the MiG-33 have been unveiled, producing consternation amongst Western suppliers.

The US has expressed concern about the appearance of low-priced ex-Soviet fighters on the export market. Malaysia was apparently offered MiG-29s at roughly $12m each. Many of the Russian target markets are those on which the US Government has imposed a sales embargo. Despite their high life-cycle costs, Russian aircraft remain an attractive prospect for certain customers. A low initial cost can secure a prestigious fleet of high performance aircraft.

Although Russia will be by far the largest supplier of arms from the former Soviet Union, other former republics are emerging as potential competitors. There have been reports in the Russian press that the Ukraine is quietly selling aircraft and helicopters internationally via German and Greek intermediaries.

It has also been suggested that much of the struggle over the Black Sea Fleet is really a struggle over whether the Russians or the Ukrainians will be able to sell it off. India and China have expressed interest in buying the former Soviet aircraft carrier *Varyag*, the 67, 500 ton sister ship of the *Admiral Kuznetsov* in the Russian Northern fleet . It is at present being fitted out at the Nikolayev Shipyard in Southern Ukraine. With the Ukrainian shipyards being nationalised and no funds available to the Russian navy, the future of capital ships under construction, including the super-carrier *Ulyanovsk* and the missile cruiser *Admiral Lobov* has become uncertain. However, construction work on the two carriers continues. Adding a super-carrier to either China or India's fleets would seriously affect the naval balance of power in the Asian Pacific or Indian Ocean regions.[6]

In January 1992, a group of military industrialists in Kazakhstan urged President Nazarbayev to promote exports to members of the Commonwealth of Independent States and other countries. It has reportedly sold 500 heavy machine guns at $15,000 each to Germany. There are also reports that a new company, Paks Alisa, intends to export SU-24 medium range bombers for hard currency. Syria was mentioned as a possible customer for the bomber and Nazarbayev has apparently explored commercial relations with India as well.

Ironically, the most direct competition the Russian defence industry may have in the promotion of Russian arms sales may be from the former Soviet military. With the deep reductions in the size of the military, surplus equipment has been building up. Yeltsin has already authorised the Commonwealth air force to sell up to 1,600 surplus aircraft through the Russian Ministry of Foreign Economic Relations, and it seems likely that the military will seek authorisation to sell other surplus hardware.

In addition, there is a burgeoning black market in Soviet military equipment which is hard to monitor or control. Many newly formed companies in Russia are thinly disguised fronts for military or former Communist party officials to sell arms for gain. Several cases of illegal transfer of property from the military to entrepreneurial structures made up of serving senior officers have been reported.

The rationale given by the former Soviet republics for this dramatic reversal in arms trade policy is the desperate state of economic collapse and the need to earn hard currency to facilitate the process of economic reform and to finance the conversion of their respective defence industries.

THE ECONOMIC SITUATION

The economic transformation which has been initiated in the former Soviet Union is unprecedented in scope and impact. The initial stages of reform have been marked by dramatic output losses. The extent of economic contraction has been far greater than Western analysts anticipated. In the territory of the former Soviet Union the drop in output is between 20–35 per cent. Lower oil production and generally weak agricultural output are major elements in Russia's economic collapse so clearly reflected in Figure 16.1.

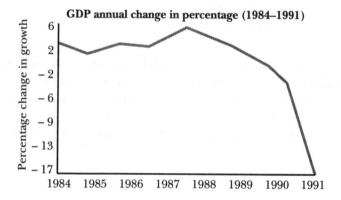

Fig. 16.1 *The dramatic collapse in GDP in the former Soviet Union since 1989*
Source: IMF data from World Economic Outlook, May 1992

The continuing decline reflects many interrelated factors, including a sharp deterioration in the terms of trade in the region following the move to world prices for inter-regional trade, the breakdown of the old command structure of supply and distribution, the lack of progress in important areas of structural reform, tight financial policies imposed by the government to achieve macroeconomic stabilisation.

These conditions have created a deep slump. Despite attempts to consolidate government budgets, the recession has resulted in a widening of fiscal deficits as tax revenues fall sharply and increasing demands are made on social security spending. External financing to aid economic transformation fell short of expectations and there have been delays in the

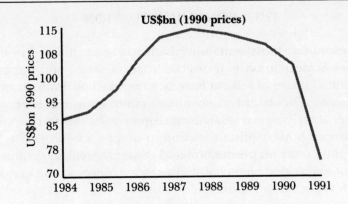

Fig. 16. 2 *Export performance 1984–91*
Source: IMF, World Economic Outlook, May 1992.

disbursements of the bilateral official assistance that was being mobilised under the auspices of the European Community.

Since price liberalisation was introduced, inflation has burgeoned. Between January and December 1991, retail prices increased by 250 per cent. The IMF estimated that inflation in 1992 would be in the order of 100 per cent. The breakdown in monetary control has eroded the rouble as a medium of exchange, resulting in a marked increase in the use of barter in transactions. In the Ukraine the government has introduced the use of coupons as a substitute for currency.

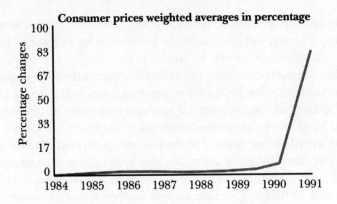

Fig. 16.3 *Percentage changes in Inflation*
Source: IMF, World Economic Outlook, May 1992

As a consequence of the currency collapse enterprises fortunate to have hard currency are keeping their foreign exchange earnings outside the country. Capital flight has aggravated the shortage of foreign exchange.

The OECD has warned that macroeconomic stabilisation policies are coming under increasing pressure because economic collapse and rising unemployment are eroding popular support for stringent stabilisation policies.[7]

The IMF in *World Economic Outlook. May 1992* expressed concern about the spiral of economic decline and appealed to the West: 'For the international community, it is a major challenge to respond to the needs of the republics for guidance and financial assistance as they struggle to overcome the legacies of the past.'

The OECD, while recognising the difficulties of making economic projections, given the uncertainty and lack of reliable data, nevertheless estimated a further decline in GDP of between 15 and 20 per cent in the former Soviet Union at the end of 1992. Such a collapse can only be offset by trade, but with large losses in oil and other raw materials the republics of the former Soviet Union will increasingly come to rely on their only other internationally competitive product – namely weapon systems.

DEFENCE CONVERSION

At the core of the problems being experienced with economic transformation are the adjustment difficulties facing the defence industries.

Due to the relative technological backwardness of the economy in the Soviet Union, military production has had a special place in Soviet planning almost from the outset. As David Holloway has noted, 'the requirements of defence (had) an important influence on the whole pattern of industrialisation', with the defence sector receiving the highest priority allocation of scarce and skilled resources.[8] This enabled the Soviet defence industry to achieve levels of technological development that far outstripped the civil economy, making Soviet military technology broadly competitive with the West.

The structure and scale of the former Soviet defence industry is often poorly understood. Apart from the ambivalent nature of existing information, production levels and pricing in a command economy were discretionary. Therefore all statistical data on output must be taken only as a rough indicator. In addition the problem of the convertibility of the rouble and the ambivalence of pricing means that information expressed in value terms must also be treated with caution.[9]

In 1988 it was estimated that the Soviet defence complex employed approximately 12 million people, of whom 7.5 million were directly engaged in industrial production, with 4.1 million directly engaged in the manufacture of weapons and other military hardware.[10]

The total gross output of the defence sector was 140 billion roubles, of which 88 billion was in military production. The sector accounted for 12 per cent of total industry and employed 10 per cent of the total workforce. It embraced 5,000 enterprises, with 20 per cent of firms engaged in civilian production. The defence complex played a substantial role in Soviet research and development (R & D), performing both civil and military R&D. Cooper suggests that there was a total of between 600-800 R&D establishments in the defence complex.

Long before the present policy of defence conversion, the Soviet defence industry had extensive civilian operations. Defence enterprises produced a wide range of civilian goods from industrial and transport equipment, oil drilling rigs, civil aircraft, ships and a spectrum of electronics goods such as computers, communications equipment and an impressive collection of consumer goods from washing machines, sewing machines, TVs, refrigerators, vacuum cleaners, to bicycles and motorbikes. Because of the more advanced state of technology in the defence sector the standard of the civil goods produced by defence firms tended to be higher than those built by civilian enterprises.[11] Thus in 1987, when the government decided to improve the consumer goods sector, it was the defence sector which assumed responsibility. In spring 1988, 230 civilian enterprises, with some 300,000 workers, were transferred to the defence sector under the control of the Military Industrial Commission known as the VPK (the Russian acronymn), giving the defence sector a near monopoly in the manufacture of refrigerators, washing machines, sewing machines and other household goods. In 1989, further civilian enterprises were transferred to the defence sector including a number of equipment suppliers, computer and medical equipment enterprises. The object of these transfers was to promote substantial technology transfer from the technologically advanced military sector to the relatively backward civilian sector.

As a consequence of these changes the defence complex expanded in terms of facilities and personnel and found itself increasingly having to meet pressing consumer and welfare needs. Under mounting political pressure to achieve quick results, resentment of these changes emerged both within and outside the defence complex.

The VPK, responsible for the defence complex, is a supra-ministerial organisation. It survived the coup in 1991, to be merged with the Ministry for Civil Machine Building Industry, thereby increasing its hold on the nation's scientific and technological resources. The technical and scientific elites which dominate the VPK and the defence complex are essentially conservative. Their priority has been to preserve their special status and privileges. Opposed to economic transformation and democratisation, due to their vested interest in the traditional system, they are proving a major obstacle to conversion.

With the dramatic cutbacks in procurement expenditure since the end of the Cold War, the defence complex is facing an unprecedented collapse in demand. Weapons production in the former Soviet Union has dropped to the lowest level in years, according to US Department of Defence statistics. Output declined significantly in nearly all major areas of weapons production.

The pervasiveness of the defence complex in Soviet industrial production means that conversion is much more a case of wholesale industrial and technological adjustment than is the case in the West: hence, the centrality of conversion to the success or failure of Russian and Ukrainian economic reform.

The Ukraine inherited about 15 per cent of the former Soviet defence industry. The defence sector is made up of 1,840 industrial enterprises which are dominated by 330 large firms, including the famous factory in Kiev and the massive Yuzmash defence enterprise at Dnepropetrovsk. The sector employs 2.7

Table 16.3 *Weapons Production 1989–91*

Weapon System	1989	1990	1991
MBTs	1700	1300	1000
Infantry fighting vehicles & APCs	4800	3600–3900	2100
Artillery pieces	2500	1900	1000
Bomber aircraft	40	30	35
Fighters and fighter bombers	650	575	350
Attack helicopters	100	70	15
Submarines and surface combatants	21	20	13
Strategic ballistic missiles	200–215	190–205	145–165

Source: Jane's Defence Weekly 26/9/92

million people, some 5 per cent of the Ukrainian population. Out of this total 1.7 million are exclusively engaged in military production. The output ranges from aircraft carriers and missile cruisers to main battle tanks, Zenith and Cyclon rockets and SS-18, SS-20, SS-23 and SS-24 nuclear missiles.

State procurement orders have reportedly dropped by 75 per cent in 1992 and enterprises depending on defence orders are struggling to survive.[12] During 1992 no military orders were placed with Ukrainian industry.[13] One source predicted that 300,000 defence sector employees would be redundant by the end of 1992.[14] If mass lay-offs were to occur at a plant such as Yuzmash – which employs 50,000 people who comprise some 30 per cent of the local population – regional collapse is possible.

So far the Ukraine has failed to implement a comprehensive conversion programme. Viktor Anatov the Minister of Machine Building, the Military Industrial Complex and Conversion estimated that the bill for conversion would be 140 bn roubles or $1bn at current exchange rate, in 1992 alone.[15] It is unclear on what basis Anatov made this calculation but in the event the cash-strapped government was only able to allocated 30 bn roubles.

Anatov attempted to raise $200 million in foreign assistance from the West. However, Western aid has been slow in arriving in Ukraine and the worsening economic situation in the country is forcing the government to review its policies towards the defence sector.

Without direction from the Ukrainian government, the situation of the defence companies has grown progressively worse, due to the scarcity of capital, difficulties in finding raw materials and the collapse of the state-controlled system of supply and distribution.

The problem of collapsing military demand is especially acute in Russia, where some 75 – 80 per cent of the former Soviet military industry is located. Between 1989–1991 Soviet military expenditure was cut by 17 per cent. Procurement expenditure took the lion's share of the cutbacks with a 20 per cent reduction. Orders for weapon systems were slashed, and projects cancelled with little or no notice in the middle of production runs. Even deeper cuts are now being made in military procurement, which has been cut according to Russian reports by at least 60 per cent from 1991 to 1992. In many cases plants are being forced to close and jobs are being lost on an alarming scale.

There are more than 5 million workers dependent on defence orders. In theory the cuts should have been offset by conversion to civilian production, or by some other form of assistance to the affected enterprises. In most cases this has not occurred.

As originally conceived by the Gorbachov government, conversion in the Soviet Union was to be established through a planned programme. Little was, in fact, achieved under this system as the military and technical élites which ran the defence sector were openly hostile to the idea of conversion. Following the coup attempt and the break-up of the Soviet Union in 1991, a new conversion policy was implemented in the Russian Republic based on privatisation and the application of free market forces; a 'bottom up' approach. But the lack of capital, monetary instability, economic uncertainty and the general breakdown in supply has not been conducive to diversification. The result of market orientated conversion has meant further chaos for the defence industries. Some Russian industrialists have warned that 1.5 million people could be thrown out of work in the military industries by the end of 1992.

Conversion and the problems of economic reform at a local level have concentrated attention on the geographical location of the production and research facilities of the Russian defence industry. It is apparent that some cities and regions of the former Soviet Union face acute problems arising from the high degree of defence dependency of their local economies. Moscow and St Petersburg are both extremely important centres of defence production. In St Petersburg some 700,000 people worked in the defence industry representing a quarter of the total employed in the city.[16] The situation in the 'closed' towns or cities, such as Chelyabinsk-40, Chelyabinsk-65 and Chelyabinsk-70, Arzamas-16, Krasnoyarsk-45, Krasnoyarsk-26, Tomsk-7, Kurchatov, Leninsk, Magadan, Norilisk and Omsk, which are exclusively or predominantly dedicated to defence production, is particularly acute.

Given the deteriorating economic circumstances and the difficulties of conversion, it is not surprising that the political leadership and individual managers of defence enterprises have turned to arms sales on their own initiative, both for direct economic gain and to preserve their high-technology capabilities, which they see as important for future economic well-being. General Mikhail Mali, Russian State Counsellor for Conversion, envisages keeping the most efficient 40 per cent of existing military industry and devoting it largely to continued arms exports for profits, which could generate the required capital to convert the remaining 60 per cent of the defence industry to civil production.

Representatives of some design bureaux are also openly advocating that exports be expanded via joint production with Western firms. Some interest has been shown by Western companies, but so far no major collaborative projects have been negotiated. Another initiative is that hard currency receipts are now retained by the bureaux and individual enterprises rather than by the VPK. This is intended to encourage individual firms to invest more effectively in civil production. But it also creates a disincentive to convert in those firms which can reap hard currency profits from exports. In reality these firms are taking advantage of previous market distortions, however, and in an economy characterised by the collapse of all but the most basic of consumer markets, successful arms exporters will be hard-pushed to find the incentives to restructure their production capabilities towards civil markets.

This is confirmed by the reluctance to give up the 'big ticket' programmes which bestow national prestige. Although Russia is short of money, certain 'core' air force programmes continued to be funded, such as the Mikoyan project 1-42, a big fighter prototype in the 30 tonne class, which includes stealth technology, composite materials and high agility. The 1-42 will compete against a design from Sukoi for the Su-27 replacement contract.

The Russian government hopes to generate from $15bn to $30bn per year from arms sales; levels comparable or greater than Soviet sales in the late 1980s. In a declining global arms market, the assumption that the Russians will be able to generate this amount of hard currency from arms sales must be called into question. The massive Soviet arms transfers of the past were rarely the source of substantial profits, given that most of the deals were financed with Soviet credits or grants, on extremely favourable terms for the buyers. Belousov has confirmed that the total outstanding debt of approximately 86 billion roubles was partly due to arms transfers.[17]

THE ARMS MARKET IN THE 1990s

The biggest limitation to the renewed drive for arms exports is that the enormous market that the Russians envisage may simply not exist. Few established Soviet clients are likely to have the finances to be major dollar customers, and it remains highly uncertain how successful Russia and the other Commonwealth states will be in finding new markets in states that did not traditionally rely on Soviet arms.

As Figure 16.4 shows, the global arms market is in decline. According to the figures of global arms exports are declining, with a fall of more than 25 per cent from 1987 to 1989. More recent figures from the Congressional Research Service show that while there was an arms sales surge in 1990–91 associated with the Gulf War, global transfers to the Third World in 1991 were even lower than in 1989.

Against this background, the success of Russian sales will depend on prices and after-sales services. In terms of price, the

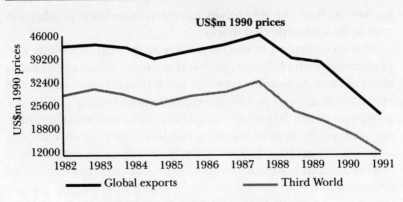

Fig. 16.4 *Global Trade in Conventional Weapons*
Source: Data from SIPRI Yearbook 1992

Russians are proving to be especially aggressive competitors. However, with the current instability in Russia, there are serious doubts about the ability of the arms producers to supply spares and other essential back-up services to keep the systems already delivered operational into the late 1990s. Uncertainty of supply has led many countries previously dependent on Soviet supplies to develop their own defence industrial capacity through import substitution policies. This is particularly true of Egypt, Iran, North Korea and India.[18]

Around 70 per cent of India's defence equipment is Soviet-made. Some 73 per cent of the total value of defence imports in 1989–90 was from the Soviet Union, mostly for the Army and the Air Force. The Army has 'indigenised' 19,000 Soviet spares over the past three years and is working to extend the life of various weapon systems.

The Indian Navy, facing spares shortages, is also planning to make them locally. Currently 27 out of the navy's 43 principal combat ships – 16 conventional submarines and 11 surface ships – are of Soviet origin and Soviet weapon systems are fitted to most frigates and corvettes.[19]

Egypt, a major importer of Soviet weapon systems in the 1980s, is another country that has attempted to become self-sufficient in military production. It has production capacity in a wide range of ammunition and other key items for land forces. It has acquired technologies such as towed artillery systems through 'reverse engineering' of the Soviet D-30. The Sakr

Factory for Developed Industries has developed and improved a version of the Soviet SA-7 'Grail' man-portable air defence system under the name Sakr Eye. The Sakr factory also produces a wide range of multiple rocket launchers based on Soviet systems and the 325mm Sakr medium artillery rocket system as a replacement for the Soviet supplied FROG-7 rockets which are now obsolescent. There is also a light anti-tank weapon, the PG-7, a development of the Soviet RPG-7 system. Abu Zaabal Engineering Industries also produce a reverse engineered copy of the Soviet ZU-23 light anti-aircraft gun system under the designation ZU-23M.[20]

Iran is expanding its indigenous defence industrial capacity. Arms production has increased threefold since 1979. The transfer of Soviet technology has been crucial to this expansion. Iran has had a policy of becoming self-sufficient in military production since 1970. The May 1989 defence and economic agreement with the then Soviet Union included wide-ranging industrial co-operation to make Iran self-sufficient in the production of MBTs, ballistic missiles and certain types of aircraft by the end of the century. Czechoslovakia, Rumania, East Germany and Poland were all in the process of helping Iran set up factories to produce armoured vehicles, anti-tank weapons and other systems. The situation of these co-production arrangements is unclear, however, since the break-up of the Warsaw Treaty Organisation and the Soviet Union.

EXPORT CONTROLS

Despite the renewed promotion of arms sales, military exports are unlikely to be completely unrestrained. With the collapse of the Soviet Union, the export control system was abandoned, including the system of grants and credits that financed many of the sales. The elimination of one export system has led to the creation of another. There is a clear consensus in Moscow against any export of nuclear, chemical or biological weapons, or the technology needed to make them. The Russian government confirmed, in January 1992, it's intention to abide by and eventually become a formal member of the Missile Technology Control Régime. Yeltsin has also expressed his support for the guidelines on conventional arms sales that the major exporters agreed in London last year, which called for restraint in particular destabilising transfers.

However, in the political and economic disorganisation now confronting many of the newly-independent states, questions remain as to whether the systems of export regulations now being set up will be adequate to control all the exports that should be limited, particularly in ambiguous dual-use areas which can require considerable expertise to monitor. A major aberration to controlling the arms trade from the former Soviet Union is the role of hard currency. In an economy desperate for hard currency, arms sales cannot but figure in policy calculations. Nor is it clear how controls can be implemented over the massive inventories of weapons in stock with the armed forces.

CONCLUSION

The governments of Russia and the Ukraine are re-entering the arms bazaar with high hopes, large stocks and incomplete export controls. They are under extreme pressure to export weapons in order to protect a large pool of industrial employment, their science and technology base and to earn foreign currency. Their leaders argue that there is nothing wrong or immoral in such exports and that, if they do not supply arms their competitors certainly will.

Notes

[1] *SIPRI Yearbook 1992*, Oxford University Press, 1992, p. 272.

[2] Official figures reported by Deputy Prime Minister Igor Belousov, in *Pravitelstyenny Vestnik* reprinted in *Foreign Broadcast Information Service* (9 January 1991), FBIS-SOV-91-006, 45. Using the SIPRI purchasing power parity conversion rate of $2.5 = 1 rouble, then total Soviet arms exports between 1986–90 are $141.750 million, which is larger than all the figures in the Table. This is almost certainly a conversion problem as Belousov also reported that Soviet arms transfers had dropped very significantly over the same period.

[3] Interview with I S Belousov published in *Pravitelstvenny vestnik* (Government News) No. 80, 2 Jan 1991. Referred to in the *SIPRI Yearbook 1991*, p. 214.

[4] *Jane's Defence Weekly* 7/3/92.

[5] *Jane's Defence Weekly* 12/9/92.

[6] *Jane's Defence Weekly* 8/2/92.

[7] OECD, *Economic Outlook*, Paris 1992.

[8] David Holloway *The Soviet Union and the Arms Race*, (2nd edition London, Yale University Press, 1983) p. 117–23.

[9] For a discussion of these problems see Julian Cooper, *Soviet Arms Exports and the conversion of the Defence Industry*, unpublished paper prepared for the United nations, Department for Disarmament Affairs, conference on Transparency in International Arms Transfers, Florence 25–8 April 1990, p. 3.

[10] For an indepth analysis of the Soviet defence industry see Julian Cooper, *The Soviet Defence Industry: Conversion and Reform*, (Pinter Publishers, London 1991).

[11] J Cooper *ibid* p. 31

[12] Robert Keatley ,Ukraine Arms Makers Seek Civilian Pursuits, *The Wall Street Journal*, 20 April 1992.

[13] Christopher K Hummel, Ukraine Arms makers Are Left on Their Own, *RPR/RL Research Report*, Vol. 1 No 32, 14 August 1992, p. 34.

[14] Quoted in Christopher Hammel, *op cit.* p. 37.

[15] *ibid* p. 34.

[16] J Cooper *The Soviet Defence Industry: Conversion and Reform*, (Chatham House Papers, Royal Institute of International Affairs, Printer Press, 1991), p. 24.

[17] Interview with I S Belousov published in *Pravitelstvenny vestnik* (Government News) No. 80, 2 Jan 1991. Referred to in the *SIPRI Yearbook 1991*, p. 214.

[18] Although rouble-rupee and counter trade agreements are valid until 1995, Moscow now expects hard currency for transactions including defence equipment exports, which India can ill afford. The Chiefs of Staff Committee Chairman General S F Rodrigues has ordered the establishments of defence plants to make spares for Soviet equipment and a switch to using simulators, wherever possible.

[19] *Jane's Defence Weekly* 2/11/91.

[20] *Jane's Defence Weekly* 14/12/91.

[21] *Jane's Defence Weekly* 1/2/92.

REGIONAL SECURITY

17

The New Face of
the United Nations

ADAM ROBERTS

Montague Burton Professor of International Relations,
Balliol College, Oxford

Euphoria does not last. By late 1992 evidence was mounting
that the United Nations (UN) could not succeed in the multiple
tasks in the field of international security which were being
imposed on it by a demanding membership. There was little
sign of anything which bore even a passing resemblance to a system of collective security emerging from the experience of the
Gulf Crisis of two years earlier; and peacekeeping operations
were in danger of failing, conspicuously, in several countries at
the same time.

States will continue, rightly, to attach importance to the UN;
and President Clinton may indeed see the UN as one possible
vehicle for setting America's global responsibilities in a multilateral context. Yet difficult questions must be faced. How will
states and individuals react to a new situation in which the limitations of the UN in the field of international security are only
too evident? What can the UN's role be in a world in which the
sadly familiar problems thrown up by an anarchical society of
sovereign states have by no means disappeared? Granted that
the UN cannot succeed in all aspects of international security,
what shape can its role take? Can the UN be expected to cope
with the problems of states which collapse into chaos? Must
member states be more modest in their demands of the UN?

In the years from about 1988 to 1992 the UN system was widely, and rightly, seen as having achieved remarkable feats in the
field of international security. A cease-fire to the terrible eight-
year war between Iran and Iraq was finally implemented in 1988;

in other regional conflicts, from Namibia to Nicaragua, the UN assisted not just in damping down hostilities, but in working towards a political settlement; UN peacekeeping forces were in huge demand, with 13 such forces being established in the years 1988 to 1992; and after Iraq invaded and occupied Kuwait in August 1990, the UN provided a framework, or at least a buttress, for international action to reverse the aggression. It could even be claimed that the UN had played some part in the transformation of the Soviet Union's world-view, and even of the Soviet Union itself. Above all, there were hopes that a largely new system of international security was emerging: in the new, veto-free world, the UN would supposedly work as the founding fathers intended.

Yet there were ample grounds for doubt as to whether the UN would be able to meet the many challenges with which it was faced. The idea that the world might be entering a new era of collective security was widely aired during and after the Gulf Crisis of 1990–91, but it was not spelt out in a way that was either intellectually persuasive or politically acceptable. The related idea that UN peacekeeping, perhaps adopting certain new tasks or forms, might succeed where traditional statecraft had failed, looked increasingly unrealistic: in Angola, Cambodia, Yugoslavia and Somalia, the UN found itself landed with a series of well-nigh impossible tasks.

In June 1992 the new Secretary-General, Boutros Boutros-Ghali, sought to initiate a debate with his interesting and in some respects symptomatic paper *An Agenda for Peace*.[1] At least in the field addressed by the paper, that of international security, the UN system is not usually good at reflecting on its own role. It lacks a strong tradition of open debate about its own philosophy and activities.

Substantial as it is, *An Agenda for Peace* reflects some of the optimism which began to dissipate towards the end of 1992. It takes as a starting point the view that it was 'the adversarial decades of the cold war' that 'made the original promise of the organisation impossible to fulfil.'[2] This implies a curiously negative interpretation of the UN's role, which had many positive aspects, in the long years of the Cold War. It also implies that the Cold War was far the most serious obstacle to the effective performance of the UN, when in fact there were many obstacles.

True, *An Agenda for Peace* does recognise the fundamental fact of the division of the world into sovereign states: but it fails to take serious account of the idea that many of the weaknesses of the UN's performance may be due to the inherent difficulties facing efforts to organise international security in a world divided, not just by the East-West divide, but by countless other divisions: between rival states, different experiences of war, colonialism and domination, and different degrees of vulnerability to internal collapse.

The same approach leads *An Agenda for Peace* to the implication – it is less than a firm proposition – that the use of the veto in the Security Council is now a thing of the past. It notes that while there have been 279 vetoes since 1945, there have been none since 31 May 1990.[3] It fails to note that an awareness of the veto power of the five permanent members has remained very lively, and has powerfully restricted what the Security Council has been able to do. Equally, it fails to note that the veto may on occasion have saved the UN from being saddled with impossible tasks.

THE UN AND COLLECTIVE SECURITY

Many events in 1988–90 reinforced the idea that the UN could be moving towards a central role in the maintenance of peace, and even developing something approaching a system of collective security. In his address to the UN General Assembly on 7 December 1988, Mikhail Gorbachev made a number of proposals indicating that the United Nations should be a principal focus of international efforts to control the use of armed force: such talk did much to focus public attention on the UN. However, it was only after the Iraqi invasion of Kuwait in August 1990 that the idea of the UN as a focus of collective security efforts began to attract attention. The spectacle of a small state being attacked, and then being liberated by a collective military action under UN auspices, was bound to re-kindle interest in the ancient and attractive idea of collective security.

Yet even against a uniquely blatant case of aggression, with little serious dissent from the proposition that Iraq's invasion and occupation ought to be brought to an end, the response of the international community marked an interesting departure from a 'pure' or 'ideal' case of collective security.

That the crisis should be handled through the UN became clear on 2 August 1990, within hours of the invasion, when George Bush and Mrs Thatcher, meeting at Aspen, Colorado, called for a collective international effort to force Iraq to end its occupation of Kuwait. As Mrs Thatcher said on that occasion: 'None of us can do it separately. We need a collective will of the nations belonging to the United Nations.'[4]

It is remarkable how little questioning there was of the decision that this crisis should be handled partly through the UN. In most Western countries, disagreements about the management of the crisis often took the form of different interpretations of the UN's proper role. It is also remarkable that, although in September 1990 both the British and US governments said that they did not need to get authority from the Security Council for the use of force (and legally they had a strong case), they both felt it advisable in the end to do so.[5]

The events which ensued, including the armed hostilities in January-February 1991, demonstrated certain strengths in acting collectively: a highly controversial military action gained in legitimacy, acquiring a character and purpose significantly different from earlier Western military action in the region; armed forces of many countries were harnessed to the cause; and opposition, whether domestic or international, was largely neutralised. Yet the case was not in itself a proof that some of the inherent problems of schemes for collective security had now been overcome in any general way.

The case of apparently successful collective action in the Gulf in 1991 should not obscure the value of other types of approach to other crises. Some threats to the peace, or even possibly acts of aggression, may best be responded to by negotiation, good offices, arbitration, or peacekeeping. There is no mechanical rule which can determine the right response of the international community to every crisis, and no substitute for that central feature of traditional statecraft, the exercise of prudential judgement to the facts of a particular case.

Even in cases where struggle is necessary, there may be some instances of other forms of action than collective military response under UN auspices. In some cases civil or non-violent methods of resistance (largely a form of pressure from below) may be a more appropriate response than military action. The campaigns, some lasting for decades, of civil resistance against one-party rule in many states of eastern Europe and the former Soviet Union are possible examples. The success of these campaigns in 1989–91 does not point to simple conclusions about the role of civil resistance in international politics, but this method of struggle should not be completely ignored.

Yet, clearly, in a new age in international relations, and after the experience of the Gulf War, ideas about collective security need to be re-examined. *An Agenda for Peace* does not discuss collective security very systematically. It contains separate sections on such topics as preventive diplomacy, peacemaking, peacekeeping, and post-conflict peace-building: but there is no section devoted to enforcement actions under Chapter VII of the UN Charter. Indeed, enforcement is discussed, illogically, within the section on 'peacemaking', which is defined as 'action to bring hostile parties to agreement, essentially through such peaceful means as those foreseen in Chapter VI of the Charter of the United Nations.'[6]

Thus, while the idea of an emerging and more collective security system imbues *An Agenda for Peace,* many of the questions associated with the idea are not explored. These questions are not new, and have arisen in connection with proposals for systems of collective security since at least the 17th century. Ten are considered here:[7]

1 *Whose collective security?* (Does the system protect only certain powers or types of power? Are there countries which, for whatever reason, feel excluded from its benefits, or even threatened by it?) The Third World response to President Bush's remarks about a 'New World Order' in his speech to Congress on 11 September 1990 provides a vivid illustration of the fears which talk of a new collective security system easily arouses. Among weaker states, especially those with recent experience of Western domination, there is inevitably a fear that they will have little say in how force is used; that the powerful will act in their own interests, as distinct from those of the international community as a whole; and that a new system of world order, however desirable it may seem, would be

a threat to the new and vulnerable sovereignty of recently decolonised states. Many in the Third World recall, with good reason, that Western colonial involvement in their countries often began with a security rationale.

2 *What is the unit (regional or global) within which a system of collective security operates?* The US and its partners were very active in the defence of order in the Gulf, but it was not obvious that they would be equally active in the event of invasions in areas where strategic and commercial interests of major powers were less sensitive: in Africa, Asia, Latin America, or other parts of the Middle East. There is a long tradition in international relations of a system of security being considered appropriate for one region, but not universally. Although the UN system is the first truly global international system, and although it involves virtually all countries in the world subscribing to a common set of principles, it is still far from self-evident that the same principles and practices regarding international order are applied consistently to different regions.

3 *Against which types of threat is a system of collective security intended to operate?* (e.g. massive aggression and annexation; cross-border incursions; acts of terrorism; human rights violations within a state; the collapse of state structures under assault from internal opposition.) Most schemes for collective security revolve around the idea of defence against massive external invasion of a state: yet the security threats which many governments most fear are different, and often it is more difficult to get international agreement in an individual case that a particular action constitutes 'aggression' and is a sufficient trigger to bring collective security into action. For better or worse, it is a fundamental truth of international relations (though sometimes glossed over in lowest-common-denominator UN statements) that different countries do see the world differently, and cannot be expected to agree on what constitutes any but the most flagrant threat to international security.

In 1991 and 1992, inspired partly by the 'safe havens' in northern Iraq, and partly by a trend of opinion, admittedly far from universal, in favour of democracy, there was increased advocacy within the UN system of some right of intervention in states even in the absence of a formal invitation. This remained a deeply contentious issue, and served as a reminder that the ends toward which collective security efforts might be directed are not fixed.

4   *What is the decision-making procedure by which threats are identified and action decided upon?* (e.g. majority of states; unanimity among a small concert of major states; key role for one major power; key role for a Secretary-General figure.) One of the great merits of the UN system, which helps to explain why it has been used so intensively in recent years regarding a wide range of security problems, is that it does have decision-making procedures – mainly within the Security Council. These procedures, which are more effective than those of most if not all regional organisations, have enabled the UN to make a diagnosis of particular threats, and to prescribe action.

Yet the Security Council's decision-making procedures, especially the existence of the veto in the hands of the permanent five, are a matter of intense controversy, and would plainly not command the consent of all states in anything like all likely or imaginable international crises. Some reform of the composition of the UN Security Council may be overdue, because of the over-representation of Europe and the northern hemisphere. However, it is still very difficult to discern the likely shape of an agreement on alternative arrangements. The most challenging ideas revolve around regional representation. The UN Charter procedures governing the matter of Charter amendment make any removal of an existing permanent member of the Security Council difficult.[8] Due to this inflexibility, dramatic change might only come at a time of severe internal crisis in the UN system.

5   *By what means is collective security enforced?* (e.g. denial of recognition; economic sanctions; use of major military force.) Traditionally, in the League of Nations era and again in the UN, collective security has been envisaged as operating, at least initially, through such forms of pressure as international condemnation backed by economic sanctions. States are

sometimes more willing to proclaim their support for economic sanctions than they are to provide combat forces.

It may be little use discussing grand schemes for collective security under UN auspices if there is not some agreement on the actual and possible future role of economic sanctions. Yet sanctions suffer from a number of well-known defects. The historical record of their effect is notoriously patchy; and has not been improved by their attempted application against Iraq since 1990 and against Serbia and Montenegro since May 1992. Sanctions can sometimes be ineffective because they are not widely implemented or fail to hurt; but sometimes, even if they do hurt, they may, like strategic bombing, have the perverse effect of making the inhabitants of a country more, rather than less, dependent on their government.

Sanctions present a further problem within the framework of the UN Charter's Chapter VII. How can the transition from economic sanctions by the many to military action by a smaller number of states be managed? It is hard to imagine any principles or procedures which could significantly reduce the intensely controversial character of any decision on this matter.

In the weeks before the outbreak of hostilities in the Gulf in January 1991, there was a remarkable failure (both in the UN, and among the Coalition powers) to explain why it was that sanctions were not likely to work. The judgement that they would not work was probably right, but the failure to explain the basis of it was one sign of weak overall direction. Among the many things which needed to be explained was the crucial distinction in sanctions between effectiveness in the sense of cutting imports and exports completely, and effectiveness in the quite different sense of getting the target country to reverse a fundamental state policy to which it was ever more deeply committed.

6 *Who commands a collective military action?* Experience seems to show that mobilising for collective security only works when one power takes the lead. But that same power may, as a result of the effort, be very reluctant to take the entire burden of collective security. After the Korean War, the US tried to set

up regional alliances to reduce its own direct commitments. After the 1991 Gulf War, the US was manifestly reluctant to get entangled in the quagmire of Iraq, and nervous about underwriting all security arrangements in the area. The desire to limit the degree of US involvement is likely to be stronger under President Clinton.

Could the UN Military Staff Committee, if life were breathed into it, usefully take on the role of coordinating military enforcement action under the Security Council? The idea that such a disparate international committee might be in charge of military operations has attracted little interest; and the Military Staff Committee is only touched on incidentally in *An Agenda for Peace*.[9] For the foreseeable future, there is no point in thinking of the Military Staff Committee as a commanding body for major military action. However, there may be more modest tasks which it, or some other body, will have to perform: including, for example, the development of rules of engagement, and the harmonisation of laws of war rules as they affect multilateral forces.

7 *How collective does enforcement have to be?* (Is complete unanimity impossible to attain, especially in the case of military action? Is there still space for some states to be neutral?) In practice there has never been, on the global level, a truly 'collective' *case* (let alone *system*) of collective security. The whole idea of collective security depends too much on the altruism of states, many of which will have no direct interest in a particular crisis.

In the Gulf Crisis of 1990-91, the key UN Security Council resolution avoided calling on all states to take military action. Instead, it merely authorised 'member states cooperating with the Government of Kuwait' to use a degree of force.[10] This wording allowed continued space for neutrality or non-belligerency in this conflict. It marks an interesting and realistic interpretation of provisions of Chapter VII of the UN Charter.

8 *How can a system of collective security actively deter a particular threat to a particular country?* In the wake of the 1991 Gulf War, there was much discussion as to how, in future, threats of

invasion could be deterred before disaster struck: this was one context for 'preventive deployment' envisaged by Boutros Ghali in his June 1992 report.[11] Yet in practice the idea of such 'preventive deployment' is fraught with difficulty. There is the risk that large numbers of states would request it; that it would be insufficient to discourage aggression; and that it might be used by a government as a means of avoiding serious moves towards its own defence, or towards conciliation with adversaries.

Yet, despite all these difficulties, there may be some residual deterrent value in the lessons of Korea 1950–53 and Kuwait 1990–91: twice, under UN auspices, the USA has led coalitions which have gone to the defence of invaded states to which the US was not bound by formal alliance commitments, and in which it had no troops deployed at the time. This curious fact may not be entirely lost on future would-be aggressors.

9 *Can the UN have forces available on a permanent basis?* The idea that the UN Security Council might have forces available on a permanent basis is often seen as one means of increasing its credibility and its power to deter. *An Agenda for Peace* envisaged that member states might 'undertake to make armed forces, assistance and facilities available to the Security Council . . . not only on an *ad hoc* basis but on a permanent basis. . . . The ready availability of armed forces on call could serve, in itself, as a means of deterring breaches of the peace since a potential aggressor would know that the Council had at its disposal a means of response.'[12] So far there has not been much response to this interesting suggestion. It appears that states remain jealous of their power to decide the exact circumstances in which their armed forces will or will not be used. At this stage, full-time, large-scale allocation of forces to the UN in advance of any crisis is improbable. However, earmarking of national military units for possible UN use is realistic. More important than this may be the training of national forces in international military co-operation: such training has taken place within NATO, and it proved to be of great value in the Gulf crisis of 1990–91.

10 *Are international forces acting on behalf of the international community subject to the same rules of restraint based on the laws of war (jus in bello) as ordinary belligerents in an inter-state war?* There is little serious dissent from the proposition that certain rules of restraint do apply to all the forces involved in collective security actions. However, the application of such rules presents special problems in a large *ad hoc* multi-national coalition typical of a collective security action, for several reasons. First, different partners may have different national standards, and be bound by different treaties. Second, the perceived legitimacy of an operation, and the maintenance of coalition unity, may depend on a public perception that warlike actions will be restrained in certain ways. Third, those rules based on an assumption that neutrality requires impartiality may conflict with the obligations of all states, including neutrals, to support the principles, purposes, and even actions of the UN. Fourth, some consequences of economic sanctions, which often hit the innocent along with the guilty, may conflict with certain underlying principles of the laws of war. Fifth, the question of possible trials in respect of war crimes often arises in large coalition actions against a state perceived in some sense as an outlaw.

The UN Security Council might usefully devote more consistent attention to laws of war matters than it has in the past, including in the Gulf Crisis of 1990–91. An Agenda for Peace avoids the subject entirely – an interesting example of the way in which laws of war matters, actively pursued in many parts of the UN system, are treated fitfully or not at all in those parts of the UN most directly involved in the management of international security.

These ten questions, taken together, are not intended to lead to the conclusion that there can never be any such thing as collective security. Rather, they suggest a more modest conclusion: collective security may properly be considered, not as a general system of international security, but rather as a form of action which is mobilised occasionally, and perfectly. Its most common use may be in response to especially glaring aggressive actions by military powers of the second rank. It is not a complete substitute for national or alliance defence efforts.

UN PEACEKEEPING

In one other area, that of peacekeeping, there had been high hopes, reflected in *An Agenda for Peace*, that the UN could play a greatly expanded role. Not only did peacekeeping expand rapidly in 1987–92, but it subtly changed its forms. In Nicaragua, Namibia and Angola it involved election-monitoring as a key feature of the attempt to end a civil war. In Cambodia, the plans for UNTAC as laid down in the 1991 Paris Agreements involved the UN peacekeeping force in taking over some of the functions of government.[13]

An Agenda for Peace discusses the problems of peacekeeping as quite largely logistic in character, and makes an eloquent plea for more resources: 'As the international climate has changed and peacekeeping operations are increasingly fielded to help implement settlements that have been negotiated by peacemakers, a new array of demands and problems has emerged regarding logistics, equipment, personnel and finance, all of which could be corrected if Member States so wished and were ready to make the necessary resources available.'[14] This plea is more than understandable: for too long, UN peacekeeping has been organised on the basis of a completely non-existent resource base, without even a supply of blue berets, let alone military equipment, personnel and finance. Yet the recent troubles of UN peacekeeping operations, many of which were looking distinctly tarnished by late 1992, suggest that there are deeper problems than those connected with resources.

One problem raised by a few UN operations in the early 1990s has been that of consent. In many countries, the fear that the UN might become an instrument for intervention under the authority of the major powers was exacerbated by such events as the establishment of the 'safe havens' in northern Iraq in April 1990. Even if this was not a peacekeeping operation within anything like the proper meaning of the word, it contributed to the growth of concern that peacekeeping forces might be imposed on a country rather than invited. Such concerns were reinforced by the passage in *An Agenda for Peace* in which peacekeeping was defined as 'the deployment of a United Nations presence in the field, hitherto with the consent of all the parties concerned, normally involving United Nations military and/or police personnel and frequently civilians as well.'[15] Those words 'hitherto with the consent' naturally caused concern. They illustrate only too clearly one of the central dilemmas of UN peacekeeping. To operate when totally dependent on the consent of the parties is to risk having to withdraw when requested, as in Sinai in 1967: accusations of weakness inevitably follow. Yet to suggest the possibility of operating without the consent of a party is to risk being an unwelcome guest on the territory of a sovereign state or a belligerent in a civil war: leading to accusations of colonialism or worse. There are no easy ways out.

In recent peacekeeping operations, however, the most serious problems have not been about the consent or otherwise of the parties to the presence of UN forces. The difficulties have arisen because of the sheer confusion of the situation; the reluctance of the parties to honour agreements entered into; the fragile character of political systems upon which, in greater or lesser degree, the success of the UN presence depends; and the tragic difficulties of notions of impartiality which UN forces have inherited from earlier, and simpler, peacekeeping operations.

Many of the recent UN peacekeeping operations have been in countries torn by civil wars which, like so many such wars, had also acquired an international dimension. Notoriously, civil wars are more bitter, and harder to end, than inter-state wars. While UN efforts have had many successes, including in El Salvador and Nicaragua, in most cases the sheer difficulty of the enterprise has undermined the heroic efforts made in the name of the UN.

Thus in Yugoslavia, UN peacekeeping efforts have run into many obstacles. The UN Protection Force (UNPROFOR) was established in February 1992 'to create the conditions of peace and security required for the negotiation of an overall settlement of the Yugoslav crisis'.[16] The reasons why the UN was called into a crisis which Europeans ought to have been able to solve are instructive: European states could not agree on a policy towards Yugoslavia, and were in any case not keen to act. The UN had two great advantages in tackling the problem: first, its reputation for impartiality; and second, its decision-making machinery in the form of Security Council procedures. Alas, neither of these assets was proof against the inherent difficulties of the Yugoslav problem.

International efforts to restore peace in Yugoslavia have had some modest successes. The presence of UNPROFOR in contested areas of Croatia was a necessary condition for the (admittedly modest and fragile) degree of improvement in relations between Serbia and Croatia. In Bosnia and Herzegovina, the UN did play a key role in providing humanitarian relief for besieged cities, most notably Sarajevo. Yet the problems associated with all these operations were huge and in some cases insoluble. To list only three:

☐ In Bosnia and Herzegovina, the member states of the United Nations recognised a state before applying the traditional and time-honoured diplomatic test of considering whether it is a functioning entity.[17] Subsequently the Security Council proclaimed its support for European Community diplomatic efforts, and recalled 'that no territorial gains or changes brought about by violence are acceptable and that the borders of Bosnia and Herzegovina are inviolable.'[18] Unfortunately, such pronouncements bore very little relation to the realities of conflict and intervention in this troubled former republic of Yugoslavia. UN peacekeepers were operating (mainly with a humanitarian mission) in an area where there was not only no peace to keep, but no real state in which to make peace.

☐ In both Bosnia/Herzegovina and Croatia, the traditional UN idea of impartiality as a basis of peacekeeping was very heavily criticised. There was simply no agreed 'cease-fire line' which could be impartially manned. Instead, there were hideous acts of 'ethnic cleansing', and other repeated violations of the most elementary rules of restraint in the conduct of hostilities. The fact that such acts were not confined to one side did not reduce the UN's vulnerability to the accusation that its impartiality, and avoidance of direct involvement in hostilities, involved it in a kind of passive complicity in the criminal actions of others.

☐ Inevitably, there were many complaints about the UN's management of peacekeeping troops operating in exceptionally difficult circumstances in former Yugoslavia. There was concern about how well thought-out the whole mission of these forces was; about the stringent rules which prevented UNPROFOR personnel from returning fire even when they were being shelled; about the adequacy of back-up in such matters as the provision of bomb-disposal officers; and about the linguistic confusion between the three main UN contingents in Sarajevo – French, Ukrainian and Egyptian.[19]

Elsewhere, in cases where the UN was involved in countries torn by civil war, comparable problems arose. In Cambodia, it was clear by autumn 1992 that the Khmer Rouge forces would not allow themselves to be disarmed or in any way administered by UNTAC forces: so UNTAC faced the daunting prospect of organising elections in 1993 against the hostility of an armed and dangerous party. This process which seemed bound to force UNTAC to move yet further into the arms of the government in Phnom Penh, reinforcing the Khmer Rouge suspicions that UNTAC was not impartial. In Angola, the UN did help monitor elections in November 1990, but could do little when the losers, UNITA, preferred to resume the struggle rather than accept electoral defeat. In Somalia, civil war and famine created conditions in which it was exceptionally hard for UN forces to work; and, as in Yugoslavia, there was tension between headquarters in New York and those having to carry out the UN's mission on the ground.

Thus, in the field of peacekeeping, the hopes which were still widespread in early 1992 have had to yield to a more pessimistic view. The United Nations, far from being at the very centre of successful efforts to transcend the pursuit of security on a purely national basis, looks more like a dust-bin into which states dump problems which they do not have the capacity or will to address directly themselves. If the veto is not being used any more, there needs to be some other system for ensuring that the UN is not saddled with an excessive number of near-impossible tasks. And if the UN is to play a central role in international security efforts, it will need to address the range of issues involved in its operations much more openly and systematically than it has in the past – even the very recent past.

Notes

[1] Boutros Boutros-Ghali, *An Agenda for Peace: Preventive Diplomacy Peacemaking and Peace-keeping*, (UN doc. A/47/277-S/24111, New York, 17 June 1992).

[2] *An Agenda for Peace*, paras. 2 and 75.

[3] *An Agenda for Peace*, paras. 14 and 15.

[4] *The Independent*, (London, 3 August 1990) p. 1. The transcript of President Bush's remarks at the Aspen Institute, as released by the White House Press Secretary on 2 August, contain no specific reference to the United Nations; but it does appear that the US needed no encouragement to handle this crisis through the UN.

[5] In Security Council Resolution 678 of 29 November 1990.

[6] *An Agenda for Peace*, paras. 20 and 34–45.

[7] The following enumeration of questions relating to collective security systems is adapted from that in Andrew Hurrell's excellent article 'Collective Security and International Order Revisited', *International Relations*, (London, March 1992).

[8] Article 108 of the UN Charter stipulates that amendments must be adopted by two thirds of the members of the General Assembly and be ratified, in accord with their respective constitutional processes, by two thirds of members of the UN, including all the permanent members of the Security Council.

[9] *An Agenda for Peace*, para. 43.

[10] Security Council Resolution 678 of 29 November 1990.

[11] *An Agenda for Peace*, paras. 28–32.

[12] *An Agenda for Peace*, para. 43.

[13] Text of the Paris Agreement on a Comprehensive Political Settlement of the Cambodia Conflict, concluded on 23 Oct. 1991, is in UN doc. A/46/608S/23177 of 30 Oct. 1991.

[14] *An Agenda for Peace*, para. 50.

[15] *An Agenda for Peace*, para. 20.

[16] Security Council Resolution 743 of 21 February 1992.

[17] Security Council Resolution 755 of 20 May 1992 recommended to the General Assembly that the Republic of Bosnia and Herzegovina be admitted to membership of the UN.

[18] Security Council Resolution 757 of 30 May 1992. The same principles were repeatedly enunciated in the documents approved by the International Conference on the Former Socialist Federal Republic of Yugoslavia, London, 26–28 August 1992.

[19] See e.g. Robert Fisk's characteristically blunt reports, 'Bungling Threatens Failure for UN Force', and 'UN Troops Battle Behind Language Barriers', *The Independent*, London, 21 and 22 Sept. 1992.

18

The Topography of Conflict: Internal and External Security Issues in South Asia

CHRISTOPHER SMITH

Senior Research Fellow, Centre for Defence Studies

Although the political map of South Asia may seem basically unchanged, the security complex has been transformed significantly. Economically, politically and physically, South Asia has undergone some fundamental changes which will both affect and define its future for many years to come. In all the changes the most common factors are economic weakness, the end of the Soviet Empire and alliances intended to form a bulwark against perceived Soviet expansionism. Not surprisingly, India and Pakistan have been most affected, other countries less so by dint of a combination of geo-political irrelevance or a state of underdevelopment and non-governance advanced enough to make common cause more a liability than an asset for external powers.

The potential for war between India and Pakistan over Kashmir or the support of separatist movements seems increasingly less likely, unless one or other side reaches an advanced level of political instability. Both sides can clearly ill-afford the luxury of a full-scale conflict and, as both protagonists become more economically exposed, their room for manoeuvre in a unipolar world grows more circumscribed. In all likelihood, diplomatic intervention, especially by the United States, Japan and possibly Germany, would restrain both sides, as the United States and the Soviet Union succeeded in doing over the 1990 Kashmir fracas.

What is clear, however, is that the combination of continued feudalism, corruption, population growth, inertia, grinding

poverty and declining governance have thrown up both
enhanced and new forms of insecurity. Abetted by some atro-
cious natural disasters in recent years, South Asia typifies the lost
decade of development. Moreover, South Asia continues to fall
apart, both metaphorically and in practice. The principal security threat lies in the interconnections between communal
tension, bad governance and sheer poverty and the potential for
such problems to mutate into more familiar types of insecurity
and conflict.

DEFENCE – THE FADING OPPORTUNITIES

Throughout the 1980s, both India and Pakistan successfully
embarked upon overdue defence modernisation programmes.
Recently, both sides have been cajoled into accepting that com-
pound economic indebtedness and continued defence
modernisation are incompatible.

Pakistan received massive tranches of US military and economic aid throughout the 1980s, totalling over $8 billion. This
allowed General Zia economic breathing space and some
defence procurement potential. In 1991, US military assistance
to Pakistan was suspended under the Pressler Amendment, for
two reasons which are difficult to disassociate from each other.
First, the Soviet withdrawal from Afghanistan sent Pakistan's
strategic value plummeting down the US foreign policy agenda.
Second, unlike Reagan, the Bush Administration took a very different view and increased significantly the US government's
efforts to prevent the horizontal spread of nuclear technology,
a resolve further strengthened by the outcome of the second
Gulf War.[1]

The effect upon Pakistan's defence capability has been little
short of devastating. Although the Pressler Amendment does
not preclude Pakistan from buying spare parts from US defence
manufacturers, it does prevent them being sold at traditional
foreign military sales (FMS) bargain-basement prices. So,
Pakistan must now pay commercial prices, which is next to
impossible – F-16 fighters, for example, are currently being can-
nibalised to keep them in service. Also, the embargo has
prevented Pakistan from receiving a further 71 F-16s on order

from the US and the penalty clauses and storage costs on some systems are adding to unnecessary expenditure and diminished readiness. Nor has Pakistan yet received the 20 M-109 self-propelled howitzers or the 200 *Sparrow* air-to-air missiles for the F-16.

A combination of military aid repayments at 14 per cent, the residual potential power of the armed forces and internal security measures have together prevented serious cuts in defence expenditure, despite demands and threats from both the IMF and bilateral aid donors. In 1991 Pakistan was instructed by the IMF to reduce its military expenditure by 9 per cent if future loans were to be forthcoming, when in fact it rose 11.6 per cent in the same year; defence expenditure and debt servicing account for 80 per cent of government expenditure.[2]

It seems difficult to see where Pakistan can go next. Although military expenditure remains high, almost Rs.77 billion in FY 1991–92 and 40 per cent of government spending, the scope for renewed procurement is extremely limited.[3] Cut off from military aid from the US, Pakistan can only trawl the international arms market in the hope of securing favourable deals to help maintain the production lines under threat after the end of the Cold War. One proposal is to sell on the F-16s and use the resources to purchase the *Mirage* 2000, assuming the US complies with the proposal.[4] Another is to persuade the French to finance the purchase of the *Mirage* 2000, given the appalling state of the French defence sector.[5] This would also act as a compensatory measure to atone for the recent decision not to go forward with plans to transfer a nuclear fuel reprocessing plant. Thus far, a financial protocol has been drawn up with France to cover the sale of 40 aircraft and three naval minesweepers but France will have to provide a great deal of credit if the deal is to survive. Even so, with bilateral donors and international finance organisations less willing than ever before to condone questionable procurement expenditures, pressure will remain until Pakistan can demonstrate the necessary economic reforms, particularly in taxation. In November 1991 the German Economic Co-operation Minister, Carl-Dieter Spranger announced that bilateral aid to Pakistan (and India) would be cut by 25 per cent in 1992 because of 'excessive armament', though Germany now appears to be backtracking.[6]

Throughout the 1980s, India undertook the most extensive modernisation programme in the country's history.[7] Though largely overlooked by the international defence community – until *Time* magazine opted to devote a cover story to India's bid for great power status[8] – the programme was quantitatively the largest in the Third World, eclipsing, by some way, similar programmes in Iraq and Saudi Arabia during the late-1980s.[9] The basis of the programme was a thorough modernisation of all sections of the armed forces coupled with a new commitment to the indigenous production base, including a comprehensive missile programme.

From 1988, however, the defence budget started to run into serious trouble and failed to keep pace with military debt repayments; a problem compounded by the declining strength and eventual devaluation of the rupee. The Army mechanisation programme ground to an ignominious halt. Equally damaging, it became known that new weapons platforms had been prematurely introduced to the Armed Forces and were practically unarmed due to foreign exchange shortages. The *Mirage* 2000 had entered service minus much of its armament and logistical back-up was poor in all sectors.[10] In addition, the end of the rupee-rouble trade has further compromised the procurement programme. In recent months, procurement has dropped away significantly. Nevertheless, curious anomalies persist, notably the ambitious decision to procure 10 C-130 transport aircraft at a cost of $12 million per unit, to be reconfigured by Israel as inflight refuelling tankers.[11] In addition, there is also a long-standing commitment to purchase an advanced trainer, most probably the *Hawk*, a requirement which has become that much more pressing as the air force currently possesses one of the worst accident rates in the world.

It seems virtually certain that India's ambitious attempt to build an indigenous Light Combat Aircraft will be either shelved or cancelled, raising the need for an interim solution of a direct replacement. The Russians have been quick to offer the Su-27 as a substitute as well as the *Yak* 141 for the Indian Navy as a means of sharing development costs, but Moscow's resolve to use defence sales as one of the few means available to acquire foreign exchange will mean that India must in future pay market prices in hard currency.

How both sides attempt to resolve the current impasse will be of enormous significance to both, once a semblance of order returns to Russia. A recent offer to provide India with $850 million of credit to purchase arms which Russia considers redundant and talk of joint tank and aircraft production intended specifically for export to the Third World are the type of defence links which could define future Indo-Russian relations. However, the international community and the US in particular may extend their current concern over Russian supply of space technology to India to encompass military equipment, should the speculative ventures proceed further. Unlike Russia, India is not politically bound by the current efforts to encourage the Permanent Five to take the lead in achieving greater transparency and control concerning weapons sales.[12] Moreover, India is capable enough of both producing under licence and exporting Russian military hardware, having itself taken the decision in the late-1980s to exploit defence market opportunities should they arise. Nor is it likely that Indian parliamentarians will find such a policy shift quite as disturbing as some of their predecessors – there is widespread desire for the country to take on a more active international role. Nevertheless, as with Pakistan, where India goes next very much depends upon the will of the international finance organisations, as well as the success or failure of the country's recently implemented structural adjustment programme.

NUCLEAR PROLIFERATION IN SOUTH ASIA

Since the end of the Second Gulf War, the question of horizontal nuclear proliferation has loomed large on the agenda of international concern. Recently, however, evidence from several quarters suggests that whilst the spectre of proliferation remains a major threat to the stability and safety of the international system, the current situation is somewhat less portentous than was assumed throughout 1991. Whilst Iraq had established a uranium enrichment programme, it had not yet reached the critical stage of enrichment cascading, namely, setting up a large number of centrifuges to operate in tandem.[13] Similarly, recent fears over the North Korean nuclear programme seem equally overstated, according to a recent evaluation within the US.[14]

Conceivably, something of the same could well be true about the two key 'nuclear hold-out' states in South Asia, India and Pakistan. Whilst the interest of both in nuclear weapons programmes cannot be denied, it is possible that the Iraq-syndrome has clouded the view of what the outside world understands is happening in South Asia.

Rolling back the Pressler Amendment now requires Pakistan to comply with a series of US requirements which together probably amount to a significant diminution and verification of the uranium enrichment programme. Well-placed sources in Islamabad suggest that this has been partially completed but not enough to convince the United States that aid should be resumed. Possibly, the sticking point concerns what nuclear policy-makers elect to do to downgrade and make unusable the highly enriched uranium core alleged to have been produced at the Kahuta plant.

The initial decision by Pakistan to cross the red light by accelerating the enrichment programme came at a particular point in the delicate history of civil-military relations in the country. Following the assassination of President Zia, Benazir Bhutto formed an elected government for the first time in nearly twenty years. Intimidated by the combined presence of President Ghulam Ishaq Khan and General Beg, then Chief of Army Staff, and despised by both, Prime Minister Bhutto played little part in decisions over the future of the nuclear programme. So much so, in fact, that she was unaware that her country had passed through the red light until informed by US intelligence. During the 1990 stand-off over Kashmir, Beg was able to order a heavily armed convoy of trucks to leave the Kahuta airbase and move towards a local airbase, where F-16s with modified bomb racks were placed on alert. To nobody's surprise this was easily picked up by US satellite surveillance and this contributed as much as anything to the sanctions.

The ousting of Benazir Bhutto failed to bring the expected return of the military under the leadership of General Aslam Beg. Thereafter, General Beg was removed from office having issued pro-Iraqi statements whilst Pakistani troops were forming a part of the Alliance force and for making irreverent comments on the nuclear issue. General Gul resigned soon after.

Together, these events weakened enormously the power of militant Islam within the country.

In addition, the demise of Beg has also weakened the pro-bomb lobby. Although the President continues to be a staunch supporter of the pro-bomb lobby, if not its virtual creator, and A Q Khan continues to add his political weight on behalf of the scientific-bureaucracy, the accession of General Asif Nawaz has markedly slowed and weakened the nuclear bomb programme. In both principle and practice, the President can act on military affairs without consulting the Prime Minister, which is how Benazir Bhutto was successfully excluded from the nuclear policy-making loop. However, it is impossible to circumvent the Chief of Army Staff.

Retired service personnel are excluded from seeking political office for a period of three years – Generals Beg and Gul are no exception. In addition, the position of Chief of Army Staff changes every three years, which means that Beg will become eligible for political office as General Asif Nawaz steps down. Thus, the establishment could simultaneously lose an anti-nuclear dove and gain a pro-nuclear hawk, which would change dramatically the configuration of the nuclear debate in Pakistan. Moreover, the link between the Islamic lobbies and the pro-nuclear lobbies should not be overlooked. Should Islamicisation acquire more than a foothold in the political life of the country, the pressure to push the nuclear programme forward would be considerable.

As a result, the next two years will be a critical period for the nuclear debate in Pakistan. Currently, the attitude towards the United States ranges from extreme chagrin to outright anger, both inside and outside government. Moreover, as non-establishment liberals are apt to point out, the United States itself has increased the prospect of nuclear proliferation through the constant waiver of the Symington Amendment over the 1980s. The general feeling is that Pakistan has been unfairly singled out now that it is of no real strategic value. Continuing to block military aid will increase the current rift even further. Nor is this situation likely to change much under the Clinton Administration: Democratic Administrations tend to take an anti-Pakistan stance on South Asian issues.

Nevertheless, it would seem that even after the departure of

General Beg, the nuclear lobby is still reasonably powerful. In all likelihood, the decision-making process is now in the hands of the President and A Q Khan, the director of the Kahuta plant. Until this changes, there is little chance of the type of movement that is needed for better relations with the US and, increasingly, Germany and Japan, both major aid donors.

In general, however, it would seem that the majority in Pakistan realise that the time has come to negotiate away the nuclear option, though this may not equate with signing the Non-Proliferation Treaty (NPT). Thus, a window of opportunity exists whilst Pakistan has an anti-nuclear Chief of Army Staff and whilst the nuclear hawks are confined to the political margins. Western policy-makers, especially in the US, appear to have overlooked this potentially valuable chance.

In India, the strength of intent on the nuclear issue is far greater. Not only is India determined to stay outside the NPT, which it considers to be inherently discriminatory, but the establishment is also determined not to relinquish the nuclear option either. Given India's evident access to nuclear materials, efforts to control India's nuclear weapon programme have centred of late upon its ballistic missile programme. In May 1992, the United States moved against both Russia and India following the former's approval to sell India cyrogenic rocket motors. The decision to apply trade sanctions against the space programmes of both countries was widely criticised within India and the feeling that commercial rather than political compulsions were at the heart of the issue were fuelled by parallel moves to punish the Indian pharmaceuticals industry over an intellectual property rights dispute. Relations with the US are currently at a low ebb.

Nevertheless, India's intermediate-range missile programme proceeds apace. Although the May 1992 launch of an *Agni* missile went wrong, more tests are in the pipeline.[15] The government's insistence that successive tests on the missile programme are nothing more than 'technology demonstrators' has failed to cut much ice within the international community and it would seem appropriate to expect that the international community will continue to question the logic of India's missile programme.

Despite India's cogent critique of the NPT over the years, the international community has all but run out of patience with an élite that it considers unduly arrogant on all matters nuclear and too ambivalent towards the country's mounting economic chaos and the links between the two. So far, all attempts to persuade India to enter the non-proliferation régime have failed and this state of affairs will continue, witness Japan's recent unsuccessful attempt to tie economic aid to discussions on the NPT.

Nevertheless, on the nuclear issue at least, India has fewer options than it might think and an acrimonious confrontation is on the horizon. During the Cold War, India successfully played East against West with considerable poise, managing never to get too ensconced in the camp of either, despite a marked dependence upon the Soviet Union for defence equipment. Geo-politically, India managed to acquire a subtle form of immunity which diplomatic efforts failed to break down, especially on the nuclear issue. Now, however, the situation is very different and India stands more politically exposed than at any time during its independence. In addition, the country's economic crisis has provided the United States with a series of political levers which the Bush Administration has proved increasingly prepared to use, as demonstrated by the recent refusal to back India's application for a soft loan from the Asia Development Bank.

In Washington, the overall feeling is that if India fails to pick up the warning signals, any form of political leverage ought to be employed and decision-makers recognise that this can be done at a low political cost. Conceivably, India may find that the advent of President Clinton reduces significantly the mounting pressure to do something/anything to convince the international community that the South Asian nuclear arms race can be controlled or even reversed. Obversely, it is more likely that members of the new Administration will take a very much tougher line than Bush on the proliferation problem.

On the nuclear issue and the political postures which surround it, the West has still much to learn and accept about South Asia. Nuclear proliferation in South Asia is a key issue which both governments and the international community must continue to confront. Nevertheless, two major issues stand out which the nonproliferation community should consider with care.

First, there exists a window of opportunity for positive movement within Pakistan which has not been exploited. The US
decision to invoke the Pressler Amendment is an obstacle more
than anything else. At present Pakistan has few options but to
stand firm against American leverage, even though the government may wish to move in the direction required by
Washington. Indeed, any capitulation would probably offer the
mullahs a golden opportunity to consolidate the linkage
between the nuclear option and Islamic fundamentalism.

Moreover, India has realised that by continuing to dismiss
any arms control initiatives, US pressure is kept up on
Islamabad, which well suits India's objectives. The blunt refusal
to give the Five Nation Conference anything more than a cur-
sory consideration and rejection was a case in point. India has
no incentive to approach the conference table. In principle,
similar levers to those used against Pakistan should work. In
practice, however, the decision- and opinion-shaping community would elect to stand firm and ride out threats to sovereignty
and independence. In sum, a US policy based upon further
leverage and coercion could alienate both Islamabad and New
Delhi from the international community and constitute an
enormous setback to non-proliferation efforts in South Asia.
Obversely, there appears to have been no thought as to how
the prevailing spiral of negative diplomacy can be reversed.
Conceivably, given the chronic economic conditions which
obtain in both countries, there is scope to entice, even bribe,
both countries to the negotiating table. What is clear is that
pressure is unlikely to work and, even if it does, the political cost
could be higher than expected.

Second, the current situation amounts to one of perverse stability, which is why both sides are keen to point out that
proliferation is a problem for the West, not South Asia. Neither
side at present seems set to deploy nuclear weapons. The
Chinese appear to have understood the process much better,
which might be why Beijing has so few problems with the *Agni*
programme, for example. Whereas the Western nuclear powers
spend a disproportionate amount of time locked in thought
and debate over how and when nuclear weapons might be used,
the absence of the equivalent in South Asia is in fact a positive,
not an unstable, element of the process, because it creates a

clear space between possessing a nuclear capability on the one
hand and the assimilation into force structures on the other.
Western strategic thinkers, who are used to equating loose ends
with instability, would do well to reassess their concerns in this
instance.

However, if one side is nudged too far, through humiliation or
through domestic pressure, a nuclear arms race could easily
result and the economic and political price would be extremely high. Therefore, the process must be stabilised. Both sides can
be encouraged to keep domestic pressures under control, which
implies a clear role for government. Transparency could be
rewarded whereas at present there only exists the opportunity to
punish non-compliance, which blocks the potential for reward-
ing progress. True, the United States can use its tremendous
relative political power to address the nuclearisation of South
Asia. In so doing, however, it should be careful not to force
either side into an anti-American/pro-nuclear posture.

At this particular point, there is an urgent need for some
imaginative thinking. In two years time, the incumbent Pakistani
Chief of Army Staff could be replaced by a more nationalist
general. Democracy may not survive in Pakistan, in the short-
term future or beyond, nor may the delicate balance between
secular and theological approaches to government. If the
Clinton Administration 'goes after' Pakistan, any or all of these
scenarios could unfold. Equally, policy-makers will at some point
have to deal with India's relentless march towards the gates of
the nuclear club, which necessitates a revisionist view of the proliferation problem in South Asia. Decisions must be taken over
how to tackle quasi-nuclear states, namely India and Israel.
Their current blurred status is a clear warning during a period
when, otherwise, the non-proliferation régime seems in reasonable shape.

Finally, there is one extremely important lesson for Britain. In
the coming months, opposition to a Comprehensive Test Ban
Treaty coupled with what borders on contempt for Article VI of
the NPT relating to nuclear disarmament is almost certain to
catch up with the government.[16] Belatedly, the importance of a
test ban is beginning to be recognised in Washington, in so far
as it would provide a political cover for the 'nuclear hold-out-
states' in South Asia and place unbearable pressure on the

Indian government to open negotiations with Pakistan. This latter view is widespread amongst decision- and opinion-shapers in New Delhi and these are developments which should be recognised and encouraged by the British government.

NON-MILITARY SECURITY ISSUES

One of the fundamental questions pertaining to South Asia is whether partition ended in 1947 or still has further to go, especially in the light of the 1971 war, which ended with the partition of Pakistan. Perhaps the main point to be understood about South Asia is how powerless the outside world will be to react if either India or Pakistan progress down the tragic route of Sri Lanka. As in the case of the former Yugoslavia, whilst the moral case for halting the loss of life and human suffering would be manifest, operational difficulties would be more than considerable. At what point could a nation's sovereignty be passed over? What would be the objectives, time limits and economic constraints? Once a semblance of order is attained, how would it be maintained?

Throughout the subcontinent, all the signs of political decay are present. The optimism that accompanied Nehru's 'tryst with destiny' has long evaporated. In particular, South Asia is now the stage for widespread ethnic conflict and instability. In Afghanistan, the toppling of President Najibullah has increased massively the ethnic disputes within Kabul, though ironically the surrounding countryside has been successfully partitioned into autonomous fiefdoms and is relatively free of conflict. Kabul itself, however, remains a political battleground and a microcosm of the complex ethnic and religious differences which have always pervaded the country's history.

Political conflict and instability now seems endemic within Kabul; it is difficult to see where the embittered battle between the government and Hekmatyer's Hesbi-Islami forces will end. Nor does any political force seem capable of wresting the rest of the country away from the war lords. Nevertheless, a large proportion of the country's six million refugees are pouring back across the borders from Iran and Pakistan, although this has been partly compensated by a flood of refugees fleeing Kabul and *mujahideen* infighting and persecution – Afghan immigration authorities have noted a large number of Pashtuns seeking refuge in Pakistan. Aid organisations have proved miserly so far and richer Islamic states, especially Iran and Saudi Arabia, have tempered their donations in the face of minimal success on influencing the country's Shia and Sunni groups. The expectation is, therefore, that Afghanistan will be left very much on its own to rebuild a shattered economy and keep the lid on the ever present threat of internecine conflict.

Pakistan, however, seems keen to offer what help it can to ensure a growth in governance and development and Islamabad is at the forefront of attempts to isolate and emasculate Hekmatyar's Hesbi-Islamic forces, which it actively supported throughout the war. In part, indulging the government in Kabul is designed to relieve the draining refugee problem from within its own borders. The intention of the government, however, is to encourage wherever possible the growth of order and stability. Underpinning Islamabad's policy in this direction is the race with Turkey to establish commercial routes into Central Asia, which it is currently losing. By using the port of Karachi and by building a rail spur through Afghanistan and Pakistan into Central Asia, Pakistan would hope to become a conduit for the massive amount of commerce and development aid which will eventually flow into the region.

Nevertheless, the potential for peaceful Pakistan-Afghan relations in the future seem remote. Within Pakistan there are still elements of support for Hekmatyar and he may still be receiving supplies from the Inter Services Intelligence (ISI) Directorate, formerly the organisation entrusted with the supply of American arms to the *mujahideen*. Whether or not the government can exercise the necessary authority to oppose this is open to question.

In the future, Pakistan's interest in Afghanistan's ethnic problems are likely to recede if Turkey continues to win the race for markets and as more refugees return home. Equally, the government's growing problems in Sindh also look set to dominate the political agenda for some time to come. In late-May 1992 under intense pressure from the Army, the government ordered 30,000 troops into Sindh to be deployed against the corrupt and violent MQM factions in Karachi and 'dacoit' groups which consistently terrorise rural areas. Although the operation has been partially successful, the possibility of open conflict between the MQM and the centre cannot be ruled out. Moreover, the MQM party – which originally held a respectable petty bourgeois power base – has degenerated into a powerful group of landowners, drug and arms dealers and corrupt power brokers. Although Karachi might have been partially 'liberated' the higher echelons of the party remained intact and the military has also uncovered MQM plans to create a separate homeland for 'mohajirs' – the Muslims who crossed over from India in 1947.

The government has attempted to cover up the less successful aspects of the mission by insisting upon an Indian connection. Clearly, however, the operation has weakened the government through defections and has bred tensions within the troika. The Sindh operation is one example of events which could so easily escalate politically rendering a foreign adventure against India an increasingly worthwhile move. Alternatively, such chaos might invite another coup.

India too has a mounting problem with separatist groups, ranging from the high profile imbroglios in the Punjab and Kashmir to the less well-known attempts to secure a separate Jharkhand state for the luckless tribals from Bihar, for example. Recent successes against Sikh terrorist leaders in the Punjab have relieved pressures to some extent but several problems remain in other parts of the country, notably Kashmir. Recent successes could all too easily be reversed by a wider dispersion of terrorist activity around the country. Sikh terrorists are alleged to be fanning out into states as far south as Maharashtra.[17]

Moreover, the problems are not just in the political sphere. Over the past decade, at least since the assassination of Mrs Gandhi, internal security problems have cost the country dearly in increased resources – paramilitary forces currently number 450,000 men and women – yet this is not seen as a part of the Indian Army's role.[18] Another marked cost has been India's increasingly frequent appearance on lists of countries which abuse human rights. The recent report by Amnesty International was particularly harmful, as was the government's repeated attempts to prevent Amnesty from gaining access to Kashmir.[19]

During the late-1980s the precarious situation in Kashmir

took an unfavourable turn for the worse, almost to the extent of bringing India and Pakistan to a war footing. Starting in December 1989, following the suppression of a peaceful demonstration by the paramilitary forces, a full scale rebellion against Indian rule began in the valley of Kashmir, involving as many as six separatist groups and a total force of 45,000 guerillas. The most frequent request is for union with Pakistan, at the very least for New Delhi to honour the plebiscite recommended by the United Nations in 1948. That India and Pakistan were able to avoid a war over Kashmir in 1990 is a tribute to the diplomatic skills of both sides and the even-handed interventions by both the Soviet Union and the United States. However, it is uncertain as to how long the Indian central government can contain the crisis and it has probably only done so do to date because of the fundamental divisions between pro-independence Jammu and Kashmir Liberation Front and the Hizb-ul-Mujahedin rebel group which seeks union with Pakistan.

More germane, perhaps, is the risk that the Kashmir issue could become a *jihad* and attract the numerous fanatical fundamentalists made redundant now the Afghan crisis has been partially solved. This is certainly not in the interests of India, which would be forced to apply tougher polices than already exist. Nor would this please Islamabad – *jihads* are there to be exported, not imported, and Pakistan hardly wants a fresh infusion of fundamentalism at this delicate point in its political history.

Under the terms of the 1971 Simla Agreement, signed in the aftermath of the war, there is scope for both sides to discuss and negotiate Kashmir. However, staying with the Indian Union or succession to Pakistan are the only two options on the agenda; there is no third alternative for independence. In Pakistan, senior officials seem inclined towards defusing tensions and, especially, from ridding the government of the costly but largely senseless dispute over the Siachin glacier. A unilateral gesture in this direction would be a major step forward for Pakistan's foreign policy and an embarrassment for India if it failed to elicit a similar act of good faith.

India's other major internal security problem concerns the rise in radical Hindu chauvinism, notably the rise of the militant Hindu-nationalist Bharatiya Janata Party (BJP) and its now permanent presence on the political landscape. Essentially, although the electoral success of the BJP was significant in Northern India, the party seems less likely to prevail against the Congress party in the south, which is imperative if the BJP is seeking outright political power. Nevertheless, the threat of violent Hindu chauvinism, typified by the dispute over the *Ayodhya* temple in Uttar Pradesh, is very real and has already cost thousands of lives. This typifies the type of dispute which inflames passions in India (which are always extremely difficult to understand and quantify). On the one hand, declining sympathy for the militant wing of the BJP, the Vishwa Hindu Parishad (VHP), is evidence that the Hindu population may not accept sustained levels of radicalism over the long term. On the other, however, Hindu chauvinism has never been far from the surface in recent years. It appeared with an ugly vengeance after the assassination of Mrs Gandhi, for example. As India becomes an economically and culturally more liberal, liberated and externally influenced polity – and there is no doubt that this is happening at great speed – the Hindu heartlands are bound to feel threatened. Whether or not India is politically cohesive enough to enter a period of fundamental confusion and debate over theological and secular approaches to government is open to question.

The remaining states of South Asia create far less cause for international anxiety, even though the conflict, misery and violence may be of no less human concern. This is because their geo-political importance and defence capability is much less than that of India or Pakistan. Nevertheless, there are signposts here for the rest of South Asia which cannot be ignored.

The most brutal example of chaos and anarchy in the region is that of Sri Lanka, racked by ethnic violence and chaos for well over a decade. In general, the superpowers have overlooked the island, save for a degree of US interest in the tank farm at Trincomalee during the 'base race' in the Indian Ocean during the 1980s. The chance of further intervention by India, following the disastrous and expensive excursion during the late-1980s, also looks remote. The international community has by and large failed to contribute towards stemming the process of ethnic fratricide, although the foreign aid community has worked hard to preserve the island's high standard of education and health care.

Although the world has become used to the stories of atro-
cious violence and ferocity coming from both sides, there is
mounting evidence that Sri Lanka is heading for an important
juncture in its ragged history. Following the receipt of light
tanks from Czechoslovakia and heavier tanks from China – Sri
Lanka's only reliable source of military equipment – the government has served notice that it intends to destroy the Tamil
Tigers. With additional firepower at its disposal, and against a
backdrop of continuing political brutalisation, the Sri Lankan
government could well succeed, especially given the Indians'
new-found resolve to eliminate the Tamil Tigers' presence in
Tamil Nadu. More than usually high collateral damage is certain
as and when the offensive begins.

At one level, the Sri Lanka situation is an intractable internal
security problem, over which external forces can have little
influence, at this stage at least. However, the fact that states such
as China and Czechoslovakia can successfully sell tanks to the Sri
Lankan government, in full knowledge of their likely use, whilst
the international community looks on, is illustrative of just how
much political energy needs to be invested in the problems surrounding the international defence trade. Preventing the supply
of tanks to Sri Lanka will do little to stem the conflict but any
means to prevent a quantum increase in violence against civilians should be pursued.

A similar brutalisation of politics can be observed in
Bangladesh, where trouble and violence is frequently centred
upon the university campuses. Also, lawlessness has risen abrupt-
ly in recent months – in August 1992 alone, the government
detained some 17,000 suspected criminals.[20]

Bangladesh's primary security problem can be summed up by
the relative volume of aid the country requires to provide basic
needs for the population. The combination of population pressure and extreme vulnerability effectively means that the
country will always depend upon the largesse of the international finance community. This is at the heart of the nation's
insecurity. At present, aid flows into Bangladesh without too
many restraints – during the mid-1980s, for example, the World
Bank was forced to confront the problem that the aid pipeline
was more than Bangladesh could, in fact, absorb.

Given that non-Third World recovery programmes are being

funded by private capital, Bangladesh will probably be able to maintain its credit-worthy status into the future without having to struggle against competing claims. Nevertheless, Bangladesh is a hostage and will remain so. In particular, the increasing attention which donor agencies devote to democracy, human rights and governance in the post-Cold War environment could all too easily work against Bangladesh should internal security problems become difficult to handle. Very much the same is true of other countries in South Asia. In addition, for Afghanistan and Pakistan there is the additional problem of religion – the future prospect of economic aid being tied to religious policies is real enough, once the United States assesses where it stands on the issue of Islamic fundamentalism.

CONCLUSION

In essence, the security environment in South Asia will rise or fall on the issue of governance. Will governments be able to organise economies, guarantee human rights, mediate ethnic disputes, stem corruption and lawlessness sufficiently to convince the international system to continue to provide an economic crutch? If they fail to succeed, will nation states become increasingly less viable and unravel into zones of ethnic conflict and chaos, as seems to be the case in Sri Lanka? The great powers are only just beginning to understand the relationship between aid and power in the post-Cold War era. Where that debate leads will have fundamental implications for South Asian security and sovereignty.

In many ways there seems little that external powers can do beyond exploiting pressure points. However, if good governance is to be encouraged then it must form a salient part of the foreign policies of those countries which wish to bring influence to bear. There is little point, for example, in adding political weight to economic aid programmes whilst maintaining *laissez faire* policies towards arms sales. Only when appropriate measures have been found to encourage greater responsibility and responsiveness will it be possible to address the myriad security problems within South Asia. Increasingly, there are quiet calls within the region, for external powers to act as brokers on, for example, Rashmir and nuclear proliferation. At present, Japan is one of the few countries which would command broad respect. The United States and Britain are largely discredited because of the serious incompatibility between their own defence policies and their expectations of others. A positive approach to nuclear testing could go a long way to establishing a more co-operative climate.

Notes

[1] Graham, T W, 'Winning the Nonproliferation Battle', *The Bulletin of Atomic Scientists*, (September 1991), p. 9.

[2] 'Pakistan', *Journal of Defense & Diplomacy*, Vol 8, No 7/8, (July/August 1990), p. 31.

[3] Wickramanayake, D 'Indian Threat Makes Defence more Important than Food', *Defence*, Vol 22, No 7, (July 1991), p. 14.

[4] McDonald, H , 'Destroyer of worlds: Concerns grow over nuclear arms potential', *Far Eastern Economic Review*, Vol 155, No 17, (30 April 1992), p. 28.

[5] 'Pakistan Defense Chief Seeks Mirage 2000', *Defence Daily*, (18 June, 1992).

[6] McDonald, H, 'Arms Audit: Germany, Soviet Union deliver double shock', *Far Eastern Economic Review*, Vol 154, No 48, (28 November 1992), p. 20.

[7] For a full account of this programme see the authors, *India's Ad Hoc Arsenal*, (SIPRI/OUP, forthcoming 1993).

[8] Munro, R H, 'Superpower Rising', *Time*, No 14, (3 April 1989 pp. 10–17.

[9] *World Armaments and Disarmament: SIPRI Yearbook 1990*, (SIPRI/OUP, Oxford, 1990), Table 7.2, p. 228.

[10] Gupta, S and P G Thakurta, 'Heading for a Crisis', India Today, Vol XIV, No 4, (28 February 1989), pp. 42–50.

[11] 'Indian inflight tankers', *Far Eastern Economic Review*, Vol 155, No 37, (17 September 1992), p. 9.

[12] For a review of these efforts see the comprehensive report by the British American Security Information Council (BASIC), 'Recent Initiatives to Control the Arms Trade', BASIC Report 92.3, (BASIC, Washington/ London, June 1992).

[13] *PPNN Newsbrief Number 17*, (Spring 1992), p. 13.

[14] Chanda, N, 'Atomic ambivalence', *Far Eastern Economic Review*, Vol 155, No 39, (1 October 1992), pp. 8–10.

[15] Ramachandran, R, 'System design problem led to Agni failure', *Economic Times*, (28 August 1992).

[16] Britain is currently a *de facto* member of the nine month moratorium on nuclear testing but only because British nuclear testing takes place in Nevada and the US has agreed to a nine month moratorium on testing.

Otherwise, British policy is unrelenting – 'The UK does not intend to declare a moratorium, nor does the . . . Act require us to do so . . .', see Pullinger, S, 'An end to Nuclear testing?' *ISIS Briefing Paper No. 30,* (October 1992).

[17] Awasthi, D, 'Expanding Turf', *India Today,* Vol XVI, No 18, (30th September 1991), p. 42

[18] Bedi, R, 'India's reluctant police', *Jane's Defence Weekly,* Vol 16, No 1, (6 July 1991), p. 22.

[19] Amnesty International, *India: Torture. Rape & Deaths in Custody,* (Amnesty International, London. March 1992), 195pp.

[20] Kamakuddin, S, 'Back to your books: Government clamps down on campus violence', *Far Eastern Economic Review,* Vol 155, No 38, (24 September 1992).

19

A Road to
an Arab-Israeli Peace?

EFRAIM KARSH AND M ZUHAIR DIAB

*Dr. Karsh is Reader at the Department of War Studies, King's
College, University of London, and Mr. Diab is a Research
Associate of the Department*

The return of the Labour Party to power in Israel in June 1992, at the head of an unprecedently large peace camp, has revived the stalemated peace process. For the moment, both Arabs and Israelis seem keen to reach an historic compromise that will resolve the protracted and bloody conflict between them. However wary of each other, there appears to be a mutual recognition that the conflict has outlived its usefulness, and that its exorbitant costs exceed by far any potential gains. Yet, despite the surprisingly positive progress of the negotiations, particularly between Israel and Syria, both sides will have to display far more innovative thinking than they have shown thus far.

In our view, the best, perhaps the only, means to break the deadlock of the Middle East conflict is to establish a regional *community*, comprising the entire Arab-Israeli sector and guaranteed by the five permanent members of the United Nations Security Council. The community would be anchored to bilateral peace agreements which would settle the outstanding problems between Israel and each of its Arab neighbours.

The plan is predicated on the following three assumptions. First, any settlement must be *comprehensive*, avoiding the all too common mistake of exclusive concentration on the Israeli-Palestinian problem. In the absence of a comprehensive peace between Israel and *all* of its Arab neighbours, especially Syria and Jordan, the collapse of any Israeli-Palestinian arrangement is a foregone conclusion. Conversely, it is extremely doubtful whether the Arab states would be willing to enter into separate peace agreements without a serious movement on the Palestinian issue; but even if they did, the perpetuation of the Palestinian problem would leave a permanent source of resentment and instability in the region, as illustrated by Saddam's 'false –linkage' during the Gulf War.

Second, an Arab-Israeli settlement must be based on mutual recognition of each other's legitimate rights and interests, namely, the Arabs' right to regain the territories lost in 1967 and the Palestinian right of self determination, on the one hand, and Israel's right for regional acceptance and secure existence, on the other. In practical terms, this means an Israeli withdrawal to the pre-June 1967 borders with agreed minimal territorial adjustments in strategic areas,[1] and the establishment of an independent Palestinian state on the West Bank and the Gaza Strip (preferably confederated with Jordan) in return for a genuine and contractual peace which includes unequivocal *de jure* recognition, full diplomatic relations, unrestricted freedom of movement and economic ties

Finally, regional actors and external powers will both have to reconcile themselves to substantial international involvement in the attainment and preservation of any peace settlement. However Middle Easterners abhor 'foreign domination', theirs is 'the most penetrated international system' and will continue to be so for the foreseeable future.[2] All of them owe much of their basic security and well-being to the political, economic, and military support of the great powers, and no solution will be feasible unless those powers will fully put their minds and hearts into it. For their part, the great powers must realise that they will not be able to shrink from their responsibility for Middle Eastern stability. Their interests in the region are simply too vast and too enduring to be left unattended.

THE PLAN

We envisage the formation of the community as a three-phased process, implemented over a period of 20 years. During this time, the parties to the conflict will move from outright hostility to neutrality, to mutual cooperation and collective security.

The *first stage*, beginning immediately after the conclusion of bilateral peace agreements between the Arab states and Israel, would take up to five years. In this stage, the foundations of a *security community* would be put in place, namely, gradual withdrawal of Israeli forces from the occupied territories and their replacement by an international supervisory force. A genuine autonomy would be implemented in the West Bank and the Gaza Strip as a corridor for the establishment of an independent Palestinian state. The Golan Heights would be placed under Syrian sovereignty and be demilitarised, but Israel would retain a defensive military presence on the Golan, along its border, for the duration of this phase.

A proposed text of a security community's treaty is presented in Appendix 'A' (page 331), suffice it to mention here that it requires the local participants to adopt a policy of permanent neutrality among themselves and to maintain and defend this policy with all the means at their disposal; to renounce any territorial claims against their neighbours and to outlaw and dissolve any irredentist movements;[3] to carry out elaborate security and arms control arrangements including the *complete* demilitarisation of the Golan Heights and the stationing of an international supervisory force there and in the newly-established Palestinian state.

The great power guarantor states, for their part, would undertake to remove the community from the sphere of great power rivalry (including the reduction and regulation of their arms transfers to the region) and to defend both its security as a whole and the territorial integrity of its individual members. It is true that the former development is already underway thanks to the end of the Cold War and the disappearance of the Soviet Union; however, as the future direction of the 'new international order' is still uncertain, it is crucial to include great power commitment to this effect in the proposed security package.

By the time the *second phase* comes into effect, the security community should have been established, Israel would have completed its withdrawal from the occupied territories (and South Lebanon), an independent Palestinian state would have been established, and complete normalisation of Arab-Israeli relations would have been accomplished. During the next 15 years, the regional actors would work to deepen and strengthen this newly-established peace by transforming the security community into a wider politico-economic entity, similar to the European Community (EC). When this process, is brought to fruition, the *third phase* of our programme would begin, namely, the emergence of a regional community with its own collaborative institutions and mechanisms in the political, economic, and military spheres. The international security guarantees would remain in force, though foreign military presence in the area would, in essence, be terminated, with the exception of small supervisory forces.

All this would undoubtedly represent a fundamental break with past patterns, and would embark the Middle East on a completely new course. But even if this final stage proved impractical within the envisaged time, or even unattainable indefinitely, the *security community* in itself would suffice to ensure a stable peace between Arabs and Israelis for the foreseeable future.

CONFIDENCE-BUILDING MEASURES

To create a more conducive atmosphere for the pre-agreement stage and to remove potential obstacles from the peace process, both parties would be well-advised to avoid public debate of contentious issues and to make a series of *mutual* political and military gestures. At the same time, a general clarification of the underlying principles of the negotiations, namely, the trading of 'land for peace' within the framework of a comprehensive regional arrangement, may be essential for a successful launching of the process.

The need to postpone discussion of the most contentious issues cannot be overstated. Take the question of Jerusalem. Were this issue to be put on the negotiating table from the start, it would be bound to derail the peace process, with Palestinians adamant on making Jerusalem the capital of their future state and Israelis equally determined to keep the city undivided. Yet, it is not inconceivable that, if left to the end of the process, both parties might be reluctant to obstruct a comprehensive settlement, even on such a sensitive issue, and might consequently modify their positions so as to give the Palestinians control over the Arab-populated part of East Jerusalem. The

Old City could then be neutralised with citizens of all states having free access to the holy sites.[4]

Concessionary gestures during the negotiating period should be reciprocal, made on a one-for-one basis. Thus, for example, the Arab states could scale down (hopefully stop altogether) the demonisation of Israel in the mass media; such a move might convince Israelis of the sincerity of Arab intentions and, at the same time, give Arab leaders more room for manoeuvre in the negotiating process. Another significant gesture on the Arab side would be the end of the economic boycott against Israel. Israel could reciprocate by avoiding any provocative statements on the final outcome of the negotiations and, more importantly, by freezing the building of settlements in the occupied territories until a solution regarding their final status has been reached.

The Palestinians would undoubtedly gain a substantial measure of Israeli goodwill by ceasing attacks on Israeli and Jewish targets, by ending the *intifada,* and, no less importantly, by revoking those clauses in the Palestinian Covenant (such as Articles 2, 5, 6) which stipulated action or the elimination of Israel, either directly or through the 'right of return.'[5] In addition, the Covenant could be amended to state that the long-term final resolution of the Arab-Israeli conflict in its ideological sense, namely, acceptance of Israel as a Jewish state and its integration into the Arab system, will be achieved through peaceful means.

Were such far-reaching gestures to be made, Israel should reciprocate by accepting the PLO as a full partner for negotiations (if it had not already done so), cease attacks on Palestinian targets, release Palestinian detainees, and, last but not least, give the Palestinians greater freedom in running their own affairs (including, perhaps, unilateral withdrawal from certain densely populated areas) as a first step towards a final settlement.

In addition to these steps, both parties would be well-advised to take certain precautionary military measures that will facilitate the implementation of the agreement, including:

☐ Restrictions on the numbers of troops and types of weapons systems deployed along the borders between Israel and its neighbours;

- □ Support for the Lebanese authorities to reassert *real* authority throughout the country by consolidating the Lebanese Army and disarming the various militia and military organisations:
- □ Establishment of monitoring and observation posts along the joint borders, manned by UN observers from the five permanent members of the Security Council;
- □ Establishment of a crisis management centre, possibly in Jerusalem, under the Security Council's auspices, to deal with emergencies and potential sources of escalation. Each of the regional states would keep representatives in this centre and keep it informed of such alarming indicators as large-scale manoeuvres or movements of troops;
- □ Working out provisions regarding mutually accepted surveillance, whether by satellite or aerial reconnaissance, to prevent any surprise attack during the process of Israeli withdrawal and the setting of the security community.[6]

This, then, is the general framework of the proposed regional community and the recommended measures to bring about its successful effectuation. In the following pages we will try to show the merits of this plan for both the great powers (especially the United States and Russia) and the regional actors.

THE VIEW FROM WASHINGTON

To successive American Administrations in the post-Second World War era, the Middle East has been a crucial link in its worldwide chain of containment around the Soviet Union. Hence the establishment of the Baghdad Pact (1955), latterly transformed into the Central Treaty Organisation (CENTO), and the Truman (1947), Eisenhower (1957), Nixon (1969) and Carter (1979) doctrines; hence too the consistent effort (with the partial exception of Jimmy Carter's presidency) to exclude the Soviet Union from the Arab-Israeli political process and the abundant aid given by the United States to the Afghan Mujahedin.

Against this backdrop, one could easily question American readiness to support any regional arrangement which envisages close collaboration with the Russians and gives Moscow an important role in Middle Eastern affairs. Just as American fears of Soviet 'expansionism' precluded superpower cooperation in the past, the disintegration of the Soviet State and the consequent elevation of the United States to the 'only remaining superpower' may diminish incentives for such collaboration in the future. Why should the United States take note of the wishes of a former (and hostile) great power, it may be reasoned, if it can readily impose a *Pax Americana* in the region?

And yet, the end of the Cold War gives room for optimism regarding the chances for future cooperation over the Middle East, as evidenced by the co-sponsorship of the Madrid peace conference in October 1991. Indeed, if there is a single major lesson to be derived from the 1990–1991 Gulf conflict, it is that, however weak it may be, Moscow can still act as a spoiler if left out of Middle Eastern affairs;[7] once made a partner to such a regional arrangement, the Russians will not only have the strongest incentives to ensure its success, but to collaborate with the United States in other regions and fields of activity. Moreover, by creating a regional system capable of responding collectively to local challenges, the proposed community largely removes the need for great power unilateralism. Given the extreme reluctance of President Bush to respond unilaterally to the Iraqi occupation of Kuwait in the summer of 1990 – a constraint likely to intensify in the future due to the growing mood of 'America first' – the contribution of this regional framework to US interests in the Middle East seems self-evident.

On top of these general advantages, the proposed scheme could offer the United States important spin-offs. So far, the Administration has remained opposed to the establishment of an independent Palestinian state, not only because of American concern about the detrimental implications of such a move for Israeli security but also (perhaps, even more so) on account of its anxiety over the stability of the Hashemite Kingdom of Jordan. Given a Palestinian majority in Jordan, on the one hand, and the growing restiveness in the Kingdom as a result of the steep and incurable economic decline, on the other, the formation of a new Palestinian state, with its possible surge of irredentism, could irreversibly upset the precarious balance which has so far kept the Hashemite Kingdom intact. In this respect the proposed community offers a measure of stability in that it gives the United States (and Jordan) greater involvement in the affairs of the Palestinian state than they might otherwise have had. Also, the multilateral and interdependent nature of the arrangement could create a chain reaction in which possible Palestinian irredentism against Israel or attempts to destabilise the Jordanian kingdom, may endanger the security and interests of other parties to the agreement (Egypt, Syria and Lebanon) who, in their turn, will do their best to curb any such tendencies. This last factor may even safeguard US interests against the irredentism of a larger Palestinian state comprising both banks of the Jordan river (i.e., including present-day Transjordan).

THE VIEW FROM MOSCOW

In January 1992, after merely seven decades in being, the Soviet Union ceased to exist. The successor states, Russia included, have been thrown into a state of disarray and are likely to remain immersed in their intractable domestic problems for the foreseeable future. However, since Russian interest in the Middle East preceded the formation of the Soviet Union and is likely to outlive its existence, for the simple reason that the region constitutes, quite literally, Russia's southern border, the leadership in Moscow will continue keenly to follow Middle Eastern developments. While it is true that Russia's commitment to its remaining regional allies will be a far cry from the extensive Soviet involvement in the Middle East during the past half a century, it will still retain the military (and to a lesser extent political) ability to get actively involved in regional affairs, whenever these will be deemed harmful to its national interests.

What could the Russians expect to gain from the establishment of an Arab-Israeli security community? Two crucial and interconnected benefits suggest themselves: stabilisation of the most volatile area along their rim and partnership with the West in this extremely important region. Compared with these abundant gains, the attendant risks of the proposed arrangement seem negligible. The abrogation of the 1980 Friendship and Cooperation Treaty with Syria, for example, one of the main requirements of the proposed community, would most probably be received by Moscow with a sigh of relief in view of its half-hearted agreement to conclude this treaty in the first place, and given the reciprocation of such a move by the abrogation of the US-Israeli Memorandum of Strategic Understanding.[8] Similarly, the dismantling of naval facilities in Tartus and the withdrawal of military advisers from the Syrian Army may not be viewed by Moscow as a negative development. Not only have the Russians always recognised the precariousness of military support as a foreign policy instrument, but the end of the Cold War and the disintegration of the Soviet Union make such a move highly convenient for the Russian Federation.[9]

THE REGIONAL ACTORS

Great power goodwill and cooperation is undoubtedly necessary for the formation and viability of the security community. But it would not be a sufficient condition. The powers could indeed push their local allies toward this arrangement and could use their political, economic and military leverage in order to raise the cost for potential violators above a tolerable threshold. However, since they cannot transform regional attitudes and perceptions, it is imperative that the local actors perceive the proposed scheme as fully conforming to their own national interests. But why should this be so?

For many Israelis, complete withdrawal from the territories occupied in 1967 is a fearful vision. With the terrifying memory of the Holocaust strongly embedded in the Israeli psyche, the longstanding Arab rejection of Israel's legitimacy (which has been partly sustained to date) has created a deep sense of vulnerability in the Israelis at large and distrust of external guarantees. This fundamental insecurity has been significantly exacerbated by the minuscule size of the country which makes it difficult to defend against a determined ground attack. The decisive majority of Israel's pre-1967 population and most of its industrial capacity are located in a 9 to 13 mile-wide strip along the Mediterranean coast from Haifa in the north to the metropolitan Tel Aviv area in the south, and in the narrow corridor leading to Jerusalem.

This 'siege mentality' explains why, in spite of the acceptance of the partition of Palestine by the mainstream Zionist movement in the 1930s, the occupation of the territories has reinforced the concept of 'Greater Israel'; namely, not on account of the 'historical right' over the land of Israel but rather because control of the territories offers greater strategic depth and thus facilitates the defence of Israel. Hence, once Israel's sense of vulnerability is alleviated by the advent of a durable peace, the attachment to the territories on grounds of security is likely to recede.

Of course, for those in Israel who would not relinquish control over the territories under any circumstances, the idea of a security community, let alone a politico-economic community, is totally unacceptable. But since a substantial proportion of the Israelis have always been willing to trade land for peace (a fact illustrated by numerous public opinion polls over the past twenty five years), whilst the rest are becoming increasingly aware of the damaging implications of the continued occupation for Israeli society as a result of the *intifada,* the main problem remains the establishment of an arrangement that would ensure Israel's security and be perceived by the decisive majority of the Israelis as such. And in this respect, it is arguable that the community offers the best solution.

In the first place and due to its comprehensive nature, this scheme would be far more stable than any partial arrangement. By taking into account the legitimate interests of all regional (and major external) parties to the conflict and intertwining them in a tangled web of commitments and interests, the community turns these actors into *status quo* powers and mitigates the reasons for revisionism; all have little to gain and a great deal to lose by violating the agreement.

In the traditional Arab perception, Israel is a colonialist state, established by Western imperialism in their midst to keep them divided and weak. The Six Day War in 1967 and consequent Israeli apprehensions over relinquishing control over the territories have been viewed by the Arabs as a vindication of the 'Zionist expansionist instinct' which, in their view, poses a detrimental threat to their national security. Hence, by offering a broader and more stable framework for Israeli withdrawal, the proposed community may deprive the Arabs of their main incentive for war against the Jewish State.

Moreover, the incorporation of the great powers into the security package as both the guarantors and supervisors of this arrangement raises the costs of violation dramatically. Should a certain state decide to defy the superpowers (and the other co-signatories to the agreement) and to embark on a belligerent/irredentist course, it will clearly identify itself as an aggressor and will run the risk of losing the political goodwill as well as the economic and military support of the international community, thereby severely compromising such a move. Hence, a security community consisting of a militarily constrained Palestinian state and a demilitarised Golan, guaranteed and strictly supervised by the great powers may satisfy Israel's security concerns and allay its apprehensions of the adverse implications of terminating the special strategic relationship with the United States caused by such a proposed arrangement.

Great power guarantees may, in turn, be reinforced by several indigenous factors and interests. For one, Israel's fears of an armed Palestinian state are shared to some extent by the Hashemite Kingdom, which perceives such a state as a potential threat to its existence. Consequently, the chances for heavy weaponry (which will continue to pose the main threat to Israeli security) crossing the Jordan River westward are virtually nil. Regarding the Golan Heights, there is a general consensus in Israel about their vital role for defence purposes. Nevertheless, a *fully demilitarised* Golan secured by great power physical presence could create a useful buffer between Israel and Syria, a milder version of the one offered in the Sinai Peninsula. By preventing direct contiguity between the Syrian and the Israeli armed forces, this buffer could reduce both the likelihood of any conflagration and the chances for a surprise attack. On the one hand, neither party would be willing to initiate hostilities as long as great power forces are stationed on the Golan Heights; on the other hand, if a certain party asked for the removal of those forces (a request that might well be declined, given the power of veto that each member of the community would have over this issue), the other side will have the necessary early warning to brace itself for possible hostilities.

These aspects of the community may be equally advantageous to the Arabs. For the *Palestinians,* it would be the instrument for the establishment of independence. It could give them a sovereign, internationally accepted and secured state, guaranteed by a multilateral arrangement. Naturally, for those who remain committed to the idea of 'a secular democratic (or for that matter, Islamic) state embracing all the territory west of the Jordan river' this agreement is blasphemous. However, for those Palestinians who recognise the futility of a zero-sum approach toward the conflict, the community offers the optimal solution. By removing most of the potentially adverse implications of a Palestinian state, the security community constitutes the best way to 'market' this idea to Israeli and American public opinion. In addition, it would give the moderates in the Palestinian camp a powerful argument against their more intransigent counterparts. For example, the scheme is far less obtrusive to Palestinian national feeling than any alternative agreement in that it would involve no Israeli military presence on Palestinian soil. The presence of an international force in the Palestinian state impinges on Palestinian sovereignty no more than the presence of UN peacekeeping forces in trouble spots throughout the world compromises the sovereignty of respective states. Moreover, it could be rightly presented as a powerful deterrent to potential Israeli attack and undue Jordanian encroachment on Palestinian sovereignty.

Similarly, the security community does not call for the complete demilitarisation of the Palestinian state but rather for the imposition of constraints, however burdensome, on its military buildup. The Palestinians may not have as strong an army as they would have wished, but they would nevertheless have a military establishment. And if small states like Austria and Finland could accept severe constraints on their military potential after the Second World War, in a situation where even a massive buildup on their part could hardly threaten their major foe, the USSR, there is no reason why the Palestinians could not live with a similar arrangement in a situation where their neighbours (Israel and Jordan) have legitimate security concerns.

Besides, just as the Austrians have used the limitations on their military buildup as a lever for economic recovery, so the Palestinian state could turn the ostensible liability of a small army into an asset. To be sure, in a Middle East which is armed to the teeth, this is small comfort. However, since the security community would be based on certain arms control measures, it is not inconceivable that a gradual transformation of values and attitudes could take place which, in turn, would make the Middle East a safer place in which to live.

The community would also serve the interests of the Hashemite Kingdom. In the two and a half decades following the 1967 Six-Day War, King Hussein has proved himself a true master of the art of 'fence-sitting.' Relinquishing little, the King has managed to keep those wishing to know his intentions at bay. A mainline school of thought in Israel has maintained (at least until July 1988, when Jordan dissociated itself from the affairs of the West Bank) that Hussein is interested in reincorporating the occupied territories into his Kingdom but has been deterred from doing so by his fear of a harsh Arab reaction. According to this line of argument, the return of the territories to Jordan would wipe out the 1967 humiliation) thereby enhancing Amman's standing in the Arab World. Such a move would also forestall the potential threat of mass expulsion of Palestinians by Israel from the occupied territories to Jordan, an act which could destabilise the Jordanian regime.

This analysis, however, can be contested. It can be argued, for example, that the King is not so much interested in getting back his lost territories as he is in keeping a measure of control over their affairs and, no less importantly, in preventing Jordan's exclusion from any solution of the Palestinian problem. Naturally, Hussein cannot sanctify Israel's control over Arab lands but the perpetuation of the *status quo* could offer him a significant advantage without jeopardising his régime, at least in the short term. For one thing, the last 25 years have witnessed the emergence of a *de facto* Jordanian-Israeli peace: not only did Israel fail to threaten the Hashemite régime but it bolstered Hussein on several occasions, most notably during the Black September of 1970, when its readiness to go to war on Hussein's behalf curbed Syrian support for the Palestinians and enabled the King to ride the most severe threat to his throne until then. Even the most alarming eventuality of Ariel Sharon's advent to premiership is unlikely to lead to a general attack against Jordan, given the Israeli state of mind following the 1982 Lebanese adventure, on the one hand, and the new international order, on the other.

Conversely, the full reincorporation of the West Bank into the

Transjordanian Kingdom would give the Palestinians a decisive
majority which, in turn, might threaten the continued survival of
the Hashemite dynasty. A separate Israeli-Palestinian agreement
leading to the establishment of an independent Palestinian state
would be equally detrimental for Jordan. For, notwithstanding
Hussein's July 1988 decision to dissociate himself from the West
Bank and his support for the Palestinians' right for self-determination, he is fully aware that such a state might contain the
seeds for the destabilisation of his kingdom. The Palestinian
threat will become especially acute if Jordan were to be kept out
of the Israeli-Palestinian dialogue since Israel might seek to
encourage the Palestinians to turn their irredentism eastward
rather than westward. Hence, as long as Israel remains
entrenched in the territories and continues to incur the exorbitant domestic and international costs of doing so, there may be
little reason for the King to concern himself in this regard.

Yet, the King can hardly remain impervious to Arab demands
to play an active role in promoting Palestinian aspirations for
nationhood. Moreover, since neither Israel's indefinite occupation of the territories nor its longstanding tacit support to the
Hashemite dynasty can be taken for granted (particularly following King Hussein's backing of Iraq during the 1990–1991
Gulf conflict), Hussein has to look for a solution that will safeguard both his throne and the security of his country; this may
be found in the form of the regional community. Such an
arrangement would give Jordan the advantages conferred by
the existing *status quo* while negating the main risks of an independent Palestinian state. It would satisfy Palestinian national
aspirations without threatening the stability of the Hashemite
Kingdom; it would give Jordan the legal and political legitimacy
(which would not exist under different circumstances) to
ensure that the Palestinian military potential remains relatively
limited; and it would create a strong Jordanian-Israeli conver-
gence of interests in containing potential Palestinian
irredentism and would give them the economic and political
mechanisms to achieve this goal. Finally, Jordan's incorporation into the proposed community would shelter it against each
of its more powerful neighbours – Iraq, Syria and Israel – especially since two of these would also participate in the proposed
bloc and would thus have a vested interest in its success.

By the same token, the community would guarantee the integrity and independence of Lebanon against any possible change in Syrian policy in the direction of forcible incorporation of large parts of that country into Syria.

Paradoxically, the friendliest Arab state toward Israel, Egypt, might fear that participation in the community might constrain its ability to play the leading role in the Arab World and damage its aid relationship with the United States. Such apprehensions, however, would be exaggerated. Since membership of the community would not call for aloofness and isolationism, it would be unlikely to constrain Egypt's manoeuverability. On the contrary, with the political and economic support of the United States and the European Community, the proposed Arab-Israeli community would become the centre of gravity of regional affairs. Nor would the scheme be likely adversely to affect US economic aid, particularly in the light of Egypt's crucial support for the American campaign against Iraq during the Kuwait crisis. And in any event, diminution in American financial support for Egypt and Israel will not be related to their inclusion within the proposed regional framework but will rather reflect the new American priorities in a fundamentally transformed international order, as well as the surge in the 'America first' mood.

Last, but not least, there is the question of Syria. From the early 1950s to date, Damascus has been one of the main champions of the Arab cause. Neither the Egyptian-Israeli peace treaty nor the Jordanian-Israeli *modus vivendi,* nor the PLO's acceptance of a two-state solution, has driven Syria to reconsider its fundamental stance on an Arab-Israeli settlement, held since Hafiz Asad's rise to power in 1970 and the October War of 1973. On the contrary, these developments only reinforced Asad's conviction that Syria was the only obstacle to what he saw as Israel's grim determination to impose its politico-military domination over the Middle East, and drove him to reject Mikhail Gorbachev's 'new political thinking' which dismissed Syria's quest for 'strategic parity' and called for a Middle East peace based on a 'balance of interests' between Israel and her Arab neighbours.

And yet, since the late 1980s, Asad has been forced to recognise the limits of Syrian power. The significant strengthening of his arch-enemy, Saddam Hussein, the reincorporation of Egypt into the Arab camp, despite its peace treaty with Israel, the collapse of the Communist bloc and the diminution of Soviet support, and the Gulf conflict; all these developments convinced the reluctant Asad of the need to become more flexible in his position. This ranged from his unconditional reestablishment of diplomatic relations with Egypt, to signalling to Israel (via American channels) of his readiness to enter into negotiations over the future of the Golan Heights, to Syria's close collaboration with the West during the Kuwait crisis and war, and to Asad's agreement to participate in the Madrid peace conference. By giving in on procedural questions in return for US undertakings to base the peace process on Security Council Resolutions 242 and 338, Asad has apparently signalled his recognition of the evolving 'new international order' and his readiness to work toward the implementation of this new political environment in the Middle East.

CONCLUSIONS

There is little doubt that the proposed scheme may appear to observers of Middle Eastern and international affairs as an incredible vision. It limits the freedom of action of the regional states in some ways and requires a level of political maturity and constructive imagination which, have been a scarce commodity in the Middle East. It also presupposes a genuine desire for peace among most parties to the Arab-Israeli conflict and assumes that all external powers are sincerely interested in resolving the conflict and, moreover, will be willing to collaborate in guaranteeing it. These assumptions may be questioned by some, both in the region and beyond it.

And yet, any solution to the Arab-Israeli conflict, perhaps the bitterest feud in the postwar epoch, has to be as unique and unusual as the situation that produced it. In any event, the ongoing transformation of the international system provides the best proof that yesterday's remote dream may readily become today's reality.

The regional community offers a timely and unorthodox solution. It does not conceive of international relations in zero-sum terms but rather as a mixed-motive game. It seeks no unilateral concessions but a fair compromise based on a balance of interests of all involved parties. It creates a situation in which each party stands to gain from the proposed arrangement (though probably not as much as it would have desired) but has a great deal to lose from its failure or non-implementation. By comprising all the interested parties both at the regional and at the global levels, the community ensures their transformation into *status quo* powers and precludes revisionism. Due to its comprehensive and interdependent nature, the scheme gives all parties concerned a vested interest in its success and raises tremendously the costs for would-be violators.

Whether or not the international community will seize this window of opportunity and adopt this solution is difficult to say. It is clear to us, however, that the old conventional formulas have led the Middle East nowhere. In the absence of new thinking on regional affairs and a far-sighted vision of peace, Arabs and Israelis are condemned to continue their all-too-familiar trail of war and bereavement.

Appendix 'A'

PRINCIPLES OF THE PROPOSED SECURITY COMMUNITY

Under this treaty, the member states of the security community will undertake the following:

1 To adopt a policy of permanent neutrality among themselves and to maintain and defend this policy with all the means at their disposal, that is:

 a Renunciation of war as an instrument of foreign policy and resort to this political course only in cases of self-defence, when subjected to an external attack (i.e., no pre-emptive or preventive wars).

 b Remaining neutral in case of war among members of the community;

 c Avoidance of any alliances or collective security arrangements that may impinge on the neutrality of the community and renunciation of such commitments that may exist at the time of this treaty;

d Prohibition of both the establishment of foreign military bases and of the stationing of foreign troops (except for the international supervisory forces and the receipt of military support in the event of an armed aggression, as mentioned below) on their territory;

e Non-intervention in civil wars and non-invitation of external military interference in such conflicts.

2 To renounce any territorial claims against their neighbours, and to safeguard the rights of the minority groups in their own territory.

3 To carry out the following security arrangements:

a Continuation of the current demilitarisation arrangement in Sinai;

b Complete demilitarisation of the Golan Heights (which will be placed under Syrian sovereignty) with the stationing in the area of an international supervisory force for that purpose, and the establishment of an appropriate demilitarised zone on the Israeli side;

c Restricted deployment of the Lebanese army in South Lebanon with the assistance of the supervisory international force;

d Restriction of the standing order of battle of the Palestinian armed forces to 30,000 troops equipped with small arms and armoured cars but lacking tanks, artillery (including surface-to-surface missiles), surface-to-air missiles and fighting aircraft. Transport planes and/or helicopters will be allowed. Adherence to these limitations would be supervised by the international force that would be installed in the newly established Palestinian state;

e Restricted deployment of the Jordanian Army along the Jordan river, supervised by the international force.

4 To accept the following arms control measures:

a To freeze their arsenals and order of battle at a measure commensurate with their individual security needs as mutually agreed;

b To embark on a process of eliminating all weapons of mass destruction, namely, nuclear, chemical, and biological, as well as medium-range missiles, under an international regime of verification.

The governments of the guarantor states, for their part, would undertake to contribute to the preservation of the security community by:

1 Removing the community from the sphere of great-power strategic rivalry, including the significant reduction and regulation of arms transfers to the entire Middle East.

2 Foregoing any attempt to bring the community in any way into a collective security agreement.

3 Avoiding both the introduction of foreign troops or military personnel and the establishment of military installations of any kind in the community.

4 Defending the independence and territorial integrity of:
   a The community as a whole against external attack;
   b Any member of the community against an attack by external factors or by other members of the bloc. The defence of the community may be carried out either jointly by all the guarantor states or part of them, or separately in the event that joint action can not be agreed upon.

5 Safeguarding the security arrangements through the deployment of an international supervisory force as follows:
   a The addition of Russian, British, French, and (if feasible) Chinese units to the Multinational Observation Force (MFO) in Sinai;
   b Deployment of at least four brigades (including minimally an American and Russian brigade) on each the Golan Heights and the newly established Palestinian state;
   c The international force in the Palestinian state will be deployed, among other places, along the passes of the Jordan River so as to ensure that no prohibited major weapons systems cross the river westwards.

6 Under the auspices of the United Nations, the supervisory force will be subordinated to an International Commission comprising representatives of the guaranteed and guarantor states, that will be established to supervise the implementation of the scheme. The removal or reduction of this force will require general consent, and each member of the Commission will have the power of veto over such a move.

Notes

1. This includes Israeli withdrawal from South Lebanon.

2. This term has been coined by historian Carl L Brown. See, his *International politics of the Middle East* (Princeton: Princeton University Press, 1984).

3. This stipulation refers not only to Arab (particularly Palestinian and Syrian) irredentist claims over Israel but also to Israeli claims over the newly established Palestinian state.

4. For a similar proposition see an article by the Jordanian Ambassador to the United Nations, Adnan Abu Awda, 'Idea for Jerusalem: Two Flags, One Undivided City,' *International Herald Tribune*, April 17, 1992.

5. Perhaps the most emotive article of faith of the PLO to date, the 'right of return' stresses the Palestinians' right to their pre-1949 dwellings thereby implying the virtual dismantling of the State of Israel. By way of preventing this 'right' from posing a lethal threat to Israel, while enabling exiled Palestinians to leave their present dwellings, the 'right of return' should be legally, politically and declaratively restricted to the newly-established Palestinian State. If citizens of Palestine (or alternatively of Israel) would like to live in the neighbouring country, they will be given the opportunity to do so in accordance with that state's established immigration policies (temporary residence etc.). An international monetary fund will be established to compensate those Palestinians who will give up their right to return to the Palestinian state, as well as Jews who were forcibly expelled from the Arab countries following Israel's establishment.

6. For further discussion of these measures see M Z Diab, 'A Proposed Security Regime for an Arab-Israeli Settlement,' in Steven L Spiegel (ed.), *The Arab-Israeli Search for Peace in the Middle East* (Boulder, Co.: Lynne Rienner, 1992).

7. There is little doubt that Moscow could easily have torpedoed the American campaign against Iraq, either by vetoing the various Security Council resolutions, or by throwing its weight behind Saddam Hussein. By siding with the United States in condemning the Iraqi occupation of Kuwait and participating in the UN sanctions against Baghdad, the Soviets have extended invaluable support to the United States.

8. For the process leading to the conclusion of the Soviet-Syrian Treaty see Efraim Karsh, *Soviet Policy towards Syria since 1970*, (London & New York: Macmillan & St Martin's, 1991), pp. 28–33.

9. For a Soviet perception of military support to the Middle East Efraim Karsh, 'Peacetime Presence and Wartime Engagement: The Soviet Case', in Steven Spiegel et.al. (eds.), *The Soviet-American Competition in the Middle East* (Lexington Lexington Books, 1986), pp. 146–57.

20

Peacekeeping in Sub-Saharan Africa: The Liberian Civil War

ABIODUN ALAO

Research Associate, Centre for Defence Studies

United Nations (UN) peacekeeping has entered a second generation of activities as the organisation takes on so many new – and different – responsibilities in the post-Cold War world. In the more demanding circumstances in which UN peacekeeping forces now operate, it is considerably more difficult to maintain traditional principles; that UN forces should operate under the mandate of the UN Security Council in accordance with the letter of relevant UN resolutions which established the force, without offensive arms, under the strictest rules of engagement, operating impartially and in a non-political way while attempts at a peaceful settlement are brokered elsewhere, and so on.

The civil war in Liberia and the peacekeeping operation established by the countries of the Economic Community of West African States (ECOWAS) provides a good example – may indeed be the test case in sub-saharan Africa – of the pitfalls of any attempt to operate peacekeeping forces in the new international environment. The ECOWAS initiative was undertaken without a sufficiently clear mandate or framework of political control. The result has been a military and political quagmire that threatens to discredit the whole enterprise of regional peacekeeping and may offer some sombre lessons for the United Nations itself.

The outbreak of the Liberian civil war in December 1989 broke a spell, since the country has been considered generally stable, in a region that was in itself considered relatively peaceful. This apart, Liberia's long history of independent existence (since 1893) has endeared it to the hearts of many Africans, who see in the country (along with Ethiopia) the black man's manifestation of independent existence and defiance of foreign rule. Located in the heart of west Africa, with an area of about 112,000 square kilometres and a population of about three million, Liberia's immediate neighbours are Côte d'Ivoire, Guinea and Sierra Leone. The country was founded by the United States for its liberated slaves, and for most of the century that followed its independence, the descendants of the slaves established a powerful oligarchy who administered the country to the total neglect of the indigenous population. Liberia, like most other African states, is composed of different ethnic groups, including the Krahns, the Manos and the Gios. All these characteristics were to play significant roles when civil conflict broke out in the country, and they were to account for a situation where, within a year of its outbreak the Liberian civil war had created considerable concern for most of the countries in the region, as the larger global concern was at the time directed to what was considered a more major conflict in the Gulf.

THE ROAD TO CONFLICT

While admitting that putting a date on the root of most conflicts is often difficult, the root cause of the Liberian civil war may nevertheless be traced to 1980, when Samuel Doe, a Master Sergeant (Staff Sergeant) in the Liberian Army, terminated the half a century rule of the Americo-Liberian 'True Whig Party' in a military coup.[2] Doe subsequently established a military administration in Liberia, after he had executed most of the key figures of the former administration of William Tolbert.

Some of Doe's policies that were to result in the civil war started not long after he assumed office. Although most of the natives, who saw in him a 'saviour' that would assist in redressing the ills of the Americo-Liberian mis-rule, initially supported him, Doe could not sustain the domestic affection that greeted his coup and he quickly became prey to corruption, nepotism and an insensitivity to criticism and brutality, all of which he had claimed to be the hallmarks of the civil régime he had overthrown.

Opposition to Doe's growing autocratic rule reached its peak in 1985, when an attempt to overthrow him was led by General Quiwomkpa of the Liberian army. Although this failed and the coup leader was subsequently executed, a number of those who collaborated with him escaped to neighbouring countries, where they remained opposed to the prevailing order in Liberia; looking for opportunities to oppose Doe's administration. For on his part, Doe did not do much to change his dictatorial and oppressive tendencies until 1987, when he organised a 'transition' to civilian rule in which he himself featured as one of the presidential candidates. He won the election and became the civil President of Liberia.[3] This metamorphosis from a military Head of State to a civil President further fuelled opposition to Doe's administration and increased the trend towards civil war.

THE OUTBREAK OF CIVIL WAR

In order to understand how the tide moved at the outbreak of the civil war, three factors must be appreciated. First, within the first few years of his rule, Doe had lost considerable support in Liberia. The hopes and aspirations raised by his rise to power had been dashed and his autocratic system of administration had fuelled enormous opposition. Thus when war did break out, any well organised opposition could expect considerable support from the civil population. Secondly, the Liberian Army had by then become considerably weakened. Although it had never been one of the battle-tested forces in the region, ethnicity, nepotism and other considerations had adversely affected the quality of the force to such an extent that when the war started, the best the Army could do was to suppress spontaneous unrest or attempted coups, rather than address a fairly sustained civil conflict. Thirdly, following a succession of failed coups against him, a substantial number of Doe's opponents were now scattered throughout most of the neighbouring states. These factors were all highly significant when the civil war eventually broke out.

The renewed opposition that finally led to war against Doe was led by Charles Taylor, a man who, like Samuel Doe, was not a stranger to controversy. Before leading the rebellion, he was the former Director General of the General Service Agency (the Government Warehouse), where he was alleged to have lived a flamboyant and corrupt life.[4] He fell out with Doe and went to the United States, where he was imprisoned while awaiting deportation. He escaped from the US in 1985, however, and arrived in Ghana, where he laid his plans to overthrow Doe. He formed the National Patriotic Front of Liberia (NPFL) which brought together a number of Liberian exiles living in neighbouring countries. The sole aim of the movement was to dislodge Doe, and the military attack towards this goal was launched on Christmas Eve 1989. Shortly after the invasion however, the rebel movement broke into two, with Yommie Johnson, one of Taylor's commanders, breaking away to form his own independent force. Unlike Taylor, Yommie Johnson was a former member of the Liberian National Army and had taken part in the 1985 abortive coup against Doe. He had evaded trial by escaping to Boukina Fasso.

Doe's immediate reaction to the invasion was to order a counter military action. He sent troops from his Krahn-dominated national army to the Nimba county, where the rebel invasion started. The remarkable brutality demonstrated by the national army was to fuel the conflict. There were confirmed reports of the massacre of civilians from the non-Krahn ethnic groups, especially the Gios and the Manos. Further brutal clampdown measures were employed against these two ethnic groups, reaching a peak in the attack on a Lutheran church, where more than 600 refugees (mostly of these groups) were killed. All this turned out to be counter-productive to Doe's cause, as many who either sought protection from or retaliation against Doe's forces joined the rebel movement.[5] The increase this brought to the numerical strength of the anti-Doe forces transformed them from the less than two hundred who had invaded the country into a force running into some thousands.

Within a few months, the war had developed a distinct political and military pattern. First, the ethnic undertone had become pronounced, with the Gios and the Manos on one side, and the Krahn on the other. A variant of ethnic cleansing had also started, with the rebels killing the Krahns and the latter doing the same to the Gios and the Manos, especially those living around the capital city. The level of discipline on all sides was very low, as looting, rape and other forms of maltreatment were rife and all the forces involved employed remarkable brutality in the pursuit of their military objectives. By the end of 1990, the war had produced up to five thousand casualties, with several thousands of displaced refugees in neighbouring countries. By this time, most of the Western European countries and the United States had evacuated their nationals from Liberia.

The Liberian war started at the time when the Cold War between the superpowers was undergoing significant changes. Liberia had a somewhat peculiar position in the region. Technically, the country did not fall under the sphere of influence of any of the 'conventional colonial powers' like Britain and France, as it was not colonised by any of them. However, its location in the midst of the former British and French colonies, and the deep relationship that existed between these former colonial powers and the United states that had founded Liberia, led to its involvement in the global politics of the Cold War, and in the sub-regional rivalry between the Anglo and Francophone countries. However, the United States held the dominant position in the country, and Liberia remained the largest recipient of American aid in Sub-Saharan Africa. In exchange for this, the United States obtained some strategic privileges. The Omega navigation station, a CIA listening post and the Voice of America's largest transmitting facility in Africa, were all placed in Liberia. The US army also had access to Liberia's main international airport for military purposes.

When the war started in Liberia, the United States did not show undue concern, as it was thought that it would only be a brief disruption. When, however, it was becoming more serious, the US decided to offer some support for Doe. A number of factors could have guided this position. First, Doe had already proved to be an ally of the United States, and as the US could not be sure of what the future would look like under a Taylor leadership, Doe was considered worth supporting. Secondly, as there were reports that the rebel forces were obtaining military support from Libya, the US have seen in the Liberian civil war, another attempt by Ghadaffi to create embarrassment for the United States in a country that Washington had come to take as a 'godchild'. Thus, even after it was confirmed that Doe's forces were guilty of atrocities, subtle American support still continued. For example, two US military personnel were sent to accompany Doe's forces, although the Bush Administration argued that the advisers were to minimise abuses by the Army and would not provide counter-insurgency advice. One wonders, however, how this could be done by two people alone if such was indeed the mission. As Holly Burkhalter and Rakiya Omaar pointed out, a more likely assignment of these two officers was to verify reports of Libyan involvement on the side of the rebels.[6]

Doe relied greatly on American support to bail him out of his domestic problems. This could be seen in the 'SOS' letter written to President George Bush, which was published in the Washington Post. In the letter, Doe pleaded for American support, claiming

> . . . My relationship with my country could be likened in some respects to that of a man who loves his wife very much, but at times is tempted to be unfaithful. I realised that people have said that I have been driven by power, greed and other unhealthy desires, but this has not been my primary motivations. . . . Our capital is named after your president Monroe. Our flag is a replica of yours. Our laws are patterned after your laws. We in Liberia have always considered ourselves step children of the United States. We implore you to come help your step children who are in danger of losing their lives and freedom.[7]

The countries in the west African sub-region however, could not wait for the outcome of this plea before a number of considerations made some form of sub-regional intervention in the Liberian civil war inevitable. Another chapter in the Liberian conflict had opened.

THE 'ECOMOG' CONNECTION: THE POLITICS AND INTRICACIES OF AN INVOLVEMENT

Even before the extent of the carnage forced member states of the Economic Community of West African States ECOWAS (a sub-regional economic union of which Liberia is a member) to consider formal intervention in the Liberian conflict, the country's civil war had attracted considerable sub-regional attention. Some of the leaders of the neighbouring states had a number of personal and national reasons to intervene. The rebel troops got most of their initial assistance from Boukina Fasso, where they were alleged to have undergone training before their invasion of Liberia in 1989. Another early sub-regional supporter of the rebel cause was President Houphouet Boigny of Côte d'Ivoire. Both leaders had personal reasons for intervention. For example, the Ivorian president had an axe to grind with Doe. In the mass execution that greeted his assumption of office, Doe had executed A B Tolbert, the son of the former President William Tolbert, who was President Boigny's son-in-law. It was thus against this background that the Ivorian leader was believed to have encouraged another of his sons-in-law, Blaise Compraore, the President of Boukina Fasso, to support the rebel cause.

Samuel Doe also had sub-regional supporters, among whom the Nigerian president, President Ibrahim Babangida, was the most redoubtable. The Nigerian leader was considered as Samuel Doe's sub-regional godfather, and the Liberian leader had named a Graduate School of International Relations and a major Liberian road after him. It was, in fact, alleged that Nigerian arms reached Doe in the early stages of the war, although this was denied by the authorities in Lagos. Another leader who the Nigerian president allegedly recruited for Doe was the deposed president of Sierra Leone, Joseph Momoh. Thus, it could be seen that, even before the official entrance of ECOMOG (the ECOWAS Monitoring Group) there had been fundamental divisions within ECOWAS over the Liberian civil war. This was to be a most determining factor in understanding ECOWAS and ECOMOG politics in Liberia.

Apart from the personal preferences however, another reason why the Liberian conflict attracted regional concern was the refugee crisis the war created for most of the neighbouring states. By the middle of 1990, hundreds of thousands of Liberian refugees were scattered in neighbouring states, especially, Côte d'Ivoire, Guinea and Sierra Leone. As most of these countries had never experienced major refugee problems before, there was practically no local network of governmental or non-governmental organisation to cope with the situation. This drove many West African governments to consider taking urgent action to resolve the situation in Liberia.

Contrary to what is often assumed, the decision to send in a peace-keeping force was not taken by the entire membership of ECOWAS. Indeed the decision was taken by the ECOWAS Mediation Committee, comprising of Ghana, Nigeria, The Gambia, Guinea and Sierra-Leone. This was to create problems later, as the Boukinabe President, Blaise Compraore, complained that the Committee did not consult ECOWAS before taking the decision. Other decisions taken by the mediation Committee included the setting up of a National Conference of Liberian Political Parties to form an Interim Government. It was further agreed that none of the warring sides should head the interim government. The peace-keeping team was composed of troops from Nigeria and Ghana, with Sierra Leone, Gambia and Guinea contributing token forces. Although more than 60 per cent of the troops were from Nigeria, the country conceded the leadership of the peace-keeping team to Ghana, and General Arnold Quiano, of the Ghanian army became the first ECOMOG Commander.

From the outset, it was obvious that some members of ECOWAS opposed the idea of sending a peacekeeping force to Liberia. Apart from Boukina Fasso, Côte d'Ivoire too was believed to be opposed to the initiative, which was largely advanced by Nigeria. Both countries were suspicious of Nigeria's intentions, the more so when it was believed that the country was supporting Doe. The age old rivalry between Nigeria and Côte d'Ivoire over sub-regional leadership also came into play in the politics of the formation of ECOMOG, as did the perennial tension between Anglo and Francophone countries. In fact, it was believed that the Nigerians initially conceded the leadership of the force to Ghana in order to avoid giving any impression that they wanted to dominate the exercise. In short, it was with considerable reluctance that some of the member states of ECOWAS supported the idea of the peacekeeping team at all. This again was to be reflected in the future activities of ECOMOG and its relationship with other warring sides in the conflict.

The reactions of the Liberian warring sides followed a predictable pattern. Samuel Doe supported the initiative, and was believed to have felt comfortable with the large number of Nigerian contingents. This apart, the invading force was making progress, and the only option left to him was to support any form of imposed truce. It was for the same reasons, however, that Charles Taylor opposed the entire peacekeeping team. He felt uncomfortable with the large number of Nigerian soldiers, who he believed were in Liberia to prop up the Doe government that was then under considerable pressure. The other rebel group (under Yommie Johnson) took an ambiguous position in this regard. Johnson had desperately wanted foreign intervention, and had in fact, held a number of foreigners hostage to provoke international attention. However, it appears that he would have preferred a non-African intervention.[8]

ECOMOG forces arrived in Liberia largely unaware of the nature of their role and the terms of their operations, beyond the fact that they were to keep the peace. Many argued, in fact, that at the time the troops arrived in the country there was literally no peace to be kept. Thus ECOMOG's first task was to establish peace. As this was the first time that most of the various national contingents had come together under the same command and control structure, there were inevitable problems over harmonising tactics and over the military reorientation of each contingent. ECOMOG had barely any adequate maps of Liberia and virtually no knowledge of the terrain. Furthermore, the legal status of their involvement was also in question. These were the circumstances under which a faction of the rebel forces (under Johnson) arrested and killed Doe whilst he was visiting the ECOMOG headquarters in Monrovia.

The actual events leading up to Doe's death are still unclear. He was believed to have gone to the ECOMOG office unannounced, apparently with the intention of discussing cooperation with the ECOMOG Commander. As the latter was not expecting him, no preparation had been made for his safety. However, to get to the ECOMOG headquarters, Doe had to pass through the territories held by Johnson, where troops got to know about his visit and stormed the ECOMOG office shortly after his arrival there. He was arrested and taken to the rebel headquarters, where he was tortured and later killed.[9] It was more than ironic that the ECOMOG force which Doe thought would offer him protection turned out to be the instrument of his arrest. This was an embarrassment from which the peace-keeping team never really recovered.

The death of Doe had three immediate impacts on the Liberian civil war. First, the ECOMOG forces thereafter took their job more seriously. They succeeded in putting an immediate end to the carnage that almost resulted in a Liberian version of ethnic cleansing. They also succeeded, with the help of ECOWAS, in establishing an interim government in Liberia. This government was headed by Amos Sawyer, a former Professor of Law at the University of Liberia.[10] The second immediate impact was that it made Yommie Johnson, the leader of the group that killed Doe, a major force, whose view and support had to be sought in any discussion on the future of Liberia. Before this, he was considered as nothing more than a rascal with an insignificant number of followers. The change in perception however, did not last for long, as the image Johnson established after he killed Doe was soon neutralised by the ECOMOG force. The third effect was that the assassination of Doe resulted in a re-arrangement of the command and control structure of the ECOMOG force. Nigeria, which hitherto had maintained a low-profile position, now became more prominent in the control structure, and since then has provided the overall commander of ECOMOG.

A new phase emerged in the Liberian conflict after Nigeria took over the supreme command of ECOMOG. The country faced a number of formidable odds both within and outside its boundaries. Militarily, Taylor's forces now controlled more than 80 per cent of Liberian territory. On the political level, there were four different groups contesting the future of the country. Apart from Taylor and Johnson, there was also the ECOWAS-backed Interim government of Amos Sawyer and the remnants of the Liberian Army that had been loyal to Samuel Doe.[11] Nigeria's problem in its peacekeeping role was further compounded by the lack of support from some members of ECOWAS, especially those who kept supplying arms to Charles Taylor. By the end of 1990, Taylor had effectively identified Nigeria as the main obstacle to the consolidation of his authority over the whole country. He therefore declared war upon the ECOMOG forces and on the civilians of those countries supplying troops to ECOMOG, who were living in

Liberia. Two Nigerian journalists were arrested and killed by his forces.[12]

Taylor based his opposition to ECOMOG and ECOWAS-sponsored peace talks on a number of grounds. First, he argued that none of the leaders of ECOMOG countries had ever bothered to talk to him about the Liberian problem. He thus wondered how they could mediate when they had refused to meet and talk to one of the major actors.[13] Secondly, he was opposed to the initiative that made Sawyer the Interim President. This, he said, was because Sawyer had earlier betrayed the cause to free Liberia from Doe's tyranny. Third, his perception of ECOMOG as a force with a hidden agenda for Liberia never actually changed. Even after Doe's death, he still believed that ECOMOG was bound to show partiality to Sawyer. But what could perhaps be seen as an encapsulation of his continued opposition to ECOMOG was his determination not to surrender through any truce organised by ECOWAS, the gains he had made through war. He was convinced that his enormous military gains would never be reflected in the outcome of any election conducted by ECOMOG. He therefore continued to prefer to fight his way forward rather than to campaign through any election.

By the middle of 1991, ECOMOG had been transformed from the peacekeeping team it set out to be into becoming part of the Liberian problem. Criticism against the organisation became more pronounced, as many observers began to see the force as being partial. Again, for most of the period they were unable to make military headway, as the Taylor faction of the rebel force confronted them with serious problems. Their rules of engagement were highly ambiguous. Beyond the capital, Monrovia, it could not be said that ECOMOG actually controlled any other part of Liberia. Although the interim president had been appointed, ECOMOG could not make any serious progress towards a ceasefire or the conduct of the election. Some of ECOMOG's problems arise from the constant changes in the leadership of the team. After Nigeria took over supreme command, different individuals were sent, each with his own perception of the role he was to perform. For example, the first Commander, Joshua Dongoyaro, was believed to have carried out his assignment in Liberia with remarkable high-handedness, so that Taylor accused him of genocide, while his successors, Rufus Kupolati and Ishaya Bakut were alleged to have given the rebel forces pretty well a free hand. In fact, Taylor humiliated the entire ECOMOG initiative when he rounded up more than 500 members of the peacekeeping team.

The problems of ECOMOG were not limited to Liberia and ECOWAS alone. Even at home opposition was mounting within the ECOMOG participating states to the human and economic cost of the war. Civilians and the media in most of these countries (especially Nigeria) started looking at Liberia as their 'Vietnam'. Thus as the countries had to consider the situation in Liberia, they also had to bear in mind that the domestic population was becoming highly critical of a war they considered unnecessary. Ironically, however, Liberia had become a prestige project for most of these countries, especially Nigeria, so that a withdrawal was considered unthinkable. Against this background, the country decided to increase its commitment to ECOMOG in order to solve the problem once and for all.

For the greater part of 1992, Taylor operated under a basic strategic calculation that there would soon be changes of government m Nigeria and Ghana – the two main sponsors of ECOMOG. This calculation was based on the fact that the military administrations in both countries had promised a transition to civilian rule. Taylor had expected that the civilian governments that would take over in these countries would reduce their commitments to ECOMOG. This however turned out to be a false assumption. Although there was indeed a transition in Ghana, the former military leader, Jerry Rawlings, became the civil president of the country, while President Babangida of Nigeria postponed yet again his handover to civil government for another eight months. Thus, the commitments of both countries to ECOMOG technically continue.

By September 1992, it appeared that ECOMOG had become determined to get over the apparent stalemate in Liberia as soon as possible. A new Commander, Olatunji Olurin was appointed, and he was alleged to have been given the instruction to dislodge Taylor and force him to comply with ECOWAS ceasefire proposals.[14] This has resulted in a situation in which ECOMOG has intensified its activities considerably, especially the aerial bombardments of Taylor-held territories. The United Nations intervened in December 1992, when the Security Council passed a resolution banning the supply of arms to the warring sides and further mandated the Secretary General to dispatch a special envoy to Liberia.

CONCLUSION

There is now a hardening of attitudes among the ECOWAS member states, based upon a broader concensus. Even Côte d'Ivoire and Boukina Fasso, which had earlier supported Charles Taylor, have now signified their intention to support and even contribute efforts to the peacekeeping team. Other countries that had earlier been tactically ambiguous have also begun to be more receptive to the ECOMOG initiative. While all this may have come as a pleasant surprise to ECOMOG countries, it is also one which they are considering with some caution. It is not known whether there is a hidden expectation of personal advantages for the Pauline conversion of some of the states. Some ECOMOG soldiers have argued (admittedly in their individual capacities) that they do not want the participation of other countries in the field. This is largely because they doubt the sincerity of such participation. They thus argued that they would be content if these countries could stop providing support for any of the warring sides in the civil war.

The options open to Taylor would be considerably reduced if Côte d'Ivoire and Boukina Fasso withdrew all their support for him. He would then have to choose between complying with the ECOWAS terms or a reversion to dissident activity against ECOMOG or any form of government installed by the sub-regional peacekeeping initiative. Militarily, the rebels do not have sufficient strength to defeat the ECOMOG force. However, neither does ECOMOG have the capacity to bring Taylor under any form of sustained military control. The best that could be achieved would be to dislodge him and frustrate any attempt he might make to march on the capital, Monrovia. Thus, in military terms, the most that can be done in the long term is the creation of a stalemate. This, by its very nature, will favour Charles Taylor and his troops since, eventually, sustained domestic opposition to the human and economic cost of the war will build up in most of the ECOMOG countries. In consequence, some of those countries would be forced, either because of that opposition or because of the extent of the human and material losses being experienced, to withdraw from the operation.

Another option open to Taylor, if his relationship with ECOMOG does develop into a stalemate, is to encourage rebel activities in some of the ECOMOG countries. This could come either in the form of support for rebel activities or the sponsorship of a military coup. Already, the Liberian civil war has heightened the civil war in Sierra-Leone, as Taylor is supporting the rebel movement against the Strasser government in that country. This may increase in the months and possibly years ahead. Another country Taylor may target in this calculation is Ghana, where he might want to exploit the recent transition to civil rule to focus disaffection in the country. Although this is an option Taylor would consider, however, it is not one that would offer much attraction, largely because of the cost that such an exercise would involve.

The other warring factions appear to be under ECOMOG control. Nevertheless, they too would attempt to break out once there was any laxity in the effective grip of ECOMOG on Liberia. Yommie Johnson is believed to be interested in becoming the Defence Minister in any future administration. Although now effectively neutralised, he could become a strong force in determining the future stability of Liberia. The remnants of Doe's force would also have to be considered in discussing the country's future.

The future of ECOMOG depends to a large extent on the commitment of Nigeria, which has contributed the largest force and has put in more money than any other country. As things now stand, the commitment of the country to ECOMOG is likely to remain total, at least until the present administration hands over, perhaps in August 1993. What eventually happens to ECOMOG thereafter depends on the position taken by the civilian administration that takes over from the present military régime. If the incoming government withdraws from ECOMOG, the peacekeeping team would almost certainly collapse, as other member states would have neither the economic nor the military strength to sustain the venture. Tactical and face-saving withdrawal from ECOMOG is an option that any civilian administration in Nigeria would almost certainly consider. The entire exercise is gradually being seen as a white elephant to which the present administration has remained committed for prestige reasons. However, in the unlikely but not impossible event that the incoming administration continues with the inherited commitment to ECOMOG, Taylor would almost certainly raise the stakes and make the entire venture even more costly in human and material terms, calculating – probably correctly – that this would fuel the type of domestic opposition to which an elected government is highly vulnerable.

Notes

[1] The affection with which the country was held could be seen in the fact that, as early as 1938, a foremost African nationalist and Nigeria's first president, Nnamdi Azikiwe, had written a book titled *Liberia in World Politics*.

[2] A more detailed study would perhaps deal with the decades of Americo-Liberian misrule at the roots of the crisis.

[3] Needless to say, there were extensive allegations of electoral malpractice in the conduct of the election.

[4] The Doe administration accused him of widespread corruption.

[5] Baffour Amkomah's detailed, though by no means unsympathetic account of the civil war gave an interesting documentation of this. See *New Africa*, October 1992, p. 11

[6] Holly Burkhalter and Rakiya Omaar 'Failure of State' *African Report*, Nov/Dec 1990, p. 27.

[7] Quoted From *African Report*, Nov/Dec. 1992.

[8] The hostages Johnson took were later released unhurt. He made it clear that he took the step to draw attention of the world to the situation in Liberia.

[9] This was the version provided by Obed Asamoh, the former Ghanian Foreign Secretary in *African Report* Nov/Dec 1990. Other accounts of Doe's death however indict the ECOMOG authorities for allegedly disarming Doe's bodyguards shortly before Johnson's force stormed the ECOMOG headquarters.

[10] Although the election of Sawyer had taken place few days before Doe's death, he had not actually taken office.

[11] Apart from these four, Harry Moniba, the late Samuel Doe's Vice President, came out of hiding to lay claim to the presidency with the legalistic argument that, since the elected President was dead, he should constitutionally become the Liberian leader.

[12] These were Krees Imobibie and Tayo Awotusin of the *Guardian* and *The Champion Newspaper* respectively.

[13] See *New Africa*, October 1992, p. 14–16.

[14] Olatunji Olurin had been part of the Nigerian team to the UNIFIL.

PERSPECTIVES ON SECURITY

21

Liberal Democracy, Global Order and the Future of Transatlantic Relations*

KEN BOOTH

Professor of International Politics, University of Wales, Aberystwyth

The history of international relations in the 20th century has been cruel to the powerful democracies. After 1918, the victorious democracies of the Great War 'lost the peace' and in just over 20 years were engaged in an even more destructive war. After 1945, the victorious 'United Nations' of World War II 'lost the peace', as the allies of that war became the adversaries of the Cold War (which threatened to be the most destructive of all 20th century wars). And now, after 1989, the victorious democratic allies of the Cold War look set to lose the peace about which so many of us were so optimistic such a short time ago.

It is not that the future portends another world or cold war within a decade or so. We have some gains for which we can be historically grateful. But our societies face a very difficult global future, and are not well equipped to meet it. Liberal democracy has been a 'triumph' in important respects but it is a failure in others, and these will hinder the development of close and productive cooperation between the transatlantic partners for the future. To adapt an old adage, we will be two continents separated by a common ideology.

The main feature of global order (and disorder) presently developing will be markedly different from those which created

---

* An edited version of a lecture given at a conference on 'Changes in Transatlantic Relations' at Loccum, Germany on 23–25 October 1992, sponsored by the Evangelische Akademie Loccum and The American Institute for Contemporary German Studies (John Hopkins)

the intense transatlantic cooperation of the past 40 years. In thinking about this problem we have to widen our perspective from the 1990s to well into the next century, and ask: What are transatlantic relations for? Why is progressive cooperation – rather than indifference or mere friendliness – important? And by what standard should we judge future transatlantic relations?

The short answer to these questions is that the standard for judging transatlantic relations should be more than indifference or mere friendliness because if the world is to overcome some of the serious and predictable problems which the future has in store, then progressive transatlantic cooperation is essential. It is essential not only because of the power which North America and Western Europe both possess (in terms of their ability to get things done) but also because it is important to recognise that we (the transatlantic partners) are a significant factor in the problem of future global order. The enemy, in part, is us. Consequently, we have to recreate ourselves, largely through the power of ideas. If we cannot recreate ourselves and cooperate progressively, then our grandchildren's world will be in an even bigger mess than our own.

THE TRIUMPH OF LIBERAL DEMOCRACY?

In terms of the history of political ideas, the context for transatlantic relations is what has been called the 'triumph' of liberal democracy, together – it must never be forgotten – with the 'triumph' of capitalism . Has it been a 'triumph'? In three important respects, it has, at least in part.

First, Fukuyama is correct in his argument that liberal democracy has triumphed over other 20th century 'systemic' challengers, notably communism.[1] This is a truly historic achievement. In the longer term however, his argument is not valid.

The problems that made the ideal of communism so widely attractive – unjustifiable inequalities, wretched poverty, and violent oppression – still exist on a global scale. We also live in an unstable world. Technological, social and other changes are so dynamic these days that prediction is a very risky business. The combination of these two features of world affairs might well breed new challenging ideologies. Furthermore, it is not even evident that liberal democracy is the most efficient way to run capitalist economies, and there is little doubt that the 'triumph of capitalism' has been both more global and fundamental than the triumph of liberal democracy. Interestingly, one of the subtexts of Fukuyama's book seems to be his admiration for the more authoritarian societies of the Far East, and the successful way they have welded their traditional societies with capitalism.

A more serious criticism still of Fukuyama's thesis is the astonishing cultural, historical and political parochialism evident in the way he considers today's 'Western' societies as the culmination of history; he appears to see the way they have developed in the last two centuries as a model for the future everywhere. Three counter points need to be emphasised, namely: that liberal democracy is probably culture specific; that historically democracy has not been a popular idea; and that there is no logical reason to suppose that Western-style liberal democracy will survive indefinitely or spread globally, through all the ups and downs of future world history.

So, in the history of political ideas, we can accept that liberal democracy meets many Western needs; that it has become a widespread norm; and that it has a certain rationality. What we cannot conclude is that we are at the end of history.

The second 'triumph' being trumpeted is the alleged congruence of liberal democracy and peace. Fukuyama wrote about this in his recent book, as had Michael Doyle a decade ago, and, of course, Immanuel Kant 200 years ago.[2] There are many supporting arguments, but the most salient points are the importance of shared values (including the mutual recognition of legitimacy between liberal democracies); the allegedly peaceful inclination of democratic foreign policies; and the common interest in peace which is said to be the consequence of commercial interdependence.

The thesis that liberal democracy is a recipe for peace is a controversial one, contradicting, if nothing else, decades of 'realist' teaching in international relations . Nevertheless the argument has some validity. Certainly the empirical evidence suggests that, for whatever reason, liberal democracies do not seem to fight each other.

But there are reasons for caution. So far there have been

rather few liberal democracies (about 25) and their historical circumstances have been propitious. The Soviet threat on the one side and the hegemony of the United States on the other were obviously conducive to peaceful cooperation, especially in, the aftermath of a terribly destructive war. Would we be so confident in the equation 'liberal democracy equals peace' if there were 100 liberal democracies across the world, inevitably bringing along with them a range of regional problems and unsettled historical rivalries? Furthermore, is liberal democracy as exportable as Fukuyama seems to suggest? And what about the brutal way liberal democracies have acted against some Third World states – including some with elected (if not transparently liberal) governments? Perhaps it is simply too soon to say that liberal democracies do not – will not – fight each other.

So, again, we must come to a qualified verdict. The alleged relationship between liberal democracy and peace cannot simply be dismissed as some sort of historical anomaly: on the other hand, it would be premature to be complacent.

The third ostensible 'triumph' of liberal democracy is in the area of values. Fukuyama sees liberal democracy as the height of political rationality, and a system which in practice has brought comfort and satisfaction to its citizens. These societies have also helped to spread certain values, such as human rights. I share such values, and am content to assert their superiority, compared with the values of a society which has offered vast sums of money for the murder of a writer who allegedly insulted god; or compared with societies which mutilate young girls as standard practice (about 90–100 million females today are said to have suffered this patriarchal torture). In short, there are some 'ethnocentric values' for which I do not think it necessary to apologise.

But Western societies have value-problems. Our societies have the vices of their virtues. Some of the key values we have privileged and operationalised over the past two centuries can be regarded as problems rather than solutions when we contemplate the global future. Michael McGwire has neatly summarised these values as 'possessive individualism', 'consumer democracy', 'the capitalist world economy', and 'unconstrained science and technology'. If these phrases accurately describe our framework of values, will it be possible to prevent the continued destruction of nature? Will it be possible to eradicate violence in all the various dimensions of South-North relations?

So, yet again, we come to a less-than-enthusiastic verdict on the 'triumph' of liberal democracy. Our Western societies have some admirable values, but if we hope to overcome major global problems, then we need to recreate ourselves. Clearly, this will not be an easy task. The qualified triumph of 'actually existing liberal democracy' has to be set some powerful evidence of failure.

Politically, we have devalued democracies. We have elections but little choice. We have universal suffrage, but limited voter interest. The 1980s were characterised by one-party democracies in many countries. Furthermore, the acceptable left has moved so far right that most of the political debate takes place within a very narrow band of conservative-capitalist-liberal-statist values.

Economically, we have a crisis of capitalism. Western societies are undergoing a long-lasting recession, with all that implies in terms of social strain and human misery. And the West runs the global economy through organisations like the World Bank and International Monetary Fund, with all that implies for the poor people of underdeveloped countries which are being forced into the shape desired by the Western economies.

And socially we have problems we do not like to advertise. There are the homeless huddled in shop doorways in London; there are riots in Los Angeles; and there is extremism in Rostock. Substantial parts of urban America are simply no-go areas for that élite which has been most triumphalist about the winning of the Cold War.

Of course, all our societies are doing better than most parts of the world, but now we have lost the Berlin Wall, and all that we could point to on the other side – which made us look so good in comparison – the achievements of liberal democracy do not look so wonderful. In hindsight, Georgi Arbatov was very prescient when in 1987 he forecast: 'We are going to do the worst thing we possibly can to America – we are going to take away their enemy' . The Iron Curtain trapped the East into oppression; but it trapped the West into complacency.

If we in the 'centre' of the world economy are going through a difficult period, parts of the 'periphery' are having an appalling time. And we in the West are not helping very effectively, either through our control of the United Nations or the running of the global economy. Does democracy in the West have to rest on debt, decay, deforestation, disease, dictatorship, destruction and death in so much of the South? As usual, women and children suffer worst. It is estimated that one child dies every hour in the Philippines to service that country's foreign debt, and that nearly a million Latin American children die each year from disease, violence, and malnutrition. We do not hear the voices of women and children in mainstream International Relations literature. What is the relationship between their plight and the triumph of liberal democracy and capitalism? Is their plight systemic, or just bad luck? Many people in the West show considerable individual generosity to suffering elsewhere; meanwhile, Britain's official foreign aid is less than half its committed target (and rumoured to be going down further), while the United States government last year supplied weapons to 59 authoritarian governments. Even if 'the West is best', it is certainly not good enough.

A fundamental problem in all this is what J K Galbraith has recently been calling the 'culture of contentment'.[3] Protecting the well off (now the majority) in Western societies has become the essential business of elections, the economy, and foreign and defence policy. In a Western election these days the most damning thing one candidate can say about another is that the latter will put up taxes. In one sense this privileging of private wants over public needs is a perfect expression of individualistic Western values, but none but the blinkered about the future could regard it as a 'triumph'.

Without the convenient Soviet threat, we have to face up to the fact that we are indeed the enemy to the extent that 'we are all natural capitalists', as the left-wing writer Martha Gellhorn once candidly put it including those who might think they are not. The consumer appetites of Western societies began to be whetted in the 18th century, and they have now gathered an apparently irresistible momentum. Reasonably-shod adolescent boys have committed murder in order to steal more fashionable footwear. We fiddle (we fiddle with our VCRs, our Camcorders and our computers) while the rain-forest burns.

Does it matter? The hard-headed tend to say: 'No. We have worked hard for what we have got; so let us enjoy it'. What those who make this argument often really mean is that their parents or grandparents worked hard – but this is not often appreciated. Instead, there is an unpleasant tendency growing in Western societies to mistake good luck for virtue, and to equate failure with unworthiness.

In short, the character of the relationship between our societies and those elsewhere does matter, and not just because we are all human beings, and therefore deserving of respect. It matters also because real security ultimately comes not from the self-interested exercise of power, but from the creation of community (as France and Germany have discovered in the last half-century). This is true at all levels. Offend a group's dignity too much and we can expect a riot. Deprive ethnic or national groups of what they consider to be their rights and we can expect terrorism. Push countries too far and we can expect the proliferation of weapons of mass destruction. The contented of the prosperous world should not forget that risking death is not the worst thing in life for the very discontented. Security grows with emancipation and community.

The consequences of failing to attend to global security issues are quite predictable, as is the further shrinking of geopolitical space between North and South as a result of the spread of modern weaponry. In military terms it might now appear like a confrontation between Northern power and Southern weakness, but in 20 years time, how many Southern Davids will have nuclear slingshots? Fear of this contingency is already driving the development of mini-nuclear weapons at the Los Alamos laboratories for possible use in Third World contingencies.

These are the outlines of the negative aspects of the situation. It can improve, of course, and there are occasional glimpses of such possibilities, as in the Middle East. But does anybody really expect the 1990s for the Western countries to be other than years of economic struggle, domestic strain, consumerism and contentment, introspection, growing environmental problems, vague and not such vague worries about the world at large, and reduced confidence about the future? Added to these features, when thinking about transatlantic relations, let us not forget that the situation no longer includes the Soviet threat or American hegemony. It is obvious then that the 1990s will be very different from the conditions in which the transatlantic partnership was forged and flourished. The 1990s do not look like providing the conditions in which that partnership will prosper and deepen in future. In the short term, at least, it is possible that introspection and a degree of pessimism in Western societies will stimulate mutual indifference, if not actual suspicion, between Western Europe and North America.

MODELS OF WORLD ORDER

How then, does the 'triumph' of liberal democracy resonate with whatever structures and processes are developing in world affairs? It is possible to identify seven recent models or images of global order; they are not mutually exclusive, but it is helpful to separate them.

The first model is global order through *collective security*. This idea resurfaced with the revival of the UN in the late 1980s, and the signs that the United States and Soviet Union could work together. They did actually make progress on several regional conflicts. But the collapse of the Soviet Union put an end to the further development of this idea. More fundamental, however, as all students of international politics are taught, is that the putting into practice of the pure theory of collective security is impossible. What is actually practical is to further the security of the powerful, rather than the security of the collectivity.

The second model began to be proclaimed as the first one faded. This was President Bush's *'New World Order'*. It was always a vague idea, but its essence seemed to be that the UN, led by the United States, would try to maintain peace and security in world affairs. The United States would be the policeman of international law (not to mention the judge and jury – but that was not mentioned). The rest of the West would provide either the posse (with the British embracing the prospect of fighting small wars in faraway places) or money (in the case of Germany and Japan). The Gulf War was described as the 'first test' of this 'New World Order', and Bush proclaimed it a victory.

The 'New World Order' always attracted criticism from outside the Bush camp. This mostly focused on the argument that the concept was simply a grandiose cloak for the pursuit of US national interests. The idea was also criticised for being hypo-critical. After all, the first aggression of the post-Cold War world was that carried out by the Bush administration in Panama. In practice, now that the dust has settled on *Desert Storm,* it is apparent that the United States does not have the means or the desire to police Bush's 'New World Order'. It provides an example of another model which has collapsed.

The third model, *Pax Americana,* could be regarded as an extension of the last: it is not a New World Order, it is the New World giving the orders. This model is based on the image of traditional United States imperialism, allied to victory in the Cold War. As the only superpower, the United States is now seen as free to exploit its power more ruthlessly than in the recent past. But this is not a world without 'enemies' for the 'single superpower'. The Soviet threat has been replaced by a variety of demons in the Third World. The latter are built up not only by the government but also by the US media, which are an accomplice of the US government and the threatened defence industries. The model of *Pax Americana* is the one articulated on the American political left. The most notable exponent of this viewpoint in the United States itself is Noam Chomsky, in his recent book *Peterrina Democracy.*[5]

There are elements of Chomsky's argument which have to be taken very seriously, such as his criticism of the inadequacies of modern democracy, including the media. Furthermore, he is to be congratulated for rubbing our noses in the memory of the brutal way we have sometimes dealt with the non-liberal demo-cratic world. But surely he exaggerates. Has not US military imperialism been more selective than he suggests? Does it not have insufficient military power to impose its will as readily as he asserts? And can any democratic government be quite as ruth-less as he asserts? On the other hand, his book could have made more of non-military imperialism, referring to the way the United States has controlled the levers of the world economy.

The fourth model is the alternative favoured on the political right. It might be called *Old World Disorder.* It sees international affairs reverting to the 1930s or 1910s. Nationalism and insta-bility are all around; and so is ambition (suspicious glances are cast towards Germany and Japan). It is regretted that there is no hegemonial power to keep order. As a result, the Cold War –

with its ostensible stability – is viewed with some nostalgia. John Mearsheimer's 'Back to the Future' thesis is the standard text for this model.[6]

On first sight there appears to be a great deal to this argument; there is indeed a great deal of disorder. But is there not plenty which is new as well as old in the situation, thereby rendering the model too simple? Compared with the 1930s or 1940s, interdependence is institutionalised these days, and war is just about unthinkable between industrialised powers. Sovereignty is no longer what it was, and we live on a 'wired planet'. The future cannot crudely be a mirror of the past.

The fifth model is that of a *tripolar world*, organised around the dollar, yen, and mark trading areas. Other regions are unhappy appendages to one or more of these blocs. There is no doubt that such regionalisation is evolving. The uncertainty is rather with the implications of the development. Will it lead to protectionist blocs? Will economic rivalry lead to military rivalry (a nuclear-armed Germany and Japan, for example)? Will ideological rivalries develop as well?

Even if more regionalisation and competition appear likely in a tripolar world, it is too simple to compare these groupings to the autarkic blocs of the past. They are more open to external trade, and interdependence is more globalised and institutionalised. And surely the leaders of major states have learned something from the terrible history of the 20th century. The world could be on a slippery tripolar slope, but it is difficult to imagine that anybody could see another Pearl Harbor as a helpful solution to future trade wars. So, we can perhaps expect more open competition, but not open conflict.

The sixth model can be described as *New World Disorder* to emphasise both the newness (in comparison with model four) and the disorder (in comparison with model two). It is a world of new as well as old problems and conflicts. It is a complex world of both localisation and globalisation, interdependence and regionalism, and conflict and cooperation. But the one common feature of this world is that everywhere one looks there seems to be what can be described as system-overload: national economies cannot cope, nor can multi-ethnic states; the environment is suffering, locally and globally; crime is increasing and weapons of mass destruction are spreading. An appropriate symbol of this overload is Kazakhstan, which in the midst of 1992 was reported as having a Foreign Ministry of eight people, while nominally in control of hundreds of ex-Soviet nuclear weapons.

The signposts of New World Disorder are all around: Somalia, Sarajevo, fundamentalism, the Russian powderkeg, Iraq, refugees, toxic whales in the St Lawrence Seaway and ozone holes above us. Such problems are undeniable. But their existence is recognised and there are some counter-trends. There is social tolerance in Eastern Europe, as well as the brutality of Sarajevo. There are attempts to control environmental destruction, as well as polluters who do not pay. The questions with these and similar problems are simple. How much time have we got? And which forces will prevail? It is the answers which are not simple.

Finally there is the *World Society* image of global order. This is a 'bottom up' rather than 'top down' view. It emphasises societies and social movements rather than states as agents of progressive change and looks towards the creation of a global civic culture rather than a global policeman. Some statist versions of global order are rather nasty. They involve 'security' between states, but not necessarily 'security' for the people who live in them. In such circumstances one's own state is the threat, not the neighbour. This has been the case in Latin America, for the most part.

The World Society view (as represented in the work of Richard Falk for example) looks to the advancement of 'world order' values such as humane governance, non-violence, human rights and ecological sustainability.[7] On political and philosophical grounds, it privileges peoples rather than states: 'statism' is seen as the enemy. The favoured solution is to bifurcate authority. People should organise smaller groupings than the state for some needs (such as cultural satisfaction) while going beyond the state to the continental or global level to create functional groupings able to deal with those problems individual states are too small to handle (the future of the oceans for example, or global warming). This would lead to a multi-layered, patchwork system of governance, which has sometimes been described as a 'new medievalism'.

Clearly, there are some trends in the World Society direction:

there are powerful non-governmental organisations, there is the erosion of state sovereignty, international régimes have evolved, and inter-regional relations, notably within Europe, increasingly resembles interdependence rather than realist images of reality. But the state is obviously a long way from withering away.

The world at present can be described as a combination of several of the models just discussed: it is a mixture of New World Disorder tempered by the qualified triumph of liberal democracy and the global grip of the capitalist world economy; there is a tendency to tripolar regionalisation, with *Pax Americana* operating in some locations; alongside the system of states there are increasingly active alternative centres of power; and all this is evolving in the context of more efficient global communications, environmental decay and population growth. The latter, incidentally, will increasingly leave the liberal democracies of the West as a global minority; in terms of people and wealth, the signs point to rapid growth in the years ahead in Asia.

THE CHALLENGE FACING
TRANSATLANTIC RELATIONS

With respect to the future of transatlantic relations, the good news is that ideological and cultural affinities, together with the lessons of the past, surely rule out any neo-realist inspired nightmare about how far any continental drift could go. The bad news is that the culture of contentment and the complex dynamics of global circumstances make progressive cooperation look unlikely, at least in the short term, and certainly to the extent of meeting the standard of recreating ourselves. There were differences between Western Europe and North America during the Cold War over issues such as how to deal with the Soviet threat. But US power and leadership together with the Western European fear of being left out in the cold in a crisis, imposed a certain discipline. But both the leadership and the fear have now gone (except perhaps over access to oil). We can therefore expect less cooperation and more competition, less deference and more disagreement, and less authority and more acrimony.

It will be easy to dismiss these arguments as over-pessimistic. We now feel as historically invulnerable as did the British Empire a century ago, or the Romans 2000 years ago, or the Greeks before them. For each of them the 'known-world' was 'theirs'. Now, the known-world seems to be 'ours'. 'Look at our wealth, at our security, at our power, at our values, at our success and at our creativity' somebody might say. But then again, look at the *Titanic.*

As the *Titanic* set sail across the Atlantic it appeared to be the culmination of the history of shipbuilding design. Its construction represented the height of rationality and applied science. And it was obviously more advanced than anything else that had hitherto put to sea. It had seen off all rival designs.

Had he been alive at the time, Francis Fukuyama would doubtless have celebrated this mighty ship, and waved it off at the quayside (with only the slightly troubling thought, perhaps, that the passengers might find the journey a little boring, compared with the less seaworthy ships of the past). The passengers on board felt good, and were made to feel good. The band played and plates were filled. The captain and crew were confident in their ship. They felt invulnerable, and hardly gave a thought to the dangers. Indeed they denied them. In transport terms, they had truly reached the end of history.

One's pessimism of the intellect when thinking about the future might be ameliorated slightly by an optimism of the spirit which sees people around who are not complacent, who do not have every faith in rationalism and science, who do not believe we in the West have a monopoly of wisdom, who do not feel invulnerable, who do think about the long-term, and who are committed to progressive world order values. In practice, the agents of hope are those progressive social movements and organisations thinking about recreating our societies, being sensitive to different thoughtways, resetting agendas, thinking globally and energising peoples (if not governments very often). These agents have to capture the vision and engage the power of the states of North America and Western Europe if the Titanic is steered away from the environmental, military, economic and social ice-fields of the future. If we do not start turning – degree by degree – then in 40, 50 or more years the world will be an even more unhappy place than today. And we should not assume that it will be the grandchildren of the culture of contentment who will have priority in the lifeboats.

Notes

1 Francis Fukuyama *The End of History and the Last Man*, (London, Hamish Hamilton, 1992). See also his earlier article which created the catchphrase, 'The End of History?' *The National Interest*, Vol. 16, Summer 1989, pp. 3–18.

2 See, Immanuel Kant, *Perpetual Peace: A Philosophical Essay* (1975), London, Swan Sonnenschein, 1903); Michael Doyle, 'Kant, Liberal Legacies and Foreign Affairs', *Philosophy and Public Affairs*, Vol 12 (3), 1983, pp. 205–35.

3 J K Galbraith, *The Culture of Contentment*, (London, Sinclair-Stevenson, 1992).

4 Martha Gellhorn, *Travels With Myself and Another*, (London, Eland, 1991, Chap. 2.

5 Noam Chomsky, *Deterring Democracy*, (New York, Verso Edition, 1991).

6 John J Mersheimer, 'Back to the Future: Instability in Europe After the Cold War', *International Security*, Vol. 15 (1), 1990, pp. 5–56.

7 Richard Falk, *Explorations at the Edge of Time: The Prospects for World Order*, (Philadelphia, Temple University Press, 1992).

22

Is There a Peace Dividend?

DAVID GREENWOOD

Director, Centre for Defence Studies, University of Aberdeen

The expression 'peace dividend' originated in the United States some 25 years ago. It was probably coined by a commentator – or maybe a Congressman – who needed a neat encapsulation of the idea that ending the war in Vietnam would permit a rapid reordering of national priorities to the immediate benefit of the civil economy.

The war had certainly required a massive commitment of additional resources to the military. In the second half of the 1960s, American defence spending and defence-related employment soared. Between 1965 and 1968 the budget of the Department of Defense (DoD) rose by a staggering 40 per cent, in real terms: from a level equivalent to less than $250 billion at today's prices (1993) to one in excess of S350 billion. The manpower engaged in the US defence effort – military personnel, DoD civilians and employees in defence industry – increased spectacularly too in these years. Fewer than 6 million Americans were so employed in 1965. By 1968 the number was over 8 million.

Not surprisingly, therefore, when it was eventually decided to end the country's involvement in South-East Asia, everyone hoped – and expected – that there would be a prompt release of resources for other purposes. Cometh the hour, cometh the catchphrase. The term 'peace dividend' entered the vocabulary of political and popular debate as a convenient shorthand for such hopes and expectations.

Nor was it just a slogan. There *was* a swift turnaround in

resource allocation. The real value of the DoD's budget dropped steadily from 1969 onwards, bottoming-out in 1976 at a level equivalent to approximately $220 billion in 1993 dollars. Numbers in defence-related employment fell even more sharply. The total was down to 6 million by 1971, below 5 million by the mid-1970s. The scale of the contraction exceeded that of the earlier expansion because the Nixon-Kissinger years were a time not only of progressive disengagement from Vietnam but also of detente with the Soviet Union. The Americans moved – albeit only briefly – to a lower 'baseline' defence effort.

Moreover, there *were* pay-offs for the civilian economy. The Johnson Administration committed itself to both tax reductions and increased public sector spending (on its so-called 'Great Society' programmes). After an interlude of counter-inflationary restraint, which precipitated the brief recession of 1970–71, the Nixon Administration too opted for expansionary fiscal and monetary action, producing a strong domestic recovery. Here was a 'peace dividend' indeed. Moreover, it was one which the American people might have enjoyed for a while longer had it not been for the (first) oil price shock of 1973–4 and the much deeper recession – plus a host of other economic problems – which followed.

There were, though, costs as well as benefits associated with the quick military rundown. Throughout the early 1970s, even when the US economy as a whole was booming, the defence cutbacks – especially those in the DoD's procurement programmes – dealt devastating blows to some industries and regions. It was in the aerospace sector that production and employment shrank most, because reduced military business coincided with big falls in orders for both commercial aircraft and work on space projects. At Boeing's plants in the Seattle area, to take a particularly vivid illustration, where there had been over 100,000 jobs in the later 1960s, there were only 30,000 or thereabouts by the mid-1970s. But the incidence of sectoral, regional and local distress was widespread. In response to it, Federal and State authorities had to devise a variety of 'adjustment' programmes: to assist large companies in diversifying or converting to civil business; to provide retraining for defence scientists and engineers; and to cushion the impact of plant rundowns and base closures on local communities. In the event, all but a few corporate 'diversification' and 'conversion' efforts ended in failure. Several schemes to aid displaced workers and some local economic development initiatives were, however, moderately successful.[1]

To summarise this American experience: there was a handsome 'peace dividend' in *macroeconomic* terms – i.e. for the US economy as a whole – following the end of the Vietnam war; but military retrenchment also necessitated many an awkward *microeconomic* adjustment. The price of peace in many places was protracted hardship.

By the later 1970s, however, no-one in the United States – or anywhere else for that matter – was much concerned about the economic consequences of military rundown. Defence budgets were rising again. Apprehension at a perceived increase in the conventional strength of the USSR and its Warsaw Pact allies, plus the appearance of new theatre nuclear weapons posing a direct threat to Western Europe, led to the NATO-wide adoption of an annual 3 per cent real growth target for military spending. This was quickly followed by an intensification of Cold War rhetoric : as it happens, the final outburst of ferocious East-West antagonism. It was exemplified in the Western camp by, on one side of the Atlantic, Ronald Reagan's celebrated characterisation of the Soviet bloc as the 'evil empire' and, on the other side of the ocean, that vehement condemnation of socialism and all its works (and in all its guises) which earned Margaret Thatcher her 'Iron Lady' tag.

THE END OF THE COLD WAR

Into this scene, though, strode Mikhail Gorbachev, championing not only *glasnost* and *perestroika* but also unilateral and negotiated arms reductions to permit, among other things, *konversiya* of the Soviet military-industrial complex. The Iron Lady said she could do business with this man; and in the arms control field Ronald Reagan did precisely that. As a result, from the mid-1980s Western governments began cautiously to revise their defence expenditure plans, opting for either level funding or reduced outlays in real terms. Later, following the wave of popular dissatisfaction with authoritarian régimes which swept

Eastern Europe in 1989 and essentially brought the Cold War to an end, Western taxpayers began to question the need for caution. If the Forty Years War was over, what about a prompt and generous 'peace dividend'?

It was – and is – a fair question. Yet throughout the West the powers-that-be have remained unwilling to slash defence budgets drastically, notwithstanding the radically changed strategic circumstances. On the whole, they have not thought it appropriate to reallocate resources on a grand scale, delivering tax cuts across the board and/or boosting outlays on social programmes all round. True, just about every government has begun modifying its national force structure, reducing force levels and revising acquisition plans. But nowhere is the extent, or the pace, of projected adjustment on a par with the American rundown after Vietnam. Nor does any Western country contemplate demilitarisation on the sort of scale that some states of the former Eastern bloc are actually implementing. The Ukraine is a case in point. According to the minister responsible for defence conversion in Kiev, whereas the value of 'military orders' in 1991 totalled 160 billion roubles, in 1992 the figure was a mere 10 billion roubles; and change from military to civil use is envisaged for a staggering 1700 factories and facilities.[2] The contrast with the situation in the United Kingdom is striking. Here it is planned that overall defence spending should fall by less than 6 per cent (after inflation) over the five-year period 1991–1995 but equipment expenditure – or 'military orders' – will remain, domestic economic conditions permitting, at some £9–10 billion per year throughout the first half of the 1990s. Moreover, not only is there no national policy – and certainly not a minister – for conversion or diversification but doom-laden prophesies accompany even the announcement of straightforward rationalisation schemes, witness the hue and cry which greeted a decision, in September 1992, foreshadowing the closure of just 17 small research establishments.[3]

REASONS FOR CAUTION

It is not simply bureaucratic inertia, or the weight of vested interests, which accounts for the measured Western response to the Cold War's end, however. For a time, though everyone recognised that the threat from the East had receded, military decision-makers felt duty bound to point out that there remained a *residual* threat, at least for as long as the USSR stayed intact. When the Soviet Union finally disintegrated, the question was whether – from the elements of the looser Commonwealth of Independent States (CIS), or from Russia alone – there could conceivably appear at some stage a *regenerated* threat. By the time planners were prepared to discount that possibility pretty heavily, Saddam Hussein's summary annexation of Kuwait was followed first by a protracted crisis then by a short, sharp conflict that led to his ejection from the sheikhdom. These events served to remind governments that they might be well advised to preserve capabilities for external intervention, and force projection generally, especially if there was going to be a 'new world order' to police. The break-up of Yugoslavia and its bloody aftermath – not to mention the possibility of similar convulsions elsewhere in the Balkans and the Levant, within the fragile CIS, or in the Baltic states – have served to reinforce this appreciation, highlighting as they have the potential for widespread disorder in the transformed strategic environment.

In these circumstances, it is unlikely that Western administrations would have chosen to dismantle their military organisations lock, stock and barrel even if the post-Cold War world had been entirely tranquil. For one thing, they would have become aware quite early in any planning for radical rundown that assets acquired, and long maintained, ostensibly to counter 'the threat from the East' – and, incidentally, paid for with tax revenues raised on that ticket – were in fact the only means available for covering even basic security needs and dealing with any contingency requiring the disposition of organised and disciplined force. Put another way, it would have dawned on them that scrapping everything assigned a Cold War rationale would mean scrapping everything, literally. They would have shrunk from that, rightly, if only to allow time for fundamental reflection on 'reasons for having armed forces' and for addressing issues which it had not been necessary to consider while force planning required doing whatever had to be done to preserve strategic nuclear parity with the USSR and maintain a conventional military balance *vis-à-vis* the Warsaw Pact.

One country which did engage in such reflection and recon-
sideration during 1991 and 1992 was the United Kingdom.
Examination of 'options for change' in the British defence
effort began in 1990, initially because of budgetary pressure
rather than any clearly perceived need for root-and-branch
strategic reappraisal. It soon became clear, however, that policy
reformulation ought to accompany revision of posture and provision. Hence the restatement of national military purpose
contained in the first major policy pronouncement of John
Major's second government.

This is most illuminating in the context of the present discussion. With a wry recognition that the post-Cold War 'bonfire
of the certainties' had rendered policy-making and planning
much more complicated than hitherto, the *Statement on the
Defence Estimates 1992* says 'there is no simple way of encompassing briefly all the tasks and activities of the armed forces'. Still,
the document goes on to define 'three overlapping roles' for
them, viz:

- [ ] To ensure the protection and security of the United Kingdom
  and our dependent territories, *even when there is no major external threat.*
- [ ] To *insure against* any major external threat to the United
  Kingdom and our allies.
- [ ] To contribute to promoting the United Kingdom's wider
  security interests through *the maintenance of international peace
  and stability.*[4]

Needless to say, disparaging remarks have been made about the
'defence for all reasons' quality of this language, especially the
phrases italicised here. Be that as it may, the British have at least
articulated a coherent rationale for future military provision
and for *not* emasculating their fighting services; and, in so
doing, they have provided a defensible justification for not
declaring an immediate and bountiful 'peace dividend' and for
thus declining to do what the Americans did 20 years ago.

It has to be remembered also that what the United States did
in the early 1970s was primarily to release the *additional*
resources which, only a few years earlier, had been so swiftly
mobilised for the conflict in Vietnam. In this respect, the much-

vaunted 'peace dividend' was no more than a prompt rebate on the massive imposition on the American economy and American society which the build-up of the later 1960s had represented. The catchphrase however, carries connotations of a return to normality and a resumption of 'baseline' provision for national security.

Western caution in reducing defence efforts since 1989 may be ascribed in part to the very different circumstances surrounding the termination of the 'Forty Years War': uncertainty all round about exactly what strictly *incremental* resource allocation the long confrontation had in fact entailed (cf. the British case); the absence of a recent military expansion crying out to be reversed by rapid demobilisation (except, perhaps, in the case of the United States); and the lack of a sound basis for gauging 'normality' and of reliable yardsticks for regular 'baseline' provision (which explains why so many nations have yet finally to decide on the size, shape, equipment and deployment of their forces for the longer term).

Nor is it just that governments appear to have lost their strategic bearings. Dealing with organisational matters and associated military-industrial complexities is problematical as well. The possibility of a regenerated threat from the East is remote, but it cannot for the time being be discounted altogether. Turbulence in and around Europe seems likely to persist; and it could worsen, requiring the commitment of more forces, more often than current calculations envisage. That is why, in the Alliance-wide strategy and force structure review which NATO completed late in 1991 and in individual countries' parallel or subsequent reappraisals of their defence provisions, much attention was – and is – paid to ensuring that diminution of national defence efforts is managed in such a way as to permit *reconstitution* of fighting strength, should circumstances require it. When the extent and pace of military contraction has to be charted with this consideration in mind, a certain conservatism is inevitable.

In fact, deciding to preserve the means to recreate military power raises a pair of key issues which have exercised administrations a great deal of late. The first arises because some capabilities are easier to reconstitute than others. Force planners must therefore identify which capabilities, once dispensed with, it would be impossible to revive, and ensure that these

remain represented in the new peacetime order of battle. For
the rest, the challenge is to strike a prudent balance between
standing forces on, the one hand, short and long-warning
mobilisable forces which can be mobilised on the other.
Prudence enters the reckoning because, while a 'mix' of minimal active forces and large standby reserves may commend itself
on financial grounds, there are attendant risks, especially since
'reconstitution' is a concept which has been discussed and not
(thus far) a procedure which has been practised.

The second issue concerns maintenance of the means to
equip both forces-in-being and formations that have been
reconstituted. Procurement planners have been thinking long
and hard about this subject, considering how acquisition is best
organised in the new strategic circumstances and how best to
preserve an adequate and appropriate defence industrial base
(DIB). Novel approaches to procurement have been advocated:
like sustaining a broad military research agenda and continuing
to develop next-generation weapons systems, but producing and
fielding state-of-the-art equipment only as, when, and if, the
modernisation of front-line forces seems absolutely necessary.
As for the DIB question, governments have been asking themselves, quite properly, what technological competence and
manufacturing capacity it is in their long-term interest to retain.
Top defence contractors, for their part, have been lobbying furi-
ously for a 'better safe than sorry' approach to this issue, in the
hope of being kept in business as the custodians of retained
competence and capacity.

It would be an exaggeration to say that governments have
been preoccupied with preserving capabilities, competence and
capacity, and with scrutinising options for what one analyst has
called – graphically, elegantly – 'inflatable armed forces' and
'reversible conversion'.[5] Nevertheless, these matters have
received a lot of attention to date and will doubtless demand
more as time goes by, keeping delivery of the 'peace dividend'
in the background a little longer.

That is where it may stay for a while, for a further and final
reason. Quite a few governments have undoubtedly decided
that, with their economies gripped by recession – the deepest
and longest-lasting in many countries' post-Second World War
experience – the last thing they want to do is add to domestic

distress by putting additional people out of work and running down industrial capacity. The opportunity to free resources from defence for worthwhile civil uses, long looked-for (and, indeed, campaigned for by the self-styled 'peace movement'), is an embarrassment when it presents itself in hard times: when cutting military spending sharply will release manpower to swell the ranks of the unemployed, and cutting production capacity will add to an already unwelcome estate of idle facilities. Moreover it is ironic that this predicament bears most heavily on administrations whose ideological disposition is to leave to 'market forces' the task of accomplishing structural adjustment in their economies. Better to have a pro-active industrial policy – for *konversiya,* or whatever – than to be committed to entrusting adjustment to an invisible hand which propels people in the direction of the dole queue.

THE NEW DISARMAMENT ECONOMICS

What the foregoing argument makes clear is that there are not only politico-strategic reasons but also economic explanations for the caution which Western governments have shown in plotting military contraction and for the fact that they have neither delivered nor plan to deliver a spectacular 'peace dividend'. This is of more than passing interest. The prospect of effecting a defence rundown in recession has thrown into sharp relief the inadequacies of the disarmament economics of the last generation.

Like earlier periods of military retrenchment the American experience after the Vietnam War was characterised, as already noted, by microeconomic costs which more or less coincided with, and were made more bearable by, simultaneous macroeconomic benefits. Some industrial sectors and some localities were hard hit. These needed, and received, remedial treatment. However, the overall economic climate was benign – at least to begin with – so compensation for the diminution in defence demand was possible, through a stimulation of consumption, tax cuts, and a boost in civil expenditure on new social programmes. This accorded with the conventional wisdom about the economics of disarmament: that one could envisage a comparatively smooth and almost instantaneous series of shifts in the use of resources from guns to butter, swords to plough-shares.

However, that is emphatically not how today's analysts view the adjustment process. Aware that a military rundown entails costs as well as benefits, and that in recessionary times the costs may initially be more apparent than the benefits, their empha-sis is on *disarmament as an investment process,* in which present costs are incurred in the expectation of future benefits.

This 'new disarmament economics' appears to have been elaborated in the deliberations of the independent experts con-vened in 1991 by the United Nations Institute of Disarmament Research (UNIDIR) to prepare a Report for the UN General Assembly, a document which was duly submitted in September 1992 with the title *Economic Aspects of Disarmament: Disarmament as an Investment Process.*[6] Certainly the most succinct and lucid statement of the 'model' is to be found in a paper prepared for this exercise by a member of the expert team, Michael Intriligator; and the approach clearly underlies each of the '12 economic principles of disarmament' that the investigation yielded.

It is worth quoting at length from Intriligator's elegant essay, which is so evidently the intellectual foundation of the UNI-DIR's work. His formal statement of the 'investment process' approach is admirably concise:

> Disarmament . . . involves initial conversion costs, including the direct adjustment costs of retraining workers and soldiers, retool-ing or building new capital, and developing the capability to produce non-defence goods and services. In addition, there are the direct and opportunity costs of unemployment of labour, cap-ital, and other inputs into the production of military goods and services. Both types of conversion costs are incurred over a tran-sition period, which may last years. They are then *followed by* benefits as inputs are reallocated to the production of civilian goods and services, which provides the ultimate 'peace dividend'. Both the initial conversion costs and the ultimate peace dividend could be measured in financial terms or, even more appropriate-ly, in real terms, as the real cost of the initial resource unemployment and reallocation and the real benefit of the ulti-

mate additional civilian output. A 'return from disarmament' can then be obtained as the implied social rate of return, taking explicit account of both the real costs and the real benefits of disarmament.[7]

Note the added emphasis here: costs are 'followed by' benefits. Note also that 'peace dividend' – in quotation marks in the original – is a label for the gross benefits from the disarmament (or rundown) experience.

Among the merits of analysing disarmament as an investment process is the value of the approach in dispelling those myths about disarmament (or military contraction) which, Intriligator notes, are 'held as strong beliefs by their proponents'.

The first myth is that there would be an immediate peace dividend that can be paid out to the citizens of the disarming country or used in some other way, such as paying off the national debt, building or rebuilding infrastructure, funding social services, reducing taxes, etc., the presumption being the reallocation of resources of labour, capital, and other inputs (including energy and other natural resources services, and material inputs of intermediate goods) can be made instantaneously and costlessly. This naive view treats military expenditure as a category of social spending and simply shifts it to another such category, like shifting money from one pocket to another. It ignores the fact that the process of conversion entails a fundamental reallocation of resources in the economy, with real adjustments to be made in employment patterns, capital utilisation, and the industrial structure.

'While there are potentially major gains' from disarmament or any reduction of defence efforts, the argument continues, 'it would be a mistake to ignore the short-term adjustment costs'.[8]

Indeed, depending on the expected pattern of costs and benefits, it is clear that – in Intriligator's words again – 'the social rate of return from disarmament, treated as an investment process, could either be very high or very low, possibly even negative'. How high or low, whether positive or negative, obviously depends on the level of so-called 'conversion' costs, the transition time to benefits, and the scale of those eventual benefits; and these factors in turn depend on 'both general economic conditions and the policies chosen by the disarming nation'.[9]

Policy prescription follows in the '12 economic principles' formulated by the UN's experts which invite selective quotation. Proposition III is interesting, in the light of the argument earlier in the present paper:

III

In order to maximise the social rate of return . . ., *reductions of military spending should be gradual and predictable*, allowing for smooth economic and social adjustments . . .' (Emphasis in the original)[10]

This amounts to endorsement of that cautious approach to reshaping defence efforts which Western governments have been practising, albeit for their own reasons rather than to maximise notional net benefits.

Other propositions are concerned, essentially, with elucidating the prerequisites for orderly adjustment. Their sentiments are unexceptionable.

IV

Overcoming the . . . constraints on conversion requires *financial commitments, managerial innovations, manpower retraining, capital retooling . . . to minimise the costs and maximise the benefits of disarmament.*

V

There should be explicit recognition of the *unprecedented economic problems of disarmament in the current world situation.* Disarmament is occurring without a prior major war . . . in several countries [it] is occurring simultaneously with a shift from a centrally planned to a market economy.

VIII

. . . Public policies which assist change and resource *re-allocation can help to minimise the costs of disarmament . . .*

Yet others lay down guidelines for maximising and distributing benefits, and are more controversial: 'disarmament requires control of military technology, especially military R&D' (Principle IX), 'increasing transparency of information regarding arms imports and arms exports is essential' (Principle X), 'Industrialised countries might use some of the benefits . . . to assist the developing countries' (Principle XI) – these are prescriptions or recommendations elevated to the status of 'principles' primarily, one suspects, because they support other policies on the United Nations' agenda.

What is most noteworthy about these commandments, however, is that the phrase 'peace dividend' occurs in none of them. The catchphrase of the post-Vietnam War era has no place in the serious 'new disarmament economics' of the post-Cold War period, except as a shorthand for the benefits which reduced allocations of resources for defence should in time deliver.

That is why the *cognoscenti* always write 'peace dividend' (in the inverted commas that suggest one is not entirely comfortable with the term) and would never write Peace Dividend.

Notes

[1] Data from US Congress, Office of Technology Assessment, *After the Cold War Living with Lower Defense Spending*, OTA-ITE-524 (Washington DC: US Government Printing Office (USGPO), February 1992), Chapter 1.

[2] Viktor Antonov, Address to the National Press Club, Washington DC, 17 September 1992 (United States Information Service (USIS) Wireless File, 18 September 1992).

[3] *Defense News*, 14 September 1992.

[4] *Statement on the Defence Estimates 1992*, Cm 1981, (London: Her Majesty's Stationery Office (HMSO), July 1992), p. 9.

[5] Bjørn Møller 'Inflatable Armed Forces and Reversible Conversion'. Editorial, *NOD [Non-Offensive Defence] and Conversion*, International Research Newsletter, No.23, August 1992, pp. 3 & 4.

[6] United Nations Document A/47/346, September 1992.

[7] M D Intriligator 'The Economics of Disarmament as an Investment Process' *UNIDIR Newsletter*, No.19, September 1992, p. 7.

[8] Ibid.

[9] M D Intriligator *op. cit.* p. 8.

[10] 'Economic Principles for Disarmament' in UN Document A/47/346 and *UNIDIR Newsletter*, No.19, pp. 21 and 22.

23

The Clinton Administration: Foreign and Defence Policy Priorities

THOMAS HALVERSON

Lecturer in International Relations, University of Keele

Bill Clinton is the first President to have been born after the Second World War, and the first inaugurated after the Cold War's end. Not since before the World War was a President elected with less defence and foreign policy campaign debate. No longer is America led by a service veteran President whose personal view of international politics derives from the Munich era: this is an important generational change. Without the Cold War glue of anti-Soviet interests to bind them, the US-led global alliance system is truly at the crossroads. Restoring America's long-term economic competitiveness has management of a global anti-Soviet coalition as the top foreign policy priority.

How does President Clinton view the world, and what international role does he see for the United States in the post-Cold War era? How will his emphasis on domestic economic regeneration influence American strategy? Will strategy and force structure be changed significantly, and what role can arms control be expected to play in the new administration? Clinton has emphasised the growing importance of Asia and the emerging opportunities for collective security and multilateral diplomacy; are fundamental strategic realignments likely? This chapter outlines the salient defence and foreign policy concepts of the Clinton Administration. It also examines these questions, and suggests how political and economic forces may influence its policy choices.

MORE OF THE SAME: AMERICA'S ROLE IN
THE CLINTON WORLD VIEW

Exactly what core intellectual assumptions about international relations President Bill Clinton brings to the job is uncertain. His statements show a marked idealistic emphasis and rejection of what he saw as the Bush Administration's *realpolitik* 'eagerness to defend potentates and dictators'.[1] Nevertheless, he clearly believes that military strength remains important, and that 'power is the basis for successful diplomacy.' America and the West today face a challenge similar in some ways to that of 1946: 'to build a world of security, freedom, democracy, free markets and growth' after prevailing in the Cold War. From his speeches, several themes emerge: the international importance of fostering democracy; the critical need for continuity in America's current international engagement; the growing importance of economic power in international relations; and the need to forge a new political consensus to support America's continued expansive foreign policy.

A global democratic revolution pervades the world today according to President Clinton, and its success is critically important. Reflecting the idealistic impulses of Presidents Wilson and Carter, he believes that 'democracies provide the best foundations on which to build international order.' They do not fight each other, sponsor terrorism or threaten each other with weapons of mass destruction. Even better, 'democracy abroad also protects our own concrete economic and security interests here at home.' As governments and peoples abandon the dead hand of communism in the former Soviet Union and Eastern Europe, and move towards democracy and market economies throughout the world, Clinton believes that America's task is to 'stand up for democracy as it remakes the world.' Reinforcing the shift towards liberal politics and economics is the defining change in the post-Cold War world, and is the best hope for international peace and security.

Successful democratic political and market-oriented economic reform within the Commonwealth of Independent States (CIS) is where this revolution is most at stake. Here Clinton believes that Russian President Yeltsin's reforms must be supported comprehensively by America and her allies for it would be 'deeply irresponsible to forgo this short term investment in our long term security.' While he recognises that the future of Russia and the CIS will be determined in this, America must 'organise and lead a long-term Western strategy of engagement for democracy.' But where will the required financial resources come from? This problem will continue to intrude on Clinton's domestic priorities, for it cannot be denied that cumulative economic weakness and fiscal constraints – not to mention political constraints – greatly reduce Washington's ability to assist Russian reform.

Although bereft of foreign policy experience, President Clinton portrays himself as a committed internationalist, in the tradition of all Presidents since the Second World War.

After his election, Clinton emphasised that 'even as America's administrations change, America's fundamental interests do not'. Emphasis and priorities might change, but continuity is the watchword. Consolidating the gains of communism's collapse requires America's continued worldwide engagement to protect enduring interests and support the global democratisation process. Like his predecessors, Clinton believes that the world is a potentially violent and dangerous place in which illiberal and undemocratic governments and non-governmental actors are willing to use force to pursue their interests. Whereas the anti-communist imperative which motivated America's internationalist post-war policy has receded, Clinton opposes a retreat into isolationism. Confident American engagement, in a leadership role, remains, Clinton believes, necessary to safeguard US and Western interests.

After the Cold War, economic power and competitiveness is more important than ever in international relations. To be powerful internationally requires domestic economic strength. Clinton's world view is founded on a belief in an outward-looking economic orientation: he supports strongly the expansion of an open and multilateral world trading system. Strong rhetoric about pressuring foreigners to open their markets and commitments to protect American industries against 'unfair' competition reflected the compromises of campaigning more than a weakness of belief in the benefits of free trade and comparative advantage – witness his qualified support of the North American Free Trade Agreement. International cooperation not only creates conditions for peace, it also helps maximise economic growth. New and more intensive cooperation is therefore necessary, beyond that which characterised the Cold War period. In addition to upholding and expanding the world trade system, initiatives for further coordination of economic policy among the G7 countries would clearly receive Clinton support. The emphasis on strengthening the domestic economy, then, is in the Clinton view, not an evasion of international responsibility, but is the necessary condition to enable America to meet its international responsibilities.

Underpinning these international commitments, Clinton and Vice President Al Gore believe it necessary to forge a new political consensus to sustain America's post-Cold War international engagement. In a world where American interests will be more fluid and difficult to define, and where threats to those interests will be less direct and dangerous, reconstructing a consensus for continued heavy international responsibilities will be difficult. In some respects this is the key question of post-Cold War US strategy: without the imperative of confronting the global communist-Soviet threat, what is the rationale for a continued internationalist and 'forward deployed' strategy? Many emerging security problems, like the crisis in the former Yugoslavia and in Somalia, will stimulate emotive calls for Washington to 'do something', not because direct US interests are at stake, but because America can, and morality requires it. This will require careful political handling. President Clinton, however, seems keen to meet this political challenge. It will require him to formulate defensible criteria to differentiate when and why America should engage in wars of interest and wars of morality. Public support will be required to sustain either.

Pronouncements about continuity and internationalism do not dispel all doubts about Clinton's judgement regarding the use of American military power in defending vital interests. His waffling about the Gulf War, when he said of the Senate vote to authorise the use of force, 'I guess I would have voted with the majority if it was a close vote. But I agree with the argument the minority made', does not reassure. Perhaps there is a fundamental weakness of will to employ military power in the new President. In a careful campaign statement in July 1992, however, Clinton's views indicated how little he differed from the prevailing views of the Bush Administration and the Pentagon. Asked when the use of US force would be justified, he said: 'When our vital interests are at stake, when there is a clear, sharply defined objective that is achievable at acceptable cost, and when you are sure you can build the support here at home.' This echoes the logic of Joint Chiefs of Staff Chairman Colin Powell, or President Bush as he rationalised America's refusal to become seriously engaged in Yugoslavia. When and where, analysts must ask, will such demanding criteria be met? Clinton's stated internationalism will surely be tested by the messier security realities which are emerging widely in South-Eastern Europe and on Russia's perimeter, for example. Observers are justified in wondering whether his view of America's international leadership role can survive the demanding criteria for the use of American military power which he professes.

SHIFTING PRIORITIES: THE PRIMACY OF DOMESTIC POLICY

If continuity is Clinton's foreign policy prescription, what will be different? There is one theme which differentiates his defence and foreign policy priorities from his predecessors': it is that America's interests cannot be properly protected or promoted without domestic economic strength. 'If we are not strong at home, we cannot lead the world we have done so much to make . . . Our economic strength must become a central defining element of our national security policy.' At a time when much of the world is turning toward market capitalism and liberal democracy, 'America's ability to lead the world and inspire others with our example has gradually been eroded by an anaemic, debt-ridden economy, an inadequate education and training system, a decaying stock of public capital, and the highest crime and poverty rate of any advanced nation.' This indicates Clinton's mandate for change, and correcting such pressing domestic problems will take precedence in attention and resources over defence and foreign policy commitments to which Presidents gave priority throughout the Cold War. For the first time in over forty years, domestic economic interests will come before foreign policy considerations.

Restoration of higher economic growth and productivity are Clinton's mission to govern. But this task will be extraordinarily difficult, as the accumulated Reagan-Bush budget deficits and vastly increased national debt have largely vitiated the government's ability to manipulate fiscal policy. A strategy for economic growth must be pursued simultaneously with an attack on the deficit, which will in itself be deflationary. Worse, tackling fundamental economic problems requires long-term solutions which do not pay off quickly. To proceed with his economic agenda will require much of the President's attention; defence and foreign policy will necessarily receive less consideration. The proposal to create an Economic Security Council similar to the National Security Council within the White House staff structure is indicative of Clinton's priorities. Exactly what this organisation will do is unclear, but that it reflects Clinton's emphasis on domestic economic restructuring is clear.

Despite Clinton's domestic priorities, the world will intrude uninvited on his domestic agenda. For international relations have become messier and more complicated after the Cold War, and the propensity for conflict is increasing, not decreasing in many areas. Developments in Europe, for example, will continue to deteriorate in the South and East, not to mention in the former Soviet Union. The resultant security problems will not directly affect American interests, yet will impinge on the security interests of her allies, engendering divergent responses. Few of these trouble spots will be amenable to outside military solutions, and the US and Western options for response will often be indirect and involve a significant economic component. Yet in a period when economic and security interests, and rivalries, become increasingly intertwined and most Western nations are strapped for cash, Clinton will find foreign and defence policy problems continually demanding more attention and resources than are available.

CLINTON ON DEFENCE

Defence policy choices during the Clinton Administration are likely to have a larger global impact in many ways than those for many years. It is ironic then, that defence received so little attention in the election campaign of 1992. President Clinton stresses continuity of strategy, of building on Cold War successes, while simultaneously restructuring forces to meet new security threats. His strategic imperative – to replace a Western coalition cemented by the need to confront the Soviet Union – is a call for America to lead a 'global alliance for democracy as united and steadfast as the global alliance that defeated communism.' What new threats does Clinton see on the horizon which this global alliance's strategy must confront? One source is armed conflicts among and between the former Soviet republics, four of which remain nuclear powers. Nuclear, chemical and biological weapons proliferation, and their delivery means, is another. Regional tensions, in the Middle East or Korea, and the increasing intensity of ethnic rivalry and separatist violence like that in the former Yugoslavia and the Horn of Africa are the major threats on Clinton's mind.

To build a new strategy, President Clinton has committed himself to retaining America's position as the world's strongest military power. In the election campaign he vowed that the Defense Department would not become a 'piggy bank' for domestic spending. His commitments bear this out: over five years Clinton's proposed defense plan would cost $1.36 trillion against President Bush's $1.42 trillion, a difference of only five per cent. Further cuts are possible, however, 'if current favourable trends in the international climate continue.'

What will America's defence forces consist of after the 'comprehensive restructuring' which Clinton desires? A US military structure in the 1990s would rest on four pillars: an 'irreducible minimum' survivable nuclear force 'to deter any conceivable threat'; rapidly deployable conventional forces capable of projecting power wherever and whenever US interests are threatened; maintaining superior personnel and technology; and development of more sophisticated, timely and accurate intelligence capabilities to analyse economic and political conditions that might fuel new conflicts. This is not a prescription for degrading American military power.

To support these four pillars, Clinton advocated several weapons programme decisions during the election campaign. He would: 'stop production' of the B-2 bomber; meet airlift needs by continuing with the C-17 transport; build new tactical fighters; increase reliance on National Guard and reserve forces; reduce from 12 to 10 aircraft carriers; and build more fast sealift ships for the Navy. What's more, Clinton actually supported several spending programmes that President Bush had abandoned, such as a second 'Seawolf' nuclear attack submarine and the V-22 'Osprey' tilt-rotor aircraft for the Marine Corps. These attempts to insulate himself from Republican charges of defence weakness partly reflected electoral concerns in the states where these weapons are built. They are therefore likely targets for reductions as budget pressures increase.

Despite this recipe for a robust defence posture, Clinton plans significantly to reduce and reorganise America's defence posture. Secretary of Defense Cheney and Colin Powell's 'base force' concept is set for a minimum reduction of 200,000 from the planned 1.6 million. Overseas bases and force structure are likely to take a disproportionate reduction because of the perceived shrinkage of the external threat, particularly in Europe. But more importantly, domestic political and economic pressures will probably combine in Congress to reject domestic base closures. America's NATO forces are earmarked for reductions significantly beyond the 150,000 personnel minimum envisaged by President Bush. Something in the vicinity of 75,000–100,000 is likely. The NATO commitment would instead be met by reinforcing Europe if necessary by rapid deployment from US bases.

Clinton accepts the view of Les Aspin that Bush's 'base force' ill fits America's changing strategic interests, and contains unnecessary redundancies. It lacks flexibility and mobility: it was designed for a now redundant concept of European war. More agile forces, of great manoeuvre and speed are needed instead. Weapons precision must, argues Clinton, be increased to reduce casualties when operating 'among civilian populations' and because the credibility of US threats will depend increasingly 'on our ability to limit the loss of life.' Structurally, separate air forces for the Marines, Army, Navy and Air Force; parallel light Army and Marine divisions; separate fighter aircraft and tactical missile programmes; and many other service inefficiencies are due to be rationalised. Comprehensive reforms of this sort have been advocated before, particularly structural service reorganisation. Clinton says he 'will order the Pentagon' to agree a new organisation 'consolidating and coordinating military roles and missions'. While laudable, this agenda will not be easy or necessarily save money. Serious structural reform, like arms control, often involves new and unforeseen spending, not to mention entrenched bureaucratic resistance.

In attempting to squeeze funds from the defence budget, Clinton claimed during the election campaign that $60 billion could be saved over five years. These 'savings' will prove illusory, $10 billion, for example, was to come from unspecified 'inventory reform'. Fifteen of the proposed $60 billion would come from one of Clinton's biggest shifts in defence policy priorities: a total reorientation of ballistic missile defence efforts. The space-based 'brilliant pebbles' programme as part of the General Protection Against Limited Strikes (GPALS) is likely to be radically reduced to save approximately $15 billion. Reflecting his closeness to Armed Services Committee chairmen Les Aspin and Sam Nunn, Clinton supports research and development to create the option to deploy a land-based ballistic missile defence designed to protect a single site inside the US from accidental or rogue missile launches. Similarly, significant funding for theatre missile defence will continue.

Whatever Clinton says about continuity in strategy and force structure, he will face severe pressures to cut further and reduce commitments. His own emphasis on domestic economic regeneration, combined with extreme fiscal constraints and pressure from Democrats in Congress all point to one outcome: lower defence spending. Hardest of all will be to provide a convincing rationale or imperative for America's large force structure and forward-deployed strategy when there is no serious opponent. A growing perception that Europe and Japan are seen more as economic rivals than strategic allies will exacerbate the pressure to foist more US international security responsibilities onto them.

Serious contractions in defence spending will inevitably cause unemployment and dislocation in industries and communities where they are located. Highly skilled defence workers are a 'vital national resource' which Clinton wants to protect. One new idea is for a civilian Defence Advanced Research Projects Agency (DARPA) to utilise these defence skills in the civilian economy. Similarly, Clinton supports legislation for defence conversion, to 'convert defense cuts into domestic economic investments.' To guarantee America's technological weapons edge will involve upgrading existing weapons and pursuing limited production of next generation technologies. Despite wanting to save money, a declared need to preserve production lines for weapons no longer being built, in case of emergency, would be very expensive. With the many other proposed defence reforms, this agenda is unlikely to be implemented comprehensively or save money: priorities must be chosen and a handful of top items must take precedence or the entire programme will get bogged down like so many before.

NEW AND OLD ARMS CONTROL PRIORITIES

After the Cold War some critics believe arms control is dead. The new administration disagrees and arms control is likely to increase in importance as an essential element in national security plans. New forms of arms control will be explored in response to changing security developments. Observance and implementation of existing arms control agreements will meanwhile remain important. What is Clinton's attitude towards arms control in today's context?

Early in the election campaign, Bill Clinton presented a set of comprehensive proposals for dealing with the nuclear dangers resulting from the Soviet collapse. His pressure on this issue stimulated President Bush's coordination of the $24 billion G7 CIS financial aid initiative of April 1992. 'No national security issue is more urgent', said Clinton in April 1992, 'than the question of who will control the nuclear weapons and technology of the former Soviet empire.' New techniques of addressing these threats, such as using economic leverage to press for central control of CIS nuclear forces and to prevent former Soviet nuclear scientists from selling their services internationally were advocated by Clinton several months before they became Bush Administration policy. With the collapse of the Soviet Union, not only has the nuclear target set evaporated, proliferation and control fears all motivate Clinton's desire to 'lock in' the greatly reduced strategic nuclear force levels negotiated between the US and CIS in July 1992. Here again, Clinton advocated banning mobile land-based and land-based MIRVed weapons well before the Bush Administration pursued such a course.

Robust support for consolidating existing arms control agreements will be a Clinton priority. Iraq's clandestine nuclear weapons programme was proof enough that the international non-proliferation régime of the Non-Proliferation Treaty (NPT) needs reinforcement. Clinton supports fortifying the NPT's essentials in a variety of ways. First, by empowering the International Atomic Energy Agency to conduct unannounced inspections of undeclared nuclear facilities. Action will be taken to reduce further America's own nuclear arsenals in line with commitments undertaken under the terms of the NPT. Countries and companies which knowingly sell nuclear technologies to proliferators are, according to President Clinton, to be punished if they violate unspecified additional 'tough, enforceable international nonproliferation agreements' which he plans to negotiate. Legislation will be sought to bar imports of goods and services from foreign companies that knowingly provide direct or indirect support for nuclear development in non-nuclear weapons states. A second major axis of attack will be greater cooperation and support for using 'economic and related leverage' to discourage potential proliferators. When the NPT comes up for renewal in 1995, its importance will certainly be critically underlined.

Beyond nuclear proliferation, the gradual erosion of the Anti-Ballistic Missile Treaty, which began with Ronald Reagan's creation of the Strategic Defense Initiative in 1983 may finally be ending. 'The ABM Treaty has well served US security interests' since its ratification. Any changes would be modest, must clearly enhance American security, and be negotiated in good faith with Russia after 'full consultation with our NATO allies'. During the campaign Clinton argued that no such changes were needed under current circumstances. Space and anti-satellite weapons that might threaten US access to and use of space will also be a target for control.

As for nuclear testing Clinton's support for a two stage phased process towards a Comprehensive Test Ban (CTB) has been pre-empted by the US Congress. His stated preference, however, was to reduce the testing threshold and cap the number of tests in order to prove that a CTB would not harm national security.

Assuming success, and no radical changes in the international security situation, a complete CTB could be negotiated. Tensions are likely here with Britain, however, which professes to need continued testing in Nevada for its Trident programme; Exactly how those needs will be accommodated, between the Administration and the emerging Congressional majority opposed to continued testing, remains to be seen.

Proliferation of biological and chemical weapons will continue to receive vigorous attention and the Clinton Administration will support implementation of the global ban on production and use of chemical weapons. Similarly, proliferation prevention and control of biological weapons will continue. As many presidents have tried before him, Clinton intends to pursue a coordinated international approach to address the supply and demand for conventional weapons which currently fuels regional conflicts. Supply restraint will require considerable skill to achieve, given the economic incentives to sell to support domestic weapons industries. To control demand, the World Bank and aid donor countries' recent linkage of aid levels to military spending will be encouraged.

The control of ballistic missile proliferation, already a major concern, will remain high on the agenda. The Bush Administration took this issue seriously for the first time. Building on the existing Missile Technology Control Régime established in 1987, President Bush sought with limited success to improve multilateral controls. President Clinton intends to intensify this effort and has also spoken of expanding the non-proliferation effort to include the problem of non-missile means of nuclear delivery. Potential proliferators are far more likely to rely 'on aircraft, cruise missiles, trucks, and other nontraditional mean of delivery of such weapons.' Exactly how control of these means would be undertaken is still unclear.

Involving the UN in a regional arms control process has also been broached. Clinton would move beyond recent proposals for a UN arms registry to bring regional adversaries together to talk and negotiate 'to restrict the number and kinds of weapons they acquire' under the aegis of the UN. Such steps would be designed to complement measures taken to address underlying issues at the heart of regional conflicts and would be intended to act as a catalyst for fundamental negotiations.

While some of this agenda will be sold as new and interesting, it is most notable for its similarity to the existing and past arms control routine. The importance of controlling ballistic missile and mass destruction weapons was, indeed, central to the Bush Administration's scheme. While there is good reason to believe that the collapse of the Soviet Union will allow unprecedented progress in reducing and controlling strategic arsenals, the intractable nature of nuclear and conventional weapons proliferation does not make their control seem markedly more likely now than in recent years – despite the lessons of Iraq. Contraction of Western defence budgets will continue to stimulate arms exports to potential aggressors, and it is difficult to see how Clinton can slake his desire to generate high-technology American jobs (of which there are many in the defence industry) whilst also controlling weapons proliferation.

FOCUS ON MULTILATERALISM AND COLLECTIVE SECURITY

Clinton wants an increased use of multilateral institutions in managing security policy. Post-Cold War opportunities include the chance to 'reinvent the institutions of collective security.' Although unwilling to surrender American freedom of action, Clinton's campaign motto was 'together where we can; on our own where we must.' The UN, argues Clinton, 'is poised to be an instrument for positive change' which requires 'stronger political leadership from the United States'. Its growing role in peacemaking and peacekeeping will be encouraged, with attention being given to undertaking new techniques of preventive diplomacy. United Nations Secretary General, Boutros Boutros-Ghali's call for a permanent UN military force may find US support, for Clinton supports creating a UN Rapid Deployment Force to: guard the borders of countries threatened with aggression; prevent mass violence against civilian populations; provide humanitarian relief; and combat terrorism. This would not be a standing force, but a small voluntary contingent called up from national armies, earmarked and suitably trained in advance. Clinton also seeks a reduction in the US share of UN peacekeeping expenses from 30.4 to 25 per cent. Responsibility sharing would be necessary too: Clinton thinks Japan and Germany should become permanent members of the Security Council, and contribute more for the privilege.

Precisely what Clinton's multilateral collective security emphasis means for regional security institutions in Europe, such as NATO, the Western European Union (WEU), and the Conference on Security and Cooperation in Europe (CSCE) is unclear – he has said almost nothing about it. All that is clear is Clinton's fundamental intention to encourage the Allies, through these institutions, gradually to increase their financial and military responsibilities for the management of European security. With Europe's economic success, there is no reason why America should continue to bear a disproportionate burden: it is time 'to insist that other nations start to shoulder more of the collective burden'. Not only, says Clinton, to save American cash, but also lives, and also because it would make these institutions more effective. This is really the old 'burden sharing' debate in new clothes. Washington hopes to retain its global leadership while offloading some risks and expenses onto its allies, mostly to Europe and Japan. Although atypical as a precedent, the Gulf War indicated the tensions which this effort might encounter as allies bridle about 'bankrolling' American policies over which they have little control.

In Europe, radical American policy changes have been explicitly shunned. Developments designed to encourage a greater European responsibility for NATO and within the WEU will be warmly received. American hostility toward the Franco-German corps is likely to recede, for Clinton is likely to accept such developments more easily than did President Bush as natural extensions of European responsibility for its own security interests. There is, however, some ambivalence in Clinton about the evolution of the European Community (EC): 'It is too early to say whether the integration of Western Europe will be a plus or minus for America' he said during the campaign. Primarily though, this reflects economic worries about possible European trade protectionism which could sour security relations. Overall, Clinton's regional policy toward Europe will be shaped more by economic and budgetary realities, and by reactions to individual problems such as Yugoslavia, than by any preconceived strategic plan.

How his interest in multilateralism and collective security manifests itself in other ways remains to be seen. Clearly he intends to work with partners whenever possible to gain legitimacy for necessary actions and to spread risks and costs. Additional multilateral initiatives for arms control is certainly one area in which to expect action. Again, though, policy will be shaped by the forces of budget constraints and the need for stronger rationales to justify politically why American military power will be needed to enforce collective security. Nevertheless, an increased emphasis on multilateralism and collective security corresponds well with the more fluid nature of contemporary international relations where alliances and threats will be more turbulent and require more adaptive American responses.

IS A LONG-TERM SHIFT TOWARD ASIA INEVITABLE?

For years analysts have speculated about whether America will shift its centre of strategic gravity from Europe to Asia. With dynamic economic growth there, and US-Asian trade already outstripping trade with Europe, does Clinton's emphasis on economics make such a shift more likely now?

Undoubtedly the level of trade with Asia has increased its importance to the United States. Faster military reductions in Europe leave an impression, fostered by reluctance to become involved in potential ethnic quagmires of the Yugoslav sort, that perhaps a strategic shift has begun. Now that the overt Soviet threat to Western interests has given way to many indirect ones, America's European reductions could become complete elimination. Here, economics is again critical, for tensions in world trade relations and economic rivalry, which have long paralysed the GATT negotiations, could well erode the ties that bind the Atlantic alliance. One need only note the hostility which has developed between Washington and Paris in the last eighteen months. Would a fracture into competing trade blocks of Asia, North America and Europe doom the American alliance with Europe? US troops will only stay in Europe if they are wanted. Would they be wanted if Washington never used them to help with threats which only directly affect Europe and if economic relationships had become continually confrontational? Perhaps.

Force reductions, however, are occurring in Asia as well as in Europe. While US-Asian trade and investment guarantee more of President Clinton's attention, this cannot destroy the ties that bind America and Europe. Historical, political and cultural links count a great deal, and the United States will retain a significant enduring geopolitical interest in Europe. Precipitous withdrawal in favour of Asia will not happen. America will stay militarily 'forward deployed', if in fewer numbers. What is to be feared is a lack of American willingness to lead or participate in resolving successive European security crises which have serious consequences for Europe, but which Washington avoids because of their potential to become political quagmires. If new EC and WEU military responsibilities were overtly sold as replacements rather than reinforcements to America's European committment, Washington's retreat would quicken. A consequence that process would be that Europeans would begin to question the Alliance and the seeds for the dissolution of the Alliance with the United States would be sown. While the relative importance of Asia in the eyes of the Clinton Administration will therefore increase, a meaningful strategic shift in emphasis is something that will first require significant European stimulus.

CONCLUSION

The reality of President Clinton's foreign and defence policies is unlikely to resemble closely what has been sketched out here. The world – and the vicissitudes of domestic politics – is always more unruly than one's plans. Nevertheless, what Clinton said before his inauguration in January 1993 tells us something about his political priorities and the way he will analyse both the expected and the surprise problems. He clearly believes that international relations are at the threshold of a new era and that current choices will shape the international security pattern for some time to come. The imperative which drives his internationalist outlook is the need to consolidate the global shift toward market economies and democratic politics. In this new era, economic power is ever more important, but unequalled American military power remains necessary. To ease America's security burden requires marginally reduced military spending and more reliance on collective security institutions and multi-lateral cooperation. These broad strategic parameters, he hopes, will guide policy choices which keep security problems minimised so that he can get on with his domestic agenda. Despite these intentions, the Clinton Administration's foreign policy results will be up for the judgement of history far sooner than will his efforts to increase the long-term health of America's economic competitiveness.

Note

Most of the quotations and material for this chapter have been taken from various campaign speeches made by President Clinton during the 1992 Presidential Election Campaign. Some were reported in the press, others were not. No attempt has been made to refer to them in detail, since they can only be interpreted as a reflection of general emphases and orientations rather than as expressions of precise policy positions.